Practical HTML5 Projects

Adrian W. West

Apress®

Practical HTML5 Projects

Copyright © 2012 by Adrian West

ISBN-13 (pbk): 978-1-4302-4275-8

ISBN-13 (electronic): 978-1-4302-4276-5

Trademarked names, logos, and images may appear in this book. Rather than use a trademark symbol with every occurrence of a trademarked name, logo, or image we use the names, logos, and images only in an editorial fashion and to the benefit of the trademark owner, with no intention of infringement of the trademark.

The use in this publication of trade names, trademarks, service marks, and similar terms, even if they are not identified as such, is not to be taken as an expression of opinion as to whether or not they are subject to proprietary rights.

While the advice and information in this book are believed to be true and accurate at the date of publication, neither the authors nor the editors nor the publisher can accept any legal responsibility for any errors or omissions that may be made. The publisher makes no warranty, express or implied, with respect to the material contained herein.

President and Publisher: Paul Manning
Lead Editor: Ben Renow-Clarke
Technical Reviewer: Andrew Zack
Editorial Board: Steve Anglin, Ewan Buckingham, Gary Cornell, Louise Corrigan, Morgan Ertel,
    Jonathan Gennick, Jonathan Hassell, Robert Hutchinson, Michelle Lowman, James Markham,
    Matthew Moodie, Jeff Olson, Jeffrey Pepper, Douglas Pundick, Ben Renow-Clarke, Dominic
    Shakeshaft, Gwenan Spearing, Matt Wade, Tom Welsh
Coordinating Editor: Jessica Belanger and Brigid Duffy
Copy Editor: Kimberly Burton
Compositor: Mary Sudul
Indexer: SPi Global
Cover Designer: Anna Ishchenko

Distributed to the book trade worldwide by Springer Science+Business Media New York, 233 Spring Street, 6th Floor, New York, NY 10013. Phone 1-800-SPRINGER, fax (201) 348-4505, e-mail orders-ny@springer-sbm.com, or visit www.springeronline.com.

For information on translations, please e-mail rights@apress.com, or visit www.apress.com.

Apress and friends of ED books may be purchased in bulk for academic, corporate, or promotional use. eBook versions and licenses are also available for most titles. For more information, reference our Special Bulk Sales–eBook Licensing web page at www.apress.com/bulk-sales.

Any source code or other supplementary materials referenced by the author in this text is available to readers at www.apress.com. For detailed information about how to locate your book's source code, go to www.apress.com/source-code.

Contents at a Glance

Contents

About the Author

Adrian West resigned as a chartered engineer to become the UK director of a correspondence school. He has been teaching in one form or another since 1982. He introduced computers into his workplace in 1987 and taught the staff how to use them. For four years, he taught undergraduates computer skills at a college in Cheshire in the United Kingdom.

Adrian lives in Colyton, a town in Devon, England, and for the last 12 years, he has designed and produced web sites for local businesses and charities. For a time, he also served as a computer technician and teacher to about 100 people in his community, until he decided to concentrate on his favorite occupation, designing web sites. To avoid disappointing his former clients, he launched a free computer-help web site at `http://www.colycomputerhelp.co.uk`.

Adrian also writes monthly computer-help articles for two local magazines.

Frustrated by a lack of information on certain aspects of web design, he researched, tested, and developed solutions for these poorly documented techniques; this book is the result.

About the Technical Reviewer

Andrew Zack is the CEO of ZTMC, Inc. (`ztmc.com`), which specializes in search engine optimization (SEO) and internet marketing strategies. His project background includes almost 20 years of site development and project management experience, including more than 15 years as a SEO and internet marketing expert.

Mr. Zack has also been very active in the publishing industry, having coauthored *Flash 5 Studio* (Apress, 2001), and serving as a technical reviewer on more than ten books and industry publications.

Working with the internet nearly since its inception, Mr. Zack continually focuses on the cutting edge, new platforms, and technology to continually stay at the forefront of the industry.

Acknowledgments

I thank my wife, Janice, for her love and support, for taking over my share of the chores so that I could concentrate on this book, for her encouragement, and for putting up with my absence as I hunched over the keyboard. I could never have managed without her meticulous proofreading, which she patiently repeated four times per chapter as each editorial stage was reached.

My thanks also goes to the magnificent team at Apress: Ben Renow-Clarke for his encouragement and for patiently explaining the editorial processes and how to use SharePoint; James Markham for tips on the layout of the chapters and for helping me conform to the Apress house style; Jessica Belanger, who coordinated everybody and ensured that I sent chapters and files on time; and Kimberly Burton, the copyeditor, who polished my chapters. I thank Andrew Zack, the technical reviewer, who checked all my code and suggested several useful resources for inclusion in the book; and special thanks to Brigid Duffy for promptly and efficiently dealing with tweaks and revisions to the page proofs.

And my thanks go to all the people who helped me and replied to my queries; to all the forums and information placed on the internet from which I learned so much; and to my clients, who graciously allowed me to use the web sites I designed for them as examples for the book. Thanks to those who gave me video clips; to Kay Banks for the loan of her iPhone to test web sites and QR codes; to Nicholas McIntyre for his encouragement and helpful tips; and to visually-impaired Douglas Hollingsworth for testing the tables in my chapter on accessibility.

—Adrian West

Introduction

This book concentrates on the practical application of HTML5 to projects that are currently not well documented. The book focuses on projects that will enhance your web sites; therefore, you will not find a history of HTML5 nor will you see a detailed discussion on things that are not commonly used by the great majority of web designers, such as APIs (application programming interface). Several books are available on the history of HTML5 and on APIs, so duplicating them is pointless. The aim of this book is to help you produce attractive and useful web sites by combining the advantages of HTML5 with exciting techniques that were previously poorly documented.

The Origin of this Book

Although I have designed many web sites over many years, I often had moments when I said to myself "how on earth do I do that?" or "how on earth did they do that?" The subjects of these "how on earth?" moments concerned techniques that were not usefully covered by any manuals that I could find. So, I assembled a collection of how-to techniques consisting of the results of my research and my practical experiments. Best of all, I compiled a collection of templates based on these techniques. These were extremely useful time-savers. The resulting volume (stored on my hard drive) was so useful that I decided it should be shared in book form with other designers. My templates were created in HTML5 and they include, where necessary, hacks to enable Internet Explorer 7 and 8 to understand HTML5 semantic tags.My quest for solutions was like an archaeological dig. I had evidence that the treasure was buried. Having eventually unearthed it, I found that these precious artifacts were fragmented and widely scattered; they were also in poor condition. My task was to assemble the fragments, then clean and polish them for public display. One problem remained, however, because many fragments were missing. I had to re-create these through trial and error.

This book was born out of frustration. Most manuals, forums, and web sites give snippets of code on the topics covered in this book, but then the web designer is left to work out how to apply that code in the real world. That means sifting through many sources to piece together sufficient information. The practical application then requires more time for trial-and-error testing.

Practical, fully-worked examples of these tools are often as rare as hen's teeth. Busy web designers should not have to plough through pages of theory or history only to discover that no practical applications are provided. Nor should they have to read a verbose paragraph five times to extract some meaning from it.

It is true that five of the book's topics are already covered in hefty, single-subject manuals, but busy designers may not wish to buy a boatload of single-topic manuals and spend time trawling through them. In this book, these manuals are summarized in one chapter each, and the chapters are more than adequate for designers who wish to quickly create something such as a PayPal page or an accessible site, a web site optimized for search engines, or to acquire an introduction to HTML5 and CSS3.

I tried to avoid those problems in this book by providing the following:

- Practical and useful real-world examples
- Screenshots of the end results
- The markup in the form of fully-worked examples

- Step-by-step guidance in plain English to explain difficult items
- Time-saving summaries of some single-topic manuals
- Downloadable templates for users to adapt in their own web sites

Is this Book for You?

- Do you want to understand and use the enhancements provided by HTML5 and CSS3?
- Are you an IT instructor or trainer looking for a set text that answers your students' questions on HTML5, provides you with many ready-made projects, and gives students a valuable resource for their personal libraries?
- Are you an IT student wishing to advance beyond the basic principles of HTML4, and CSS2?
- You could spend many days and weeks searching the internet for how-to techniques. Would you rather have a collection of fully-worked examples of these otherwise hard-to-find tools?
- Some of the projects in this book could eventually be constructed by piecing together snippets from a number of single-topic computer textbooks and web sites. Would you prefer to have them ready-constructed and described step-by-step in one book?
- Many single-topic web design manuals are big and verbose. It takes time to trawl though them. Would you like the practical content adequately summarized in one chapter?
- You will find several ways of doing the same job by searching for a technique on the internet or in books. I tested several of the techniques and chose the most straightforward methods that do the job well. Do you think the tried and tested techniques in this book will save you research and testing time?
- Would you like a downloadable toolkit consisting of free, easily-adaptable templates?
- Do your clients ask you to add enhancements to their web sites, but you're not sure how to do it?
- Do you need to know how best to update your client's older web sites because they contain deprecated markup or because they are not accessible to the disabled?
- Perhaps your prospective client used a paint-by-numbers kit, that is, a content management system (CMS) such as Joomla!, Textpattern, WordPress, or CMS Made Simple. Would you prefer to take full control of his web sites? This book will help you to break free from the limitations of the CMS templates and software. (Although if the web site is a blog or is database driven, the CMS approach may be a better choice.)

What this Book Does and Does Not Cover

The great majority of web site owners want a web site for the following reasons:

- To sell a service or a product

- To provide information

- To publicize an organization such as a charity, a church, or a society

This book caters to the great majority of web site owners. The book does not cover techniques that are adequately described and illustrated in readily available resources. It does, however, summarize four bulky manuals that are very time-consuming to read and extract information.

This book does not discuss RSS feeds, nor does it have much discussion on JavaScript-driven APIs. The great majority of owners would be horrified if users could tinker with their web sites. Business owners would not have the time or inclination to moderate entries in blogs. The only interactive elements covered in this book are the truly practical ones, such as methods of payment (for example PayPal), secure feedback forms, page-printing buttons, audio and video controls, go-back buttons, and accessibility features.

This book does not deal with blogs or database-driven web sites using SQL or MySQL. To learn how to take control of a CMS blog, I recommend *Blog Design Solutions* (Apress, 2006).

The Layout

Each chapter is self contained so that generally you can complete a task without jumping from chapter to chapter. I had to compromise occasionally when deciding where to locate a sub-topic; for example, where should I put CSS3 rounded corners: in the CSS3 chapter or in the chapter on rounded corners? I eventually placed it in the chapter on rounded corners.

The chapters are in no special order and they do not have to be read in a particular order. Just dive in anywhere to discover what you want to learn. However, if you have little knowledge of HTML5, start with the first chapter. It will introduce you to HTML5 and it provides worked examples to practice on.

I avoided unproductive detail such as the history of HTML5 or how a particular technique evolved. Instead, I concentrate on practical application. Some topics do need the *how* explained—such as how screen readers help the blind to read a web site—but my general aim has been to "cut to the chase" (as film producers say), that is, cut the waffle and get to the exciting bit as soon as possible.

My hope is that by collecting and presenting the tools, techniques, summaries, and templates in one book, web designers, students, and teachers will be spared many hours of research and testing.

The Level of Skill Required

The instructions in this book are intermediate level; that is, it is assumed that you already have a working knowledge of HTML4 and CSS2.

HTML5 and CSS3

Many HTML5 and CSS3 manuals have been published recently. They are good at describing the history behind the new recommendations and they tend to concentrate on less commonly used items such as APIs and the new canvas element. Worked examples in HTML5 were scarce, and very few were relevant to the real world. Most of the manuals dealt extensively with APIs, something that the vast majority of web site owners know nothing about and would not want anyway. This book emphasizes the practical aspect of HTML5, CSS2, and CSS3. I have cut to the chase and provided fully-worked projects covering all the most useful new features.

▨ **Note** CSS3 and HTML5 are not dependent on each other; they are totally separate recommendations.

Updates for CSS3

At the time of writing, Mozilla Firefox, Safari, and Chrome needed `-mozkit-` and `-webkit-` hacks in order to support some CSS3 features. When newer versions of these browsers are released, they may no longer need the hacks.

Minimum Use of Scripts

I have tried to reduce the use of scripts to a minimum. If there is a CSS solution, this will be used instead of a script. HTML5 and CSS3 offer script-free solutions for several new web site enhancements. The latest versions of most browsers support them.

PHP

Some PHP is used in two of the projects—visitor counters and forms—but no knowledge of PHP is required. Even though the script is fully explained, you can skip the explanations and simply insert your own details in the templates where indicated in the PHP markup.

JavaScript

To enable some HTML5 features to work in IE 7 and IE 8, a snippet of JavaScript is essential. This script is available for you to download from the book's Apress web site.

A small number of topics in this book use a little JavaScript; for example, CSS2 rounded corners (Chapter 7), enciphered email addresses (Chapter 11), and audio and video (Chapter 6), but no knowledge of JavaScript is required. The JavaScript files can be downloaded from the companion web site and placed in the root folder of your web site. Eventually, rounded corners will be achievable without scripts by using CSS3. Some browsers already support this technique. Cross-browser audio and video will eventually be achieved without scripts by using the new HTML5 `<audio>` and `<video>` tags. Meanwhile, a fallback solution is provided to enable audio and video to play using IE 7 and IE 8.

Conventions Used in this Book

The words *code, listing,* and *markup* are used in the book to mean the same thing. Code that should be replaced by the reader's own markup is shown in bold italics. For instructional purposes, bold adds emphasis to some markup.

The words *client* and *web site owner* are used synonymously to mean a person (or organization) commissioning you to produce a web site.

The words *tag* and *element* are also used interchangeably.

Resources

Many helpful books and free software programs are mentioned in this book. Wherever possible, freeware or open-source software has been chosen and fully tested.

▨ **Tip** Install a text editor such as Notepad ++, which has several enhancements compared to MS Notepad.

When a piece of CSS markup cannot be contained on one line, a left-pointing arrow is used to indicate that the two lines belong together; for example:

```
#header { width:920px; height:180px; padding:0; margin: 20px auto; ⬅
border:10px white solid; background: url(images/header3.jpg) no-repeat;
        }
```

Using the Book's Markup and Templates

Most of the worked examples are practical templates that readers can view and download from the companion web site. Readers can easily and quickly adapt these examples for their own use. No permission is required for using the markup or the templates in a web site. Permission will be required if you include the markup examples in media for sale, that is, printed matter or a CD. If you use markup examples in a web site offering instruction on web design, permission is required and you will be asked to acknowledge where you found the code. The attribution should give the source, as follows: *Practical HTML5 Projects* by Adrian West. Copyright 2012 Adrian West. Published by Apress Media, LLC. ISBN 978-1-4302-4275-8.

If you think that your particular use of the book's markup is not covered by this paragraph, please contact permissions@apress.com.

WYSIWYG Web Design Programs

WYSIWYG programs can be an excellent way of quickly starting a web page and a good way of learning the grammar and syntax of HTML. But don't always believe what you see. Sometimes layouts, when viewed in the design pane of a WYSIWYG program, are not what you expect to see. Until the WYSIWYG programs catch up, this particularly applies to pages using HTML5 or XHTML5 DOCTYPES. Don't struggle with the WYSIWYG layout, images, or menu bars; instead, test the page in Internet Explorer, Mozilla Firefox, Safari, Chrome, and Opera. You may be pleasantly surprised to see the layout, images, and menus displayed properly despite their odd appearance in the WYSIWYG editor.

I use MS Expression Web. It has an excellent error checker. Pressing the F9 key in code view reveals and explains the errors step-by-step. However, any WYSIWIG editor may need either updating or upgrading to error check HTML5 pages.

Web Design Programs and CMS

Web design programs and content management systems (CMS) claim that you don't need to learn HTML. They are the paint-by-numbers kits in the world of web site design.

I agree that you can design web sites using these programs without ever using or understanding HTML or CSS; however, you will be forced to use the templates that thousands of others are using. Your ability to adapt or fine-tune your web sites will be severely limited because most CMS use proprietary markup as well as JavaScript and PHP. All CMS sites load an enormous amount of baggage into your root folder; this may swallow up most of your available hosting capacity. For example, a basic five-page web site using HTML5 and CSS2 results in only two folders and six files. Using a CMS package for the same web site results in 17 folders with an average of 30 files in each, plus ten PHP files and several additional files for administering the web site.

If you need to move a CMS site to another web master, you may have difficulty finding someone willing to take on the learning curve necessary to grapple with the complexities of fine-tuning a CMS web site.

Encouraging beginners to use CMS (or online web site generators) is like saying to someone, "So, you're going to France on business for three months? Don't bother to learn French, just take a translator with you." Should beginners wish to fine-tune a CMS web site, they will eventually need to learn HTML, JavaScript, and PHP. Web sites that can be designed online can be even more restrictive. These are mainly JavaScript-based, resulting in even less designer control. Online methods and CMS sites also use JavaScript navigation menus that prevent search engines from probing past the home page.

You will never be in full control of your web design process unless you learn some HTML and CSS. If you want to produce unique, lean, clean, easily managed web sites, then HTML and CSS are the only way. HTML is not difficult, 40 words of HTML language will suffice, and all of them are English words or abbreviations of English words. Several free WYSIWYG web design programs are available to help you learn the syntax and grammar. Public libraries usually have HTML and CSS manuals on their shelves.

Which Browsers?

Currently, a majority of ordinary users surf with Internet Explorer because it comes free with Windows. A recent computer magazine poll showed that Internet Explorer, Mozilla Firefox, and Chrome are equally popular. Computer magazines cater to a small proportion of the population, so their survey results are rather biased. When considering IE, we need to be aware of the four versions in use.

I assumed we could dismiss the ten-year-old IE 6. Any people still using IE 6 deserve what they see on their screens. However, I had a shock when I designed a web site for a group supporting my local public library. The county library's computers were still using IE 6 despite its great age and vulnerability. The web site looked a mess on library computers; I fixed this with an IE conditional hack, (details of these hacks are provided in this book). Now *I always check to see which browsers my clients are using.*

User inertia ensures that older browsers and operating systems will be in use for the next five years. Many businesses and home users will stay with Windows XP, IE 7, and IE 8 until at least 2014. They will continue to use IE 7 and IE 8 because IE 9 is not compatible with XP. People buying new computers from mid-2011 will have IE 9 pre-installed. Over the next decade, IE 9 and later versions may increasingly be the most-used versions of Internet Explorer. Internet Explorer 9, which was released in March 2011, will be compatible with the most useful new HTML5 and CSS3 features. People who are savvy enough to download and use Mozilla Firefox, Opera, Safari, and Chrome will normally continue to download the latest versions. Designers should, therefore, test on the most recent versions.

For the present, so that your web sites reach the maximum audience, make sure they work in the five most popular browsers. They are, in order of importance, Internet Explorer 8 and IE 9+, Chrome, Mozilla Firefox, Safari for Windows, and Opera. They may not (and need not) display in an identical manner, but as long as they communicate the web site's message effectively, small differences are not important. After 2015 you may able to forget about hacks for IE 8.

Tip See the Appendix for a table showing the browser usage in the United States, the United Kingdom, and Europe. This is useful if you are targeting a particular area.

CHAPTER 1

Moving to HTML5

The projects in this book use HTML5. In this chapter, readers who are not familiar with HTML5 will be introduced to its essential features and will learn how it differs from HTML4/XHTML. You will also discover how to:

- Convert an HTML4/XHTML page or an entire web site to HTML5
- Create HTML5 pages that will display correctly in Internet Explorer 7 and 8
- Take advantage of the enhanced features in HTML5

HTML5 is the most exciting step forward in web development since the launch of XHTML 1.0 in the year 2000. HTML5 is the future of web design, but it can be implemented right now; and yet it does not make any of your current knowledge of HTML4 or CSS2 redundant. It is a welcome enhancement that increases the flexibility and usefulness of HTML. It also solves some problems; for instance, it can dispense with plugins for embedded video and audio clips, and the number of video file formats is drastically reduced. A raft of new semantic tags makes coding and maintaining a web site much easier. The number of DOCTYPES is reduced from six to two, and the HTML5 DOCTYPES are so brief that you can easily commit them to memory.

HTML5 has brought agreement between the browser vendors because they participated in its formulation. This means that the way they handle coding errors is now standardized; all those little differences are ironed out. A browser's parsing rules as specified by HTML5 ensure that all existing web sites continue to function as before; HTML5 is backwardly compatible.

Because this chapter focuses on the aspects of HTML5 that will enhance the most common types of web site, you will not find a comprehensive discussion on APIs (Application Programming Interfaces); nor will you find a history of the development of HTML5. Several books are available on APIs and the history of HTML5. They cover those topics very well; duplicating them would be pointless (see the tip at the end of the chapter for a list of resources).

The chapter ends with a brief mention of some APIs, but it is probably safe to assume that the great majority of web designers and site owners are not yet implementing them on traditional web sites. This view is reinforced by a recent poll taken by CSS Tricks (http://css-tricks.com). Two years after the release of the APIs, the poll asked web designers the following question: Which HTML5 features have you implemented on production sites?

The results were as follows:

Semantic tags	58%
Forms	36%
Audio/video	30%
Other	16%

1

The "Other" 16 percent was split between nine APIs: Canvas, Web Workers, Web Storage, Geolocation, Drag and Drop, ContentEditable, History, and Microdata. The total adds up to more than 100 percent because most respondents implemented more than one feature.

Moving to HTML5

Now is the time to take advantage of the new features in HTML5; by trying the projects in this and subsequent chapters, you will discover the benefits and enhancements made possible by the new version of HTML. The emphasis of this book is the word *Practical* in the title; therefore, I have "cut to the chase" and provided fully-worked projects covering all the most useful new features of HTML5. I expect you are eager to get started, so let's move on!

The HTML5 and XHTML5 DOCTYPES

HTML 4/XHTML have several DOCTYPES, but HTML5/XHTML5 have only one DOCTYPE each, as follows:

HTML5:
```
<!doctype html>
<html lang=en>
<head>
<title>HTML5 test document</title>
<meta charset=utf-8>
        meta details go here
</head>
```

XHTML5:
```
<!DOCTYPE html>
<html xmlns="http://www.w3.org/1999/xhtml" lang="en">
<head>
<title>XHTML5 test document</title>
<meta charset="utf-8" />
        meta details go here
</head>
```

■ **Note** The simpler HTML5 DOCTYPE can be used for a page containing XHTML markup and it will validate. In fact, you can ignore the XHTML5 DOCTYPE altogether. HTML5 does not care whether you use closed tags (such as `<br />`) or not. The examples in this book do not use the closed tag; however, if you have been using XHTML, you may prefer to continue using closed tags—HTML5 will it accept either way.

HTML5 DOCTYPES specify the English language with lang=en. For other languages, see

http://wwww.iana.org/assignments/language-tags/language-tags.xml.

To change web pages to HTML5 or XHTML5, just change the DOCTYPE. The markup won't be broken, but you will be able to use the more useful elements such as `<audio>` and `<video>` (even in IE 7 or IE 8 with a little bit of JavaScript) and your pages will validate.

■ **Caution** The current HTML5 and XHTML5 validators are `http://validator.w3.org` and `http://html5.validator.nu`. These are still experimental and you should be aware that they may change as time goes by.

To keep up with the development and release of HTML5 items visit

`http://html5doctor.com`

Remy Sharp is one of the experts at the HTML5 Doctor web site. Read his useful article at

`http://html5doctor.com/html-5-boilerplates/`

where he writes that the following markup is "completely valid HTML5":

```
<!doctype html>
<title>Small HTML 5</title>
<p>Hello world</p>
```

Amazing! No <html>, no <body>, no language, no charset, no quote marks, how can it be so lax? It will validate, but it will not support current screen readers, so stay with the following structure for HTML5 markup:

```
<!doctype html>
<html lang=en>
<head>
<title>HTML5 test document</title>
<meta charset=utf-8>
        meta details go here
</head>
<body>
        content goes here
</body>
</html>
```

■ **Note** HTML5 attributes do not have to be wrapped in quotes, and many MIME types can now be omitted in HTML5—but leave the quotes and MIME types in for XHTML5.

A web site can contain a mixture of pages, provided the DOCTYPE for each individual page is correctly specified. This can be useful if you wish to use the new <audio> and <video> tags on only one or two HTML5 pages on an existing web site.

Table 1-1 shows the DOCTYPE of an XHTML page that was changed to an HTML5 DOCTYPE. This page was submitted to the W3C HTML5 validator. It validated and displayed exactly the same as the original page in all browsers. The two DOCTYPES are compared in Table 1-1.

Table 1-1. The DOCTYPE of an XHTML page is changed to an HTML5 DOCTYPE

The original DOCTYPE	The new HTML5 DOCTYPE
```<!DOCTYPE html PUBLIC "-//W3C//DTD XHTML 1.0 Transitional//EN" "http://www.w3.org/TR/xhtml1/DTD/xhtml1-transitional.dtd"> <html xmlns="http://www.w3.org/1999/xhtml"> <head> <title>Old DOCTYPE</title> <meta http-equiv="Content-Type" content="text/html; ↵ charset=utf-8" /> </head>```	```<!doctype html> <html lang=en> <head> <title>New DOCTYPE</title> <meta charset=utf-8> </head>```

Table 1-1 shows the HTML5 DOCTYPE that I experimented with. Figure 1-1 shows the webpage that I used.

Figure 1-1. The web page I used to experiment with the HTML5 DOCTYPE from Table 1-1

In this experiment, the original XHTML page (starter-page.html) validated in the usual W3C HTML4 validator. An identical page, but using the HTML5 DOCTYPE, validated in the W3C HTML5 validator. Both pages were in XHTML format and only the DOCTYPE was changed. The photographs are used by the kind permission of Sandra and Ruth Gould, owners of the Bonehayne Farm holiday accommodations web site at http://www.bonehayne.co.uk

Try this same experiment yourself.

- Use either one of your own validated XHTML or HTML4 web pages, or

- Download the page for Figure 1-1 from the book's page at `www.apress.com`. Amend the DOCTYPE on the page to the HTML5 DOCTYPE.

- Test it on both of the HTML5 validators.

User-inertia will ensure that older browsers and operating systems will be in use for several years to come. Pages in HTLM5 should be readable in older browsers because **the new DOCTYPE is backwardly compatible**. It may be some time before all the browsers catch up with all the new enhancements. Test your HTML5 and XHTML5 pages in various browsers before uploading to the host.

HTML5 is very tolerant, and like HTML4 transitional, it accepts unclosed tags. It will also accept self-closing tags or a mixture, and currently, the pages will validate. Although you can use the HTML5 DOCTYPE instead of the XHTML5 DOCTYPE on a page using XHTML, some time in the future the HTML5/XHTML5 validator may be more strict, so continue to check with the experimental W3C validator for changes.

I have shown that you can take advantage of the shorter HTML5 DOCTYPE without adopting any semantic elements. Having changed an existing page to the new DOCTYPE, you are probably eager to try out the new semantic elements, so let's begin.

The New Elements in HTML5

The following are a few things I'd like to note:

- Most semantic tags are covered in this chapter

- Audio/video are covered in Chapter 6

- Forms are covered in Chapter 10.

Regarding JavaScript and HTML5: on one hand, the new recommendations remove the need for some JavaScript (good); on the other hand, HTML5 has an increased number of APIs needing quite complex JavaScript (not so good). If you intend to take advantage of the new APIs, you should be—or you should strive to be, proficient in the use of JavaScript.

The New Semantic Tags

Semantic concerns the meaning of words. The new semantic tags describe the content of the tags; they include the following:

`<article>`, `<aside>`, `<audio>`, `<details>`, `<figcaption>`, `<figure>`, `<footer>`, `<header>`, `<hgroup>`, `<mark>`, `<nav>`, `<section>`, `<summary>`, `<svg>`, `<time>`, and `<video>`.

A few other semantic tags are proposed. You can investigate them at:

`http://www.w3schools.com/html5/tag_progress.asp`.

There you will find definitions for the tags: bdi, comment, keygen, meter, output, progress, and track. The current browser support for these is also given on the W3CSchools web site.

■ **Caution** CSS assumes that elements are *display:inline;*. This will need to be changed. To ensure that the semantic tags behave as blocks in all browsers, adjust the display property by inserting the following line in the linked CSS sheet.

`article,aside,details,figcaption,figure,footer,header,hgroup,nav,section { display:block; }`

IE 7 and IE 8 will misbehave if you don't do this.

Who benefits from semantic tags? Everybody does; semantic tags make life easier for the web site developer. The standardization of tag names can only be a good thing, and design teams will have no problem locating tags if they use ubiquitous names such as nav or header or article, and so forth. Search engines will be able to home in on the <nav> tag to locate pages linked to the home page. The number of <div>s and ids will decrease, which simplifies development and coding. I recommend that you use semantic tags wherever you can, even though a little JavaScript is needed to enable IE 7 and IE 8 to recognize them. Then, when these two browsers become extinct, you will have become adept at using and styling semantic tags.

Semantic Tags Are Intended to Dispel Ambiguities

Some dispel ambiguity and some do not. Some tags have a presentational connotation, as well as a meaning indicating content.

- Unambiguous HTML5 tags include <article>, <aside>, <audio>, <figure>, <figcaption>, <hgroup>, <mark>, <nav>, and <video>.

- Semi-ambiguous HTML5 tags include <header> and <footer>. These would be unambiguous if there was only one of each per page. They would not only be semantic, but also presentational because they state the element's location on a page. However, an HTML5 page can have several headers and footers. Each article can have a header and footer; these tags are, therefore, ambiguous.

- Another semi-ambiguous HTML5 tag, <section>, is discussed in "The <section> vs. <article> Controversy" section of this chapter.

Since 1997 the recommendation has been that tags should relate to the tag's content, *not* to the content's position or style. Only the new unambiguous tags exactly obey that rule, the others do not.

Headings

In HTML5, the restriction to one <h1> tag per page has been abandoned. Each article or section can have headings <h1> to <h6>. How this affects accessibility is a problem that must be resolved because screen readers use the hierarchy of the headings to guide the sight-impaired person through a web page.

Best Practice

Neither the site owner nor ordinary users will care whether you use semantic tags, but as a web designer, you should care and try to use HTML5 and semantic HTML5 tags where you can. For at least the next half-decade, you will need a JavaScript work-around for IE 7 and IE 8 when using semantic tags. Designers can become overly obsessive about avoiding *ids* and *classes* that describe presentation. Try not to be smitten with this OCD (obsessive-compulsion disorder). For instance, consider a page with a content panel with two columns. Surely `<div id="leftcol">` and `<div id="rightcol">` are more meaningful to a design team than `<div id="some-content">` and `<div id="some-different-content">`. A client wishing to change something in `"leftcol"` will say, "Please amend the left-hand column." She would not know any other name for that column. **Do whatever communicates unambiguously with the client, the designer, and the team members.**

Search Engines and HTML5

Searches will be improved because of the new semantic elements; this is true of the `<nav>` tag and perhaps the `<video>` tag. A search engine could locate the footer and apply a lower weighting because the footer is less likely to include the information the user is looking for.

Summary

The doubly welcome semantic tags are those that embody another advantage in addition to being semantic. A new tag will be a great improvement if it removes the need for hacks and JavaScript work-arounds. Internet Explorer 7 and 8 do not understand the semantic tags; therefore, web designers must either ignore HTML5 semantic tags for a few years or use semantic tags with a JavaScript work-around.

I strongly recommend that you use the semantic tags and the JavaScript hack until IE 7 and IE 8 are no longer widely used.

Simple Examples of Page Layout with Semantic Tags

The first three projects in this section show simple page layouts using HTML5 and semantic tags. The examples use a JavaScript snippet to enable IE 7 and IE 8 to recognize the semantic tags.

⬛ **Note** The navigation menus in the next three examples are primitive; more-sophisticated menus are revealed later in this chapter. HTML5 rollover menus are explained fully (with working examples) in Chapter 4.

Figures 1-2 and 1-3 show the effect of semantic tags.

Figure 1-2. Displayed in IE 9, Firefox, Safari, Opera, and Chrome

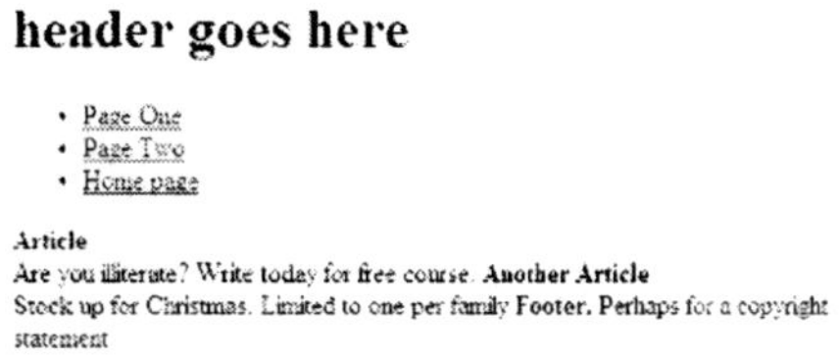

Figure 1-3. Displayed in IE 7 and IE 8

This simple page uses semantic elements <header>, <footer>, and <article>. The markup uses no <div>s. An internal style is used for instructional purposes only.

Listing 1-2 creates Figure 1-2 and Figure 1-3; the difference in appearance is caused by the different browsers.

Listing 1-2. A Simple Semantic Page for Testing in Various Browsers (simplistic-html5.html)

```
<!doctype html>
<html lang=en>
<head>
<title>Simplistic HTML5</title>
<meta charset=utf-8>
<style>
body { width:500px; margin:auto;
}
header, nav, article, footer { display:block;
}
header { width:500px; background-color:#FF9966; text-align:center; margin:auto;
}
nav { float:left; width:25%; background-color: #FF9966; margin-bottom:10px;
}
article { float:right; width:70%; background-color:#FF9966; margin-bottom:10px;
}
footer { clear:both; background-color:#FF9966; text-align:center;
}
h2 { font-size:large; font-weight:bold; margin-top:0; margin-bottom:0;
}
</style>
</head>
<body>
<header>
<h1>header goes here</h1>
</header>
<nav>
<ul>
        <li><a href="page-one.html" >Page One</a></li>
        <li><a href="page-two.html" >Page Two</a></li>
        <li><a href="index.html" >Home page</a></li>
</ul>
</nav>
<article>
<h2>Article</h2>
Are you illiterate? Write today for free course.
</article>
<article>
<h2>Another Article</h2>
Stock up for Christmas. Limited to one per family.
</article>
<footer>
Footer. Perhaps for a copyright statement
</footer>
</body>
</html>
```

The Solution for Internet Explorer 7 and 8

IE 9 will support HTML5 semantic tags, but IE 7 and IE 8 need a "conditional" that forces them to recognize semantic tags. Use Remy Sharpe's JavaScript snippet in the markup so that you can test a page for IE 7 or IE 8 support in the IETester software.

▓ **Tip** IETester from `http://www.my-debugbar.com/wiki/IETester/HomePage`. See Chapter 19 for details. In addition to IETester, other tools are available for testing your pages for older browser support. You might try Adobe BrowserLab, Microsoft Expression's SuperPreview, and IE NetRenderer (`http://netrenderer.com`).

Remy Sharp devised a solution that is free for anyone to use. It converts the semantic tags into something that IE 7 and IE 8 can understand. It covers most HTML5 tags, including:-

<article>, <aside>, <audio>, <canvas>, <figcaption>, <figure>, <footer>, <header>, <hgroup>, <mark>, <nav>, <section>, <time>, and <video>.

▓ **Tip** See Remy Sharp's B:log at `http://remysharp.com/2009/01/07//html5-enabling-script`. See also *Introducing HTML5* by Bruce Lawson and Remy Sharp (New Riders Press, 2010).

Download the JavaScript file `html5.js` and put a copy in the host folder. The pages on the web site must contain a <body>…</body> tag for the JavaScript to work, even though the <body> tag is no longer required for HTML5. In the <head> section on every page, add an IE conditional statement and a link to the JavaScript, as shown in bold type in the following snippet:

```
<!doctype html>
<html lang=en>
<head>
<title>HTML 5 complete</title>
<meta charset=utf-8>
<link to a style sheet goes here…>
        <!--[if lte IE 8]>
                <script src="html5.js">
        </script>
        <![endif]-->
</head>
<body>
<p>Oh no! not another Hello World</p>
</body>
</html>
```

▓ **Caution** `html5.js` is not written as "htm plus 15" but as htm plus lower case L and the number five.

Even the JavaScript MIME type; type="text/javascript" can be omitted from HTML5. New browsers recognize the JavaScript file's *.js ending and apply the appropriate MIME type by default.

■ **Note** The conditional and the script must be in the <head> section and placed after any link to a style sheet, as shown in Figure 1-4.

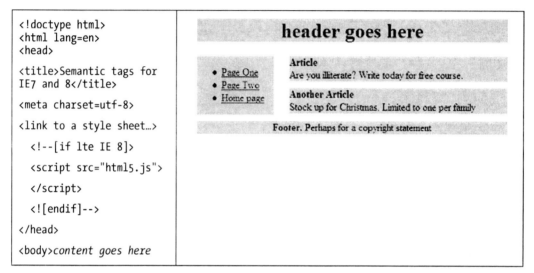

Figure 1-4. The right-hand panel shows the display in IE 7 and IE 8 using JavaScript

Listing 1-4 contains a snippet of JavaScript that allows IE 7 and IE 8 to understand semantic tags. The result can be seen in Figure 1-4.

Listing 1-4 A simple semantic page with JavaScript fallback for IE 7 and IE 8 (simplistic-html5-java.html)

```
<!doctype html>
<html lang=en>
<head>
<title>Semantic tags with JavaScript support for IE 7 and 8</title>
<meta charset=utf-8>
<style>
body { width:500px; margin:auto;
}
header, nav, article, footer { display:block;
}
header { width:500px; background-color:#FF9966; text-align:center; margin:auto;
}
nav { float:left; width:25%; background-color: #FF9966; margin-bottom:10px;
}
article { float:right; width:70%; background-color:#FF9966; margin-bottom:10px;
```

```
}
footer { clear:both; background-color:#FF9966; text-align:center;
}
</style>
        <!--[if lte IE 8]>
                <script src="html5.js">
                </script>
        <![endif]-->
</head>
<body>
<header>
<h1>header goes here</h1>
</header>
<nav>
<ul>
        <li><a href="page-one.html" >Page One</a></li>
        <li><a href="page-two.html" >Page Two</a></li>
        <li><a href="index.html" >Home page</a></li>
</ul>
</nav>
<article>
        <b>Article</b><br>Are you illiterate? Write today for free course.
</article>
<article>
        <b>Another Article</b><br>Stock up for Christmas. Limited to one per family
</article>
<footer>
<strong>Footer.</strong> Perhaps for a copyright statement
</footer>
```

Columns

The simple example shown in Listing 1-4 is all very well, but suppose we want a more readable layout with the *article* blocks in vertical columns, as shown in Figure 1-5.

Figure 1-5. *Vertical side-by-side article blocks. No problem with semantic tags.*

Listing 1-5 creates the the two vertical "article" columns shown in Figure 1-5. The key features are shown in bold type. An internal style sheet is used for instructional purposes only.

Listing 1-5. Using the Semantic `<article>` *tag to Create Columns (simplistic-side-by-side.html)*

```
<!doctype html>
<html lang=en>
<head>
<title>Semantic tags with two articles side by side</title>
<meta charset=utf-8>
<style>
body { width:500px; margin:auto;
}
header, nav, footer { display:block;
}
article { display:inline;
}
header { width:500px; background-color:#FF9966; text-align:center; margin:auto;
}
h1 { margin-bottom:10px;
}
nav { float:left; width:25%; background-color: #FF9966; margin-bottom:10px;
}
article { float:left; width:33%; background-color:#FF9966; margin:0 0 0 10px; ↵
padding:6px;
}
footer { clear:both; background-color:#FF9966; text-align:center;
}
h2 { font-size:large; font-weight:bold; margin-top:0; margin-bottom:0;
</style>
        <!--[if lte IE 8]>
                <script src="html5.js>
                </script>
        <![endif]-->
</head>
<body>
<header>
<h1>header goes here</h1>
</header>
<nav>
<ul>
        <li><a href="page-one.html" >Page One</a></li>
        <li><a href="page-two.html" >Page Two</a></li>
        <li><a href="index.html" >Home page</a></li>
</ul>
</nav>
<article>
<h2>Article</h2>Are you illiterate? Write today for a free course.<br>Easy payment terms.
</article>
<article>
<h2>Another Article</h2>Stock up for Christmas. Limited to one per family.<br>
Free Delivery &pound;2
</article>
<footer>
<strong>Footer.</strong> Perhaps for a copyright statement
</footer>
```

```
</body>
</html>
```

The <nav> Tag

Web sites have traditionally used a <div> with many different *id* attributes for the navigation menu; for example, menu, nav, links, navmenu, navigation, and so on. HTML5 introduces a semantic tag <nav> that standardizes the navigation menu. The <nav> tag must act as a container surrounding a block of unordered links, that is, the <ul> </ul> tag must sit inside the <nav> </nav> container. Figure 1-6 shows a menu block created with the semantic <nav> tag.

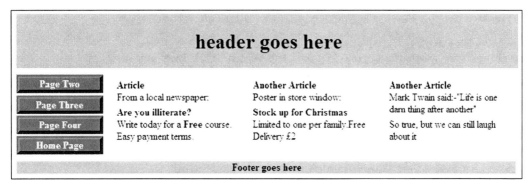

Figure 1-6. A set of navigation menu buttons created using the HTML5 <nav> tag

Listing 1-6a introduces 3D buttons using the HTML5 Semantic <nav> tag

Listing 1-6a. Inserting a 3D Navigation Menu Using the <nav> tag (html5-nav.html)

```
<!doctype html>
<html lang=en>
<head>
<title>The nav tag</title>
<meta charset=utf-8>
<link rel="stylesheet" type="text/css" href="nav-style.css">
    <!--[if lte IE 8]>
    <script src="html5.js">
    </script>
    <![endif]-->
</head>
<body>
<div id="container">
<header>
<h1>header goes here</h1>
</header>
<nav>
<ul>
            <li><a href="#" title="Page 2">Page Two</a></li>
            <li><a href="#" title="Page 3">Page Three</a></li>
            <li><a href="#" title="Page 4">Page Four</a></li>
```

```
                <li><a href="#" title="Home page">Home Page</a></li>
</ul>
</nav>
<div id="content">
<article>
<strong>Article<br></strong>From a local newspaper:<p><strong>Are you ⏎
illiterate?</strong><br>Write today for a <strong>Free</strong> course. ⏎
<br> Easy payment terms. </p>
</article>
<article>
<strong>Another Article</strong><br>
Poster in store window:<p><strong>Stock up for Christmas</strong><br>
Limited to one per family.<br>Free Delivery &pound;2</p>
</article>
<article>
<strong>Another Article</strong><br>Mark Twain said:&quot;Life is one ⏎
darn thing after another&quot;<p> So true, but we can still laugh about it</p>
</article>
</div></div>
<footer>
<strong>Footer goes here</strong>
</footer>
</body>
</html>
```

Listing 1-6b provides the CSS presentation for the navigation menu

Listing 1-6b. *Using the <nav> Tag in the CSS for Listing 1-6a (nav-style.css)*

```
    #container { width:780px; margin:auto;
    }
    #content { width:640px; margin-left:140px;
    }
    header, nav, footer, article, section { display:block;
    }
    header { width:780px; background-color:#FF9966; text-align:center; ⏎
    margin:5px auto 10px auto; padding:2px;
    }
    article { float:left; width:190px; margin:0 0 0 10px; padding:6px;
    }
    footer { clear:both; background-color:#FF9966; text-align:center; ⏎
    width:780px; margin:auto;
    }
    p { margin-top:5px; margin-bottom:5px;
    }
    /* set navigation menu position and style*/
    nav { float:left; width:130px; background-color : white; margin: 0 7px 5px -30px;
    }
    nav ul {float:left; width:130px;}
    /* set general side button styles */
    nav li { margin-bottom: 3px; text-align: center; list-style-type:none; width:125px;}
    /* set general anchor styles */
    nav li a { display: block; color: white; font-weight: bold; ⏎
    text-decoration: none }
```

```
/* specify state styles */
/* mouseout (default) */
nav li a { background:#946055; color: white; border: 5px outset #C96E6B;}
/* mouseover */
nav li a:hover { background: #9F7562;    border: 5px outset #C96E6B;}
/* onmousedown */
nav li a:active { background:maroon;  border: 5px inset maroon }
}
```

A More Complex Example Using Semantic Tags

The next example uses the page illustrated earlier in Figure 1-1. Figure 1-7 provides a reminder of its appearance.

Figure 1-7. The same web page as shown previously in Figure 1-1 now includes semantic tags

Here, we'll convert the page shown previously in Figure 1-1 to HTML5 semantic elements.

In real life, you don't need to convert an existing page. Your current pages in HTML4 or XHTML will display properly in all browsers without the HTML5 DOCTYPE for at least a decade. However, if you wish to take advantage of the semantic tags, the next project describes how to incorporate them by amending an existing XHTML or HTML4 page.

■ **Note** Your current WYSIWYG web site editing program may not display HTML5 semantic elements properly. As a result, you need to test each step in web browsers. You could write the code direct into a text editor, such as Notepad or Notepad++, and then test in the browsers. You might be able to upgrade your WYSIWYG program so that it is compatible with HTML5. Some WYSIWYG editors claim to be HTML5 compatible, including the Bordeux/HTML-5 WYSIWIYG editor at `https://github.com/bordeux/HTML-5-WYSIWYG-Editor`, the Aloha editor at `http://aloha-editor.org`, and Mercury Editor at `http://jejackson.github.com/mercury/`. In any case, check your HTML5 pages with the validator at `http://validator.w3.org` or `http://html5.validator.nu`

The Conversion Steps

Perform the following steps to convert a page to HTML5:

1. Make a copy of an existing (X)HTML4 page (one with no semantic markup) and name it something like *HTML5-test-page.html*. I have called my copy `starter-page.html` and it can be downloaded from the book's page at `http://www.apress.com`.

2. Make a copy of the page's style sheet and name it something like *html5-style.css*. I have called my copy `starter.css` and it can be downloaded from the book's page at http://www.apress.com.

3. Look for logical blocks in the page you are intending to convert. Also, review a checklist of the new tags to see how the page could be adjusted to accommodate them. The page I'm working on has no stand-alone items, therefore we can't use `<article>`s. The logical blocks will eventually become the semantic blocks. In this exercise the suitable blocks are as follows:

    *   The header with its white border (currently labelled `<div id = "header">`).

    *   The far right column with its menu block can be replaced with `<nav>`.

    *   The semantic `<footer>` can replace the current `<div id="footer">`.

4. Change the DOCTYPE to

    ```
    <!doctype html>
    <html lang=en>
    <head>
    <title>Your title</title>
    <meta charset=utf-8>
    ```

5. Change the link in the HTML page to point to the name of your copied and renamed CSS file.

6. To support IE 7 and IE 8, add a link for Remy Sharp's JavaScript snippet in the `<head>` section.

    ```
    <!--[if lte IE 8]>
    <script src="html5.js">
    </script>
    <![endif]-->
    ```

7. Download and install html5.js in the main folder of the web site. It's available from www.apress.com or from

    http://remysharp.com/2009/01/07//html5-enabling-script

8. Add this line into the CSS file:

                header, nav, footer, article, { display:block; }

After converting my starter files to semantic tags, I renamed them HTML5-Ch1-7.html and HTML5-style-2.css. These are listed below and can be downloaded from the book's page on the Apress web site.

Listing 1-7a. The new HTML5 listing (HTML5-Ch1-7.html)

```
<!doctype html>
<html lang=en>
<head>
<title>Test page for semantic tags </title>
<meta charset=utf-8>
<link rel="stylesheet" type="text/css" href="HTML5-style-2.css">
        <!--conditional Javascript added-->
        <!--[if lte IE 8]>
        <script src="html5.js">
        </script>
        <![endif]-->
</head>
<body>
<header><!--<div id="hdr"> changed to <header>-->
  <h1>Devon's Rural Retreats</h1>
</header>
<!--close top section - content area starts -->
<div id="content">
    <h2>Award winning accommodation, self catering or bed and breakfast</h2>
<div id="leftcol">
<h3>Cottages, converted barns, caravans</h3>
<img alt="Cottage interior" title="Cottage interior" height="225" ↵
src="images/cotdining300.jpg" width="300"><br>The superb interior ↵
of one of our cottages
</div>
<nav><!--use the semantic tag <nav>-->
<ul><!--start of menu list-->
<li class="btn"> <a href="accommodation.html" title="Accommodation">Accommodation</a></li>
<li class="btn"><a href="maps.html" title="Location Maps">Maps</a>
</li><li class="btn"><a href="faqs.html" title="Frequently Asked Questions">Information</a> ↵
</li>
<li class="btn"><a href="attractions.html" title="Local attractions">Attractions</a></li>
<li class="btn"><a href="contact.html" title="Contact us">Contact Us</a></li>
<li class="btn"><a href="index.html" title="Return to Home Page">Home Page</a></li>
</ul><!--end of menu list-->
</nav><!--</div> removed and replaced with </nav>-->
<div id="midcol">
    <h3>Situated in the UK's beautiful Devon countryside</h3>
<img title="Devon countryside" alt="Devon countryside" src="images/devon398.jpg" ↵
height="229" width="398">
</div>
```

```
<br class="clear">
</div><!--content section closed-->
<!--<div id=footer"> changed to <footer>-->
<footer><p>Footer goes here</p>
</footer>
</body>
</html>
```

Listing 1-7b. The Revised CSS Sheet **for Figure** 1-7 *(html5-style-2.css)*

(The key items are picked out in bold type.)

```
/*equalise for various browsers and change #header to header*/
div body header #content { margin:0; padding:0; border:0;
}
body { background:#FFF url(images/green-grad.jpg) repeat-x; margin:auto;
}
/*add display attributes for the semantic tags*/
header, footer, section, article, nav { display:block;
}
/*remove the # from #header*/
header {width:920px; height:180px; padding:0; border:10px white solid; ↵
background: url(images/header3.jpg); margin:10px auto;
}
h1 { font-size:300%; color :white; position: relative; left:90px; top: 55px;
width:480px;
}
#rosette { position:relative; left:750px; top:5px;
}
#content { background-color:transparent; border-left:10px white solid; ↵
border-right:10px white solid; border-bottom:10px white solid; width: 904px; ↵
margin-top:10px; margin-left:auto; margin-right:auto; padding:8px; ↵
font-size:medium; color:maroon;
}
h2 { font-size:x-large; color:white; margin:0 0 10px 0;
}
h3 { font-size:large; color:white; margin:0 0 6px 0;
}
#leftcol { float:left; width: 310px; vertical-align:top;
}
#rightcol { width: 135px; float:right; height: 252px; margin-right:10px;
}
#midcol { margin-left:315px; margin-right:145px; margin-top:10px; ↵
vertical-align:top;
}
/*set nav block position and width and remove the #menu item*/
nav ul { margin:10px 0 10px 0; width:135px; float:right;
}
/*Set un-ordered list style within the menu block only. This removes bullets*/
nav li { list-style-type:none;
}
/* set general side button styles */
li.btn { margin-bottom: 3px; text-align: center; width:130px;
}
```

```
/* set general anchor styles and include the zoom fix for IE6*/
li.btn a { display: block; color: white; font-weight: bold; ↩
text-decoration: none; zoom:1;
}
/* specify mouse state styles */
/* mouseout (default) */
li.btn a { background:#559a55; color: white; border: 5px outset #559a55; ↩
padding-bottom:3px;
}
/* mouseover */
li.btn a:hover { background: red; color:white; border: 5px outset red;
}
/*mouse active*/
li.btn a:active { background:maroon; border: 5px inset maroon;
}
br.clear { clear:both;
}
#midcol img { margin-left:10px;
}
/*change #footer to footer */
footer { clear:both; color:maroon; text-align:center;
}
```

▩ **Note** The semantic tags do not altogether dispense with the *id* and *class* identifiers. An HTML5 page can have several articles that can be separately identified with their own *id*s and *classes*.

The <section> vs. <article> Controversy

You may wonder why I have not used the <section> element in any example so far. When I wrote this chapter, there was considerable confusion over the difference between <section> and <article>. This arose because some manuals and web sites described the <section> element as being like a chapter in a book. This suggested that it was like a wrapper containing chunks of content. As a result, one HTML5 manual and some HTML5 forums used <section> as a styled wrapper or container. This surrounded several <article> elements. Another HTML5 manual used a <div> for the container or wrapper; this enclosed <article> elements, which in turn enclosed <sections>.

Which practice is correct? I tried them all and they all worked because HTML5 is currently quite lax.

Even my favorite HTML5 gurus at HTML5 Doctor *(http://html5doctor.com)* discovered they had been using the <section> element incorrectly; their revised web site stated: "…we realize that we've been using the <section> element incorrectly all this time. Sorry, what we've been doing wrong is using <section> to wrap content in order to style it, or to demarcate the main content area from the <nav>, <header>, <footer> etc. These are jobs for <div>, not <section>."

The http://www.whatwg.org specification was revised as follows: "The <section> element is not a generic container element. When an element is needed for styling purposes…authors are encouraged to use the *<div>* element instead."

See the full version of the W3C statement on this topic at

http://www.w3.org/TR/html5/sections.html#the-section-element

<section> is best used as a sub-section of an <article> and should always contain and enclose a heading, something like the following:

```
<article>
<h1>A heading, any level from h1 to h6</h1>
        <section>
                <h1>A heading, any level from h1 to h6</h1>some content
        </section>
        <section>
                <h1>A heading, any level from h1 to h6</h1>some content
        </section>
    <article>
```

HTML5 Doctor gives the following helpful rules for using <section>:

- Don't use <section> as a target for styling or scripting; use a <div> for that.

- Don't use <section> if <article>, <aside>, or <nav> is more appropriate.

- Don't use <section> unless there is *naturally* a heading at the start of the section.

Check your page in http://gsnedders.html5.org/outliner/. If you see an "untitled section" notice referring to a <section>, it means you omitted a heading for that <section>.

The <article> Element

An <article> is a stand-alone item, such as a self-contained piece of information that could be lifted from the page and published in a forum, magazine, RSS feed, or newspaper. It should contain and enclose a heading (h1 to h6) and it can contain two or more sections. The key words are STAND ALONE. This is the essential characteristic of the <article> element. The www.whatwg.org specification states: "Authors are encouraged to use the <article> element instead of the <section> element when it would make sense to syndicate the contents of the element."

A blog containing ongoing and interesting discussions on this topic is at

http://www.brucelawson.co.uk/2010/html5-articles-and-sections-whats-the-difference/

The controversy still simmers. Blogger/web developer Estelle Weyl of Standardista also speaks on the subject at http://www.standardista.com/html5-section-v-article

Estelle uses the analogy of a newspaper containing sections such as sport, fashion, food, and so forth. Each section contains articles that contain sections. The sections in a newspaper are "main topics," the articles are sub-topics. Each sub-topic is complete in itself which matches the W3C definition of <article>. However, the analogy falls down if one web page deals with only one topic (which is best practice). One topic (article) per web page makes a better user experience and it helps search engines to index a page. To add to the confusion, it could be said that a section (such as sport) in a newspaper is complete in itself and is, therefore, a large article which could be syndicated.

Although a page seems to work whether you have an article inside an article, a section inside an article, or an article inside a section, Bruce Lawson's model provides a useful guideline.

My own solution is to forget <section> and use <div>; after all, the two new tags <article> and <section> are for the benefit of browser vendors, blogs, and web sites that provide RSS feeds; they are not particularly helpful for traditional web sites. Because <article> is unambiguous and clearly defined, I sometimes use it in HTML5 pages together with the JavaScript hack for IE 7 and IE 8.

> ▓ **Note** The `<section>` element is treated as `display:inline;`. In current browsers, this may change eventually, but meanwhile set the `<section>` element to `display:block;`.

The <aside> Tag

The `<aside>` tag separates a piece of text from the main content. It can have a border and/or a background color to make it stand out from the surrounding text. This means the `<aside>` can contain an interesting extract to tempt a user to read the main body of text. An `<aside>` with a border is shown in Figure 1-8.

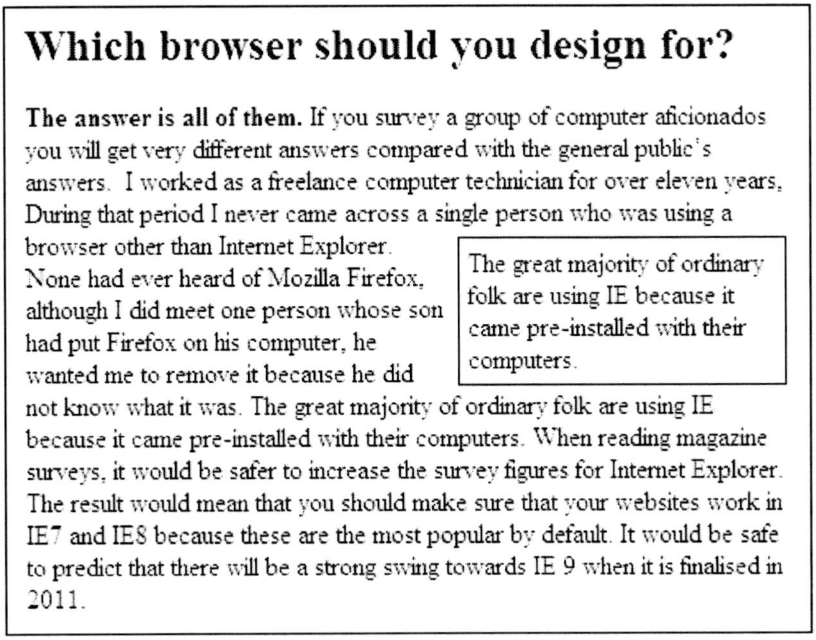

Which browser should you design for?

The answer is all of them. If you survey a group of computer aficionados you will get very different answers compared with the general public's answers. I worked as a freelance computer technician for over eleven years. During that period I never came across a single person who was using a browser other than Internet Explorer.

None had ever heard of Mozilla Firefox, although I did meet one person whose son had put Firefox on his computer, he wanted me to remove it because he did

> The great majority of ordinary folk are using IE because it came pre-installed with their computers.

not know what it was. The great majority of ordinary folk are using IE because it came pre-installed with their computers. When reading magazine surveys, it would be safer to increase the survey figures for Internet Explorer. The result would mean that you should make sure that your websites work in IE7 and IE8 because these are the most popular by default. It would be safe to predict that there will be a strong swing towards IE 9 when it is finalised in 2011.

Figure 1-8. The aside element can create a pull quote (shown inset with border).

Listing 1-8 provides the pull quote separated from the main body of text.

Listing 1-8. Demonstrating the Semantic `<aside>` Tag (aside.html)

(The text has been abbreviated and an internal style is used to save space)

```
<!doctype html>
<html lang=en>
<head>
<title>HTML5 exercise, an aside</title>
<meta charset=utf-8>
<style type="text/css">
```

```
h1 { font-size:160%; font-weight:bold;
}
aside, section, article { display:block;
}
section { width:450px; margin:auto;
}
article { width:445px; text-align:left;
}
aside { width:180px; padding:5px; margin:5px 0 0 5px; float: right; border:1px black solid;
}
</style>
        <!--[if lte IE 8]><!--conditional Javascript added-->
        <script src="html5.js" type="text/javascript">
        </script>
        <![endif]-->
</head>
<body>
<section>
<h1>Which browser should you design for?</h1>
        <article>
        <b>The answer is all of them.</b> If you survey a group of computer ↵
         aficionados you will get very different answers…Internet Explorer.
                <aside>
                The great majority of ordinary folk are using IE because it came ↵
                pre-installed with their computers.
                </aside>
        None had ever heard of Mozilla Firefox…a strong swing towards IE 9 from 2011.
        </article>
</section>
</body>
</html>
```

The <mark> Tag

Highlighting certain words or phrases can be achieved either by formatting them or giving them a colored background. In HTML5 you can use the <mark> tag; the effect is similar to using a highlighter pen on printed text, as shown in Figure 1-9.

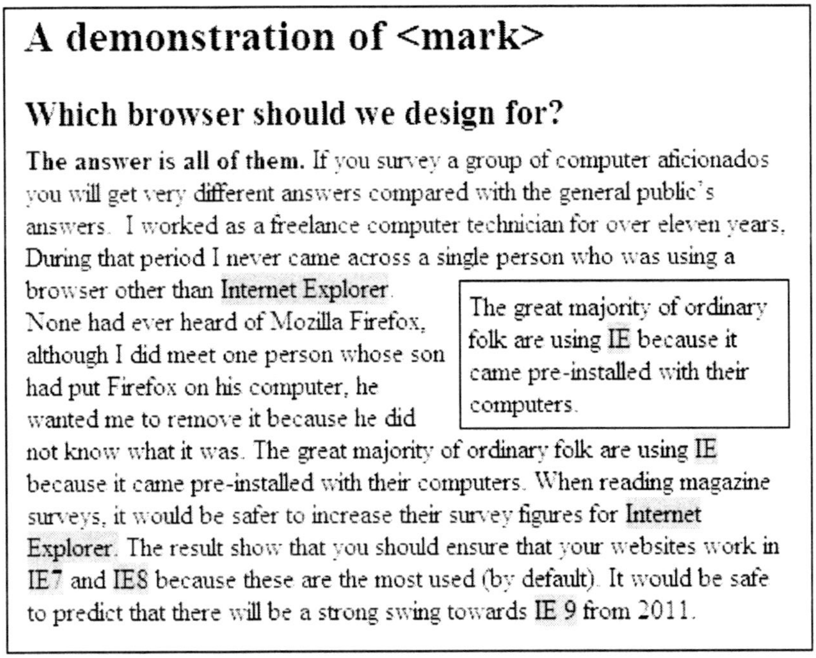

A demonstration of <mark>

Which browser should we design for?

The answer is all of them. If you survey a group of computer aficionados you will get very different answers compared with the general public's answers. I worked as a freelance computer technician for over eleven years. During that period I never came across a single person who was using a browser other than Internet Explorer. None had ever heard of Mozilla Firefox, although I did meet one person whose son had put Firefox on his computer, he had put Firefox on his computer, he wanted me to remove it because he did

> The great majority of ordinary folk are using IE because it came pre-installed with their computers.

not know what it was. The great majority of ordinary folk are using IE because it came pre-installed with their computers. When reading magazine surveys, it would be safer to increase their survey figures for Internet Explorer. The result show that you should ensure that your websites work in IE7 and IE8 because these are the most used (by default). It would be safe to predict that there will be a strong swing towards IE 9 from 2011.

Figure 1-9. The mark tag can be used to highlight text.

■ **Tip** The <mark> tag could be used in conjunction with a search, perhaps by employing Stuart Langridge's *searchhi* script, which can be downloaded from http://www.kryogenix.org/code/browser/searchhi/

In Listing 1-9 for the <mark> tag, the markup uses the full word <mark>. Some manuals offer the abbreviation <m>, but because the abbreviated version does not behave itself in all browsers, it is better to use the full word.

Listing 1-9. Creates Text With Certain Words Highlighed as Shown in Figure 1-9 (mark.html)

(The text in the listing has been abbreviated to save space and an internal style sheet is used.)

```
<!doctype html>
<html lang=en>
<head>
<title>HTML5 exercise, mark</title>
<meta charset=utf-8>
<style type="text/css">
h1 { font-size:160%; font-weight:bold; margin-top:5px; margin-bottom:0;
}
h2 { font-size:130%; font-weight:bold; margin-top:0; margin-bottom:5px;
}
```

```
aside, section, article { display:block;
}
#content {width:450px; margin:auto;
}
article { width:445px; text-align:left;
}
aside {width:180px; padding:5px; margin:5px 0 0 5px; float: right; border:1px black solid;
}
mark { background-color:#FFCC66;
}
</style>
        <!--[if lte IE 8]><!--conditional Javascript added-->
        <script src="html5.js" type="text/javascript">
        </script>
        <![endif]-->
</head>
<body>
<div id="content">
<h1>A demonstration of &lt;mark&gt;</h1><br/>
<h2>Which browser should we design for?</h2>
<article>
<strong>The answer is all of them.</strong> If you survey a group of computer ↵
aficionados you will get very different answers compared with the general public's ↵
answers.  I worked as a freelance computer technician for over eleven years, ↵
During that period I never came across a single person who was using a browser other ↵
than <mark>Internet Explorer</mark>.
<aside>
The great majority of ordinary folk are using <mark>IE</mark> because it came pre-installed
with their computers.
</aside>
None had ever heard of Mozilla Firefox, although I did meet one person whose son had ↵
put Firefox on his computer,
he wanted me to remove it because he did not know what it was.
The great majority of ordinary folk are using <mark>IE</mark> because it came ↵
pre-installed with their computers. When reading magazine surveys, it would be ↵
safer to increase their survey figures for <mark>Internet Explorer.</mark> The ↵
results show that you should ensure that your web sites work in <mark>IE7</mark> ↵
and <mark>IE8</mark> because these are the most used (by default). It would be ↵
safe to predict that there will be a strong swing towards <mark>IE 9</mark> from ↵
2011.
</article>
</div>
</body>
</html>
```

The <figure> Tag

The <figure> tag can be used to connect captions to illustrations, diagrams, photos, and code listings. The caption stays fixed to the element no matter where the element is relocated on the web page. For a full explanation and examples using this element see:-

http://www.w3.org/TR/html5-author/the-figure-element.html

Figure 1-10 shows how the new <figure> tag can provide a caption for a photograph.

Fig 10 Using the HTML5 figure tag

Figure 1-10. An example of the new <figure> element. The caption is enclosed within the white border and is an integral part of the <figure> block element.

In Figure 1-10, the <figure> tag combines an image and its descriptive text into a single block element. Like any other block, it can be given borders and it can be positioned. No matter where it is positioned, the descriptive text (caption) stays with the image. The element works in all browsers if the conditional JavaScript is included in the markup. In Listing 1-10 you will see that the actual caption is enclosed in a <figcaption> tag, this is the companion tag to the <figure> tag. To save space an internal style sheet is used in Listing 1-10.

Listing 1-10. The HTML Markup Using the <figure> Tag That Links a Caption to an Element (figure.html)

```
<!doctype html>
<html lang=en>
<head>
<title>Using the figure and caption tags</title>
<meta charset=utf-8>
<style type="text/css">
figure, hgroup { display:block;
}
figure {width:300px; padding:10px; border:1px black solid;
}
</style>
<!--[if lte IE 8]>
<!--conditional Javascript added-->
<script src="html5.js" type="text/javascript">
</script>
<![endif]-->
</head>
<body>
<figure>
<img alt="The river Coly" height="196" src="images/colrivblu.jpg" width="298">
        <figcaption><br>
        Fig 10 Using the HTML5 figure tag
```

```
        </figcaption>
    </figure>
    </body>
    </html>
```

The <hgroup> Tag

The tag `<hgroup>` `</hgroup>` is a container for two or more headings (h1, h2, h3 ,h4, h5, and h6). It indicates that the headings are closely related, so it will be used to group together headings with subheadings, titles, and subtitles. Prior to the release of the `<hgroup>` tag, grouping headings resulted in problems with the outline of a document; this problem was called *phantom nodes*. Using `<hgroup>` avoids this problem because it combines the two headings into one node. The `<hgroup>` tags can only contain headings. The following is an example:

```
<article>
<hgroup>
<h1>I put our holiday dates and address on a social network</h1>
<h2>An idiot's tale</h2>
        </hgroup>
<p>We returned to a ransacked house, even the furniture was taken.<br> Your friend,
<br>Loopy Lou</p>
</article
```

This tag would most probably be used within the header, but it can also be used within any of one or more `<article>` `</article>` tags on the same page.

The New HTML5 Form Controls

The HTML5 recommendation for forms is almost complete. HTML5 forms are not straightforward because other factors affect them. A hack-proof form needs a handler in PHP, ASP.NET, or Perl. The handler must match the new HTML5 form tags. Accessibility will be compromised unless great care is taken to integrate the new HTML5 form elements with the requirements of screen readers. For some time, IE conditionals and alternative style sheets will have to be used so that surfers using IE 7 or IE 8 can see and use HTML5 forms. At the time of writing, IE 9 does not support HTML5 forms. IE 10 will most likely support the current forms as well as HTML5 forms.

Only Opera 9.5+ supports *all* the new form elements at the time of writing.

Mozilla Firefox 5+ supports most of the HTML5 form elements. Safari supports most of the form elements except for autocomplete. Chrome supports all elements except autocomplete and list.

To see which browsers currently support forms, visit:-

http://www.w3schools.com/html5/html5_form_input_types.asp.

The new form input controls are backwardly compatible so that you can use the new input for fields such as e-mail addresses. Browsers that don't yet support `<input type="email">` will read it as if it was `<input type="text">`.

■ **Note** Even though formatting checks are built into HTML5, robots and criminals can still enter dodgy URLs. Therefore, you still need the protection of an anti-hack form handler for some fields.

The list of new HTML5 input controls includes the following:

date (such as date of birth)	datetime	search
email (e-mail address)	datetime-local	time
number (a number)	color	url
tel (a telephone number)	range	week
		month

The first four input controls in the left-hand column will probably be the most useful. The url input control in the right-hand column is positively dangerous because it will allow users to insert an address linked to a nasty web site. I never include a field for URL. If the user wants me to access a URL because no URL field is provided, they email me to request permission to send a URL; a robot can't do that.

The HTML5 form controls also have the following new attributes:

autofocus	autofocus="autofocus"
required	required="required"
maxlength	maxlength="25"

Opera has a demo page that gives an indication of how the new inputs might eventually work. Open the demo in Opera 9.5 or later and try it out at:-

http://devfiles.myopera.com/articles/4582/html5-forms-example.html.

The forms have a different appearance in different browsers, but they all function in the same way. The appearance in Opera is shown in Figures 1-11, 1-12, and 1-13.

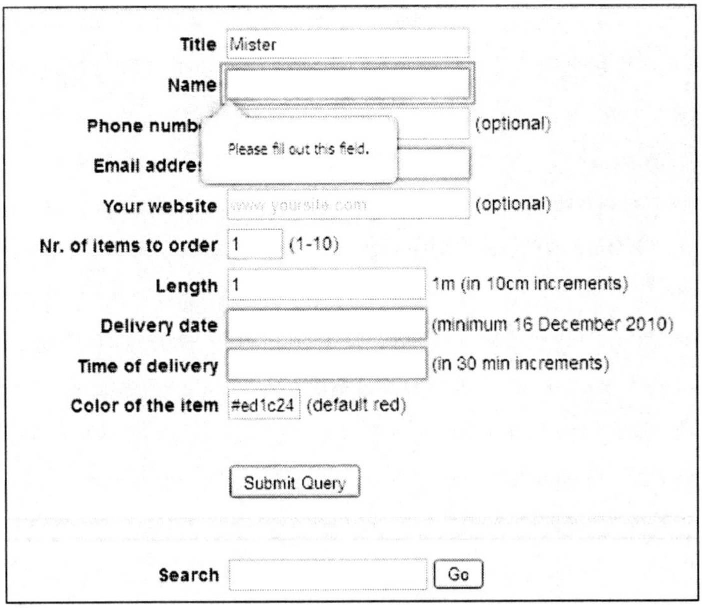

Figure 1-11. The Opera HTML5 form demo shows what happens after you click the submit button.

In this case, I did not fill out an essential field. As a result, that field is surrounded with a double red border and a drop-down warning appears.

In Opera, *required* fields have a red border, as shown in Figure 1-12.

If the field is filled in correctly, a green border appears.

Figure 1-12. *In this case, the e-mail address contained an illegal space.*

Although not displayed in this Opera demo, other Opera demos show that in some fields a drop-down choice is presented when the field is clicked. Other fields have a color picker or a slider for a range of values. Clicking a date field brings up a calendar to choose a date, as shown in Figure 1-13.

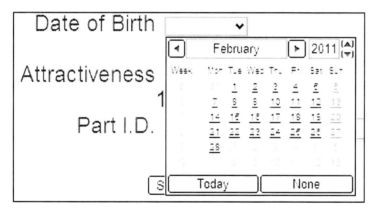

Figure 1-13. *When the date-of-birth field is clicked, a calendar pops up, permitting the user to select the date of birth.*

As I stated at the start of this section, Opera has produced a demo page and some guidelines that describe how the Opera browser applies the HTML5 form elements.

Listing 1-13 was taken from the Opera guide. It creates the interface shown in Figure 1-11 and will produce the error messages and the drop down list shown in Figures 1-11 through 1-13.

Listing 1-13. *Taken from the Opera Demo Page and Guide. In this case, only the main elements are listed (new_form_features_in-html5.html).*

```
<body>
<h1>HTML5 forms example</h1>
<p>This is an example for the <a href="http://dev.opera.com/articles/view/new-form-features-
in-HTML5/"></a> article</p>
```

```
<form id="form-order" onsubmit="this.checkValidity(); return false;">
<div>
<label for="title">Title</label>
<input type="text" list="mydata" name="title" id="title" placeholder="Select one or enter your
own" required>
<datalist id="mydata">
        <option label="Mr" value="Mister">
        <option label="Mrs" value="Mistress">
        <option label="Ms" value="Miss">
</datalist>
</div>
<div>
<label for="name">Name</label>
<input type="text" name="name" id="name" placeholder="John Doe" required>
</div>
<div>
<label for="phone">Phone number</label>
<input type="tel" name="phone" id="phone" placeholder="+1 23456789" pattern="[0-9]{10}">
(optional)
</div>
<div>
<label for="email">Email address</label>
<input type="email" name="email" id="email" placeholder="foo@bar.com" required>
</div>
<div>
<label for="web site">Your web site</label>
<input type="url" name="web site" id="web site" placeholder="www.yoursite.com"> (optional)
</div>
<div>
<label for="numberexample">Nr. of items to order</label>
<input type="number" name="numberexample" id="numberexample" min="1" max="10" value="1" ↵
required>  (1-10)
</div>
<div>
<label for="rangeexample">Length</label>
<input type="range" name="rangeexample" id="rangeexample" min="1" max="10" value="1"
step="0.1">
<output onforminput="value=rangeexample.value" for="rangeexample">1</output>m ↵
(in 10cm increments)
</div>
<div>
<label for="deliverydate">Delivery date</label>
<input type="date" name="deliverydate" id="deliverydate" min="2010-12-16" required> ↵
(minimum 16 December 2010)
<!-- with some server-side scripting we'd prefill the min attribute with today's ↵
date ... in this static example it's simply hardcoded -->
</div>
<div>
<label for="timeexample">Time of delivery</label>
<input type="time" name="timeexample" id="timeexample" step="1800" required> ↵
(in 30 min increments)
</div>
<div>
```

```
<label for="colorexample">Color of the item</label>
<input type="color" name="colorexample" id="colorexample" value="#ed1c24"> ↵
(default red)
</div>
<input type="submit">
</form>
<form id="form-progress-meter" onsubmit="return false;">
<div>
<label for="progress">Progress</label>
<progress id="progress" value="25" max="100"><span>25</span>%</progress>
</div>
<div id="meter_demo">
<label>Disk usage</label>
<meter min="0" value="50.3" max="232.57">50.3 GB used out of 232.57 GB</meter>
<meter min="0" value="193.44" max="232.57">193.44 GB used out of 232.57 GB</meter>
<meter min="0" value="232.57" max="232.57">232.57 GB used out of 232.57 GB</meter>
(3 <code>meter</code> values)
</div>
</form>
</body>
```

Mobile Devices

The HTML5 form controls will improve the inputs for touchscreen mobile devices that have no proper keypad. For instance, the date input control would pop up a calendar so that the user can select a date to avoid the tedium of typing it in from the touchscreen. When the e-mail field is focused, an @ symbol will be included in the touchscreen keyboard.

SVG Images

So many HTML5 manuals refer to SVG (scalable vector graphic) images that you could be forgiven for thinking they are a new feature. They are not new, SVG images have been around since 1999, and they are currently experiencing a revival in association with new browser releases. Also an <svg> tag has been included in the list of new HTML5 elements. You can use it inline; previously, it was always a tricky add-on—usually requiring a plug-in to display properly. Now it's a native part of HTML5, therefore, I have included SVG in this chapter to match other HTML5 resources. All the latest browsers support SVG except IE 7 and IE 8.

SVG images can be compressed, and as their name suggests they can be scaled; they look equally clear and sharp on a hand held device or when expanded to any size on a desktop screen. The images are just *drawings*. They are constructed by drawing from point to point and no pixels are involved.

SVG files are entirely text. The following is the code for a colored square (mysvg.svg), as shown in Figure 1-14.

```
<?xml version="1.0" encoding="UTF-8"?>
    <svg version="1.1" baseProfile="full" ↵
    xmlns=http://www.w3.org/2000/svg  width="100px" height="100px">↵
    <rect x="10" y="10" fill="red" width="100px" height="100px" />
    </svg>
```

Figure 1-14. An SVG Image

The file must be saved as an .svg file. I have saved it as mysvg.svg in the companion web site.

The red square can be seen by simply right clicking mysvg.svg and opening it in a browser (but not Safari, IE 7 or IE 8). It will not open by double-clicking the file. Adobe Photoshop and GIMP (GNU Image Manipulation Program) can import and display an SVG image. The file cannot be regarded as a normal image; for example, this won't work, <img="images/mysvg.svg">.

Currently IE 9, Mozilla Firefox, and Chrome support inline SVG code like Listing 1-14 (that is, there is no need for <object>).

Listing 1-14a. Using an SVG image Inline for Modern Browsers (svg-inline-square.html)

```
<!doctype html>
<html lang=en>
<head>
<title>Embed an SVG square inline</title>
<meta charset=utf-8>
</head>
<body>
<svg>
<rect x="10" y="10" fill="red"
width="100px" height="100px" />
</svg>
</body>
</html>
```

Items such as <object> are called embedding elements, they pull files into the page and display them. The <object> tag can be used to embed an SVG file into a page, as in Listing 1-14b:

Listing 1-14b. Using <object> to embed an SVG Image for Modern Browsers (svg-object-square.html)

```
<!doctype html>
<html lang=en>
<head>
<title>Embed an SVG square using object</title>
<meta charset=utf-8>
</head>
<body>
<object width="100px" height="100px" type="image/svg+xml" data="mysvg.svg"></object>
</body>
</html>
```

▩ **Note** The MIME type for SVG is `type="image/svg+xml"`.

A large range of shapes can be created using SVG such as triangles, ellipses, rectangles with rounded corners and circles. We only have space here for demonstrating the SVG circle.

Figure 1-15. *SVG can draw circles*

The SVG file for a circle can be saved as follows:

```
<?xml version="1.0" encoding="UTF-8"?>
<svg version="1.1" baseProfile="full" xmlns="http://www.w3.org/2000/svg" >
<circle cx="100" cy="50" r="40" stroke="black" stroke-width="2" fill="blue"></circle>
</svg>
```

I saved the file in the companion site as *svg-object-circle.svg*

Listing 1-15a uses the inline technique to embed an SVG circle in an HTML5 page.

Listing 1-15a. *Creating a Page with an SVG Inline Image of a Circle (svg-inline-circle.html)*

```
<!doctype html>
<html lang=en>
<head>
<title>Embed an SVG circle inline SVG</title>
<meta charset=utf-8>
</head>
<body>
<h1> SVG </h1>
<svg xmlns="http://www.w3.org/2000/svg" version="1.1">
<circle cx="100" cy="50" r="40" stroke="black" stroke-width="2" fill="blue">
</svg>
</body>
</html>
```

In Listing 1-15a, the items *xmlns="http://www.w3.org/2000/svg" version="1.1"* appear to be optional in modern browsers, just using <svg> is sufficient.

Listing 1-15b demonstrates the <object> method for embedding the SVG circle in an HTML5 page.

Listing 1-15b. Using `<object>` to embed an SVG image of a circle (svg-object-circle.html)

```
<!doctype html>
<html lang=en>
<head>
<title>Embed an SVG circle using object</title>
<meta charset=utf-8>
</head>
<body>
<object type="image/svg+xml" data="blue-circle-svg.svg"></object>
</body>
</html>
```

The colored square shown in Figure 1-14 is entirely constructed from text; the `.svg` file exists only as code on the page. If the SVG file is huge, it would be better to save it as an `.svg` file and import it with `<object>`. Otherwise the page would be filled with incomprehensible code, making it difficult to work on.

SVG is not suitable for complex images such as photographs, but it can be used for sophisticated drawings. Figures 1-16 and 1-17 are my very poor substitutes for the well-known SVG images of a butterfly and a tiger. Be sure to see the real thing at www.croczilla.com

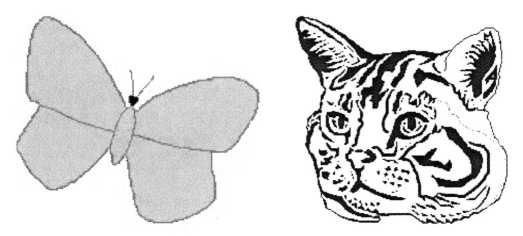

Figure 1-16. Butterfly   *Figure 1-17. Tiger*

The proper SVG images for Figures 1-16 and 1-17 can be downloaded from

```
http://croczilla.com/bits_and_pieces/svg/samples/
```

Visit the site to examine the enormous amount of code that makes up each image. Bitmap images can be converted to SVG files using a free program from

```
http://inkscape.en.softonic.com
```

SVG Images Can Be Created for Text

Figure 1-18 is an outline text created as an SVG image.

Figure 1-18. *Text created as an SVG image*

This technique is only satisfactory for large font sizes and won't work in IE 6, IE 7, or IE 8.

The next snippet of code creates the text shown in Figure 1-18 *(outine-text.svg)*

```
<?xml version="1.0" encoding="UTF-8"?>
<svg version="1.1" baseProfile="full" xmlns="http://www.w3.org/2000/svg" ↵
width="500px" height="60px">
<text x="20" y="50" style="font-family:times new roman; font-size:36pt; ↵
font-weight:bold; stroke:black; fill:white; ">Tour Devon</text>
</svg>
```

The previous snippet of code produces the image, but how do you incorporate it into an HTML5 page? Listing 1-18 shows how this is done:-

Listing 1-18. *Embeds an SVG Image of Some Text Into a Web Page (svg-text-embed-html5.html)*

```
<!doctype html>
<html lang=en>
<head>
<title>Embed an SVG text into an HTML5 page</title>
<meta charset=utf-8>
</head>
<body>
<svg version="1.1" baseProfile="full" xmlns="http://www.w3.org/2000/svg" ↵
width="500px" height="60px"><text x="20" y="50" style="font-family:times new roman; ↵
font-size:36pt; font-weight:bold; letter-spacing:20px; stroke:black; ↵
fill:white; ">Tour Devon</text>
</svg>
</body>
</html>
```

The <details> and <summary> Tags

The <details> and <summary> tags provide a hide/show technique, but only Chrome supported them at the time of writing. When it is eventually fully supported, you will be able to show a page of headlines that, when clicked, expand to reveal detailed information. The element is also useful for expanding the details of a copyright or similar content. Meanwhile, a JavaScript version is provided in Chapter 13 of this book. The Opera display is shown in Figures 1-19 and 1-20.

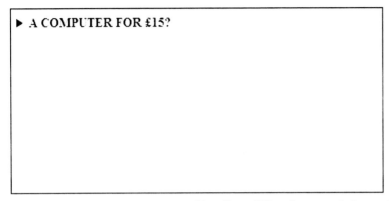

Figure 1-19. This could be a series of headlines filling the page. Only one is shown for clarity.

The next Figure 1-20 shows the expanded text after clicking the heading.

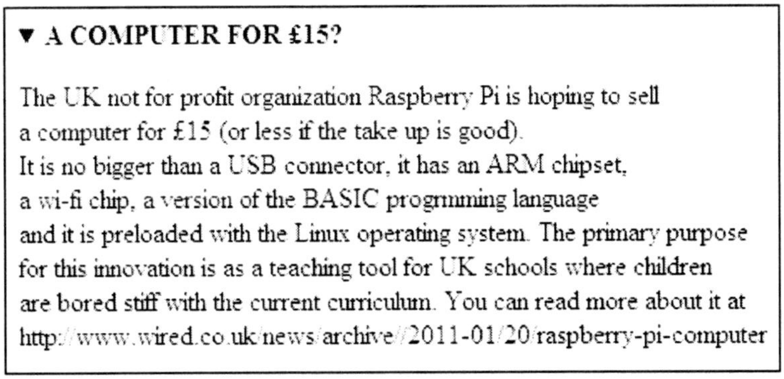

▼ A COMPUTER FOR £15?

The UK not for profit organization Raspberry Pi is hoping to sell
a computer for £15 (or less if the take up is good).
It is no bigger than a USB connector, it has an ARM chipset,
a wi-fi chip, a version of the BASIC programming language
and it is preloaded with the Linux operating system. The primary purpose
for this innovation is as a teaching tool for UK schools where children
are bored stiff with the current curriculum. You can read more about it at
http://www.wired.co.uk/news/archive/2011-01/20/raspberry-pi-computer

Figure 1-20. This shows the result of clicking the arrow next to the headline.

The <summary> tag must be the first child of the <details> tag, as shown in Listing 1-18.

Listing 1-19. Create a Headline That Displays Expanded Text When Clicked (summary-details-tags.html)

```
<!doctype html>
<html lang=en>
<head>
<title>The summary and details tags</title>
<meta charset=utf-8>
</head>
<body>
<details>
<summary><b>A COMPUTER FOR &pound;15?</b></summary>
<p>The UK not for profit organization Raspberry Pi is hoping to sell<br> a computer for ↵
&pound;15 (or less if the take up is good).<br>It is no bigger than a USB connector, it ↵
has an ARM chipset, <br>a wi-fi chip, a version of the BASIC programming language <br>and ↵
it is preloaded with the Linux operating system. The primary purpose <br>for this ↵
```

```
innovation is as a teaching tool for UK schools where children <br>are bored stiff with ↵
the current curriculum. You can read more about it at ↵
<br>http://www.wired.co.uk/news/archive//2011-01/20/raspberry-pi-computer</p>
</details>
</body>
</html>
```

APIs (Application Programming Interfaces)

APIs are usually grouped with HTML5; however, they are actually separate W3C recommendations. The great majority of web owners sell or promote something. They certainly don't want users messing with their carefully-crafted web sites. Therefore, at this point in time, clients are unlikely to demand APIs on their sites. The following is a list of some of the APIs and brief definitions:

Canvas: Provides a rectangular drawing surface on a web page. Using JavaScript you can draw, paint, and fill the area. Currently, it is primarily used for games and graphs.

ContentEditable: Allows users to select and edit items on a section of a web page.

Drag and Drop: The user can control the dragging and dropping of any element on the screen. For a live demonstration, see http://html5demos.com/drag . For more information, see http://html5doctor.com/native-drag-and-drop.

Geolocation: Tells you a user's geographical location (with the user's permission) and can track whether the user has moved. It can interact with maps to show a location. Conversely, the user can ask you whether you will allow him to know your location. If you agree, a map could appear with an indicator pointing to your location (or it could display the latitude and longitude).

Microdata: Allows machine-readable data to be embedded in HTML documents so that browsers and search engines can extract data from the page.

Offline and Manifest: Creates and manages a local cache so that you can work offline. The files, CSS, and images are stored in the manifest so that the web site can be viewed offline.

Web Storage: This is a more powerful form of cookie. It can store a large amount of data on the client side. It can store up to 5MB of data, whereas a cookie is limited to about 4KB.

Web Workers: Allows a JavaScript operation (or multiple operations) to work in the background without interfering with the user's browsing.

▧ **Tip**   If you wish to learn more about the new APIs, try the following resources:*HTML5: Up and Running* by Mark Pilgrim (O'Reilly Media, 2010); *Pro HTML5 Programming* by Peter Lubbers, Brian Albers, and Frank Salim (Apress, 2011);

Introducing HTML5 by Bruce Lawson and Remy Sharp (New Riders Press, 2010);

HTML5: Designing Rich Internet Applications by Matthew David (Focal Press, 2010).

A Strategy for Moving to HTML5

Web designers could begin by experimenting with the new tags one page at a time. The best time to start using HTML5 and its semantic tags would be when you add a new page to a current web site, or when you begin a new web site. When adding a new page, you only need to markup that particular page as HTML5—you can leave the rest of the pages as HTML4 or XHTML. However, you will also need to link that page to a modified CSS sheet. This is not a suitable strategy if you work within a team (unless you enjoy creating confusion). The new `<form>` tags will not be completely hack-proof, a form handler with a filter will still be required for some of the form tags. The new HTML5 form elements are mentioned again in Chapters 11 and 14.

Summary

In this chapter you were introduced to the difference between HTML4 and HTML5. You will have understood that IE 7 and IE 8 cannot understand the semantic tags unless some JavaScript is included in the markup. I hope this introduction to HTML5 has inspired you to start exploring the exciting possibilities offered by HTML5. When exploring the rest of this book, the following rules will be helpful:

- If an HTML5 page contains one or more semantic tags, use the Remy Sharp JavaScript snippet in the page. This will enable users of IE 7 and IE 8 to see the page as you intend it to be seen.

- If a page contains one or more semantic tags, use the display block setting to support IE 7 and IE 8 in the linked CSS sheet as follows:

  `header, nav, article, section, footer { display:block; }`

- If a page contains no semantic tags, Internet Explorer 7 and 8 do not require the JavaScript snippet.

■ **Note** The HTML5 <video> and <audio> tags are covered in Chapter 6.

A Rollover Picture Gallery

Artists or retailers of greetings cards may ask you to create a rollover picture gallery. These galleries are also great for almost any project, including retailers with multiple pictures of products, restaurants with menus, non-profit organizations with pictures of events, and so on. The rollover effect works when the cursor is hovered over a thumbnail picture, this causes an enlarged version of the image to pop up. This chapter demonstrates how this can be achieved using CSS without resorting to tables or complicated scripts.

I am most grateful to the portrait artist Ann Roe Jones for allowing me to use the images from the web site I created for her. The cards depicted are based on her superb paintings. These images are used in all the examples in this chapter.

Visit her web site at http://www.annroejones-artist.co.uk. To see the rollover gallery in action, click the Cards button in the menu.

An Introduction to the Technique

The number of columns or rows can vary, and photo sizes cannot always be uniform—some may be wider or shorter. A universal template is, therefore, not possible. You can adopt the solution given next, or resize and/or crop the thumbnail images to a uniform size.

Create two versions of each image, a thumbnail of the image and a large version of the image. I have labeled the pairs in this manner alithumb.jpg and alibig.jpg. Each column of thumbnails is achieved by means of an unordered list. Each list element has a target link, <a>…</a>, which is instructed by the CSS style sheet to respond to the cursor hovering over its thumbnail.

Create the link from each thumbnail image to its large version using CSS, like this:

```
<ul id = "col-1">
<li>
<a href="#">
<img src = "alithumb.jpg" title="Ali" alt="Ali">
<img class = "hid" src="images/alibig.jpg" alt=" ">
</a>
</li>
</ul>
```

Some things to note include the following:

- The two lines containing the images are enclosed in <a> tags. This is so that they can be made to respond to the cursor hovering over the thumbnail.

- The line for the larger image contains the class="hid" and an empty alt, i.e., alt=" ".

- The CSS instructs any class="hid" element to remain hidden until the cursor hovers over the thumbnail.

- The target columns in the markup will be col-1, col-2, col-3, and so forth, so that the CSS can position them on the page.

Image Size and Format

The technique is easiest if all the thumbnails have the same format and dimensions, and all the enlarged images have the same format and dimensions.

However, life is never that simple. You may have some images in landscape format, some in portrait format, and some may have a square format. If you need to use different formats and sizes, see the instruction associated with Figures 2-4 and 2-5 later in this chapter.

A Single-Column Gallery

Figures 2-1 and 2-2 show a single column gallery.

Figure 2-1. Three thumbnails in one column   *Figure 2-2. Hovering over the cat thumbnail*

Listing 2-1a for this example creates a single column of thumbnail images. Each thumbnail image is a live link to a larger version of the image. The larger image appears when the cursor is rolled over the thumbnail. It appears on the same page and in the place reserved for it by the markup.

Listing 2-1a. Creating a Column of Thumbnail Images (gallery-one-col.html)

```
<!doctype html>
<html lang=en>
<head>
<title>Rollover Gallery, one column</title>
```

```
<meta charset=utf-8>
        meta details go here
<link rel = "stylesheet" type = "text/css" href = "gallery-one-col.css">
</head>
<body>
<ul id = "col-1">
        <li><a href="#"><img src ="images/alithumb.jpg" alt="Ali" title="Ali"> ↵
        <img class = "hid" src ="images/alibig.jpg" alt=" "></a></li>
        <li><a href="#"><img src ="images/catthumb.jpg" title="Cat" alt="Cat"> ↵
        <img class = "hid" src ="images/catbig.jpg" alt=" "></a></li>
        <li><a href="#"><img src ="images/beachthumb.jpg" title="Beach" alt="Beach"> ↵
        <img class = "hid" src ="images/beachbig.jpg" alt=" "></a></li>
</ul>
</body>
</html>
```

▒ **Note** No 'alt' is needed for the large image because the image vanishes when the cursor hovers over it.

In the CSS Listing 2-1b, the first block of MouseOut state code reserves a space on the page that will be occupied by the expanded images, but the expanded images are hidden from the user by the visibility:hidden; property. When the mouse is hovered over a thumbnail, the CSS markup in the second MouseOver state block reveals the expanded image.

Listing 2-1b. The CSS Style Sheet for Listing 2-1a (gallery-one-col.css

```
/*reset browsers to give cross browser uniformity*/
html, body, p, lu, li { margin:0; padding:0;
}
img { border:0;
}
/* Set general thumbnail styles */
/*place the column on the page*/
#col-1 { position: absolute; top: 0; left: 0;
}
/*remove bullets from the list elements*/
li { margin: 10px; list-style-type:none;
}
/* MouseOut state (default) - create a space for the larger images and hide them*/
#col-1 a img.hid { width: 260px; height:390px; position: ↵
absolute; top: 10px; left: 140px; visibility: hidden;
}
/* MouseOver state (hover)- reveal larger image */
#col-1 a:hover { background: white;
}
#col-1 a:hover img.hid { visibility:visible;
}
```

A Two-Column Gallery

By adding a second column and inserting the appropriate rollover code for it, we can create a two-column gallery, as shown in Figure 2-3.

Figure 2-3. *A two-column gallery. The cursor is hovering over the top-right thumbnail.*

Figure 2-3 has an additional feature, the enlarged image has some descriptive text. To do this, resize the *canvas* for the enlarged image in your image manipulation software (e.g., Adobe Photoshop, Corel PaintShop Pro, or GIMP). Add about 20 to 30 pixels of white canvas area at the bottom of the image. Add the text using the image manipulation software and take note of the new image height.

Add canvas to give a consistent aspect ratio to the larger images. In this example, all the enlarged images have been created 260 pixels wide. Add canvas to all the enlarged images to give them the same height; this will ensure consistency of appearance—that is, none of the enlarged versions will look squashed or stretched.

It would seem appropriate to use the new ‹figure› ‹figcaption› tags here, but sadly, they fail because the caption becomes attached to the thumbnail instead of the large image. If you try surrounding the large image with ‹figure› ‹figcaption› using the following snippet of markup, you will see what I mean:

```
<li><a href="#"><img src = "images/take-cardthumb.jpg" title="Take a card" ↵
alt="Take a card">
        <figure>
        <img class = "hid" src = "images/take-cardbig.jpg" alt="">↵
        <figcaption>Take a card</figcaption>
        </figure></a>
</li>
```

Listing 2-3a and its CSS style sheet Listing 2-3b will create a rollover gallery with two columns.

Listing 2-3a. Creating a Rollover Gallery with Two Columns (gallery-2col.html)

```
<!doctype html>
<html lang=en>
<head>
<title>Two column rollover Gallery</title>
<meta charset=utf-8>
        meta details go here
<link rel = "stylesheet" type = "text/css" href = "gallery-2col.css">
</head>
<body>
        <ul id = "col-1">
        <li><a href="#"><img src ="images/alithumb.jpg" alt="Ali" title="Ali">↵
        <img class = "hid" src ="images/alibig.jpg" alt=" "></a></li>
        <li><a href="#"><img src ="images/catthumb.jpg" alt="Cat" title="Cat"/> ↵
        <img class = "hid" src ="images/catbig.jpg" alt=" "></a></li>
        <li><a href="#"><img src ="images/beachthumb.jpg" alt="Beach scene" ↵
        title="Beach scene"><img class = "hid" src ="images/beachbig.jpg" alt=" ">↵
        </a></li>
        </ul>
        <ul id = "col-2">
        <li><a href="#"><img src ="images/fernsthumb.jpg" alt="Ferns" title="Ferns"> ↵
        <img class = "hid" src ="images/fernsbig.jpg" alt=" "></a></li>
        <li><a href="#"><img src ="images/nicohumb.jpg" alt="Nico" title="Ferns"/>↵
        <img class = "hid" src ="images/nicobig.jpg" alt=" "></a></li>
        <li><a href="#"><img src ="images/cliffthumb.jpg" alt="Cliff" title="Cliff">↵
        <img class = "hid" src ="images/cliffbig.jpg" alt=" "></a></li>
        </ul>
</body>
</html>
```

Listing 2-3b presents the thumbnails as two columns and creates a space for the expanded images.

Listing 2-3b. The CSS Style Sheet for Listing 2-3a (gallery-2col.css)

```
/*reset browsers to give cross browser uniformity*/
html, body, p, lu, li {margin:0; padding:0;
}
/*set images to have no borders*/
img { border:0;
}
/*place the column on the page*/
#col-1 { position: absolute; top: 0; left: 0; width:85px;
}
/* Set general thumbnail styles and remove bullets from the list elements*/
li { margin: 5px; list-style-type:none;
}
/* MouseOut state (default) - create and position a space for the larger images ↵
and hide them*/
#col-1 a img.hid { width: 260px; height:390px; ↵
position: absolute; top: 10px; left: 250px; visibility: hidden;
}
```

```
/* MouseOver state (hover)- reveal larger picture */
#col-1 a:hover { background: white;
}
#col-1 a:hover img.hid { visibility:visible;
}
/*--THE 2ND COLUMN STARTS 85 PIXELS FURTHER TO THE RIGHT ---*/
#col-2 { position: absolute; top: 0; left: 85px; width:85px;
}
li { margin: 5px; list-style-type:none;
}
/* MouseOut state (default) - hide larger picture */
#col-2 a img.hid { width: 260px; height:390px; ↵
position: absolute; top: 10px; left: 155px; margin-left:10px; visibility: hidden;
}
/* MouseOver state (hover)- reveal larger picture */
#col-2 a:hover { background: white;
}
#col-2 a:hover img.hid { visibility:visible;
}
```

A Mixture of Sizes and Formats in Three Columns

If the images all have portrait format, or all have landscape format or are all square, the thumbnails should all be created with the same height per row to give neat rows. This way you will have neat rows and columns of thumbnails, a minimum of markup, and very little CSS hassle.

However, the height of each *row* can vary. The thumbnails may then have different widths per column, but if the widths don't vary too widely, you will probably have an acceptable display. Column widths can vary to accommodate groups of thumbnail images with almost the same thumbnail width.

If some of the thumbnails have different heights, arrange them so that each row contains similar height images. For instance, if you have twelve thumbnails and four of them have a height of 80 pixels, put those four in one row. If four thumbnails have a height of 90 pixels, put those four in the next row. If the final four thumbnails have a height of 95 pixels, put those in the last row. This way you will create neat rows of thumbnails.

Differing Formats

Real life, however, is never easy: images come in different formats, such as portrait, landscape, and square. If your thumbnails have various formats, put the *portrait* formats in one column, the *landscape* formats in another column, and the s*quare* formats in another column (as shown in Figure 2-4). Try to match the thumbnail heights to the row heights as described in the previous paragraph. For the expanded versions of the images, the formats (portrait, landscape, and square) will need to be treated differently so that the expanded images are not distorted due to squashing the various formats into one inappropriate size.

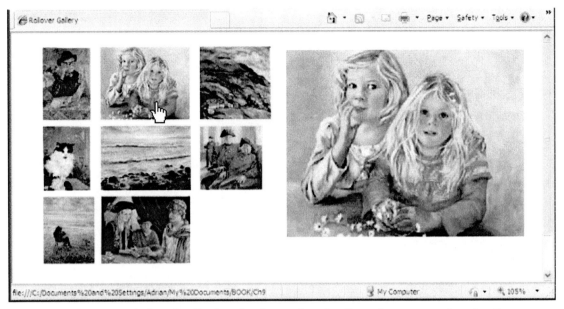

Figure 2-4. *Three portrait thumbnails, three landscape thumbnails, and two square thumbnails. The cursor is hovering on the top landscape thumbnail, revealing the large version in landscape format.*

Figure 2-4 demonstrates that shapes and sizes can be mixed. Each row has a slightly different thumbnail height: all the thumbnails in the top row have a height of 103 pixels, the thumbnails in the second row have a height of 91 pixels, and those in the bottom row all have a height of 95 pixels. I made the bottom thumbnail in the first column a little wider than the upper two thumbnails to demonstrate that you need not be ultra fussy about widths.

Three formats of expanded image were created to match the three variations in format (portrait, landscape, and square) of the thumbnails. Three different column widths were provided to take the three formats.

In the third column, the top thumbnail is a 103×103 pixels square, the second thumbnail is 91×91 pixels square. The last row of thumbnails is the best place to present odd sizes because readers are used to a ragged right. Putting the odd sizes in the final column ensures that the gaps between all the other thumbnails are reasonably consistent.

Figure 2-5 shows the same page as Figure 2-4 but the cursor is hovering over the square image. The space reserved for the expanded images must be able to accommodate various image formats.

Figure 2-5. The cursor now hovers over the third column, second row to reveal a larger version as a square image. The large versions of the first column will appear as in Figures 2-1 and 2-2.

In Listing 2-5a, which corresponds to Figures 2-4 and 2-5, one thumbnail has been deliberately omitted from the bottom of the third column. This demonstrates that you don't need to fill every column with thumbnails; for instance, your client may have provided you with an awkward number of pictures for her gallery.

Listing 2-5a. Creating Three Columns of Mixed Format Images with Rollover (gallery-3col-mix.html)

```
<!doctype html>
<html lang=en>
<head>
<title>Three column mixed image shapes</title>
<meta charset=utf-8>
<link rel = "stylesheet" type = "text/css" href = "gallery-3col-mix.css">
</head>
<body>
<ul id = "col-1">
<li><a href="#"><img src = "images/alithumb.jpg" title="Ali" alt="Ali">
        <img class = "hid" src = "images/alilarge.jpg" alt=""></a>
</li>
<li><a href="#"><img src = "images/catthumb.jpg" title="Cat" alt="Cat">
        <img class = "hid" src="images/catlarge.jpg" alt=""></a>
</li>
<li><a href="#"><img src = "images/beachthumb.jpg" title="Beach" alt="Beach">
        <img class = "hid" src = "images/beachlarge.jpg" alt=""></a>
</li>
</ul>
<ul id = "col-2">
```

```
<li><a href="#"><img src = "images/childrenthumb.jpg" title="Children" alt="Children">
      <img class = "hid" src = "images/childrenbig.jpg" alt=""></a>
</li>
<li><a href="#"><img src = "images/seathumb.jpg" title="Seascape" alt="Seascape">
      <img class = "hid" src = "images/seabig.jpg" alt=""></a>
</li>
<li><a href="#"><img src = "images/take-cardthumb.jpg" title="Take a card" alt="Take a card">
      <img class = "hid" src = "images/take-cardbig.jpg" alt=""></a>
</li>
</ul>
<ul id = "col-3">
<li><a href="#"><img src = "images/walesthumb.jpg" title="Wales" alt="Wales">
      <img class = "hid" src = "images/walesbig.jpg" alt=""></a>
</li>
<li><a href="#"><img src = "images/pensthumb.jpg" title="Chelsea pensioners" ↵
alt="Chelsea pensioners">
      <img class = "hid" src = "images/pensbig.jpg" alt=""></a>
</li>
</ul>
</body>
</html>
```

Listing 2-5b provides the CSS presentation information for a three column gallery

Listing 2-5b. The CSS Style Sheet for Listing 2-5a (gallery-3col-mix.css)

```
/*set images to have no borders*/
img { border:none;
}
/*place the first column on the page*/
#col-1 { position: absolute; top: 0; left: 0; width:85px;
}
/*remove bullets from the list elements*/
li { margin: 5px; list-style-type:none;
}
/* MouseOut state (default) - create and position a space for the larger images and
hide them*/
#col-1 a img.hid { width: 250px; height:340px; position: absolute; top: 10px; left:
400px; visibility: hidden;
}
/* MouseOver state (hover)- reveal larger picture */
#col-1 a:hover { background: white;
}
#col-1 a:hover img.hid { visibility:visible;
}
/*--------------------------------------------------*/
/* Set 2nd column of thumbnails 85px further over to right*/
#col-2 { position: absolute; top: 0; left: 85px; width:135px;
}
li { margin: 5px; list-style-type:none;
}
```

```
/* MouseOut state (default) - hide larger picture */
#col-2 a img.hid { width: 350px; height:265px;  position: absolute; top: 10px; left:
315px; margin-left:0;   visibility: hidden;
}
/* MouseOver state (hover)- reveal larger picture */
#col-2 a:hover { background: white;
}
#col-2 a:hover img.hid { visibility:visible;
}
/*----------------------------------------------------*/
/* Set 3rd column of thumbnails 170px further over to right*/
#col-3 { position: absolute; top: 0; left: 230px; width:108px;
}
li { margin: 5px; list-style-type:none;
}
/* MouseOut state (default) - hide larger picture */
#col-3 a img.hid { width: 260px; height:260px; position: absolute; top: 10px; left:
175px; margin-left:0; visibility: hidden;
}
/* MouseOver state (hover)- reveal larger picture */
#col-3 a:hover { background: white;
}
#col-3 a:hover img.hid { visibility:visible;
}
```

More Columns and More Rows

Increasing the number of columns and rows is just a matter of adding similar blocks of HTML code and matching blocks of CSS code. The mathematics for positioning columns and hidden enlargements becomes more complex, but if your mathematical skills are low, positioning by trial and error is not too difficult if you have a good WYSIWYG editor.

Placing the Gallery Within a Real Web Page

Figure 2-6 shows a three-column gallery in a practical HTML5 web page.

Figure 2-6. *A web page with a gallery of three columns and three rows of thumbnails. The cursor is shown hovering on the first image in the second row.*

Three semantic tags are used in this HTML5 markup: <header>, <nav>, and <footer>. The Remy Sharp JavaScript snippet is used to ensure that the page is displayed correctly in IE 7 and IE 8. Also, a conditional is used for positioning the gallery block in IE 7. You will notice in Figure 2-6 that I have displayed the new HTML5 validation logo. I have incorporated my snippet of code into the listing to enable users to check that the page validation is genuine. See Chapter 18 for further discussion of HTML5 validation.

Listing 2-6a is the HTLM markup for the rollover three column gallery shown in Figure 2-6.

Listing 2-6a. *Creating a Three Column Rollover Gallery with HTML5 Validation Logo (gallery-page-validated.html)*

```
<!doctype html>
<html lang=en>
<head>
<title>Complete Gallery page</title>
<meta charset=utf-8>
<link rel = "stylesheet" type = "text/css" href = "gallery-page-HTML5.css">
        <!--[if lte IE 7]>
        <link rel = "stylesheet" type = "text/css" href = "gallery-ie7.css">
        <![endif]-->
        <!-- conditional Javascript added -->
        <!--[if lte IE 8]>
        <script src="html5.js" type="text/javascript">
        </script>
        <![endif]-->
</head>
```

```
<body>
<header>
<h1>A full page roll-over gallery of greetings cards</h1>
<h2>Hover the mouse over a small picture to see an enlarged version</h2>
</header>
<nav>
<ul>
<li class="btn"><a href="#">Page Two</a></li>
<li class="btn"><a href="#">Page Three</a></li>
<li class="btn"><a href="#">Page Four</a></li>
<li class="btn"><a href="#">Home Page</a></li>
</ul>
</nav>
<div id="rightcol">
        Secondary information<br><br>
        <p><a href="http://validator.w3.org/check?uri=referer">
<img src="http://www.w3.org/html/logo/img/mark-word-icon.png" width="64" height="64" ↲
alt="Validated HTML5" title="Validated HTML5"></a>
</p>
<p>
a href="http://jigsaw.w3.org/css-validator/"><img src="images/vcss-blue.gif" width="88" ↲
height="31" title="Valid CSS!" alt="Valid CSS!"></a>
<span class="small"><br><br>Markup Validated by the World Wide Web Consortium</span>
</p>
<br class="clear">
<p class="advert">Web Design by Fred Bloggs</p></div>
<div id="midcol">
<div id="gallery-block">
<ul id = "col-1">
<li><a href="#"><img src = "images/alithumb.jpg" alt="Ali" title="Ali">
<img class = "hid" src = "images/alibig.jpg" alt=""></a></li>
<li><a href="#"><img src = "images/catthumb.jpg" alt="Cat" title="Cat">
        <img class = "hid" src = "images/catbig.jpg" alt=""></a></li>
<li><a href="#"><img src = "images/beachthumb.jpg" alt="Beach" title="Beach">
        <img class = "hid" src = "images/beachbig.jpg" alt=""></a></li>
</ul>
<ul id = "col-2">
<li><a href="#"><img src = "images/fernsthumb.jpg" alt="Ferns" title="Ferns">
<img class = "hid" src = "images/fernsbig.jpg" alt=""></a></li>
<li><a href="#"><img src = "images/nicothumb.jpg" alt="Nico" title="Nico">
        <img class = "hid" src = "images/nicobig.jpg" alt=""></a></li>
<li><a href="#"><img src = "images/childbeachthumb.jpg" alt="Child and Beach" ↲
title="Child and Beach">
<img class = "hid" src = "images/childbeachbig.jpg" alt=""></a></li>
</ul>
<ul id = "col-3">
<li><a href="#"><img src = "images/ancientthumb.jpg" alt="Ancient and modern" ↲
title="Ancient and Modern">
<img class = "hid" src = "images/ancientbig.jpg" alt=""></a></li>
<li><a href="#"><img src = "images/felixthumb.jpg" alt="Felix" title="Felix">
        <img class = "hid" src = "images/felixbig.jpg" alt=""></a></li>
<li><a href="#"><img src = "images/cliffthumb.jpg" alt="Cliffs" title="Cliffs">
<img class = "hid" src = "images/cliffbig.jpg" alt=""></a></li>
```

```
</ul><br class="clear">
</div><!--gallery block closed-->
</div><!--midcol closed-->
<footer>
        Footer goes here
</footer>
</body>
</html>
```

Listing 2-6b provides the CSS presentation instructions for a 3 column gallery set in a real world page.

Listing 2-6b. The CSS Style Sheet for Listing 2-6a (gallery-page.css)

```
/*set attributes for consistent appearance in all browsers*/
html, body, p, ul, li, h1, h2 { margin:0; padding:0;
}
/*set images to have no borders*/
img {    border:0;
}
/*add display attributes for the semantic tags*/
header, footer, section, article, nav { display:block;
}
/*SET FONTS*/
span.small { font-size:small;
}
h1 { font-size:x-large; font-family:"times new roman"; text-align:center;
}
h2 {font-size:large; font-family:"times new roman"; text-align:center;
}
/*PAGE LAYOUT*/
body {margin:auto; width:970px;
}
header { width:970px;
}
nav { float:left; margin-left:10px; width:115px;
}
nav ul { margin-left:0; border:0; width:115px;
}
/*set far right column for ads*/
#rightcol { width:150px; float:right; text-align:center;
}
#rightcol p.advert {font-size:small; margin-top:190px;
}
/*set middle column for main content*/
#midcol { margin-left:135px; margin-right:155px;
}
/*set gallery block position*/
#gallery-block { position:relative; left: 30px; top:10px;
}
/*set footer*/
footer { clear:both; color:black; text-align:center; width:970px;
}
.clear { clear:both;
}
```

```
/*set menu buttons*/
li.btn a { display:block; background-color :#66CCFF; color:black; font-weight:bold; ↵
padding:4px; margin-left:0; text-align:center; list-style-type:none; ↵
text-decoration:none; width:110px;
}
li.btn a:hover { background-color:blue; color:white;
}
li.btn { width:110px;
}
/*SET THUMBNAIL GALLERY BLOCK*/
/* Set general thumbnail styles */
#col-1  { position: absolute; top: 0; left: 0; width:85px;
}
/*place the first column on the page*/
li { margin: 5px; list-style-type:none;
}
/*remove bullets from the un-ordered list elements and create the ↵
MouseOut state (default) - create and position a space for the larger images and ↵
hide them*/
#col-1 a img.hid { width: 260px; height:390px; position: ↵
absolute; top: 10px; left: 330px; visibility: hidden;
}
/* MouseOver state (hover)- this reveals larger picture */
#col-1 a:hover { background: white; }
#col-1 a:hover img.hid { visibility:visible;
}
/*--------------------------------------------------*/
/* set 2nd column of thumbnails 85px further over to right*/
#col-2 { position: absolute; top: 0; left: 85px; width:85px;
}
li { margin: 5px; list-style-type:none;
}
/* MouseOut state (default) - hide larger picture */
#col-2 a img.hid { width: 260px; height:390px; ↵
position: absolute; top: 10px; left: 245px; margin-left:0;visibility: hidden;
}
/* MouseOver state (hover)- reveal larger picture */
#col-2 a:hover { background: white; }
#col-2 a:hover img.hid { visibility:visible; }
/*--------------------------------------------------*/
/* set 3rd column of thumbnails 170px further over to right*/
#col-3   { position: absolute; top: 0; left: 175px; width:95px; }
li { margin: 5px; list-style-type:none;
}
/* MouseOut state (default) - hide larger picture */
#col-3 a img.hid { width: 260px; height:390px; ↵
position: absolute; top: 10px; left: 155px; margin-left:0; visibility: hidden;
}
/* MouseOver state (hover)- reveal larger picture */
#col-3a:hover { background: white;
}
#col-3 a:hover img.hid { visibility:visible;
}
```

▨ **Note** `position:absolute;` is used within the gallery. But to locate the gallery block on the page, `position:relative;` must be used for the gallery block itself, otherwise the gallery block will overlap the menu on large screens and large resolutions.

Listing 2-6c. Conditional CSS for Listing 2-6a to Support Browser IE 7 (gallery-ie7.css)

```
/*set the gallery block 10px further to the right*/
#gallery-block { position:absolute; left: 165px; top:50px;
}
```

▨ **Tip** Lightbox is an alternative method of creating a gallery. If you are reasonably proficient at using JavaScript, access `http://www.lokeshdhakar.com/projects/lightbox2/` There you will find a demonstration, the full code, and detailed instruction. You will also be able to download the various scripts. The pop-up picture unfortunately covers the thumbnails, but some controls are presented to enable the user to move to the next thumbnail rather like a slide show. By pressing the Escape key, you can return to the thumbnails.

Summary

The rollover effect described in this chapter is superior to the older method of enlarging pictures from a gallery of thumbnails. The older method involved clicking a picture that sent you to a new page—if you had 12 thumbnails, you would have to create 12 pages. In this chapter, you explored a rollover gallery that needed only one page to display both the thumbnails and the enlarged image. This method also has the advantage of leaving the thumbnails visible—no additional controls or keystrokes are required.

The placement of thumbnail images in columns was covered, as well as how to accommodate different image shapes and sizes. The process for creating the rollover effect was also demonstrated. Other ways of showing off your photographs, including collages and galleries with captions, are described in Chapter 9.

In the next chapter, you will discover the visual possibilities for styling backgrounds using CSS gradients. You will also learn how to create multiple background images, transparent backgrounds, overlaid images and overlaid text.

CHAPTER 3

Backgrounds

This chapter gives working examples of popular web page enhancements using various CSS background techniques. Many types of backgrounds are covered, including images, gradients, multiple backgrounds, rollover menu buttons, and watermarks. We will also look at the creation of multiple backgrounds using the new CSS3 background properties.

Overview

CSS provides a whole range of backgrounds to enhance web pages. The web has come a very long way since the days of `<body bgcolor="#00ffff">`. For instance, backgrounds can be:

- gradients, solid colors, or images
- positioned precisely on a page
- repeated (tiled) vertically or horizontally to fill a column, a row or a page
- overlaid with text and multiple images
- set to allow the button background appearance to change in rollover menus (more on this in Chapter 4)
- watermarks (these should be used with great care; they can make superimposed text difficult to read)

Note If no background property is given to an element, it will default to

`background-color: transparent; position: top left; background-repeat: repeat;`

Create Gradient Backgrounds

A gradient background looks best when it fades from a color at the top of a page to white at the bottom. However, if the web site has a solid background color (say, a cream color), a background gradient can be superimposed on this and the gradient should fade to cream. Using CSS, the gradient can be made to expand to fill any screen width.

■ **Note** Several backgrounds are described later in this chapter, but see Chapter 5 for information on CSS3 background gradients.

Most paint programs—such as GIMP, Adobe Photoshop, and Corel PaintShop Pro—can create an image for a colored gradient. The free online ColorZilla gradient generator produces the CSS code for you to copy and paste. If you tick the box labeled IE9 Support, it provides the code for an IE 9 conditional statement. You need to use Mozilla Firefox, Safari, or Chrome to access this online generator, which can be found at

http://www.colorzilla.com/gradient-editor/

The ColorZilla generator does not provide a gradient image; it provides CSS code that generates a gradient in a selected HTML element.

Transparent gradients are also possible; these can be created using the ColorZilla online gradient generator. Rest the cursor on the little pointed sliders to determine what each one does. To create a transparent gradient in ColorZilla, click and adjust the Opacity Stop slider on the horizontal bar just below the Presets section. The ColorZilla interface is shown in Figure 3-1.

You could make a useful resource by creating a few gradients in ColorZilla and saving the code to produce printouts. By examining the printed code, you learn how to produce your own generated gradients.

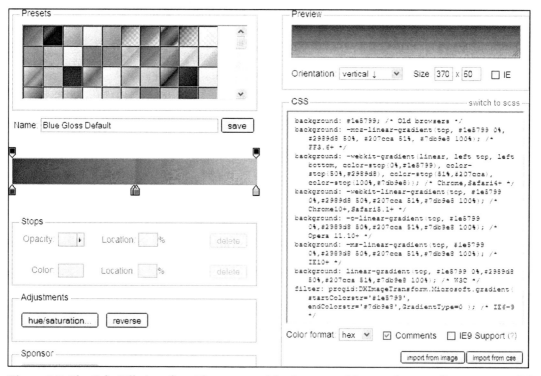

Figure 3-1. The ColorZilla interface. The content of the Stops panel is grayed out until you move a slider.

Using a Gradient Image

A gradient image works in all browsers, and the images can be created in most paint programs. The gradient image green-grad.jpg used in Figure 3-1 has a width of 3 pixels and a height of 600 pixels. The color fades to white quickly from top to bottom so that the fade was noticeable even on a short web page such as the home page. A gradient image can be saved as a .gif, .png or a .jpg file. The CSS markup repeat-x spreads the gradient images from left to right; the x-axis refers to the horizontal axis, as on a Cartesian graph.

```
body { background-color: #FFF; background-image: url(images/green-grad.jpg); ↵
background-repeat: repeat-x; margin:auto;
}
```

This can be written in CSS shorthand like this:

```
body { background: #FFF url(images/green-grad.jpg) repeat-x; margin:auto;

}
```

The background color is set to white (#FFF;) and the green gradient fades to white, as shown in Figure 3-2.

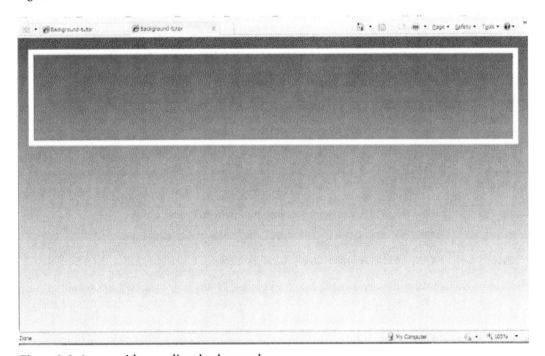

Figure 3-2. A page with a gradient background

The listing for Figure 3-2 demonstrates the use of a gradient image 3 pixels wide that is repeated horizontally. The white border used here indicates where we will eventually insert a background image and some text.

Downloading Examples

If you download the background examples from the book's web page, please note that many examples have an external style sheet. Be sure to also download the style sheet. All the examples work in all the popular browsers.

░ **Note**   Add the JavaScript file html5.js to the folder containing any of the following projects.

Listing 3-2 produces the gradient and the white framed header depicted in Figure 3-2.

Listing 3-2. Creating a Gradient Background and a Framed Header (background-ex1.html)

```
<!doctype html>
<html lang=en>
<head>
<title>Gradient background and white border</title>
<meta charset=utf-8>
      meta details go here
<link rel="stylesheet" type="text/css" href="gradient-style.css">
      <!--Add conditional Javascript-->
      <!--[if lte IE 8]>
      <script src="html5.js" type="text/javascript">
      </script>
      <![endif]-->
</head>
<body>
<header>
</header>
</body>
</html>
```

Listing 3-2b. The CSS Markup for HTML Listing 3-2a (gradient-style.css)

```
body { background:#FFF url(images/green-grad.jpg) repeat-x; margin:auto;
}
header, nav, footer, article, section { display:block;
}
header {width:920px; height:160px; border:10px solid white ; margin:20px auto;
}
```

A Background Header Image

Figure 3-3 shows a header banner as a background image.

Figure 3-3. *A background image has been added to the header.*

The HTML for Figure 3-3 *(background-ex2.html)* is the same as for Figure 3-2 except that it links to a new style sheet. The new style sheet inserts a background image, as shown in Listing 3-3.

Listing 3-3. *CSS for new style sheet (gradient-pic.css)*

```
body, header { margin:0; padding:0; border:0;
}
/*add display attributes for the semantic tags*/
header, footer, section, article, nav { display:block;
}
body { margin:auto; background:url(images/green-grad.jpg) repeat-x;
}
header {width:920px; height:180px; padding:0; border:10px white solid; ↵
background: url(images/header3.jpg); margin:10px auto;
}
```

The code in bold type adds the image to the header. The image header3.jpg was created wider than the header because we may wish to change to a liquid layout at a later date using percentages. A full discussion of fixed, liquid, and semi-liquid layouts can be found in Chapter 12.

The height of the image is the same height as the header, in this case the image was 1024 × 180 pixels. This time we don't want the header image to repeatedly tile across the header container, so the CSS markup uses background-repeat:no-repeat; or in shorthand; background: url(images/header3.jpg) no-repeat;.

You may not want a border around the header, as shown in Figure 3-4.

Figure 3-4. *White border removed*

To remove the border, just delete the CSS markup *border:10px solid white;*.

Overlay a Background Image with Text

The white border is used in the next example, shown in Figure 3-5.

Figure 3-5. Text has been added to the background image and positioned by means of CSS.

In Listing 3.5a, the text is added to the header and is positioned accurately upon the header image by means of CSS. The CSS style sheet also sets the size, format, and color of the text.

Listing 3-5a. Adding and Positioning the Text on the Header's Backgound (background-ex4.html)

The added text is shown in a bold font in the listing.

```
<!doctype html>
<html lang=en>
<head>
<title>Web page with gradient, picture and text.</title>
        <meta charset=utf-8>
<link rel="stylesheet" type="text/css" href="grad-pic-text.css">
<!--Add conditional Javascript-->
        <!--[if lte IE 8]><script src="html5.js">
        </script>
        <![endif]-->
</head>
<body>
<header>
        <h1>Devon&#39;s Rural Retreats</h1>
</header>
</body>
</html
```

Listing 3-5b uses CSS relative positioning to place the heading text as shown in Figure 3-5.

Listing 3-5b. The CSS Style Sheet for Listing 3-5a (grad-pic-text.css)

```
body, header, #content, { margin:0; padding:0; border:0;
}
header, footer, section, article, nav { display:block;
}
body { margin:auto; background:url(images/green-grad.jpg) repeat-x;
}
header {width:920px; height:180px; padding:0; border:10px white solid; ↵
background: url(images/header3.jpg); margin:10px auto;
}
h1 { font-size:300%; color :white; position: relative; left:90px; top:55px; width:480px;
}
```

■ **Note**   The text is positioned relative to the header to prevent the text from poking out of the left margin of the header on wide screens.

Superimpose an Image on the Header

We now superimpose an image of a rosette on the header background as shown in Figures 3-6a and 3-6b. The rosette image is added into the HTML Listing and it takes up its natural position within the header (Figure 3-6a). This position is not very suitable because it looks uncomfortable wedged between the white frame and the text. Therefore by means of an addition to the CSS style sheet the rosette will be repositioned as shown in Figure 3-6b.

Figure 3-6a. This shows the location of the rosette before relative positioning is applied. The rosette is added between the <header> tags

An image can be placed on the header by including it between the header tags, as shown in the following snippet of code.

```
<header>
<h1>Devon's Rural Retreats</h1>
        <img id="rosette" alt="Rosette" title="Rosette" height="127"↵
```

```
            src="images/rosette-128.png" width="128">
      </header>
```

The next task is to move the rosette to the right as shown in Figure 3-6b.

Figure 3-6b. *The rosette is now relatively positioned. The HTML listing was amended so that it linked to a revised style sheet.*

By using the *position* property in the CSS, the image can be placed precisely where we want it to be. The HTML Listing 3-6a is similar to the previous examples but it links to a CSS style sheet containing instructions for repositioning the rosette. The link to the revised style sheet is shown in bold type

Listing 3-6a. *Linking to the Revised CSS Style Sheet (background-ex5b.html)*

```
<!doctype html>
<html lang=en>
<head>
<title>Header with re-positioned rosette</title>
<meta charset=utf-8>
<link rel="stylesheet" type="text/css" href="rosette.css">
<!--Add conditional Javascript-->
<!--[if lte IE 8]>
<script src="html5.js">
</script>
<![endif]-->
</head>
<body>
<header>
```

```
<h1>Devon&#39;s Rural Retreats</h1>
<img id="rosette" alt="Rosette" title="Rosette" height="127" ↵
src="images/rosette-128.png" width="128">
</header>
</body>
</html>
```

Listing 3-6b includes the instruction for re-positioning the rosette, this is shown in bold type.

Listing 3-6b. The Revised CSS for Re-positioning the Rosette (rosette.css)

```
body { background: #FFF url(images/green-grad.jpg) repeat-x; margin:auto;
}
header, nav, footer, article section { display:block;
}
header {width:920px; height:180px; padding:0; border:10px white solid; ↵
background:url(images/header3.jpg); margin: 20px auto;
}
h1 { font-size:300%; color :white; position: relative; left:90px; top: 55px; ↵
width:480px;
}
#rosette { position:relative; left:750px; top:5px;
}
```

Relative positioning relocates the item *relative* to its original position. For a more detailed explanation of relative and absolute positioning, see the Appendix.

What About Backgrounds in Semi-Liquid Layouts?

No problem. Take the same HTML, rename it `background-ex6-liquid.html`, link it to a new style sheet, `liquid.css`. The CSS listing 3-6c limits the maximum width to 1024 pixels and the minimum width to 900 pixels.

Listing CSS 3-6c. The CSS Style Sheet for a Semi-Liquid Version of the SamePage (liquid.css)

```
body { background: #FFF url(images/green-grad.jpg) repeat-x; margin:auto;
}
header, nav, footer, article section { display:block;
}
header { width:95%; max-width:1024px; min-width:900px; height:180px; ↵
padding:0; border:10px white solid; background:url(images/header3.jpg); ↵
margin:20px auto;
}
h1 { font-size:300%; color :white; ↵
position: absolute; left:15%; top: 55px; width: 480px;
}
#rosette { position:relative; left:85%; top:120px;
}
```

The width of the header image is 1024 pixels; therefore, the header in this example must not exceed 1024 pixels. With a wider image, the max-width of the header could be enlarged to match. The liquid version can be seen in this book's page at `http://www.apress.com`.

Transparent Backgrounds

In the next example, the background within the white border is transparent so that the green gradient is visible, as shown in Figure 3-7.

Figure 3-7. Several backgrounds are used in this layout.

Figure 3-8 shows a collection of background effects. The problem with this screenshot is that the bottom border is hardly visible against the faded part of the gradient. The moral of this story is to avoid gradient backgrounds if you want to have a layout with a white border; use a solid background color instead. With a solid background color, the page can be any length, and a white bottom border will be clearly visible.

The photographs used in Figures 3-2 to 3-7 are used by the kind permission of Sandra and Ruth Gould, owners of the Bonehayne Farm holiday accommodation web site http://www.bonehayne.co.uk

---

▨ **Note** Any IE conditionals must be placed after the main CSS links. The JavaScript follows after the conditionals. Placing them in a different order may result in weird behavior in IE 7 and IE 8.

In Listing 3-7a, a transparent CSS background has been used *within* the lower white bordered area. This allows the gradient background to show through. The rosette (not a background item) overlaps the heading and the lower content as if it is pasted on top of them. The rollover menu buttons don't actually exist as images, they are produced by a CSS background method called *dynamic pseudo styling* (this is described fully in Chapter 4).

Listing 3-7a. Creating an Element with a Transparent Background (background-ex7-transp.html)

```
<!doctype html>
<html lang=en>
<head>
<title>Page with transparency and gradient background.</title>
<meta charset=utf-8>
<link rel="stylesheet" type="text/css" href="transparent.css">
        <!--Add conditional Javascript-->
        <!--[if lte IE 8]><script src="html5.js">
        </script>
        <![endif]-->
</head>
<body>
        <header>
        <h1>Devon&#39;s Rural Retreats</h1>
        <img id="rosette" alt="Rosette" title="Rosette" height="127" ⏎
        src="images/rosette-128.png" width="128">
        </header>
<div id="content">
        <h2>Award winning accommodation, self catering or bed and breakfast</h2>
<div id="leftcol">
        <h3>Cottages, converted barns, caravans</h3>
        <img alt="cottage interior" height="225" src="images/cotdining300.jpg" ⏎
        width="300"><br>The superb interior of one of our cottages
</div>
<div id="rightcol">
<nav>
        <ul>
                <li><a href="accommodation.html" title="Accommodation"> ⏎
                Accommodation</a></li>
                <li><a href="maps.html" title="Location Maps">Maps</a></li>
                <li><a href="faqs.html" title="Frequently Asked Questions"> ⏎
                Information</a></li>
                <li> <a href="attractions.html" title="Local attractions">⏎
                Attractions</a></li>
                <li><a href="contact.html" title="Contact us">Contact Us</a></li>
                <li><a href="index.html" title="Return to Home Page">Home Page</a></li>
        </ul>
</nav>
</div><!--end of side menu column-->
<div id="midcol">
        <h3>All situated in the beautiful rolling countryside of Devon</h3>
        <img alt="Devon countryside" height="229" src="images/devon420.jpg" ⏎
        width="419">
</div>
        <br class="clear">
</div><!--content closed-->
<footer>footer goes here
</footer>
</body>
</html>
```

CSS listing 3-7b contains code that creates a transparent content box, this code is shown in bold type.

Listing 3-7b. The CSS Style Sheet for Listing 3-7a (transparent.css)

```
/*equalise all the margins, paddings and borders built into various browsers*/
div body #header #content { margin:0; padding:0; border:0;
}
body { background:#FFF url(images/green-grad.jpg) repeat-x; margin:auto;
}
/*add display attributes for the semantic tags*/
header, footer, section, article, nav { display:block;
}
header {width:920px; height:180px; padding:0; border:10px white solid; ↵
background: url(images/header3.jpg); margin:10px auto;
}
h1 { font-size:300%; color :white; position: relative; left:90px; top: 55px; width:480px;
}
#rosette { position:relative; left:750px; top:5px; }
#content { background-color:transparent; border-left:10px white solid; ↵
border-right:10px white solid;
border-bottom:10px white solid; width: 904px; margin-top:-10px; margin-left:auto; ↵
margin-right:auto; padding:8px; font-size:medium; color:maroon;
}
h2 { font-size:x-large; color:white; margin:0 0 10px 0;
}
h3 { font-size:large; color:white; margin:0 0 6px 0;
}
#leftcol { float:left; width: 310px; vertical-align:top;
}
#rightcol { width: 135px; float:right; height: 252px; margin-right:10px;
}
#midcol { margin-left:315px; margin-right:145px; margin-top:10px; vertical-align:top;
}
/* set side menu block position and width*/
nav { margin:10px 30px 0 10px; width:135px; float:right;
}
/*Set list style within the menu block only. This removes bullets*/
nav li { list-style-type:none;
}
/* set general side button styles */
nav li { margin-bottom: 3px; text-align: center; width:130px;
}
/* set general anchor styles and include the zoom fix for IE6*/
nav li a { display: block; color: white; font-weight: bold; text-decoration: none; zoom:1;
}
/* specify mouse state styles */
/* mouseout (default) */
nav li a { background:#559a55; color: white; border: 5px outset #559a55; padding-bottom:3px;
}
/* mouseover */
nav li a:hover { background: red;  color:white; border: 5px outset red;
}
/*mouse active*/
nav li a:active { background:maroon;  border: 5px inset maroon;
}
br.clear { clear:both;
```

```
}
#midcol img { margin-left:10px;
}
footer { clear:both; color:maroon; text-align:center;
}
```

Background Bullets

Figures 3-9 and 3-10 show how menu lists can be enhanced using background images.

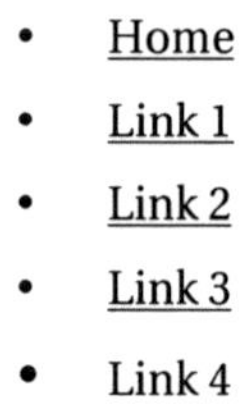

- Home
- Link 1
- Link 2
- Link 3
- Link 4

Figure 3-8.

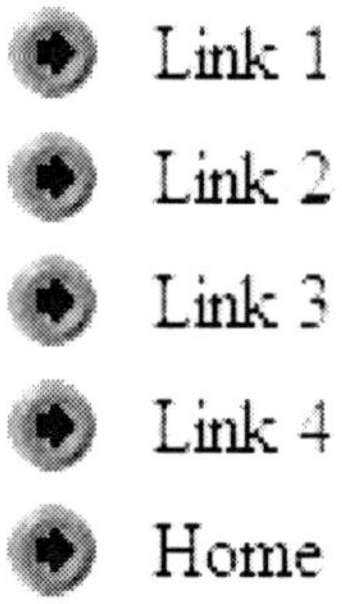

Link 1

Link 2

Link 3

Link 4

Home

Figure 3-9.

A plain, unordered list for a menu would look like Figure 3-8. Graphical background bullets can enhance a menu list, as shown in Figure 3-9. The underline beneath the links is removed by using text-decoration:none;. The standard bullets can be replaced with background images by using the CSS code background-image:url(images/*image*.gif).

In the CSS Listing 3-9b, I used a background image (menu-bullet.gif) 18 ×18 pixels. The whole area—that is the bullet and its text—responds to the mouse. A sensible gap between each menu item helps the disabled to avoid accidentally clicking the wrong link.

Listing 3-9a. Providing a Basic Navigation Menu by Using an Un-ordered List (bullet-images.html)

```
<!doctype html>
<html lang=en>
<head>
<title>Using images for bullets</title>
<meta charset=utf-8>
<meta details go here>
<link rel="stylesheet" type="text/css" href="bullets.css">
        <!--Add conditional Javascript-->
        <!--[if lte IE 8]><script src="html5.js">
        </script>
        <![endif]-->
</head>
<body>
<nav>
        <ul>
```

```
                  <li><a href="#">Link 1</a></li>
                  <li><a href="#">Link 2</a></li>
                  <li><a href="#">Link 3</a></li>
                  <li><a href="#">Link 4</a></li>
                  <li><a href="#">Home</a></li>
         </ul>
</nav>
</body>
</html>
```

Each href="#" is a dummy link and should, of course, be replaced by the correct path to a web page.

Listing 3-9b. The CSS for Listing 3-9a for Replacing Bullets with Images in an Un-ordered List (bullets.css)

```
/*add display attributes for the semantic tags*/
header, footer, section, article, nav { display:block;
}
/*remove bullets*/
nav ul { list-style:none; width:120px;
}
/*place background image in each menu item. The top margin spaces links 10 pixels apart*/
nav li { height:20px; margin-top:10px; background-image:url(images/menu-bullet.gif); ↵
background-repeat:no-repeat;
}
/*remove underline. Push text 30px to the right to clear the image*/
nav li a { color:black; text-decoration:none; padding:0 5px 0 30px;
}
```

Multiple Backgrounds Using HTML5 and CSS2

It is possible to combine several background images. Figure 3-10 shows three combined images.

Figure 3-10. Multiple backgrounds

Multiple backgrounds in CSS2 are not only possible but the procedure is simple using <div>s. This method works in all popular browsers. The solution using CSS2 requires four <div>s. Three images are used here: a gradient, a clipboard, and a beetle. Listing 3.10a creates the <div>s for three background images.

Listing 3-10a. Creating Three Divs to Contain the Three Background Images (multiple-css2.html)

```
<!doctype html>
<html lang=en>
<head>
<title>multiple background with css2</title>
<meta charset=utf-8>
        meta details go here
<link rel="stylesheet" type="text/css" href="multiple-css2.css">
</head>
<body>
        <div id="wrapper">
        <div id="background-container">
        <div id="clipboard">
        <div id="beetle">
        </div>
        </div>
        </div>
        </div>
</body>
</html>
```

Listing 3-10b. The CSS2 that Places the Background Images in the Divs (multiple-css2.css)

```
#wrapper { width:320px; height:420px; margin:auto;
}
#background-container { width:300px; height:400px; margin:auto; ↩
background:url(images/blugrad500.jpg) repeat-x;
}
#clipboard { width:300px; height:400px; ↩
background: url(images/clipbrd.gif) no-repeat 50% 50%;
}
#beetle {width:300px; height:400px; ↩
background:url(images/Beetle.gif) no-repeat 50% 55%;
}
```

Multiple Backgrounds Using CSS3

CSS3 can provide multiple background images using only one div. At the time of writing, Mozilla Firefox, Safari, Chrome, and Opera support this feature. Internet Explorer 7 and 8 cannot understand this most welcome simplification of the markup. Figure 3-11 and Figure 3-10 are identical in appearance but Figure 3-11 is the result of using the CSS3 multiple image module, this does not require three <div>s.

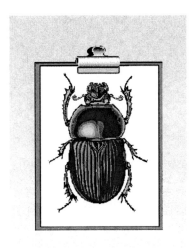

Figure 3-11. *Multiple background images using CSS3*

Listing 3-11a has only one <div> for the three background images, this is indicated in bold type.

Listing 3-11a. Providing One Div for Three CSS3 Background Images (multiple-css3.html)

```
<!doctype html>
<html lang=en>
<head>

<title>Multiple background with css3</title>

<meta charset=utf-8>

        meta details go here

<link rel="stylesheet" type="text/css" href="multiple-css3.css">

</head>

<body>

<div id="example">
</div>

</body>

</html>
```

Listing 3-11b. This CSS3 Style Sheet Provides Three Background Images for Listing 3-11a (multiple-css3.css)

```
#example {width:300px; height:400px; margin:auto;background: ↵
url(images/Beetle.gif) no-repeat 50% 55%, url(images/clipbrd.gif) no-repeat 50% 50%, ↵
url(images/blugrad500.jpg) repeat-x;
}
```

■ **Note** The URL for each background image must be separated by commas.

The background images must be listed in reverse order, that is, the bottom layer (the gradient) is last and the beetle is listed first in the markup. The shorthand version of the background attributes has been used.

Multiple CSS2 and Images in a Real-World Page

The next worked example combines the techniques described earlier. I chose to use the CSS2 solution with three <div>s because it is much easier to position the squares accurately than with the CSS3 method. To assist positioning with CSS3, be sure to zero all the margins, padding, and borders like this:

```
body { margin:0; padding:0; border:0 }
```

The result of the three <div>s technique is shown in Figure 3-12.

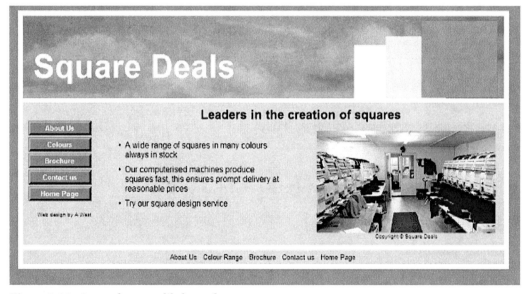

Figure 3-12. A page for an unlikely product

■ **Note** The CSS3 method was not used in Figure 3-12 because CSS3 is not supported by IE 7 or IE 8.

The multiple background image produced by Listing 3-12a and its style sheet Listing 3-12b consists of the sky and three squares that vary in size and color. Three <div>s contain the three colored squares. The semi-liquid layout is limited to 1200 pixels maximum width and 960 pixels minimum width.

Listing 3-12a. Creating a Page with Multiple Background Images (squares-html5.html)

```
<!doctype html>
<html lang=en>
<head>
<title>Squares for sale</title>
<meta charset=utf-8>
        meta details go here
<link rel="stylesheet" type="text/css" href="squares-html5.css">
        <!--Add conditional Javascript-->
        <!--[if lte IE 8]><script src="html5.js">
        </script>
        <![endif]-->
</head>
<body>
<div id="container">
<header>
<h1>Square Deals</h1>
        <div id="white"></div>
        <div id="red"></div>
        <div id="yellow"></div>
</header><br>
<div id="mainpanel"><br>
<nav>
   <ul>
        <li><a href="square-deals-about.html" title="Square Deals, About Us">About ↵
        Us</a></li>
        <li><a href="square-deals-colours.html" title="Squares, range of colours"> ↵
        Colours</a></li>
        <li><a href="square-deals-contact.html" title="Square Deals, brochure">↵
        Brochure</a></li>
        <li><a href="square-deals-contact.html" title="Square Deals, Contact Us">↵
        Contact us</a></li>
        <li><a href="index.html" title="Return to Home Page">Home Page</a></li>
   </ul><br>
</nav>
        <h2>Leaders in the creation of squares</h2>
<div id="midpanel">
<div id="midleft"><br>
   <ul>
        <li>A wide range of squares in many colours always in stock</li>
        <li>Our computerised machines produce squares fast, this ensures prompt delivery ↵
        at reasonable prices</li>
        <li>Try our square design service</li>
   </ul>
</div>
<div id="midright" class="cntr">
<span class="small"><br></span>
```

```
<img alt="Our machines" title="Our machines" height="193" src="images/machines.jpg" ↵
width="349">
<div class="cntr">
<span class="tiny">Copyright © Square Deals</span>
</div>
</div>
<br class="clear"/>
</div>
</div>
<footer>
        Footer goes here
</footer>
</div>
</body>
</html
```

In the CSS listing 3-12b, the three squares are indicated by bold type.

Listing 3-12b. *The CSS Style Sheet for Placing Three Squares in the Header (squares-html5.css)*

```
body, header, div, #content, { margin:0; padding:0; border:0;
}
body{background: #39F; color: navy; font: medium Arial;
}
/*add display attributes for the semantic tags*/
header, footer, section, article, nav { display:block;
}
h1,h2,p{margin: 0; padding: 0;
}
h1 { font-size: 380%; color: #FFF; font-family:Arial; font-weight:bold; color:white; ↵
letter-spacing: 1px; width:560px; position:absolute; top:55px; left:20px;
}
h2 { font-size: 150%; color:navy; margin-top:-10px;
}
.small { font-size:small;
}
.tiny { font-size:x-small; text-align:center;
}
#container { position:relative; width:95%; max-width:1024px; min-width:920px; ↵
margin: 0 auto 10px auto; padding:10px; text-align:left; background:#FFF;
}
#mainpanel { width:100%; margin:auto; margin-bottom:0; margin-top:-10px; ↵
background:#bad0ff; text-align:center;
}
header { padding-top:0; width:100%; height:156px; margin:0 auto 0 auto; ↵
background-image:url('images/bluepan.jpg'); background-repeat:no-repeat; ↵
background-position:-20px left;
}
#red { position:absolute; right: 15px; top:14px; ↵
background-image:url('images/red-square.png'); width:160px; height:160px; z-index:3;
}
#yellow { position:absolute; right: 120px; top:44px; ↵
background-image:url('images/yellow-square.png'); width:123px; height:125px; z-index:2;
```

```
}
#white {position:absolute; right: 200px; top:61px;  ⏎
background-image:url('images/white-square.png'); width:105px; height:109px; z-index:1
}
#midpanel{margin-left:160px; margin-right:5px; margin-top:0; padding:0 10px 10px 0;  ⏎
background:#bad0ff; color:navy;}
#midleft { width:45%; float:left; background:#bad0ff;
}
#midleft li { text-align:left; margin:0 0 10px 10px; width:330px; list-style-type:disc;
}
#midright { float:right; width:350px; text-align:left; background:#bad0ff;
}
footer { clear:both; width:99%; background:#bad0ff; padding:5px; margin-top:10px;  ⏎
text-align:center; font-size:small}
nav { float:left; width:140px; margin-left:0; margin-top:20px; background:#bad0ff;
}
/* set vertical button menu position */
nav ul { float:left; width:130px; margin-left:10px; padding-left:0;  ⏎
list-style-type :none;
}
/* set general side button styles */
nav li { width:115px; line-height:20px; margin-bottom: 3px; text-align: center;
}
/* set general anchor styles */
nav li a { display: block; width:115px; color: white;  font-family:arial;  ⏎
font-size: small; font-weight:bold; text-decoration: none
}
/* specify mouse state styles */
/* mouseout (default) */
nav li a { background: #1A9CE0;  border: 4px outset #AABAFF;}
/* mouseover */
nav li a:hover { display:block; background: #0A4ADF; border: 4px outset #8ABAFF;  ⏎
width:115px;}
/* onmousedown */
nav li a:active { background:#AECBFF; border: 4px inset #AECBFF;
}
br.clear { clear:both
}
.lft { text-align:left;
}
.cntr { text-align:center;
}
```

The Rules for CSS Background Images

These rules cover normal, non-repeating background images, such as those used in banner headings and also tile images that are used to fill an area on the page. You can use any of the background-image properties in <div>s, table cells, and paragraphs.

Positioning a Single Non-Repeating Background Image

Background images can be positioned within containers, as illustrated in Figure 3-13.

Figure 3-13. An image positioned in various locations within a container

Background images can be positioned relative to the edges of a container using key words, pixels, ems, or percentages. Listing 3-13, uses internal styling and key words to position the images as shown in Figure 3-13. The internal style sheet is used here to simplify the instructions, in a real-world page you would use an external style sheet.

Listing 3-13. Positioning Images Relative to Their Containers (image-position.html)

```
<!doctype html>
<html lang=en>
<head>
<title>Positioning images in containers</title>
<meta charset=utf-8>
        meta details go here
<style type="text/css">
/*The containers in Figure 3-13 are dealt with from left to right */
#container1 {border:2px black solid; margin-top:50px; margin-right:10px; float:left; ↵
width:200px; height:200px;background-image: url("images/tile.jpg"); ↵
background-repeat: no-repeat; background-position: left top;
}
#container2 {border:2px black solid; margin-top:50px; margin-right:10px; ↵
float:left; width:200px; height:200px; background-image: url("images/tile.jpg"); ↵
background-repeat: no-repeat; background-position: right bottom;
}
#container3 {border:2px black solid; margin-top:50px; margin-right:10px; float:left; ↵
width:200px; height:200px;background-image: url("images/tile.jpg"); ↵
background-repeat: no-repeat; background-position: center center;
}
#container4 {border:2px black solid; margin-top:50px; margin-right:10px; ↵
float:left; width:200px; height:200px;background-image: url("images/tile.jpg"); ↵
background-repeat: no-repeat; background-position: left bottom;
}
</style>
</head>
<body>
        <div id="container1"></div>
```

```
            <div id="container2"></div>
            <div id="container3"></div>
            <div id="container4"></div>
</body>
</html>
```

Using pixels or ems provides more versatile positioning than key words. The first pixel or em dimension will place the image horizontally from the left. The second dimension will place the image relative to the top edge of the container.

The following code will display the image 150 pixels from the left-hand edge and 100 pixels below the top edge:

```
#container1 { background-image: url("tile.jpg"); background-repeat: no-repeat; ↵
background-position: 150px 100px;
}
```

▓ **Note** If only one value is specified, it sets the horizontal position. If two values are specified, the second value sets the vertical position.

Specifying a Repeating Tiled Background

Tiling means to repeat an image either horizontally or vertically. A typical tile is shown in Figure 3-14.

Tiling can be done with any `.jpg`, `.png`, or `.gif` image. Tiling the whole page or container is usually achieved with a repeated tile image of about 100×100 pixels, as shown in Figure 3-14.

Figure 3-14. A typical tile (tile.jpg)

To fill the entire background of a page or container, the tile is repeated both horizontally and vertically, as follows:

```
body { background-image: url("tile.jpg"); background-repeat: repeat;
}
```

The following code will tile the background image horizontally across the page (one tile high):

```
body { background-image: url("tile.jpg"); background-repeat: repeat-x;
}
```

The following will tile the background image vertically down the page (only one tile wide):

```
body { background-image: url("tile.jpg"); background-repeat: repeat-y;
}
```

The <div>s' widths and depths for horizontal or vertical strips of tiles do not have to be multiples of the tile size. Also it would not be very practical to have a banner that was only one tile deep or a sidebar only one tile wide. The next examples will demonstrate that tiling fills any width or depth of a <div> or its semantic equivalent. Three examples of tiling are shown in Figures 3-15, 3-16, and 3-17.

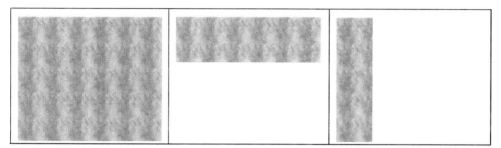

Figure 3-15. A full page   *Figure 3-16. A horizontal strip*   *Figure 3-17. A vertical strip*

Figure 3-15 has a container filled with tiles. The horizontal banner in Figure 3-16 is filled with 100 pixel square tiles, but it is only 180 pixels deep; this demonstrates that containers do not have to be multiples of the tile size. Similarly, the width of the sidebar in Figure 3-17 is not a multiple of the tile width but is just 150 pixels wide. Internal styles have been used in the examples, but in a web site the style sheets would be external.

Listing 3-15 fills a container with tiles. If the <body> is the container, the entire screen will be tiled.

Listing 3-15. Filling a Container with Tiles (tile-whole-page.html)

```
<!doctype html>
<html lang=en>
<head>
<title>Tile the whole container</title>
<meta charset=utf-8>
<style type="text/css">
#container { width:600px; height:500px; background-image: url("images/tile.jpg"); ↵
background-repeat: repeat;
}
</style>
</head>
<body>
<div id="container">
</div>
</body>
</html>
```

Listing 3-16 creates a horizontal strip of tiles that fills a <div>. The tiles will be constrained by the boundary of the <div>. For example, using tiles 100 pixels square in a horizontal <div> with a height of 150 pixels, you will see a horizontal strip only one and a half tiles high.

Listing 3-16. Create a Horizontal Strip of Tiles (tile-horizontal-strip.html)

```
<!doctype html>
<html lang=en>
<head>
```

```
<title>Horizontal strip of tiles</title>
<meta charset=utf-8>
<style type="text/css">
#container { width:600px; height:500px;
}
header {width:600px; height:180px; background-image: url("images/tile.jpg"); ↵
background-repeat: repeat;
}
header, footer, section, article, nav { display:block;
}
</style>
<!--Add conditional Javascript-->
<!--[if lte IE 8]>
<script src="html5.js">
</script>
<![endif]-->
</head>
<body>
<div id="container">
<header>
</header>
</div>
</body>
</html>
```

Listing 3-17 creates a vertical strip of tiles that will fill a <div> but not spill outside the boundary of the <div>. In this example the vertical column is a side bar for a navigation menu.

Listing 3-17. Create a Verical Strip of Tiles (tile-vertical-strip)

```
<!doctype html>
<html lang=en>
<head>
<title>Vertical strip of tiles</title>
<meta charset=utf-8>
<style type="text/css">
#container { width:600px; height:500px;
}
nav {width:150px; height:500px; background-image: url("images/tile.jpg"); ↵
background-repeat: repeat;
}
header, footer, section, article, nav { display:block;
}
</style>
<!--Add conditional Javascript-->
<!--[if lte IE 8]><script src="html5.js">
</script>
<![endif]-->
</head>
<body>
<div id="container">
<nav>
</nav>
</div>
```

```
</body>
</html>
```

Creating a Static Watermark as a Background Image

Watermarks must be very faint or they will make overlaid text difficult to read. A background image will normally scroll with the page. However, by using the property background-attachment: fixed;, the watermark will remain in the same place on the screen when the user scrolls up or down. The CSS for this is as follows:

```
body { background-image: url("image.jpg"); background-attachment: fixed }
```

Figures 3-18 and 3-19 show a fixed watermark in action.

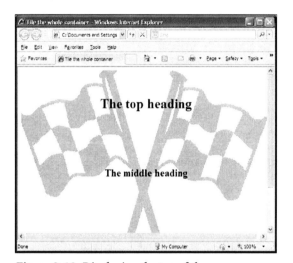

Figure 3-18. Displaying the top of the page

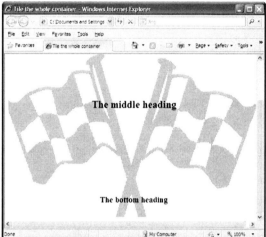

Figure 3-19. The user has scrolled down, but the watermark has not moved down.

Listing 3-18. Create a Background Watermark but Fix its Position on the Screen.(watermark.html)

```
<!doctype html>
<html lang=en>
<head>
<title>A fixed watermark</title>
<meta charset=utf-8>
<style type="text/css">
#container { text-align:center; width:600px; height:500px; ↵
background-image: url("images/cheqflags.jpg"); background-attachment:fixed
}
</style>
</head>
<body>
<div id="container">
        <br><br>
<h1>The top heading </h1>
```

```
            <p> </p>
            <p> </p>
            <p> </p>
    <h2>The middle heading</h2>
            <p> </p>
            <p> </p>
            <p> </p>
            <p> </p>
            <p> </p>
    <h3>The bottom heading</h3>
    </div>
    </body>
    </html>
```

■ **Note** A background color fills the padding and border areas of a box element, not just the content area. The background color will be visible between the dots or dashes if you choose a dotted or dashed border.

Summary

You have seen how backgrounds can convert an ordinary page into a visually exciting page. Using the techniques described in this chapter, you now have complete control over style and positioning of backgrounds using CSS. You learned how to place background images within containers such as <div>s or their semantic equivalents. You were shown how to combine backgrounds with text and how to superimpose images over a background. Multiple background images were demonstrated using CSS2 and CSS3. Using a background image as a watermark was also demonstrated. Backgrounds will feature in many of the other chapters in this book.

In the next chapter you will discover how to create many types of rollover menus, including horizontal menu bars, vertical blocks of buttons, and tab menus.

CHAPTER 4

Rollover Menus

Rollover menus consist of hyperlinks that change in some way when the cursor hovers over them. The hyperlinks enable the user to visit other pages on a web site. Navigation menu blocks can be horizontal or vertical, or a page can contain both types. This chapter deals with the basic principles for the most popular types. It then lists resources to enable you to create variations on the main themes. It deals with several horizontal menus because this type can be tricky. Vertical menus are well behaved; worked examples of vertical menu blocks are included later in the chapter.

All the examples use the CSS *pseudo-classes*, such as :link,:hover, and :active, combined with a display:block attribute or the display:inline-block;. The entire area in the example buttons is clickable, not just the text. Script is used in only one example because search engines ignore navigation menus that use JavaScript to target links. The one example that uses a script does not affect search engines. The CSS method is much easier to master than script-based techniques.

Note To meet accessibility standards for the disabled, choose text and button colors that give a contrast ratio of at least 5:1 (see Chapter 14 for details on color contrast).

Horizontal Rollover Navigation Menus

Horizontal menus are suitable for pages with menus containing fifteen menu buttons or fewer per row. Obviously, this depends on the length of the labels and the size of the text used on the buttons. With very short labels, more buttons could fit across a page (for instance, if the labels were page numbers 1, 2, 3, 4, etc.). The horizontal tab menus on the http://www.bbc.co.uk web site has fourteen tabs in one row and two other rows with seven links on each. This shows that many more links can be fitted into a page if you can accept several rows. The rows need to be distinctly separated by a divider or by using navigation bars with different colors.

Horizontal menus can be challenging because the commonly advocated inline or float methods each have their problems. Floated menus can be difficult to center on the page, inline menus traditionally could not have equal size buttons. However, now that all the browsers support the much-neglected attribute { display:inline-block; }, horizontal menus are no more difficult than vertical menus, and dimensions can be very easily applied to give equal size buttons, or buttons that automatically vary to accommodate the content.

Recipes for horizontal menus often use { display:inline: }, but the resulting buttons are unsatisfactory. All browsers now support { display:inline-block; }.

The attribute { `display:inline:` } did not allow width, height, margins, or padding to be set. By using { `display:inline-block;` }, buttons can be displayed inline and have their dimensions set. This provides the best of both worlds, as shown by the second row of buttons in the basic menu in Figure 4-1.

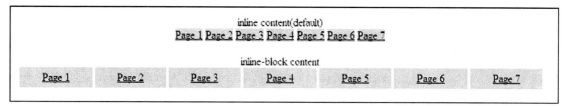

Figure 4-1. The top row of this basic menu shows the unsatisfactory appearance of `display:inline`. In the second row, the `display:inline-block` buttons can be given height, line-height, and padding.

The very basic menus shown in Figure 4-1 are not a rollover menus; that is, they do not change color when the cursor hovers over the buttons. Also, they use paragraphs instead of the traditional unordered lists.

Listing 4-1a contains two rows of menu buttons. The top row is unaffected by the CSS style sheet. The CSS style sheet 4-1b, is linked only to the bottom row of buttons and the style gives the text plenty of horizontal space. This demonstrates the value of the `display:inline-block` code compared with the default `display:inline;`.

Listing 4-1a. Creating the Structure for Two Rows of Menu buttons (inline-block.html)

```
<!doctype html>
<html lang=en>
<head>
<title>Inline-block content</title>

<meta charset=utf-8>
      meta details go here
<link rel = "stylesheet" type = "text/css" href = "inline-block.css">
</head>
<body>
<div id="container">
    <p> </p>
    <p>inline content (default)</p>
    <p>
        <a href = "#">Page 1</a>
        <a href = "#">Page 2</a>
        <a href = "#">Page 3</a>
        <a href = "#">Page 4</a>
        <a href = "#">Page 5</a>
        <a href = "#">Page 6</a>
        <a href = "#">Page 7</a>
    </p><p> </p>
    <p class = "inline-block">inline-block content<br>
        <a href = "#">Page 1</a>
        <a href = "#">Page 2</a>
        <a href = "#">Page 3</a>
        <a href = "#">Page 4</a>
        <a href = "#">Page 5</a>
```

```
                    <a href = "#">Page 6</a>
                    <a href = "#">Page 7</a>
            </p><p> </p>
            </div>
            </body>
            </html>
```

The # symbol in the href items must be replaced by your own page URLs.

Listing 4-1b is the style sheet that targets the second row of menu buttons and applies the style display:inline-block; to enable the width of the buttons to be adjusted.

Listing 4-1b. Applying the display:inline-block; *Style to the Second Row of Buttons (inline-block.css)*

```
/* Set styles to equalise the browser rendition*/
html, body, h1, h2, h3, h4, h5, p, ol, ul, li { padding: 0; margin: 0;
}
body { font-size: 100%; font-weight: normal;
}
ul { padding-left: 0;}
/* end of style equalisation */
p { background:white  margin:auto; text-align:center;
}
#container { margin:auto; text-align:center; width:97%; min-width:800px; ↵
max-width:1200px;
}
a { background: orange; color:navy;
}
.inline-block a { display:inline-block; width:110px; height:30px; ↵
line-height:30px; text-align:center;
}
```

The Types of Horizontal Menu

Horizontal navigation menus are as common as vertical sidebar menus. They present a few more design problems compared to sidebar menus, but these are easily dealt with by the judicious use of CSS. Horizontal navigation bars take the following three forms:

- simple 2D buttons
- 3D buttons
- tab menus

Simple 2D Button Menu

The previous example, Figure 4-1, was not a rollover menu. The next project demonstrates the basic rollover technique. Also, it uses an unordered list for creating equal-width buttons.

Figure 4-2 shows a simple, two-dimensional menu with rollover buttons of equal width.

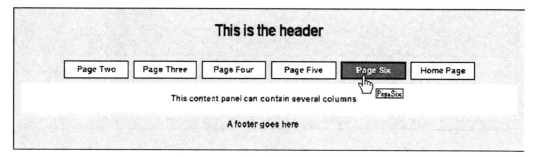

Figure 4-2. *A simple, horizontal, rollover menu. The cursor is hovering over the Page Six button.*

When the cursor hovers over a button, the color changes and a tool tip appears.
Listing 4-2a displays the equal width buttons shown in Figure 4-2. It works in all browsers including IE
7 and IE 8—provided the Remy Sharp JavaScript snippet is included.

Listing 4-2a. *Creating a row of equal-width menu buttons (horizontal-equal-2d.html)*

```
<!doctype html>
<html lang=en>
<head>
<title>Equal width buttons horizontal menu</title>
<meta charset=utf-8>
<meta details go here>
<link rel="stylesheet" type="text/css" href="equal-2d.css">

        <!--Add conditional Javascript-->
        <!--[if lte IE 8]>
        <script src="html5.js" type="text/javascript">
        </script>
        <![endif]-->
</head>
<body>
<div id="wrapper">
<header>
        <h1>This is the header</h1>
</header>
<nav>
  <ul>
        <li><a href="#" title="Page Two">Page Two</a></li>
        <li><a href="#" title="page Three">Page Three</a></li>
        <li><a href="#" title="Page Four">Page Four</a></li>
        <li><a href="#" title="Page Five">Page Five</a></li>
        <li><a href="#" title="Page Six">Page Six</a></li>
        <li><a href="#" title="Return to Home Page">Home Page</a></li>
  </ul>
 </nav>
<!--[if lte IE 7]><br>
<![endif]-->
<div id="main-content">
<br>This content panel can contain several columns<br/><br>
</div>
```

```
<footer>A footer goes here
</footer>
</div>
</body>
</html>
```

The # symbol in the href items must be replaced by your own page URLs.

■ **Note**   A line break is required for IE 6 and IE 7 (shown in bold in Listing 4-3). Fixed-width buttons on a horizontal menu can be difficult to center on the page. However, by using percentage or pixel positioning on a fixed-width page, or percentage positioning on a limited liquid page, this problem can be overcome (see the percentage positioning shown bold in Listing 4-2b).

Listing 4-2b introduces rollover styling so that the button color changes when the cursor is hovered over the button. The rollover effect is achieved by the code nav a:hover shown in bold type.

Listing 4-2b. Styling Equal-width Buttons with Rollover Color Change (equal-2d.css)

```
/* Set styles to equalise browser renditions*/
html, body, h1, h2, h3, h4, h5, h6, p, ol, ul, li { padding: 0; margin: 0;
}
body { font-size: 100%; font-weight: normal; background-color:#99FF66; ↵
font: 100% arial;
}
header, footer, section, article, nav { display:block;
}
#wrapper {position:relative; top:0; left:0;width:950px; margin:auto; ↵
text-align:center;
}
header {width:100%; height:80px; color:black; background-color:#FFCC00; ↵
padding-top:10px;
}
h1 { font-size:200%; font-weight:bold; margin-top:20px;
}
#main-content {width:950px; margin:50px auto 0 auto; background-color:white; ↵
color:black; text-align:center; font-weight:bold;
}
footer {margin:10px auto 0 auto; width:950px; font-weight:bold; ↵
text-align:center; background-color:#FFCC00; color:black; clear:both;
}
nav ul {position:absolute; top:100px; left:9%; width: 780px; ↵
list-style: none; height: 36px;
}
nav li { float: left; width: 120px; margin:0 5px 0 5px;
}
nav a { color: #000; font-size: 100%; font-weight:bold; text-decoration: none; ↵
text-align:center; border: 1px solid #000; padding: 5px; display: block; ↵
background-color: white;
```

```
}
nav a:hover { font-weight: bold; background-color:green; color:white;
}
.clear { clear:both;
}
```

A Variable-Width Horizontal 2D Button Menu

It is not always possible to accommodate some of the labels on equal-width buttons. This requires buttons that expand to fit the size of the labels. Figure 4-3 shows a menu with variable-width buttons.

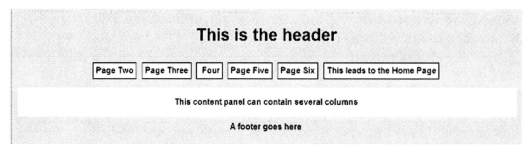

Figure 4-3. *The home page button has expanded to accommodate the text.*

Listing 4-3a and its CSS Listing 4-3b show you how to create variable-width buttons. The buttons will expand to accommodate the text. This project works in all browsers, including IE 6, IE 7, and IE 8. You may need to increase the width of the menu block to ensure that all your text is accommodated in the buttons.

Listing 4-3a. *Displays Variable Width Buttons and a Rollover Effect (horizontal-variable-2d.html)*

```
<!doctype html>
<html lang=en>
<head>
<title>Horizontal menu with variable width 2D buttons </title>
<meta charset=utf-8>
      meta details go here
<link rel="stylesheet" type="text/css" href="variable-2d.css">
<!--[if IE 6]>
<link rel="stylesheet" type="text.css" href="ie-6-style.css">
<![endif]-->
      <!--Add conditional Javascript-->
      <!--[if lte IE 8]>
      <script src="html5.js" type="text/javascript">
      </script>
      <![endif]-->
</head>
<body>
<div id="wrapper">
<header>
    <h1>This is the header</h1>
</header>
```

```
<nav>
  <ul>
    <li><a href="#" title="Page Two">Page Two</a></li>
    <li><a href="#" title="page Three">Page Three</a></li>
    <li><a href="#" title="Page Four">Four</a></li>
    <li><a href="#" title="Page Five">Page Five</a></li>
    <li><a href="#" title="Page Six">Page Six</a></li>
    <li><a href="#" title="Return to Home Page">This leads to the Home ↵
    Page</a></li>
  </ul>
</nav>
<!--[if lte IE 7]>
<br>
<![endif]-->
<div id="main-content">
    <br>This content panel can contain several columns<br><br>
</div>
<footer>A footer goes here
</footer>
</div>
</body>
</html>
```

Listing 4-3b. The CSS for Listing 4-3a Giving Rollover and Variable Width Buttons (variable-2d.css)

```
/* Set styles to equalise browser renditions*/
html, body, h1, h2, h3, h4, h5, h6, p, ol, ul, li { padding: 0; margin: 0;
}
body { width:960px; margin:auto; background-color:#99FF66; font: 100% Arial; ↵
font-size: 100%; font-weight: normal;
}
header, footer, section, article, nav { display:block;
}
#wrapper {position:relative; top:0; left:0; width:950px; margin:auto; ↵
text-align:center;
}
header {width:100%; height:80px; color:black; background-color:#FFCC00; ↵
padding-top:10px;
}
h1 { font-size:200%; font-weight:bold; margin-top:20px;
}
#main-content {width:950px; margin:60px auto 0 auto; background-color:white; ↵
color:black; text-align:center; font-weight:bold;
}
footer {margin:10px auto 0 auto; width:950px; font-weight:bold; ↵
text-align:center; background-color:#FFCC00; color:black; clear:both;
}
nav {position:absolute; top:100px; left:78px; width: 785px; padding: 5px; ↵
list-style: none; height: 35px;
}
nav li { display:inline; padding: 5px; padding-top:15px; margin:5px 0 0 2px; ↵
height:25px;
}
```

```
nav a {height:25px; color: #000; font-size:80%; font-size: 100%; ↵
font-weight:bold; text-decoration: none; border: 1px solid #000; ↵
padding:5px 5px 0 5px; display: inline-block; ↵
background-color: white; zoom: 1;
}
nav a:hover { font-weight: bold; background-color:green; color:white;
}
.clear { clear:both;
}
```

Note The style `display:inline-block;` allows top and bottom padding. Without padding, the labels in the buttons would butt against the top edge of the buttons. If `display:block` is used, the buttons would be hidden one behind the other, and they would sprawl across the width of the container.

3D Rollover Button Menus

The menu bars in the previous examples can be made more interesting by adding a 3D effect. This is achieved with a little extra code in the CSS border attributes, as listed next.

Note Some trial and error must be used to produce good border colors. The default method uses the same color for both the background and the outset border, like the blue button scheme shown in Figure 4-4.

```
/*mouseout state (default)*/
li.hbtn a { background: #0080a0;  border: 4px outset #0080a0; }
```

However, a better result was achieved by using a different outset color, as follows (also see Figure 4-4):

```
/*mouseout state (see Figure 4-4)*/
li.hbtn a { background: #0080a0;  border: 4px outset #aabaff; }
```

Figure 4-4. Menu buttons produced using CSS pseudo-classes. Any part of a button is clickable.

Caution When using the outset and inset attributes, browsers render the border colors differently. For instance, a good color scheme in IE will show as very pale borders in Mozilla Firefox. One way around this would be to design good colors for Mozilla, then have an IE conditional link to a style sheet that gives good colors in IE. However, this requires a great deal of trial and error. A better solution would be to specify the four borders individually, as shown in the next code snippet.

The snippet of code for specifying border colors individually.
(A downloadable file is not provided for this brief code snippet for 3D buttons.)

```
/*mouseout state*/
li.hbtn a { background: #0080a0;  border-top: 4px color-one solid; ↵
border-right: 4px color-two solid; border-bottom:4px color-two solid; ↵
border-left:4px color-one solid; }
```

Note The attributes `color-one` and `color-two` would, of course, be replaced by hexadecimal or RGB color codes.

Variable-Width 3D Menu Buttons

Figure 4-5 shows a 3D version of the 2D buttons used previously in Figure 4-3.

Figure 4-5. *Variable-width 3D buttons created by means of additional style attributes*

Listing 4-5a is the same code as the 2D buttons in Listing 4-3a, except that it has a different title and is linked to a different style sheet, called `variable-3d.css`, as noted in bold.

Listing 4-5a. *Creating Variable Width 3D Menu Buttons with Rollover (horizontal-variable-3d.html)*

```
<!doctype html>
<html lang=en>
<head>
<title>Horizontal variable width 3D buttons</title>
<meta charset=utf-8>
<meta details go here>
<link rel="stylesheet" type="text/css" href="variable-3d.css">
<!--Add conditional Javascript-->
<!--[if lte IE 8]>
<script src="html5.js" type="text/javascript">
</script>
<![endif]-->
</head>
<body>
<div id="wrapper">
```

```
<div id="header">
        <h1>This is the header</h1>
</div>
 <nav>
   <ul>
    <li><a href="two.html" title="Page Two">Page Two</a></li>
    <li><a href="three.html" title="page Three">Page Three</a></li>
    <li><a href="four.html" title="Page Four">Four</a></li>
    <li><a href="five.html" title="Page Five">Page Five</a></li>
    <li><a href="six.html" title="Page Six">Page Six</a></li>
    <li><a href="index.html" title="Return to Home Page">This leads to the ↵
    Home Page</a></li>
  </ul>
   </nav>
<!--Add a conditional for IE 7 and IE 8 to push the content below the menu-->
        <!--[if lte IE 7]>
        <br>
        <![endif]-->
<div id="main-content">
        <br>This content panel can contain several columns<br><br><br>
</div>
<div id="footer">A footer goes here
</div>
</div>
</body>
</html>
```

In the CSS Listing 4-5b, the code shown in bold type gives the 3D effect. The style sheet also creates the variable width buttons.

Listing 4-5b. The CSS for Listing 4-5a Giving the 3D Buttons with Variable Width (variable-3d.css)

```
/* Set styles to equalize browser rendition*/

html, body, h1, h2, h3, h4, h5, h6, p, ol, ul, li {  padding: 0; margin: 0; ↵
font-size: 100%; font-weight: normal;
}
img { border: 0; }
ul { padding-left: 0; }
/* end of style equalization */
/* Layout */
body { width:960px; margin:auto; background-color:#99FF66; font: 100% Arial;
}
#wrapper {position:relative; top:0; left:0; ↵
width:950px; margin:auto; text-align:center;
}
#header {width:100%; height:80px; color:black; background-color:#FFCC00; ↵
padding-top:10px;
}
h1 { font-size:200%; font-weight:bold; margin-top:20px;
}
#main-content {width:950px; margin:65px auto 0 auto; background-color:white; ↵
color:black; text-align:center; font-weight:bold;
}
```

```
#footer {margin:10px auto 0 auto; width:950px; font-weight:bold; ↵
text-align:center; background-color:#FFCC00; color:black; clear:both;
}
nav ul {position:absolute; top:100px; left:3.6%; width: 866px; padding: 5px; ↵
list-style: none; overflow: hidden; height: 35px;
}
nav li { display:inline; padding: 5px; padding-top:15px; margin:5px 0 0 2px; ↵
height:25px;
}

nav a {height:25px; color: #fff; font-size:80%; font-size: 100%; ↵
font-weight:bold; text-decoration: none; background-color: #72b720; ↵
border: 4px outset #5edd51; padding:5px 5px 0 5px; display: inline-block;
}
.clear { clear:both;
}
#mainNav a:hover { font-weight: bold; background-color:green; color:white;
}
```

▨ **Note** You may have to juggle with the widths, heights, border widths, padding, spacing, and margins to cure problems like float drop or missing borders. Because 3D borders are thicker, the width of the <nav> must be increased to accommodate them. This means that the absolute position of the <nav> must be amended to center the menu on the page.

A 3D Version with Equal-Width Buttons

Figure 4-6 illustrates a menu with equal-width 3D buttons.

Figure 4-6. *Fixed-width 3D buttons created from Listing 4-3 by means of a new style sheet (fixed-3d.css)*

The 3D version Figure 4-6 with equal-width buttons was created by linking the same page as Listing 4-6 (horizontal-variable-2d.html) to the style sheet, Listing 4-6b (horizontal-fixed-3d.css). Be sure to shorten the home page button's text to fit in the equal-width button. In Listing 4-6a , the text *This leads to the Home Page* was shortened to *Home Page* to fit into its equal-width button.

Listing 4-6a provides the structure for the menu with 3D equal-width buttons as shown in Figure 4-6.

Listing 4-6a. Creating the structure for a menu with 3D Equal Width Buttons (horizontal-fixed-3d.html)

```
<!doctype html>
<html lang=en>
<head>
<title>Horizontal fixed width 3D buttons</title>
<meta charset=utf-8>
<meta details go here>
<link rel="stylesheet" type="text/css" href="fixed-3d.css">
<!--Add conditional Javascript-->
<!--[if lte IE 8]>
<script src="html5.js" type="text/javascript">
</script>
<![endif]-->
</head>
<body>
<div id="wrapper">
<header>
        <h1>This is the header</h1>
</header>
<nav>
  <ul>
        <li><a href="#" title="Page Two">Page Two</a></li>
        <li><a href="#" title="page Three">Page Three</a></li>
        <li><a href="#" title="Page Four">Four</a></li>
        <li><a href="#" title="Page Five">Page Five</a></li>
        <li><a href="#" title="Page Six">Page Six</a></li>
        <li><a href="#" title="Return to Home Page">Home Page</a></li>
  </ul>
  </nav>
  <!--[if lte IE 7]>
  <br>
  <![endif]-->
<div id="main-content">
        <br>This content panel can contain several columns<br><br>
</div>
<footer>A footer goes here
</footer>
</div>
</body>
</html>
```

Listing 4-6b shows the CSS that is linked to Listing 4-6a for displaying equal-width 3D buttons.

Listing 4-6b. The CSS Providing the Presentation of 3D Equal Width Buttons (fixed-3d.css)

```
/* Set styles to equalise browser rendition*/
html, body, h1, h2, h3, h4, h5, h6, p, ol, ul, li {  padding: 0; margin: 0;
}
header, footer, section, article, nav { display:block;
}
body { width:960px; margin:auto; background-color:#99FF66; font: 100% Arial; ↵
font-size: 100%; font-weight: normal;
}
```

```
#wrapper {position:relative; top:0; left:0; width:950px; margin:auto; text-align:center;
}
header {width:100%; height:80px; color:black; background-color:#FFCC00; padding-top:10px;
}
h1 { font-size:200%; font-weight:bold; margin-top:20px;
}
#main-content {width:950px; margin:65px auto 0 auto; background-color:white; ↵
color:black; text-align:center; font-weight:bold;
}
footer {margin:10px auto 0 auto; width:950px; font-weight:bold; text-align:center; ↵
background-color:#FFCC00; color:black; clear:both;
}
nav {position:absolute; top:100px; left:3.6%; width: 866px; padding: 5px; ↵
list-style: none; overflow: hidden; height: 35px;
}
nav li { display:inline; padding: 5px; padding-top:15px; margin:5px 0 0 2px; ↵
height:25px; width:100px;
}
nav a {height:25px; width:100px; color: #fff; font-size:80%; font-size: 100%; ↵
font-weight:bold; text-decoration: none; background-color: #72b720; ↵
border: 4px outset #5edd51; padding:5px 5px 0 5px; display: inline-block;
}
.clear { clear:both;
}
nav a:hover { font-weight: bold; background-color:green; color:white;
}
```

Incidentally, Rollover Menus Can Be Achieved By Using a Definition List

This is an interesting alternative way of creating 3D buttons that validates despite being unorthodox. The snippet of code that follows shows how this is done.

Using a Definition List Instead of an Unordered List

```
<nav>

<dl>
    <dt><a title="Page 1" href="page1.html">Page One</a></dt>
    <dt><a title="Page two" href="page2.html">Page Two</a></dt>
    <dt><a title="Page Three" href="page3.html">Page Three</a></dt>
    <dt><a title="Return to the opening page" href="index.php">Home Page</a></dt>
</dl>
</nav>
```

The CSS code snippet for a Definition List

```
/*MENU set horizontal menu and button general style*/
nav {margin-left:-5px; margin-rignt:0; height:35px; text-align:center; ↵
width:710px; margin:auto;
}
nav dl {display:block; margin:auto; float:left; text-align:center; padding:3px;
}
nav dt a {display:block; text-decoration:none; color:white; ↵
background-color:#0080a0; font-weight:bold; padding:4px;
```

```
}
/*mouseout state (default)*/
nav dt a { background: #0080a0; border: 4px outset #aabaff;
}
/* mouseover state*/
nav dt a:hover { background: #0060a0; color:yellow;  border: 4px outset #8abaff;
}
/* mousedown state*/
nav dt a:active { background:#abcbff; border: 4px inset #abcbff;
}
```

The definition list, though unorthodox, has the merit of automatically removing bullets and the left margins. No additional CSS markup is required to achieve the removals. Depending on how many buttons you want and the amount of text on each, you will need to juggle with the <nav> items through trial and error on the width and margin-left figures. Otherwise, the horizontal menu may not be centered on the page and a button might jump out of line.

Which 3D Buttons to Choose: ul/li or dl/dt?

Both methods give exactly the same appearance. Both methods are accessible to screen readers, both methods will validate. Although the unordered list method requires extra CSS attributes for the <nav> items, nearly all web sites use the unordered list method. Two proposed HTML5 recommendations, if adopted, will hijack the <dt> tag, which could cause confusion in the future.

Tabbed Horizontal Menus

Figure 4-7 shows a tab menu with variable-width tabs. Note the width of the middle tab.

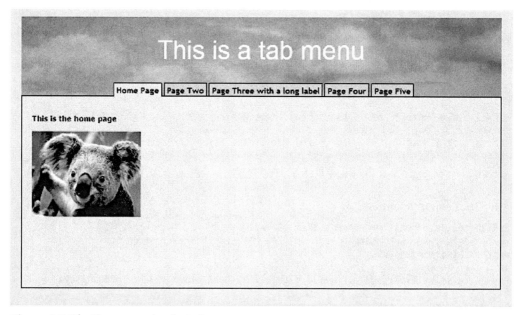

Figure 4-7. The Home page is selected.

Figure 4-7 illustrates how the Home tab becomes part of the Home page. Figure 4-8 shows what happens when a different tab is clicked. In the following section, we will run through a quick tutorial using Figures 4-7 and 4-8 as the basis of the instructions.

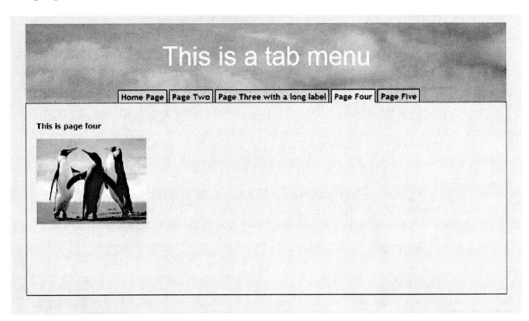

Figure 4-8. Now, page four is selected.

Tutorial for the Tabbed Menu

Tab menus are popular because thousands of well-known sites use them, and visitors are familiar with them. In Figures 4-7 and 4-8, the selected tab indicates clearly which page is currently being viewed. The tabs appear to become part of the content area.

The menu in this tutorial is my adaptation of Joshua Kaufman's CSS tab menus at

`http://unraveled.com/publications/assets/css_tabs/`

They are licensed under `http://creativecommons.org/licenses/by/3.0/` and are free to use and modify.

Create five simple pages using Listing 4-7a and Listing 4-8a as a basis and name them `index.html`, `page2.html`, `page3.html`, `page4.html`, and `page5.html`.

On each page, amend the page title and move the item `class="active"` down one line so that it sits alongside the relevant page. On the index.html markup I have shown the `class="active"` in bold.

In the following listings, to change the images on each page in this example, I used the sample images in Windows XP.

Listing 4-7a. Creating the Home Page for the Tab Menu (index.html)

```
<!doctype html>
<html lang=en>
<head>
```

```
<title>The home page. Square tabs</title>
<meta charset=utf-8>
<meta name="author" content="Ian Andolina">
        meta details go here
<link rel="stylesheet" type="text/css" href="squaretabs.css">
        <!--Add conditional JavaScript-->
        <!--[if lte IE 8]>
        <script src="html5.js" type="text/javascript">
        </script>
        <![endif]-->
</head>
<body>
<div id="container">
<header>
        <h1>This is a tab menu</h1>
</header>
<nav>
  <ul>
        <li><a class="active" href="index.html">Home Page</a></li>
        <li><a href="page2.html">Page Two</a></li>
        <li><a href="page3.html">Page Three with a long label</a></li>
        <li><a href="page4.html">Page Four</a></li>
        <li><a href="page5.html">Page Five</a></li>
  </ul>
</nav>
<div id="content">
<b>This is the home page</b>
<p><img title="Koala" alt="Koala" height="165" src="images/Koalasmall.jpg" ⏎
width="220"></p><p> </p><p> </p><p> </p>
</div></div>
</body>
</html>
```

The middle block of code in Listing 4-8 would change as shown in bold.

Listing 4-8a. (page4.html)

```
<!doctype html>
<html lang=en>
<head>
<title>Page four. Square tabs</title>
<meta charset=utf-8>
<meta name="author" content="Ian Andolina">
        meta details go here
<link rel="stylesheet" type="text/css" href="squaretabs-.css">
        <!--Add conditional JavaScript-->
        <!--[if lte IE 8]>
        <script src="html5.js" type="text/javascript">
        </script>
        <![endif]-->
</head>
<body>
<div id="container">
<header>
```

```
            <h1>This is a tab menu</h1>
    </header>
      <nav>
          <ul>
                  <li><a href="index.html">Home Page</a></li>
                  <li><a href="page2.html">Page Two</a></li>
                  <li><a href="page3.html">Page Three with a long label</a></li>
                  <li><a class="active" href="page4.html">Page Four</a></li>
                  <li><a href="page5.html">Page Five</a></li>
          </ul>
      </nav>
  <div id="content">
  <b>This is the home page</b>
  <p><img alt="Penguins" height="165" src="images/Penguinsmall.jpg" width="220"> ⏎
  </p>
  <p> </p><p> </p><p> </p>
  </div>
  </div>
  </body>
  </html>
```

Repeat the process for each page. The completed pages can be viewed and downloaded from the companion web site.

▦ **Tip**   If one tab drops below or behind the others, increase the width of the menu bar.

All five tab menu pages use the same style sheet Listed as 4-7b. This creates the style that changes the selected tab so that it blends into the content panel.

Listing 4-7b. The CSS Listing for Changing the Tab for the five Tab Menu Pages (squaretabs.css)

```
/* Set styles to equalise browser rendition*/
html, body, h1, h2, h3, h4, h5, h6, p, ol, ul, li {  padding: 0; margin: 0;
}
header, footer, section, article, nav { display:block;
}
body {text-align:center; margin: 20px; background: #bee8ff; font: medium arial;
}
#container {width:960px; margin:-10px auto 0 auto;
}
header {margin-top:0; height:156px; width:100%; ⏎
background-image:url('images/bluepan.jpg'); background-repeat:no-repeat; ⏎
background-position:center; border-bottom:0;
}
h1 {font-family:Arial; font-size:320%; color:white; font-weight:normal; ⏎
text-align:center; padding-top:35px; margin-bottom:-10px; height: 94px; margin:auto;
}
/*set the generic tab style--and move menu upwards so that it overlaps the header*/
nav {position:relative; top:-13px; color: navy; border-bottom: 1px solid black; ⏎
margin: -25px 0 0 0; padding: 0px; padding-left: 10px z-index: 1; }
```

```
/* use display:inline to remove IE6 double margin bug*/
nav li { display: inline; overflow: hidden; list-style-type: none;
}
/*set tab colour*/
nav a, a.active { color: navy; background: #81d9f6; font: bold 1em Arial; ↵
border: 1px solid black; padding: 2px 5px 0px 5px; margin: 0; text-decoration: none;
}
/*make a 3px wide bottom border on tab the same colour as the page*/
nav a.active { background: #cfecf5; color:navy; border-bottom: 3px solid #cfecf5;
}
/*hovering over a non-active tab shows an aqua tab*/
nav a:hover { background: aqua;
}
nav a:visited { color: navy;
}
/*hovering over the active tab shows navy text*/
nav a.active:hover { background: #cfecf5; color: navy;
}
/*set the position of the content to move it close up to the menu tabs*/
#content {margin-top:0; font : 0.9em/1.3em "bitstream vera sans", verdana; ↵
position:relative; top:-13px; text-align: left; background: #cfecf5; ↵
padding: 20px; border: 1px solid black; border-top: none; z-index: 2;
}
```

Horizontal Menus with Rounded Tabs

The tab menus in Figures 4-9 and 4-10 have tabs with rounded corners; all browsers support them.

▓ **Note**   Chapter 7 covers rounded tabs using CSS3.

Figure 4-9. The Home page is selected.

Figure 4-10. *Now the Services page is selected.*

Alessandro Fulciniti developed this JavaScript solution that works in all browsers, including IE 6. The technique is free to use for personal and commercial use and Fulciniti asks you to credit him as the author and to provide his web site address, which is:

http://www.html.it/articoli/niftycube/index.html.

The script has *no effect on search engine optimization* because the JavaScript is applied to the tab corners and not to the navigation itself.

■ **Note** The following files must be included in the folder containing your web page: niftyCube.js and niftyCorners.css. They can be downloaded from Alessandro Fulciniti's web site or from this book's companion web site.

The tabs and the dark bar behind the tabs can be any color you choose. The bar behind the tabs **must not have a named color** such as green or navy; be sure to use hexadecimal notation. The selected tab will automatically have a color to match the loaded content area. In Listing 4-9b, white is the chosen color for the content area. The selected tab changes to white to match the content area.

The code for the pages can be downloaded from the companion web site.

■ **Caution** The Nifty Corners JavaScript will not respond to semantic targets, hence the element <div> and the identity id="nav";.

Listing 4-9a sets the structure for the home page, it is also the template for all other pages. Of course the title and the content will change on each page. The "active" class will be placed against a different link to match the page (this will be explained later).

Listing 4-9a. Creates the Page for a Tab Menu Using Nifty Corners (home-nifty.html)

```
<!doctype html>
<html lang=en>
<head>
```

```
<title>Home page Nifty Corners tabs</title>
<meta charset=utf-8>
<meta details go here>
<link rel="stylesheet" type="text/css" href="nifty-tabs.css">
    <script type="text/javascript" src="niftycube.js"></script>
    <script type="text/javascript">
    window.onload=function(){
    Nifty("ul#nav a","top");
    }
    </script>
            <!--Add conditional Javascript-->
            <!--[if lte IE 8]>
            <script src="html5.js" type="text/javascript">
            </script>
            <![endif]-->
</head>
<body>
<header>
    <h1>This is a tab menu</h1>
    <h2>Based on the technique devised by Alessandro Fulciniti</h2>
    <h3>http://www.html.it/articoli/niftycube/index.html</h3>
</header>
<nav>
  <ul id="nav">
    <li id="home" class="activelink"><a href="#">Home</a></li>
    <li id="about"><a href="about-nifty.html">About</a></li>
    <li id="prod"><a href="prod-nifty.html">Product</a></li>
    <li id="serv" ><a href="serve-nifty.html">Services</a></li>
    <li id="cont"><a href="cont-nifty.html">Contact us</a> </li>
  </ul>
</nav>
</body>
</html>
```

▦ **Note** The activelink class is added to each page against the appropriate page name together with
`<a href="#">`; for example, it appears against the Services link (shown bold) in the following snippet of markup.

```
<nav>
    <ul id="nav">
        <li id="home"><a href="home-nifty.html">Home</a></li>
        <li id="about"><a href="about-nifty.html">About</a></li>
        <li id="prod"><a href="prod-nifty.html">Product</a></li>
        <li id="serv" class="activelink"><a href="#">Services</a></li>
        <li id="cont"><a href="cont-nifty.html">Contact us</a> </li>
    </ul>
</nav>
```

Listing 4-9b provides the CSS style sheet to create the rounded corners. It also changes the color of
the selected tab and merges the tab into the content panel.

Listing 4-9b. *The CSS Setting the Page and Tab Style Using "Nifty Corners" (nifty-tabs.css)*

```
body { background: #FFF; color:black; padding:0; margin:0; font: 100% Arial;
}
header, footer, section, article, nav { display:block;
}
header { padding-top:-10px; margin-top:-10px; height:156px; width:100%; ↵
max-width:1017px; min-width:960px; margin:auto; text-align:center; ↵
background-image:url('images/bluepan.jpg'); background-repeat:no-repeat; ↵
background-position:center; border-bottom:0;
}
h1 { font-family:Arial; font-size:250%; color:white; font-weight:normal; ↵
margin-top:0; margin-bottom:5px; padding-top:10px;
}
h2 { font-family:Arial; font-size:180%; color:white; font-weight:normal; ↵
margin-top:0; margin-bottom:5px;
}
h3 { font-family:Arial; font-size:150%; color:white; font-weight:normal; margin-top:0;
}
nav { float:left; width: 100%; margin-top:0; padding-top:5px; background:#002455;
}
ul#nav { margin-left: 60px; width:750px;
}
ul#nav li { float:left; margin-right: 3px; text-align: center; ↵
list-style-type:none;margin:0;padding:0;
}
ul#nav a { float:left; width:7em; padding: 6px 0; text-decoration:none; ↵
color: #000; font-weight:bold;
}
ul#nav a:hover { color: #000;
}
ul#nav li.activelink a { background: #FFF;
}
ul#nav li.activelink a,ul#nav a:hover { color: #000; font-weight:bold;
}
li#home a { background: #FF749C;
}
li#about a { background: #DF3694;
}
li#prod a { background: #4D80FF;
}
li#serv a { background: #80FF4D;
}
li#cont a { background: #FFCB4D;
}
```

▨ **Note** If you wish to use the Listing 4-9a HTML and CSS markup, obviously the name home-nifty.html would have to be changed to index.html in every page and style sheet. The file name home-nifty.html was used to avoid duplicating an index.html file used in an earlier example.

Horizontal Tab Menus Using an Image

Figure 4-11 illustrates a simple solution using a tab image. The rollover effect only changes the color of the text. The method is simple because clicking a tab does not result in the tab merging with the content panel.

Figure 4-11. *Using an image for the tabs. The active page has red tab text. Rollovers also result in red text. Designed by Free CSS Templates (www.freecsstemplates.org). Released for free under a Creative Commons Attribution 2.5 License.*

This solution uses a fixed-width tab image. The tab image used in Figure 4-11 is shown on the right. It is 130 pixels wide × 39 pixels high. The black background for the header and content panel background is created from a rectangle that is 50 pixels wide × 450 pixels high; it is tiled over the page. The images can be downloaded from the book's page on the http://www.apress.com web site. The colors of the tabs and the background can be changed in a paint program.

The item `class="current_page_item"><a href="#">` must be applied to the relevant page name on each page. The item `<a href="#">` in statements like `<li><a href="#">Home</a></li>` must, of course, be changed to the target page name, like in the following example for the Photos page:

```
<nav>
    <ul>
        <li><a href="index.html">Home</a></li>
        <li><a href="blog.html">Blog</a></li>
        <li class="current_page_item"><a href="#">Photos</a></li>
        <li><a href="about.html">About</a></li>
        <li><a href="links.html">Links</a></li>
        <li><a href="contact.html">Contact</a></li>
    </ul>
</nav>
```

Listing 4-11a configures the header for the home page. The class for the current page is shown in bold type.

Listing 4-11a. *Creating the Structure of the Template for all the Pages (yosemite.html)*
```
<!doctype html>
<html lang=en>
<head>
```

```
<title>Yosemite by Free CSS Templates</title>
<meta charset=utf-8>
        meta details go here
<!--Design by Free CSS Templates http://www.freecsstemplates.org ↵
Released for free under a Creative Commons Attribution 2.5 License ↵
Name : Yosemite-->
<link rel="stylesheet" type="text/css"  href="style-yosemite-2.css">
        <!--Add conditional Javascript-->
        <!--[if lte IE 8]>
        <script src="html5.js" type="text/javascript">
        </script>
        <![endif]-->
</head>
<body>
<div id="wrapper">
    <nav>
        <ul>
                <li class="current_page_item"><a href="#">Home</a></li>
                <li><a href="#">Blog</a></li>
                <li><a href="#">Photos</a></li>
                <li><a href="#">About</a></li>
                <li><a href="#">Links</a></li>
                <li><a href="#">Contact</a></li>
        </ul>
    </nav>
<header>
        <div id="logo">
        <h1>Yosemite</h1>
        <p> design by <a href="http://www.freecsstemplates.org/"> ↵
        Free CSS Templates</a></p>
        </div>
</header>
<div id="page">
<div id="page-bgtop">
<div style="clear: both;"></div>
</div>
</div>
<footer>
<p>Copyright (c) 2008 Sitename.com. All rights reserved. Design by ↵
<a href="http://www.freecsstemplates.org/">Free CSS Templates</a></p>
</footer>
</div>
</body>
</html>
```

Listing 4-11b is the CSS style sheet for the HTML markup Listing 4-10a. It uses the same tab image as background images for all the tabs. It places them in the correct location on the pages. It also styles the rollover effect and indicates where the user has landed.

Listing 4-11b. This CSS Styles Listing 4-11a. It also Creates the Rollover Effect (style-yosemite-2.css)

```
/* Set styles to equalise browser rendition*/
html, body, h1, h2, h3, h4, h5, h6, p, ol, ul, li {  padding: 0; margin: 0;
}
```

```
header, footer, section, article, nav { display:block;
}
body { background: url(images/img01.gif) repeat-x left top; font-family: Arial; ↵
font-size: 100%; color: black;
}
h1, h2, h3 { font-weight: normal;
}
h1 { font-size: 2em; color:white;
}
h2 { font-size: 2.4em;
}
h3 { font-size: 1.6em;
}
p, ul, ol { margin-top: 0; line-height: 180%;
}
ul, ol {
}
a { text-decoration: none; color: white;
}
a:hover { color:red;
}
#wrapper { width: 980px; margin: 0 auto; padding: 0;
}
header { width: 980px; height: 280px; margin: 0 auto; padding: 0px; ↵
background: url(images/img06.gif) no-repeat left top;
}
#logo { float: right; margin: 0; padding: 0; color: #000000;
}
#logo h1, #logo p { margin: 0; padding: 0;
}
#logo h1 { float: left; padding-top: 210px; letter-spacing: -1px; ↵
text-align: right; text-transform: lowercase; font-size: 3.8em;
}
#logo p { float: left; margin: 0; padding: 250px 0 0 10px; ↵
font: normal 14px Georgia, serif; font-style: italic; color: #FFFFFF;
}
#logo a { border: none; background: none; text-decoration: none; color: #FFFFFF;
}
nav { width: 980px; height: 90px; margin: 0 auto; padding: 0;
}
nav ul { margin: 0; padding: 50px 0px 0px 0px; list-style: none; line-height: normal;
}
nav li { float: left;
}
nav a { display: block; width: 130px; height: 30px; margin-right: 1px; ↵
 padding: 9px 0px 0px 0px; background: url(images/img02.gif) no-repeat left top; ↵
 text-decoration: none; text-align: center; font-family: Arial; font-size: 100%; ↵
 font-weight: bold; color: #FFFFFF; border: none;
}
nav a:hover, nav .current_page_item a { text-decoration: none; color:red;
}
nav .current_page_item a { padding-left: 0;
}
```

```
#page { width: 940px; margin: 0 auto; padding: 0px 0px 0px 40px; ↵
background: url(images/img03.gif) repeat-y left top;
}
#page-bgtop { padding: 20px 0px;
}
#content { float: left; width: 580px; padding: 30px 0px 0px 0px;
}
footer { height: 30px; margin: 0 auto; padding: 0px 0 15px 0; background: white; ↵
        border-top: 1px solid #DEDEDE; font-family: Arial;
}
footer p { margin: 0; padding-top: 20px; font-size: small; text-align: center; ↵
        color: black;
}
footer a { color: #8A8A8A;
}
```

▸ **Tip**   Tabs can be given rounded corners by means of CSS3. See Chapter 7.

Using Button Images for Tabs

Buttons can be downloaded from the internet for constructing menus like Figure 4-12.

Figure 4-12. Using button images. Adapted from the web site at:
        http://cssportal.com/horizontal-menus/13styles2.htm.

CSS Portal (http://cssportal.com) is a great resource for menu images. Figure 4-12 does not do justice to the quality of the tabs. They are gradient images giving 3D, shiny tabs that change to a pale gradient when hovered over, and to a teal color when selected. Suitable images can be created without too much difficulty in most image-manipulation programs.

The following are the button images for Figure 4-12.

Figure 4-12a and 12b. The pale button images   *Figure 4-12c. The full color button image.*

Buttons can be found in abundance on the internet, but if you wish to create your own with background gradients, try http://colorzilla.com/gradient-editor/.

■ **Note**   The active page has the attribute class="current" shown bold in Listing 4-12a.

Listing 4-12a provides the HTML for the *cssportal.com* menu illustrated in Figure 4-12.

Listing 4-12a. Setting up the Structure for a Page with Tabs Using Images (index2.html)

```
<!doctype html>
<html lang=en>
<head>
<title>Turquoise home page</title>
<meta charset=utf-8>
        meta details go here
<link rel="stylesheet" type="text/css" href="turquoise.css">
        <!--Add conditional Javascript-->
        <!--[if lte IE 8]>
        <script src="html5.js" type="text/javascript">
        </script>
        <![endif]-->
</head>
<body>
<div id="container">
<header>
<h1>Turquoise tabs</h1>
<nav>
<ul>
  <li><a href="about.html" title="">About Us</a></li>
  <li><a href="news.html" title="">News</a></li>
  <li><a href="events.html" title="">Events</a></li>
  <li><a href="volunteers.html" title="">Volunteers</a></li>
  <li><a href="services.html" title="">Services</a></li>
  <li><a href="membership.html" title="">Membership</a></li>
  <li><a href="index2.html" title="" class="current">Home</a></li>
</ul>
</nav>
<br class="clear">
</header>
<div id="main-content">
<h2>This is the home page</h2>
<div id="left-col">This is the left panel<br><br>
</div>
<div id="right-col">This is the right hand panel<br>
</div>
```

```
<div id="mid-content">This is the middle panel<br><br><br>
</div>
<br class="clear">
</div>
</div>
</body>
</html>
```

■ **Note** All references to index2.html in every page of this example must be changed to index.html. The name index2.html was used to prevent confusion with another index.html file in this chapter.

Figure 4-13 shows what happens when the *Events* tab is clicked.

Figure 4-13. *The Events page is selected*

The markup for creating the Events page is the same as Listing 4-12a, except for the title, which changes to *Events page*, also the menu list on that page has modified markup as follows:

This code snippet shows the class *current* is now placed next to the link for the Events page.

```
<nav>
<ul>
  <li><a href="about.html" title="About Us">About Us</a></li>
  <li><a href="news.html" title="News">News</a></li>
  <li><a href="events.html" title="Events" class="current">Events</a></li>
  <li><a href="volunteers.html" title="Volunteers">Volunteers</a></li>
  <li><a href="services.html" title="Services">Services</a></li>
  <li><a href="membership.html" title="Membership">Membership</a></li>
  <li><a href="index2.html" title="Home Page">Home</a></li>
</ul>
</nav>
```

Of course, the content of the mid-content panel will be different because it relates to the actual events. Listing 4-12b provides the CSS styling for all the pages.

Listing 4-12b. *Providing the CSS Styling for all the Pages that Use the cssportal.com Menu (turquoise.css)*

```
html, body, h1, h2, h3, h4, h5, h6, p, ol, ul, li {  padding: 0; margin: 0;
}
header, footer, section, article, nav { display:block;
}
body { background-color:#bbFFaa; color:black; font-family:Arial;
}
#container { width:97%; margin:auto; min-width:800px; max-width:1100px;
}
header { background-image:url("images/panew.jpg"); background-repeat:no-repeat; ↵
height:190px; background-position:top left;
}
nav ul {padding-top:230px;padding:0;list-style-type:none; margin:auto; ↵
display:block;height:36px;text-transform:uppercase; font-size:12px; ↵
font-weight:bold; background:url('images/bgOFF.gif') repeat-x left top; ↵
font-family:Helvetica,Arial,Verdana,sans-serif; border-bottom:4px solid #336666; ↵
border-top:1px solid #C0E2D4; position:relative; top: 70px; left: 0;
}
nav ul li { display:block;float:left;margin:0;padding:0;
}
nav ul li a { display:block; float:left;color:#874B46; text-decoration:none; ↵
padding:12px 20px 0 20px;height:24px; ↵
background:transparent url("images/bgDIVIDER.gif") no-repeat top right;
}
nav ul li a:hover{ background:transparent url("images/bgHOVER.gif") no-repeat top right;
}
nav ul li a.current,ul#main-menu li a.current:hover { color:#fff; ↵
background:transparent url("images/bgON.gif") no-repeat top right;
}
#main-content { text-align:center; background-color:white; color:black; margin-top:35px; ↵
border-bottom:4px solid #336666; border-left:4px solid #336666; ↵
border-right:4px solid #336666; border-top:none;
}
#left-col { float:left; width: 180px;
}
#right-col { float:right; width:180px;
}
#mid-col { margin-left:185px; margin-right:185px;
}
h1 {font-family:Arial; font-size:300%; padding-top:60px; padding-left:60px; margin-top:0; ↵
margin-bottom:0; color:white;
}
h2 { font-size:150%; margin-top:0; margin-bottom:5px; color:black;
}
br .clear { clear:both;
}
```

The code for all the pages and the CSS can be downloaded from the companion web site.

Sliding Doors Technique

The sliding doors technique gives an attractive horizontal tab menu, but it can be tricky to implement. The tabs expand horizontally and vertically to fit the labels: this feature is the main characteristic of sliding doors. The method has another advantage in that when partially-sighted users increase the text size using the browser's zoom facility, the tabs will expand horizontally and vertically to accommodate the larger text.

The tabs can have a flat color or can have 3D top and side edges (see Figure 4-14). The technique takes advantage of two properties of background images:

1. a background image cannot extend beyond the boundaries of its containing element, the boundary in the case of a tab menu is provided by the li element of an unordered list.

2. one background image can be made to slide over another image. The images that slide over one another are right and left-hand slices of a tab image (see Figures 4-15 and 4-16).

The method was developed by Douglas Bowman. Full details can be found at

http://www.alistapart.com/articles/slidingdoors

and *http/.*www.alistapart.com/articles/slidingdoors2

For the latest developments, see http://cssportal.com/horizontal-menus/alistapart.htm.

Figure 4-14 is an example of a sliding doors menu. It shows the starting point before adding the ability to have the active tab look as though it was part of the page's content panel (this is shown in Figure 4-15).

Figure 4-14. The starting point that was created using Listing 4-14a. Notice how the tabs have expanded to accommodate various amounts of text.

The expandable tabs are created from images consisting of two parts of a single image, a left-hand slice, let's say 6 pixels wide × 100 pixels high, and a right-hand slice 294 pixels wide × 100 pixels high. Figures 4-15 and 4-16 show an image before and after slicing it in a paint program.

Figure 4-15. The original tab image

Figure 4-16. The sliced image

A selection of these images can be downloaded from

http://www.exploding-boy.com/images/cssmenus2/menus.html.

It is rather tricky to get at the information. Access the web site, choose a menu style (let's say Tab Menu 6), then view the source code. Copy the style and the HTML markup for that menu to Notepad and save it. Next go to

http://www.exploding-boy.com/images/cssmenus2

Click the relevant .gif files, such as tableft6.gif and tabright6.gif, then right-click them and save them.

Listing 4-14a exploits one other aspect of a tab menu. Normally, you cannot give an element two styles; for instance, you would not expect to be able to give the li element two background images (the left-hand slice and the right-hand slice). But the li element also contains an <a href…> tag; therefore, we can send the left-hand slice to the <a href… tag, and the right-hand slice to the li element. The rollover feature is set by a color change; the text changes from white to red.

Listing 4-14a. Providing an Example of the Sliding Door Tab Menu Technique (sliding-doors-start.html)

```
<!doctype html>
<html lang=en>
<head>
<title>Sliding Doors Navigation, starting point</title>
<meta charset=utf-8>
<!--conditional Javascript added-->
<link rel="stylesheet" type="text/css" href="sliding.css">
<!--[if lte IE 8]>
<script src="html5.js" type="text/javascript"></script>
<![endif]-->
</head>
<body>
<a id="top"></a>
<div id="container">
 <header>
 <h1>Coly Computer Help</h1>
 </header>
<nav>
  <ul>
<!-- REPLACE EACH href="#" SO THAT THEY POINT TO YOUR WEB PAGES.-->
        <li><a href="#">Home Page</a></li>
        <li><a href="#">Jargon</a></li>
        <li><a href="#">How To Do Things</a></li>
        <li><a href="#">Troubleshoot</a></li>
        <li><a href="#">Donate</a></li>
        <li><a href="#">Contact Us</a></li>
```

```
    </ul>
</nav>
<div id="content">
        <h2> </h2>
        <h2>Here is the page's content</h2></div>
</div>
</body>
</html>
```

Listing 14b styles the page created by Listing 4-14a and causes the sliding door tabs to expand or contract to fit the text on the tabs.

Listing 4-14b. Providing the CSS that Controls the Behavior of Sliding Door Tabs (sliding.css)

```
/*add display attributes for the semantic tags*/
header, footer, section, article, nav { display:block;
}
body { background-color:#D7FFEB; font-family: 'Trebuchet MS'; ↩
font-size: 70%; margin: 20px;
}
#container { width:960px; margin:auto;
}
header { background-position:35% top; ↩
background-image:url('images/compbkgcrop.jpg'); background-repeat:no-repeat; ↩
height:160px; padding-bottom:0;
}
h1 { padding-top:110px; padding-left: 310px; font-family :"times new roman"; ↩
font-size: 450%; color: #0080a0;; font-weight:bold;
}
h2 { text-align:center;
}
/* Navigation */
nav { height:37px; border-bottom: 2px solid #506BB1; margin: auto; margin-top:10px; ↩
width: 900px;
}
nav ul { margin-left:70px;
}
/*THE RIGHT HAND SLICE IS NOW PINNED TO THE TOP RIGHT CORNER OF THE TAB*/
nav li {border-bottom: 2px solid #506BB1; list-style: none; float: left; ↩
background: #FFF url(images/right_side.png) no-repeat right top; ↩
margin-right: 5px; height: 37px;
}
/*THE LEFT HAND SLICE IS NOW PINNED TO THE TOP LEFT CORNER OF THE TAB*/
nav a { display: block; padding: 7px 15px 4px 15px; background-image: ↩
url(images/left_side.png); background-repeat: no-repeat;background-position: left top; ↩
text-align: center; text-decoration: none; color: #FFF; font-weight: bold; ↩
font-size: 1.2em; text-transform: uppercase;
}
nav a:hover { color:yellow;
}
/*THE NEXT TWO STATEMENTS ARE INCLUDED READY FOR THE NEXT STAGE
```

```
#active { border-bottom: none; color:navy; list-style: none; float: left; ↵
        background: #FFF url(images/right_side-pale.png); background-repeat:no-repeat; ↵
        background-position: right top; margin-right:  5px; height:39px;
}
#active a { display: block; border-bottom:none; padding: 7px 15px 4px 15px; ↵
        background: url(images/left_side-pale.png); background-repeat: no-repeat; ↵
        background-position: left top; text-align: center; text-decoration: none; ↵
        color: navy; font-weight: bold; font-size: 1.2em; text-transform: uppercase; ↵
        height: 28px;
}
#content { width:900px; border: 2px navy solid; margin:-15px auto 5px auto; border-top:0;
}
```

■ **Caution** In Listing 4-14b take a look at this piece of code:

`nav li {border-bottom: 2px solid #506BB1; list-style: none; float: left;` ↵

`background: #FFF url(images/right_side.png) no-repeat right top; margin-right: 5px;` ↵

`height: 37px; }.` The `float:left;` item might be mistaken for a printing error because it is associated with the right-hand slice. However, the `float:left` applies to the `li` (the tab), not to the right-hand background image.

The two remaining steps to complete the sliding door menu are:

1. prepare two more tab images and modify them;
2. amend the HTML5 markup so that the tab for the selected page is highlighted when that page is active.

The modified images are the tricky part. Make a copy of the left and right slices, and name the copies something like `left_side-pale.png` and `right_side-pale.png`. Modify them in your image-manipulation program to leave just the rims showing, as illustrated in Figure 4-17 and Figure 4-18.

Figure 4-17.   *Figure 4-18.*
left_side-pale.png   *right_side-pale.png*

In Figure 4-17 the tab's background color was replaced by the page's background color. An alternative solution would be to make the pale area transparent so that the page's color is visible in the tab. The new images will be used to highlight the active page, as shown in Figure 4-19.

Figure 4-19. *The Jargon page has been selected (it is now active) and the tab appears to be part of the page.*

To achieve the color change and to make the tab appear to be part of the content panel, the markup has to be modified just like the previous examples of tabbed navigation menus. Each page must have the id="active" attribute added alongside the link for that page.

The following code snippet amends the markup of the page links on the Jargon page. The Jargon page has been made the active page by means of the identity id="active"

```
<nav>
   <ul>
        <li><a href="">Home Page</a></li>
        <li id="active"><a href="jargon.html">Jargon</a></li>
        <li><a href="">How To Do Things</a></li>
        <li><a href="">Troubleshoot</a></li>
        <li><a href="">Donate</a></li>
        <li><a href="">Contact Us</a></li>
   </ul>
</nav>
```

Vertical Rollover Navigation Menus

A vertical block of menu buttons can appear on the left or right of the page.

In Figure 4-20 the menu is floated to the left of the page.

Figure 4-20. *A vertical menu*

No images are used and because it is drawn by CSS markup, the colors of the menu buttons and font can be changed throughout the web site by one simple change in the CSS style sheet.

A vertical side-menu is normally contained within a column called <nav>. The column width will determine the button width, but don't rely on this. In the CSS markup, give the buttons a width and use zoom:1; to prevent unsightly gaps appearing in IE 6. The snippet of vertical menu button code that follows has semantic tags and it is assumed that the Remy Sharp JavaScript snippet is included in the head section of the HTML5 page.

```
<nav><!--side menu column contains the vertical menu-->
<ul>
<li><a href="southbury-parish-aboutus.html" title="About us">About Us</a></li>
<li><a href="southbury-parish-who.html" title="Who's Who in Southbury ↵
Parish">Who&#39;s Who</a></li>
<li><a href="southbury-parish-location.html" title="Location of the parish"> ↵
Find us</a></li>
<li><a href="southbury-parish-churches.html" title="Description of each ↵
church">Churches</a></li>
<li><a href="southbury-parish-activities.html" title="Parish activities ↵
and organisations">Activities</a></li>
<li><a href="southbury-parish-faqs.html" title="Frequently Asked Questions ↵
(Baptisms, Funerals, Weddings)">FAQs</a></li>
<li><a href="index.html" title="Return to Home Page">Home Page</a></li>
</ul>
</nav><!--end of side menu column-->
```

Part of the the CSS style sheet for the vertical menu with 3D buttons (Figure 4-20)

```
nav {width:130px; float:left;
}
ul{  margin-left:0; padding-left:0;
}
/* set general side button styles */
li { width:115px; list-style-type :none; margin-bottom: 3px; text-align: center;
}
/* set general anchor styles */
li a { display: block; width:115px; color: white; font-weight: bold; ↵
text-decoration: none
}
```

```
        /* specify state styles. */
        /* mouseout (default) */
        li a { background: #1A9CE0;  border: 4px outset #aabaff;
        }
        /* mouseover */
        li a:hover  { display:block; background: #0a4adf; border: 4px outset #8abaff; ↵
        width:115px;
        }
        /* onmousedown */
        li a:active { background:#aecbff; border: 4px inset #aecbff;
}
```

Create an Active-Page Button

An *active-page button* gives users a visible indication of where they have landed. Some clients ask for an active-page button on each active page, others prefer not to have this feature for the sake of consistency. Figure 4-21 shows a button that appears to be depressed, indicating the active page.

The Contact Us button in Figure 4-21 appears to be inset. This indicates to the user that she is viewing the Contact Us page. Don't rely entirely on this. The page should also have a prominent Contact Us heading.

Figure 4-21. Showing the depressed Contact Us button

In Listing 4-21a, the Contact Us link has a new class (indicated in bold font). This class is a CSS style that makes the button appear to be depressed. Listing 4-21a creates the appearance of a depressed button on a 3D menu. In this listing the depressed button appears on the "Contact Us" page. A depressed button can appear on any page by placing the code class="insetbtn" in the menu link for that page. See the example in bold type in Listing 4-21a.

Listing 4-21a. Making the "Contact Us" Button Appear Depressed (active-page.html)

```
<!doctype html>
<html lang=en>
<head>
<title>Active page for a depressed button</title>
<meta charset=utf-8>
```

```
                          meta details go here
<link rel="stylesheet" type="text/css" href="inset-active.css">
<!--Add conditional Javascript-->
<!--[if lte IE 8]>
<script src="html5.js" type="text/javascript">
</script>
<![endif]-->
</head>
<body>
<div id="container">
<nav>
  <ul>
    <li><a href="aboutus.html" title="About Us">About Us</a></li>
    <li><a href="membership.html" title="Membership form">Membership</a></li>
    <li><a href="volunteers.html" title="Volunteers needed">Volunteers</a></li>
    <li><a href="services.html" title="The Services">Services</a></li>
    <li><a href="news.html" title="News and events">News-Events</a></li>
    <li class="insetbtn"><a href="#" title="Contact Us">Contact Us</a></li>
    <li><a href="links.html" title="Links to related sites">Links</a></li>
    <li><a href="index.html" title="Return to Home Page">Home Page</a></li>
  </ul>
</nav>
</div>
</body>
 </html>
```

Listing 4-21b is the CSS style sheet for Listing 4-21a. It creates the appearance of a depressed button on the selected page so that the user knows where he has landed.

Listing 4-21b. *The CSS Style Sheet for Making A button Appear to be Depressed (inset-active.css)*

```
html, body, h1, h2, h3, h4, h5, h6, p, ol, ul, li { padding: 0; margin: 0;
}
header, footer, section, article, nav { display:block;
}
#container { margin-left:20px; margin-top:20px;
}
nav { width:140px;
}
nav ul { width: 115px; float:left;margin-left:0;
}
nav li { margin-bottom: 1px; text-align: center; list-style:none; padding-bottom:3px;
}
nav li a { display: block; color: yellow; font-weight: bold; text-decoration: none; zoom:1;
}
/* mouseout (default) */
nav li a { background: #946055;  border: 4px outset #c96e6b;
}
nav li a:hover { background: #9f7562; color:white;  border: 4px outset #c96e6b;
}
nav li a:active { background:#aecbff;  border: 4px inset #aecbff;
}
/* set general inset button styles */
nav li.insetbtn { border:none;
```

```
}
nav li.insetbtn a { display: block; color:orange; font-weight: bold; ↵
text-decoration: none; cursor:default; margin-bottom: 0; text-align: center; ↵
list-style:none; padding-bottom:3px; background:#744035; border-top: 4px #5e2100 solid; ↵
border-left: 4px #5e2100 solid; border-right:3px #bfa5a2 solid; ↵
border-bottom:3px #bfa5a2 solid;
}
```

■ **Note** The attribute for the cursor in the inset class is set as *default* to indicate that the inset link is not clickable.

On each page, the appropriate button is given the class insetbtn; for example, on the next page named links.html, the inset class would be applied like this:

```
<li class="btn"><a href="contact.html" title="Contact Us">Contact Us</a></li>
<li class="insetbtn"><a href="#" title="Links to related sites">Links</a></li>
<li class="btn"><a href="index.html" title="Return to Home Page">Home Page</a></li>
```

Horizontal and Vertical Menus on the Same Page

A combination of horizontal and vertical menus needs to be applied with care. If the horizontal menu is not made prominent enough by means of larger buttons, it can be overlooked by the user. Figure 4-22 shows a typical page with both types of menu.

Figure 4-22. A horizontal and a vertical menu on the same page. Use the horizontal buttons for the main items and make those buttons bigger to reflect their importance.

■ **Tip**   To avoid confusion during the design stage, use a `<div>` for one menu and the `<nav>` tag for the other. In the Listing 4-22a for Figure 4-22, I chose to use the semantic `<nav>` tag for the vertical menu, and a `<div>` for the horizontal menu.

Some users have difficulty when confronted by two menus on one page, The horizontal menu can seem invisible because users tend to look only at the vertical block out of habit. However, the technique is a good way of having more buttons without overcrowding them. The drawback can be overcome by making the horizontal buttons much larger than the vertical buttons, as in Listings 4-22a and 4-22b.

Listing 4-22a. Displaying a Page with Horizontal and Vertical 3D Button Menus (horiz-vert-menu.html)

```
<!doctype html>
<html lang=en>
<head>
<title>Contact page for the parish of Southbury, Devon</title>
<meta charset=utf-8>
        meta details go here
<link rel="stylesheet" type="text/css" href="horiz-vert-menu.css">
        <!--Add conditional Javascript-->
        <!--[if lte IE 8]>
        <script src="html5.js" type="text/javascript">
        </script>
        <![endif]-->
</head>
<body>
<div id="container">
<header>
        <h1>THE PARISH OF SOUTHBURY</h1>
</header>
<div id="hnav"><!--start of horizontal menu-->
  <ul>
        <li><a title="Southbury Church Services" href="southbury-church-services.html"> ↵
        Services</a></li>
        <li><a title="What's On" href="southbury-parish-whatson.html">What&#39;s On</a></li>
        <li><a title="Contact Us" href="southbury-parish-contact.html">Contact Us</a></li>
  </ul>
</div><!--end of horizontal menu-->
<br class="clear"/><br>
<div id="main-content"><br>
  <nav><!--vertical menu starts-->
    <ul>
        <li><a href="southbury-parish-aboutus.html" title="About us">About Us</a></li>
        <li><a href="southbury-parish-who.html" title="Who's Who in Southbury Parish">↵
        Who&#39;s Who</a></li>
        <li><a href="southbury-parish-location.html" title="Location of the parish">↵
        Find us</a></li>
        <li><a href="southbury-parish-churches.html" title="Description of each ↵
        church">Churches</a></li>
```

```
        <li><a href="southbury-parish-activities.html" title="Parish activities and ↵
        organisations">Activities</a></li>
        <li><a href="southbury-parish-faqs.html" title="Frequently Asked Questions ↵
        (Baptisms, Funerals, Weddings)">FAQs</a></li>
        <li><a href="index.html" title="Return to Home Page">Home Page</a></li>
    </ul>
  </nav><!--end of vertical menu-->
<!--start of far right column-->
<div id="creditcol"><br>
        <img alt="Church logo" title="Church logo" src="images/churchlogo.jpg">
        <p><a href="http://validator.w3.org/check?uri=referer"><img class="cntr"↵
        src=http://www.w3.org/Icons/valid-xhtml10-blue alt="Valid XHTML 1.0 ↵
        Transitional" height="31" width="88"></a>
        <span class="tiny">Validated by the World Wide Web Consortium</span></p>
        <p><span class="tiny">Website design and production by<br>
        A West Web Design</span></p>
</div>
<div id="midcontent">
        <h2>CONTACT US</h2><br>
<div id="mid-left-col">
        <h2>Contact James Miller</h2>Vice Chairman of the Parochial Church Council<br>
        Tel: 01234 333 555<br><br>
        <h2>Church Office Postal Address:</h2>Church Office, Southbury Parish<br>
        Sunday School Building, The Churchyard<br>Church Lane, Southbury, SX24 6JM
</div>
<div id="mid-right-col">
<img class="cntr" title="Southbury Church" alt="Southbury Church" height="172" ↵
src="images/southbury220.jpg" width="220">
</div>
</div>
</div>
<br class="clear">
<footer>
        Footer goes here
</footer>
</div>
</body>
</html>
```

Listing 4-22b. The CSS for Presenting Both Horizontal and Vertical Menus. (horiz-vert-menu.css)

```
html, body, h1, h2, h3, h4, h5, h6, p, ol, ul, li { padding: 0; margin: 0;
}
header, footer, section, article, nav { display:block;
}
body {text-align:center; background: #bee8ff; font-family:"times new roman"; ↵
font-size:medium; color:navy;
}
#container {width:97%; max-width:960px; min-width:780px; margin:auto;
}
#main-content { width:100%; margin:0; padding:0;
}
```

```
header {width:100%; height:156px; background-image:url('images/header2.jpg'); ⏎
text-align:center; background-repeat:no-repeat; background-position:center top;
}
img { border:0;
}
#creditcol { float:right; width:125px; text-align:center;
}
#midcontent { margin:0 135px 0 145px; text-align:center;
}
footer {text-align:center; clear:both;
}
br.clear { clear:both;
}
#mid-left-col {width:47%; float:left; text-align:left;
}
#mid-right-col {width:47%; float:right; text-align:left;
}
h1 { padding-top:30px; margin:0; text-align:center;
}
h2 { margin:0 0 5px 0; font-size:large; font-weight:bold;
}
p.lft {text-align:left;
}
p.cntr {text-align:center;
}
/*set horizontal menu buttons general style*/
#hnav {display:inline-block;  margin:10px auto 10px auto; width:450px; height:42px;
}
#hnav li {margin:10px; float:left; text-align:center; padding:5px;  list-style-type:none;
}
/*set general anchor style to fill the container*/
#hnav li a {text-decoration:none; color:white; font-weight:bold; width:120px; ⏎
padding:5px; text-align:center;
}
/*mouseOut state (default)*/
#hnav li a { background: #1A9CE0; border: 4px outset #AABAFF; text-align:center; ⏎
margin-right:5px;
}
/* mouseover */
#hnav li a:hover { background: #0A4ADF; border: 4px outset #8ABAFF; width:120px;
}
/* onmousedown */
#hnav li a:active { background:#ABCBFF;  border: 4px inset #ABCBFF;
}
/* set vertical button menu position */
nav {width:130px; float:left;
}
ul { margin-left:0; padding-left:0;
}
/* set general side button styles */
li { width:115px; list-style-type :none; margin-bottom: 3px; text-align: center;
}
```

```
/* set general anchor styles */
li a { display: block; width:115px; color: white; font-weight: bold; text-decoration: none
}
/* specify state styles. */
/* mouseout (default) */
li a { background: #1A9CE0; border: 4px outset #AABAFF;
}
/* mouseover */
li a:hover { display:block; background: #0A4ADF; border: 4px outset #8ABAFF; width:115px;
}
/* omousedown */
li a:active { background:#AECBFF; border: 4px inset #AECBFF;
}
br.clear { clear:both; }
/*various font sizes and colours*/
.tiny { text-align: center; font-family: Arial; font-size: 8pt; color: #000000;
}
p.cntr { text-align:center;
}
p.lft { text-align:left; margin-top: 1px;
}
p.right {text-align:right;
}
```

Summary

This chapter provided you with many rollover menu projects. Several of the techniques are used again in subsequent chapters. Many resources for rollover menus were listed. They will help you find further information and also enable you to download button images. Chapter 7 will feature a project using CSS3 to produce rounded corners on tab menus.

In the next chapter, you will discover the enhancements offered by CSS3. These include CSS3 gradients, the ability to modify the opacity of colors, drop capitals, and striped data tables. The next chapter also discusses the CSS3 font selectors that provide server-side fonts for a tighter control of the fonts used in web sites.

CHAPTER 5

Moving to CSS3

CSS3 is a *separate* recommendation and not a component of HTML5. Not only does CSS3 offer a very exciting prospect, but browsers (other than IE 7 and IE 8) have already picked up most of the CSS3 features. IE 7 and IE 8 just ignore CSS3; for instance, pages with CSS3 rounded corners display square corners.

This chapter contains a selection of CSS3 modules. Other CSS3 modules are described in their appropriate chapters, as follows:

- CSS3 multiple backgrounds: Chapter 3
- CSS3 tabbed menus with rounded corners: Chapter 7
- CSS3 rounded corners: Chapter 7
- CSS3 drop shadows: Chapter 8
- CSS3 multiple columns: Chapter 15
- W3C validation of CSS3: Chapter 19
- CSS3 quick reference: Appendix

■ **Tip**   The following web sites provide additional information on CSS3: `http://www.cssportal.com/css3-preview` is a must see resource that gives excellent examples, templates, and explanations for CSS3 modules. `http://www.css3generator.com` allows you to choose a CSS3 module and see the markup for each example, you can also discover which browsers support them.
`http://www.css3.info/preview/` provides the latest news and examples.
`http://www.css3.info/modules/` is updated frequently and has a comprehensive list of modules and their progress.
`http://css-tricks.com/examples/` offers excellent demos and good code snippets.
`http:/mashable.com/2010/06/04/awesome-css3-techniques/` provides news and examples.

CSS3 Gradients

At the time of writing, CSS3 gradient support was untidy. CSS3 gradients needed browser specific hacks. The examples in this section give an insight into how useful CSS3 gradients will be when the browser vendors are able to remove their hacks. Mozilla has to use a `-moz-` hack and the `-webkit-` hack is needed for Safari and Chrome. Even their markup differs. Opera has no support at the time of writing and IE 7 and IE 8 must fall back to a CSS2 gradient image. Currently, CSS2 gradient images work in all browsers, thus eliminating the need for the CSS3 solution for some time ahead. To create gradients with CSS2 see Chapter 3. Gradient generators are available at `http://gradients.glrzad.com/` and `www.colorzilla.com/gradient-editor/`.

I advise you to play with the examples now, but delay using CSS3 gradients until vendor-specific hacks are no longer needed. For IE 7 and IE 8, use CSS2 and a gradient image.

The W3C recommendations on CSS3 gradient can be seen at `http://dev.w3.org/TR/2011/WD-css3-images-20110908` and at `http://css-tricks.com/examples/CSS3Gradient/`

CSS3 gradients can be incorporated into backgrounds instead of using images. They can also be used in the new CSS3 border image.

Linear Gradients

Figures 5-1 and 5-2 show gradients achieved by CSS3 without using a paint program.

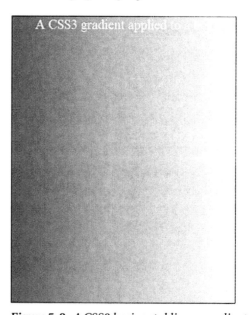

Figure 5-1. A CSS3 vertical linear gradient   *Figure 5-2. A CSS3 horizontal linear gradient*

Listing 5-1 results in a vertical gradient. An internal style is used for instructional purposes. The relevant code is shown bold and you will see that currently the `-moz-` and `-webkit-` hacks are needed. At some time in the near future we can expect Mozilla Firefox, Google, and Safari to support the gradients without the hacks.

Listing 5-1. Creating a Vertical Linear Gradient with CSS3 (css3-gradient-vert.html)

```
<!doctype html>
<html lang=en>
<head>
<title>A vertical CSS3 gradient applied to a box</title>
<meta charset=utf-8>
        meta details go here
</head>
<style type="text/css">
#gradient-box {margin:auto; text-align:center; font-size:x-large; color:white; ↵
border:1px black solid; width:400px; height:500px; ↵
   background: -moz-linear-gradient(100% 100% 90deg, white, green);
   background: -webkit-gradient(linear, 0% 0%, 0% 100%, from(green), to(white));
}
</style>
</head>
<body>
<div id="gradient-box">
A CSS3 gradient applied to a box</div>
</body>
</html>
```

■ **Note** The -moz- and -webkit- markups are very different; also, Firefox works from bottom to top, the others work from top to bottom. (Another fine mess, Stanley.)

Listing 5-2 results in a horizontal gradient. Note that this does not work in any version of IE, not even IE 9 or IE 10.

An internal style is used for instructional purposes. The relevant code is shown in bold and you will see that currently the -moz- and -webkit- hacks are needed.

Listing 5-2. Creating a horizontal Linear Gradient with CSS3 (css3-gradient-horiz.html)

```
<!doctype html>
<html lang=en>
<head>
<title>A horizontal CSS3 gradient applied to a box</title>
<meta charset=utf-8>
        meta details go here
<head>
<style type="text/css">
#gradient-box {margin:auto; text-align:center; font-size:x-large; color:white; ↵
border:1px black solid; width:400px; height:500px; ↵
background: -moz-linear-gradient(100% 100% 180deg, white, green); ↵
background: -webkit-gradient(linear, left top, right top, from(green), to(white));
}
</style>
</head>
<body>
```

```
<div id="gradient-box">A CSS3 gradient applied to a box</div>
</body>
</html>
```

▓ **Note** Because the -moz- and -webkit- markups are very different, it would be pointless to give a detailed explanation until browser vendors implement the W3C recommendations without vendor specific hacks. Until then, use CSS2 gradient images created in a paint program. The W3C recommendations for future browsers will have something like the following format: background:linear(green, white); or linear-gradient(green, white);. For the latest developments in gradients visit: http://dev.w3.org/csswg/css3-images/#linear-gradients Meanwhile search the internet to follow developments in browser support for gradients, a good starting point would be: http://www.css3gradients.com/

Radial Gradients

Figures 5-3 and 5-4 show radial gradients achieved by CSS3 without using a paint program.

Figure 5-3. Gradient in Mozilla Firefox

Figure 5-4. Gradient in Safari and Chrome

Mozilla Firefox gives the best gradient, the other browsers currently depict the gradient as a ball.

The code in bold type in Listing 5-3 produces a radial gradient, again -moz- and -webkit- hacks must be used in the current browsers that support CSS3 gradients. The relevant code is shown in bold. This does not work in any version of IE, not even IE 9.

Listing 5-3. Creating a Radial Gradient With CSS3 (css3-gradient-radial.html)

```
<!doctype html>
<html lang=en>
<head>
<title>A radial CSS3 gradient applied to a box</title>
<meta charset=utf-8>
        meta details go here
<style type="text/css">
#gradient-box {margin:auto; text-align:center; font-size:x-large; color:white; ↵
border:1px black solid; width:400px; height:500px; ↵
background: -moz-radial-gradient(center 45deg, circle closest-corner, ↵
white 0%, green 100%);
background: -webkit-gradient(radial, center center, 0, ↵
center center, 200, from(white), to(green));
}
</style>
</head>
<body>
<div id="gradient-box">
A CSS3 gradient applied to a box</div>
</body>
</html>
```

The W3C recommendations for future browsers will have something like the following format:

```
background:radial-gradient(green, white);
```

A circular gradient would be something like this:

```
Background:radial-gradient(circle, green, white)
```

CSS3 Opacity and RGBA Colors

These two modules are discussed together because their differences need explaining. The opacity declaration concerns a whole element, including its child elements. The RGB (Red, Green, Blue) declaration describes a color and opacity for one element; child elements are not affected. However, with RGBA, the designer can choose which child elements are transparent or opaque.

■ **Tip**   For a good explanatory slide show covering RGBA and opacity see:

```
http://leaverou.me/2009/03/css3-colors-today-mediacampathens-session/.
```

In the following three examples, an internal style sheet is used for instructional purposes only. Figure 5-5 is the starting point for the examples shown in Figures 5-5, 5-6, and 5-7.

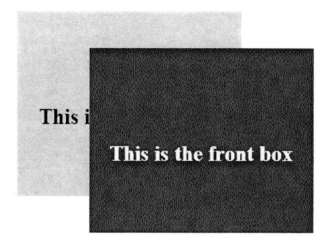

Figure 5-5. *Two plain, box elements using CSS3 and RGB to set the background colors*

For reasons that will become clear later in Figure 5-7, the front box has been given a 4-pixel wide border in the same color as the background, the border is therefore not visible in Figure 5-5.

Listing 5-5 shows the HTML and CSS3 for the Figure 5-5. The code in bold type creates the opaque boxes. The boxes have an identical appearance in any browser. Because IE 7 and IE 8 do not support CSS3 you would expect a problem to occur. However, because the default for IE 7 and IE 8 is *opaque,* and because the Listing does not specify any transparency, all browsers will display opaque boxes.

Listing 5-5. *Creating Two Overlapping Opaque Boxes Using RGB (css3-opaque.html)*

```
<!doctype html>
<html lang=en>
<head>
<title>Opaque boxes in CSS3</title>
<meta charset=utf-8>
        meta details go here
<style type="text/css">
#back-box {position:absolute; top:20px; left:20px; z-index:1; text-align :center; ↵
font-size:x-large; font-weight:bold; color:black; border:0; width:250px; ↵
height:200px; background-color: rgb(255,255,0);
}
#back-box p { margin-top:100px;
}
#front-box {position:absolute; top:60px; left:100px; z-index:2; text-align:center; ↵
font-size:x-large; font-weight:bold; color:white; border:4px red 0; width:250px; ↵
height:200px; background-color: rgb(255,0,0);
}
#front-box p { margin-top:100px;
}
</style>
</head>
<body>
<div id="back-box">
```

```
<p>This is the back box</p>
</div>
<div id="front-box">
<p>This is the front box</p>
</div>
</body>
</html>
```

The next project displays CSS3 opacity/transparency. IE7 and IE 8 do not support this. The effect of CSS3 transparency (aka opacity) is shown in Figure 5-6.

Figure 5-6. Using CSS3, the entire front box element has been given 0.5 opacity (transparency), This degree of opacity applies equally to all the elements of the front box including the child elements, the invisible 4-pixel border, and the white text.

The back box can be seen through the transparent front box. The background color of the back box is visible in the white text of the front box.

In Listing 5-6, the CSS3 attribute opacity:0.5; relates to the whole #front-box element, including any child elements such as border and paragraphs. The opacity can be set as 1 (fully opaque) or 0 (not at all opaque; that is, completely transparent) and anything in between, such as 0.5 for half opaque.

Listing 5-6. Creating a Front Box with 0.5 Opacity (css3-opacity.html)

```
<!doctype html>
<html lang=en>
<head>
<title>Opacity and CSS3</title>
<meta charset=utf-8>
        meta details go here
<head>
<style type="text/css">
#back-box {position:absolute; top:20px; left:20px; z-index:1; text-align :center; ↵
font-size:x-large; font-weight:bold; color:black; border:0; width:250px; ↵
height:200px; background-color: rgb(255,255,0);
}
```

```
#back-box p { margin-top:100px;
}
#front-box {position:absolute; top:60px; left:100px; z-index:2; text-align:center; ↵
font-size:x-large; font-weight:bold; color:white; border:4px red solid; width:250px; ↵
height:200px; background-color: rgb(255,0,0); opacity:0.5;
}
#front-box p { margin-top:100px;
}
</style>
</head>
<body>
<div id="back-box">
<p>This is the back box</p>
</div>
<div id="front-box">
        <p>This is the front box</p>
</div>
</body>
</html>
```

The next project demonstrates the flexibility of the CSS3 RGBA element. The "A" stands for alpha, a feature that allows the designer to chose which child elements will have various degrees of opacity.

Figure 5-7 shows that transparency/opacity can be selectively applied to child elements.

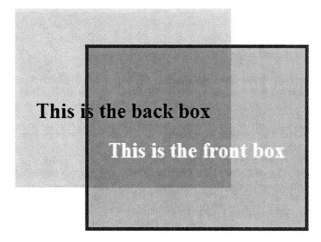

Figure 5-7. *RGBA has been applied selectively to the front box. This time, only the background color of the front box is made transparent.*

The two child elements, the 4-pixel border and the white text, remain fully opaque. The 4-pixel border was included earlier but was not visible in the previous examples.

▨ **Note** The colors of the border and text can be made opaque or transparent by applying RGBA to the individual children, for instance the border color and the text. This gives great flexibility because the designer can select which bits of an element should be given opaque values.

In Listing 5-7, the selected element is the background color of the front box which is made transparent. The child elements, such as border and paragraphs, are not affected by the opacity of the background. The opacity can be set from 1 (fully opaque) to 0 (not at all opaque; completely transparent). In Figure 5-7, the background color of the front box is set as background-color: rgba(255,0,0,0.5); .

Listing 5-7.Applying CSS3 Opacity Selectively to the Front Box (css3-rgba.html)

```
<!doctype html>
<html lang=en>
<head>
<title>CSS3 and RGBA</title>
<meta charset=utf-8>
        meta details go here
<head>
<style type="text/css">
#back-box {position:absolute; top:20px; left:20px; z-index:1; text-align :center; ↵
font-size:x-large; font-weight:bold; color:black; border:0; width:250px; ↵
height:200px; background-color: rgb(255,255,0);
}
#back-box p { margin-top:100px;
}
#front-box {position:absolute; top:60px; left:100px; z-index:2; text-align:center; ↵
font-size:x-large; font-weight:bold; color:white; border:4px red solid; width:250px; ↵
height:200px; background-color: rgba(255,0,0,0.5);
}
#front-box p { margin-top:100px;
}
</style>
</head>
<body>
<div id="back-box"><p>This is the back box</p>
</div>
<div id="front-box"><p>This is the front box</p>
</div>
</body>
</html>
```

▨ **Note** The RGBA and opacity modules are exciting and long awaited. Unfortunately, they are not supported by IE 6, IE 7, and IE 8. As a result, an IE conditional has to be used to present an alternative display for these versions of IE. The conditional IE style link must be placed after the main style link in the HTML markup and it could provide a uniform color or a gradient made by tiling a gradient image.

New CSS3 Selectors and Elements

Many new selectors are available in CSS3. These can be found in the downloadable cheat sheet mentioned at the end of this chapter.

The following examples are a few of the most useful pseudo-class selectors and pseudo-elements. A drop capital is shown in Figure 5-8.

::first letter

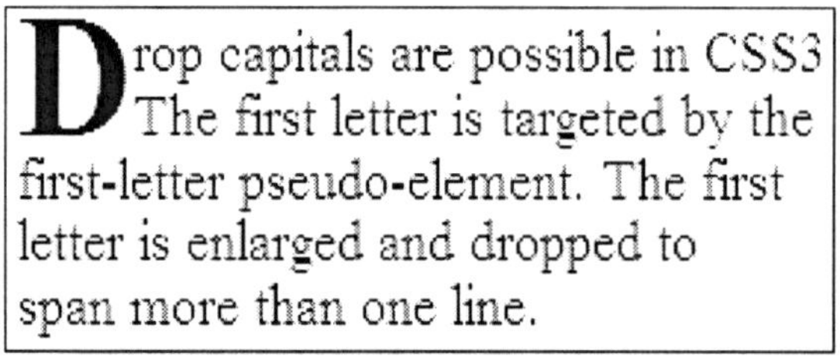

Figure 5-8. *A drop capital using CSS3*

The drop capital shown in Figure 5-8 is produced by the pseudo-class selector indicated in bold in Listing 5-8. The height of the drop cap varies in each of the modern browsers. Mozilla Firefox gives the best display.

Listing 5-8. *Applying a Drop Capital to the First Letter of a Paragraph (CSS3-drop-cap.html)*

```
<!doctype html>
<html lang=en>
<head>
<title>Drop cap initial letter</title>
<meta charset=utf-8>
<style type="text/css">
    p { font-size: large; line-height: 1.1
    }
    #dropcap-section p::first-letter { font-size: 300%; font-weight: bold; float: left
    }
</style>
</head>
<body>
surrounding paragraph
<div id="dropcap-section">
  <p>Drop capitals are possible in CSS3<br>
  The first letter is targeted by the <br>
  first-letter pseudo-element. The first<br>
  letter is enlarged and dropped to<br>
  span more than one line. <br></p>
</div>
  surrounding paragraph
 </body>
</html>
```

■ **Note** You may have to juggle a little with the font size and line height to get the desired effect. The first letter may be given a different color. You are unlikely to want dropped capitals throughout the entire web site, hence the `<div id="dropcap-section">` to select only the paragraphs that do need dropped capitals.

::first line

`::first line` affects the entire first line of a paragraph; however, this seems more cumbersome than using a `<span>` on the first line.

::before

The `::before` pseudo-element can generate some content at the start of certain paragraphs; however, this can also be achieved in CSS2 (see the Appendix).

:nth-child()

`:nth-child()` styles selective items in a list or a table. Information in table form is easier to read and understand if alternate rows are colored; this is particularly true in wide, multi-column tables.

The `:nth-child` attribute simplifies the creation of alternately colored rows. For instance, `ul :nth-child(even)` will style every second, fourth, sixth, eighth, and so forth, item in a *list* of items. Note the space between `ul` and `:nth-child`; this is important in a list.

The parenthesis can contain various keywords, such as *odd*, *even*, or *number* to select particular items.

In Figure 5-9, the second, fourth, and sixth rows have been colored using `nth-child(even)`.

Place	Hotel	Cost
London	Kingfisher	£200
Colyton	Leofric	£30
Coventry	Ritz	£150
Charmouth	Palace	£100
Daventry	De Luxe	£150
Rugby	Royal Grand	£180

Figure 5-9. Using CSS3 nth-child(even) to add stripes

A wide table can be made easier to read by using alternate stripes. In Listing 5-9, the code in bold produces the alternate stripes shown in Figure 5-9. IE 7 and IE 8 do not support CSS3 striped tables.

Listing 5-9. Creating Colored Stripes in Even Rows in a Table (table-1.html)

```
<!doctype html>
<html lang=en>
<head>
```

```
<title>Table 1</title>
<meta charset=utf-8>
<style type="text/css">
        table { width: 500px; border:1px black solid; border-collapse:collapse;
        }
        td { border:1px black solid; padding:0 5px;0 5px
        }
        th { border:1px black solid;
        }
        caption { font-weight:bold;
        }
        table tr:nth-child(even) { background-color: #C8F0F0;
        }
        .right { text-align:right; }
</style>
</head>
<body>
<table summary="Table with stripes">
<caption>Table 1. Using CSS3 nth-child(even) to add stripes</caption>
        <tr><th>Place</th><th>Hotel</th><th>Cost</th></tr>
        <tr><td>London</td><td>Kingfisher</td><td class="right">&pound;200</td></tr>
        <tr><td>Colyton</td><td>Leofric</td><td class="right">&pound;30</td></tr>
        <tr><td>Coventry</td><td>Ritz</td><td class="right">&pound;150</td></tr>
        <tr><td>Charmouth</td><td>Palace</td><td class="right">&pound;100</td></tr>
        <tr><td>Daventry</td><td>De Luxe</td><td class="right">&pound;150</td></tr>
        <tr><td>Rugby</td><td>Royal Grand</td><td class="right">&pound;180</td></tr>
</table>
</body>
</html>
```

Figure 5-10 shows a table with alternate striped rows starting with the 3rd row by using CSS3.

Place	Hotel	Cost
London	Kingfisher	£200
Colyton	Leofric	£30
Coventry	Ritz	£150
Charmouth	Palace	£100
Daventry	De Luxe	£150
Rugby	Royal Grand	£180

Figure 5-10. Using CSS3 and nth-child(2n+3) to add stripes

In Listing 5-10, the formula for the stripes is more complicated, but quite logical. The markup **table tr:nth-child(2n+3)** means: apply the style to every second row starting at row 3.

Listing 5-10. Using CSS3 to Create a Striped Table Starting From the 3rd Row (table-2.html)

```
<!doctype html>
<html lang=en>
<head>
```

```
<title>Table 2</title>
<meta charset=utf-8>
<style type="text/css">
        table { width: 500px; border:1px black solid; border-collapse:collapse;
        }
        td { border:1px black solid; padding: 0 5px 0 5px;
        }
        th { border:1px black solid;
        }
        caption { font-weight:bold;
        }
        table tr:nth-child(2n+3) { background-color:#C8F0F0;
        }
        .right { text-align:right;
        }
</style>
</head>
<body>
<table summary="Table with stripes">
<caption>Table 2. Using CSS3 nth-child(2n+3) to add stripes</caption>
        <tr><th>Place</th><th>Hotel</th><th>Cost</th></tr>
        <tr><td>London</td><td>Kingfisher</td><td class="right">&pound;200</td></tr>
        <tr><td>Colyton</td><td>Leofric</td><td class="right">&pound;30</td></tr>
        <tr><td>Coventry</td><td>Ritz</td><td class="right">&pound;150</td></tr>
        <tr><td>Charmouth</td><td>Palace</td><td class="right">&pound;100</td></tr>
        <tr><td>Daventry</td><td>De Luxe</td><td class="right">&pound;150</td></tr>
        <tr><td>Rugby</td><td>Royal Grand</td><td class="right">&pound;180</td></tr>
</table>
</body>
</html>
```

Font Selectors

The CSS3 `@font-face` module can instruct a browser to use a particular font even if it is not installed on the user's computer. However, it presents difficulties in download speed and possible copyright infringement. If the font is not installed on the user's computer, it has to be downloaded from the web site's server, where it is stored. Because font sets can be huge, the download speed will be affected and the text will not be visible on the page until the download is complete. Unless you have permission to use the font, you could be accused of piracy by downloading copies without permission. IE 6, IE 7, and IE 8 do not support the `@font-face` module unless you do the following:

- Employ JavaScript,

- Use .eot (embedded open type) fonts, or

- Try the technique found at

   http://jontangerine.com/log/2008/10/fontface-in-ie-making-web-fonts-work

Let's say you want your site to use a font called `mickealmouse.ttf` and you also have an `.eot` version of the font. Your markup might look like the following:

```
@font-face { font-family: 'mickealmouse';
        src: url('mickealmouse.ttf') format(truetype);
        src: local(mickealmouse'), src: url('mickealmouse.eot');
```

```
      }
body { font-family: mickealmouse; Arial, Helvetica, sans-serif; font-size: medium;
color:black;
}
h1 { font-family: mickealmouse; Arial, Helvetica, sans-serif; font-size: x-large; ↵
color:black;
}
h2 { etc…
```

If the user's browser does not support @font-face, it can fall back to Arial, Helvetica, or sans-serif. If the user has the mickealmouse font already installed, the src: local(mickealmouse') item will instruct the browser to use the installed version so that the font does not have to be downloaded. No format is needed for .eot fonts.

The WOFF file format is another font face suitable for @font-face, which W3C, Microsoft, Opera, and Mozilla expect to become the "single, interoperable (font) format" supported by all browsers. It seems this file format is 40 percent smaller than the equivalent TTF file.

▪ **Tip**   For a useful resource on this topic, see Chapter 10 of the book *Pro HTML5 and CSS3 Design Patterns* by Michael Bowers, Dionysios Synodinos, and Victor Sumner (Apress, 2011).

Although not CSS3, an alternative solution provided by Google is well worth trying;

visit: http://google.com/webfonts You can choose a free open source font and download its code. The code will be a link to an on-line style sheet, the link must be the first item in the <head> section of a page. Then add the font style to the list of font styles in your CSS; say you downloaded the Diplomata font, the CSS font family could look like this: h1 { font-family: 'Diplomata', 'times new roman', serif; }

Using Current, Future, and Other Modules

Remember that CSS3 is not part of HTML5; it can, therefore, be used with HTML4 and XHTML1.0. However, it is only partially supported by the latest browsers at the moment. The following CSS3 modules are not supported by IE 7 and IE 8, and not all the CSS3 modules are currently supported by IE 9:

- *Outline*: Provides various border appearances, such as, ridge, outset, inset, groove. (Has a good CSS2 equivalent.)

- *Border images*: Surrounds a block element with a border made of tiny images (Not very useful.)

- *Grid layout*: A shorthand CSS method for creating a page layout grid.

- *Template layout*: Appears to duplicate a grid layout.

- *Media Queries*: CSS2 used the media types screen, speech, and print; the CSS3 module will extend the usefulness of media types.

- *Marquee-style*: Deals with overflowing text presented as a moving marquee.

- Speech (this module defines the improved rendering of documents into speech and also the use of aural recognition of spoken commands)

- Transitions and animation (improved control of animations)

■ **Tip** See the CSS3 cheat sheet at `http://www.smashingmagazine.com/2009/07/13/css-3-cheat-sheet-pdf`

Summary

CSS3 has exciting possibilities, but they are spoiled by the fact that IE 7 and IE 8 cannot make use of them. However, you now know the advantages CSS3 will offer when IE 7 and IE 8 are superseded by IE 9. Be sure to look at the other CSS3 recommendations covered in Chapters 3, 7, 8, and 15.

In the next chapter, you will learn about the new audio and video tags that are provided with HTML5. This is one of HTML5's most exciting and useful enhancements, particularly as video is such an important feature in modern web sites. You will also learn how the new tags permit a great reduction in the number of video formats. Fallback tips enable IE 7 and IE 8 to utilize the new tags. Two methods for creating slide shows are also described.

CHAPTER 6

Audio, Video, and Slide Shows

The first part of this chapter deals with the use and misuse of audio and video in web sites. The chapter then provides instructions for embedding an audio clip into a web page and for recording a speech clip. The current file formats for video are mentioned briefly and this is followed by information about the HTML5 <video> tag, the files that it uses, and instructions for embedding video clips into an HTML5 web page.

The problem presented by the lack of support in IE 7 and IE 8 for the <video> tag are resolved by various fallback methods, fully worked examples of fallbacks are provided. These include YouTube and Vimeo because they provide a relatively easy way of adding video to a web site. You will discover how these two online video stores can be used either alone or as fallbacks.

The chapter then provides two other methods of dealing with HTML5 video for IE 7 and IE 8 using the free downloadable JavaScript files, Flowplayer and OS FLV.

The chapter concludes with various methods for creating and embedding slideshows.

When to Use Audio and Video (AV)

Great care should be taken not to use audio and video gratuitously. Some web site designers insert a video just because they can and because it is fun. Creating and embedding a video can enliven a ho-hum day, but it may not please the client who commissioned the web site. The following are some valid reasons for including AV in a web site:

- An AV clip can sometimes explain something much better than text or images, providing there is no background music drowning the speaker's commentary.

- If the client is a film/TV production unit, a video clip can illustrate the quality of the product.

- If your page gives instructions for programming, making, fitting, or repairing something, then an AV clip could be helpful. However, most users will not remember the instructions on the video when they come to put them into practice (unless they have two computers, one to show the video and the other to carry out the instructions). Always provide a printable set of instructions in addition to the video.

- Audio can be used to good effect if your web site sells ringtones or doorbells with various sounds. Prospective customers can listen to the options and choose the one that pleases them.

- A video can present a product or service, but be warned: a poorly produced video will have a negative effect. Avoid inappropriate background music like the plague, as this is the biggest turn off. Why video and documentary makers wish to drown the presenter's commentary is a mystery.

- A slide show or video is ideal for displaying hotel accommodations, real estate, or tourist attractions.

- Pop groups, folk bands, and choirs looking for fixtures can give a brief sample of their stage presentation and music style by using a video clip; or the web site could just present an audio clip of music.

- As an example of the helpful use of AV, a web site for bird watchers could incorporate a video of birds and birdsong.

Using Other People's Video, Music, or Sound

Don't steal AV clips. You will need a genuine license (or permission from a non-commercial source) to incorporate AV on your web site. Musicians and filmmakers will certainly sue you and you may have to sell your house to pay the penalty. Owning a video tape, a CD, or DVD does not give you the right to use the music or video on it. Downloaded clips cannot be used without a genuine license, or unless they are offered for free use. So-called "royalty-free clips" are misnamed and normally have to be paid for.

If using video from another URL (with permission, of course), the owner of the source would supply you with the URL that points to the video file on her web site.

Test Your AV

Some AVs work on the internet, but they fail or misbehave when tested on your local computer. Always upload and test on the internet.

What to Avoid

Videos can be intensely annoying if used at the wrong time or in the wrong place.

- **Strongly resist the temptation to put a video on the home page.** It will dictate the focus and distract the viewer's attention away from the more important items on the page, such as your navigation menu. In addition, a video or audio clip might cause a MIME type problem or a coding error; both problems would prevent proper access to your all-important home page.

- **Do not use autostart.** Autostart causes the sound or video to automatically begin when the page is loaded. It is particularly bad practice on the home page and a bad idea on any page. The sudden burst of sound can startle users, especially blind users. Users will either immediately switch away from your web site or frantically search for a way to turn off the AV clip. They will probably never return to your site again.

- **Video and audio clips must have user controls.** Make sure the AV can only begin when the user clicks the start button on the video controls. Autostart might be acceptable if it loads a short but *quiet* arpeggio. Perhaps a *quiet* and soothing piece of background music might be tolerable in a video as long as it does not repeat in a never-ending loop, and as long as it is appropriate. At the first hint of a thumping, disco-type background, the great majority of users will hit the mute button, or more likely, abandon the site.

- **Do not use** onmouseover **sounds or videos.** A blind or partially-sighted person will receive a fright if she inadvertently mouses over an onmouseover sound link. Even sighted persons can accidentally mouse over a sound link and they won't be pleased with the sudden burst of sound. For the user's sake, always use onmousedown or a control console to launch audio or video.

Audio for a Non-Semantic HTML5 Page

Audio clips can be embedded in non-semantic HTML5 pages to save having to convert audio files to other formats. However, I encourage you to start using semantic tags as soon as practicable to keep up with modern web design techniques.

Figure 6-1 shows the controls for three sounds depicted in Internet Explorer 8.

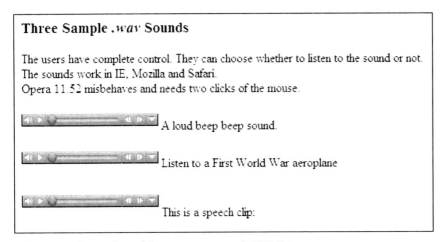

Figure 6-1. Screenshot of three, non-semantic HTML5 pages

Listing 6-1 uses the once deprecated <embed> tag. These three .wav sounds are audible in Internet Explorer, Mozilla, Safari, and Chrome; therefore, about 95 percent of computer owners will be able to hear the sounds. Unfortunately, to start the sounds in Opera 11.5, the user needs to click the starter button twice.

Listing 6-1.Creating Three Sounds in a Non-semantic Page (example-sound1.html)

```
<!doctype html>
<html>
<head>
<title>Sounds example 1</title>
<meta charset=utf-8>
</head>
<body>
<h3>Three Sample <i>.wav</i> Sounds</h3>
The users have complete control. They can choose whether to listen to the sound or ↵
not.<br>The sounds work in IE, Mozilla and Safari.<br>Opera 11.52 misbehaves and needs two
clicks of the mouse.<br><br>
<embed src="sounds/beepbeep.wav" width="180" height="25" autostart="false" ↵
repeat="false" loop="false"> A loud beep beep sound.
```

```
</embed><br><br>
<embed src="sounds/planeflyby.wav" width="180" height="25" autostart="false" ↵
loop="false"> Listen to a First World War aeroplane
</embed><br><br>
<embed src="sounds/adrianspoem.wav" width="180px" height="40" autostart="false" ↵
loop="false">This is a speech clip:
</embed>
</body>
</html>
```

Audio for a Semantic HTML5 Page

The next project demonstrates how the three sounds can be played using an HTML5 page using semantic tags. Figures 6-2a and 6-2b show the controls displayed in IE 7 and IE 8 and in Mozilla Firefox.

■ **Tip**   The .wav files were converted to .mp3 and .ogg files using the online converter at `http://media.io/` For best results, convert the files first to .mp3 then convert the .mp3 files to .ogg. These two file formats are necessary to enable the HTML5 audio tag to support browsers other than IE 7 and IE 8.

The .ogg file will arrive with about half a mile of figures and letters appended like this:

`beep-beep.ogg;jsessionid=0113CF8JM5SD16M37…` and so on. Rename the file and delete everything after .ogg

---

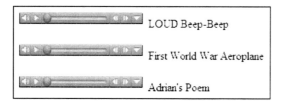

Figure 6-2a. *The controls displayed in IE 7 and IE 8*

Figure 6-2b. *The controls in Firefox*

In Listing 6-2a/2b, the three sounds and their controls are contained in three `<div>`s . Each `<div>` contains a semantic audio section and a fallback for IE 7 and IE 8. The latest HTML5 spec seems to suggest that autobuffer will be replaced by `preload="auto"`. Some designers are playing safe and including both, as follows:

```
<audio controls autobuffer preload="auto">
```

Listing 6-2a/2b. *Creating Three Sounds in a Page with Semantic Tags (example-sound2a-and-2b.html)*

```
<!doctype html>
<html>
<head>
<title>Example sound2a and 2b</title>
<meta charset=utf-8>
        <style type="text/css">
        div { margin-left: 20px;
        }
```

```
        </style>
</head>
<body>
#container { margin-left: 20px; width:500px;
}
<div>
        <p>
        <audio controls autobuffer>
        <source src=sounds/beepbeep.ogg type="audio/ogg">
        <source src=sounds/beepbeep.mp3 type="audio/mp3">
                <object>
                <embed src="sounds/beepbeep.wav" width="180" height="25" ↵
                autostart="false" repeat="false" loop="false">
                </embed>
                </object>
        </audio> LOUD Beep-Beep</p>
</div>
<div>
        <p>
        <audio controls autobuffer>
        <source src=sounds/planeflyby.ogg type="audio/ogg">
        <source src=sounds/planeflyby.mp3 type="audio/mp3">
                <object>
                <embed src="sounds/planeflyby.wav" width="180" height="25" ↵
                autostart="false" loop="false">
                </embed>
                </object>
        </audio> First World War Aeroplane</p>
</div>
<div>
        <p>
        <audio controls autobuffer>
        <source src=sounds/adrianspoem.ogg type="audio/ogg">
        <source src=sounds/adrianspoem.mp3 type="audio/mp3">
                <object>
                <embed src="sounds/adrianspoem.wav" width="180" height="25" ↵
                autostart="false" loop="false">
                </embed>
                </object>
        </audio> Adrian's Poem
        </p>
</div>
</div>
</body>
</html>
```

Creating a Speech Clip

Windows has in-built voice recorder software. Laptop computers have integral microphones, but a desktop computer will usually need a cheap microphone. Microphone/earphone kits have two plugs attached to them; use only the pink plug. Insert the pink plug into the pink socket on the computer. If the computer's sockets are not color-coded, look for the microphone symbol next to the socket. Some internal dial-up modems have colored sockets, but don't plug into those.

Starting the Recording

To start the recording in XP, do the following: Click Start ➤ All Programs ➤ Accessories ➤ Entertainment ➤ Sound Recorder.

To start the recording in Windows 7, do the following: Click Start ➤ All Programs ➤ Accessories ➤ Sound Recorder.

For either operating system, click the stop/start button and speak your message. Your message can be up to one minute long. Speak naturally and clearly with the microphone about six inches from your mouth. Click the button with the black rectangle to stop recording.

In XP, click the button with the right-pointing triangle to hear your message. Then, click File ➤ Save As... Give the file a name and save it.

In Windows 7, save the file with an appropriate name in the appropriate folder. Find the file and double-click it to hear it.

Video Overview: Yesterday's Video Formats

Video was a web designer's nightmare. With fourteen video file formats, four popular media players, and five main browsers with four plug-ins, the best description would be "a dog's breakfast". Personally, video and audio caused me more head scratching and frustration than any other aspect of web design and production. The following are a few of the common video formats current at the time of writing:

- The .flv format is a Flash file from Adobe. It must be located within an .swf container.

- The .mov format was developed by Apple and the files are known as QuickTime movies. The free QuickTime player has to be installed to play these movies on a Windows computer.

- The .rm or .ram format is produced by RealMedia for streaming online radio and internet TV. Its low bandwidth requirement means that it is good, but not top quality.

- The .swf format (Shockwave Flash) is the container for playing .flv Flash video or animation files.

- The .wma format from Microsoft is very versatile and can be highly compressed. It can be tailored to any download speed. It can be any size and is used for streaming radio and video.

- The .wmv format from Microsoft is popular, but can only be played on Windows computers using the Windows Media Player.

But Things Have Improved!

The following four methods for embedding videos are available right now:

- The new HTML5 <video> tag.

- Online video hosting (YouTube or Vimeo).

- HTML5 using the new video tag with only three file types and a fallback for IE 7 and IE 8.

- JavaScript players such as Flowplayer or OS FLV.

File Types for the HTML5 Semantic Video Tag

HTML5 introduces a <video> tag that will eliminate the need for plug-ins and JavaScript. It is supported in all the latest browsers, but not in IE 7 or IE 8. The HTML5 video tag uses only three video formats; a welcome reduction from 14 file types. To play a video, the browser unzips a video file.

▓ **Tip** For a useful resource, read *The Definitive Guide to HTML5 Video* by Silvia Pfeiffer (Apress, 2010).

HTML5 video uses the new video containers (files) .webm, .mp4, and .ogv. A video container has several components; a video component, one or more audio tracks, some metadata specifying various dimensions, the title and the file language. A video player uses codecs that enables the video player to decode the information in the container so that it a can be seen and heard.

Browsers that support HTML5 video use one or more of the following file types:

- Safari, Chrome and IE 9 play .mp4 (aka H.264).

- Mozilla Firefox and Chrome play .webm.

- IE 9 plays .webm using a plug-in (the WebM Media Foundation components), which rather defeats the purpose of the HTML5 video tag because it was intended to remove the need for plug-ins.

- Mozilla Firefox, Chrome, and Opera play .ogv.

HTML5 video is remarkably simple, but you will need some video file conversion programs.

Converting File Formats

To convert between .flv and .swf, download the free FoxTab video converter from http://www.foxtab.com. This is my favorite converter because it can convert almost any format.

To convert files to .webm, .ogv, and .mp4, download the free Miro Video Converter at http://mirovideoconverter.com Apparently, Miro will eventually offer an iPad version of their converter.

To convert files to .wmv format, download the free program, Freemake, from http://freemake.com; this site also offers a useful sound file converter.

To convert files to .mp4, .webm, and .ogv formats, download HandBrake, a free program, from http://handbrake.fr.

The first three video converters mentioned are easy to use. The last one is trickier, but it gives complete control of the conversion process. I have managed so far without HandBrake. For an excellent, fully detailed, and illustrated set of instructions on HandBrake, visit Mark Pilgrim's site at http://diveintohtml5.info/video.html. You should also check out Mark Pilgrim's book, *HTML5: Up and Running* (O'Reilly Media, 2010).

The Base HTML5 Video Code Format

The new <video> tag can be used right now provided you have a fallback to enable IE 7 and IE 8 users to view your videos. When users eventually cease using IE 7 and IE 8, the HTML5 video tag will make life so much easier for web designers. Then the fallback for IE can be abandoned and only three file formats will be needed. Later in this chapter you will learn how to use various fallbacks. The next snippet of code demonstrates the simplicity of the markup when using the HTML5 video tag without a fallback.

```
<video width="320" height="240" controls>
    <source src=somevideo.mp4 type='video/mp4; codecs="avc1, 42Eo1E, mp4a.40.2" '>
    <source src=somevideo.webm type='video/webm; codecs="vp8, vorbis" '>
    <source src=somevideo.ogv type='video/ogg; codecs="theora, vorbis" '>
</video>
```

I have found that the codecs can be omitted because they seem to be embedded in the browsers, but they are shown in the previous snippet for completeness. The sources can therefore be written as:

```
<video width="320" height="240" controls>
    <source src=somevideo.mp4 type='video/mp4;'>
    <source src=somevideo.webm type='video/webm;'>
    <source src=somevideo.ogv type='video/ogg;'>
</video>
```

Eventually, IE 7 and IE 8 will dwindle away and die; when this happens, you can see from the previous code snippets that embedding video will be as simple as adding an image to a web site page. Let's hope that one day soon, the media player creators will get together and agree to use only one audio format and one video format.

The wagon and butterfly video clips used in the following projects were kindly provided by the artist Roger Laughton and his daughter Helena of the Dolphin House Gallery, Colyton, Devon, United Kingdom. Their web site is at http://www.dolphinhousegallery.co.uk

You can try out the new <video> tag by downloading the files for this chapter from the book's page at http://www.apress.com, then load video-tag.html with any browser other than IE 7 or IE 8. Figure 6-3 shows a screenshot of the video using the new <video> tag and created by the Listing 6-3.

Figure 6-3. The HTML5 <video> tag displays a video in Mozilla Firefox. Note that no logo or other unwanted markings are shown.

Mozilla Firefox, IE 9, Chrome, Opera, and Safari support the new <video> tag and each browser has controls that are familiar to the user. Listing 6-3 is the markup for Figure 6-3 and the video files are assumed to be in a folder named video.

■ **Note** The dimensions in the listing line `<video width="480" height="385" controls="controls">` are important. When you produce the three video files, the videos must have the same frame size, and the frame dimensions must be included in the markup, otherwise the videos may not play.

Listing 6-3. Using the HTML5 Video Tag Without a Fallback for IE 7 and IE 8 (video-tag.html)

```
<!doctype html>
<html lang=en>
<head>
<title>Using the new HTML5 video tag</title>
<meta charset=utf-8>
<style type="text/css">
body { text-align: center; font-family:Arial; font-size:100%; font-weight:bold;
}
</style>
</head>
<body><br><p>HTML5 video tag with embedded YouTube fallback</p>
<video width="480" height="385" controls="controls">
                <source src=" video/wagon3.mp4" type="video/mp4">
                <source src=" video/wagon3.webm" type="video/webm">
                <source src=" video/wagon3.ogv" type="video/ogg">
</video>
</body>
</html>
```

Mixing Pages

Just because a new W3C standard is released, does not mean you have to change a whole web site to meet that standard. Provided the DOCTYPE for each individual page is correctly specified, a web site can contain a mixture of pages in HTML, HTML5, XHTM, and XHTML5. This can be useful if you only wish to use the new `<audio>` and `<video>` tags on one or two pages of an existing web site. Just use HTML5 on the video pages until you are ready to change the other pages to HTLM5. Meanwhile, in the next section we will investigate interim solutions that will allow IE 7 and IE 8 users to watch your videos.

What About the Problem of IE 7 and IE 8?

Internet Explorer 7 and IE 8 do not understand the HTML5 `<video>` tag; therefore, various solutions have been developed using workarounds called *fallbacks*. For the next few years, because it will take a while for IE 7 and IE 8 to be replaced by IE 9, you should continue to ensure that videos play in IE 7 and IE 8.

Meanwhile, don't panic! Your current pages using the `<object>` and `<embed>` tags in HTML4 and XHTML 1.0 pages will continue to function for the next decade or even longer.

The next two projects provide instructions for using YouTube and Vimeo as the sole video players and also as fallback solutions when using the HTML5 `<video>` tag.

Online Solutions: Using YouTube or Vimeo

Storing short video clips online in YouTube or Vimeo makes good sense because when the code for the video is added to an HTML5 page, the videos can be viewed in all the main browsers. We can be sure that, for commercial reasons, YouTube and Vimeo will keep abreast of any new web standards. YouTube and Vimeo codes now use the `<iframe>` tag and this works in all browsers, including IE 7 and IE 8.

▦ **Caution** Regularly check the YouTube and Vimeo web sites for changes in registration and upload/download procedure, and especially for changes in the terms and conditions under which you can use these products. There may be a charge (or a change in the cost) for using the videos on a web site that sells goods or services. The permitted size of a video file may also change.

The next two projects describe how to create a YouTube or Vimeo account, how to upload a video to YouTube or Vimeo, and how to embed the YouTube or Vimeo code into a web page.

Using YouTube

When uploading your video files, YouTube prefers MPEG-2 or H.264 (aka MPEG-4, aka .mp4). YouTube will also accept .wmv files. Videos should have 30 frames per second, and a size of 640 × 360 (at 16:9 aspect ratio) or 480 × 360 (4:3 aspect ratio). The preferred audio format is MP3 or ACC.

Hosting Limits on the Size of a Video

Web site hosts restrict the size of a web site. A basic low cost web site hosting package will probably allow a total upload of 1GB (including all the other web site files). The most expensive hosting packages will allow up to 20 GB. Video files can be huge; therefore, storing videos elsewhere, such as on YouTube, can keep a web site within the limit specified by the host.

Warn prospective clients that each video on YouTube is limited to a maximum of 1 GB, with a maximum play time of 15 minutes (1 to 3 minutes is preferred). To keep up-to-date on these limits, visit http://www.youtube.com and look for the *Help* button, since Google completely revised the YouTube web site the help link seems to have been relegated to the bottom of a very lengthy home page. It may even be easier to visit the Google home page and click the YouTube item on the top menu. Again you will then need to scroll down to the bottom of a very long page to find the Help button.

Signing up for a YouTube Account

If you have a Google account, use the Google login details to login because Google owns YouTube. Otherwise, on the YouTube home page, click Create an Account and fill in the details required. Give the email address of your client (or yourself if the video is for your web site) so that your client (or you) can receive the email verifying the account details. You will be asked to invent a username and password. When you receive the e-mail, click the verification link to activate your new account.

⬚ **Caution** You cannot upload a duplicate of something you have already uploaded; this applies even if you change the file name. Google/YouTube tends to change things occasionally, so the following procedure will probably go out of date. At the time of writing Google has made what was a user-friendly site into a magical mystery tour. All the configuration tricks have vanished. The most irritating omission is the user's ability to refuse a gallery of related videos being displayed when your own video plays. This has made YouTube a non-starter for my clients.

To host a video with YouTube, log in at `http://www.youtube.com`, click the Upload item on the top menu. At this point the previous, more user-friendly version allowed you to configure the video before uploading it, sadly that feature has now been removed.

After clicking Upload on the top menu bar, click the button labelled *Select files from your computer*. A small window will allow you to navigate to where your video is stored on your hard drive. Click the video and then click the Open button. On the right of the next screen select *Unlisted, anyone with the link can view*. After a while the video will have finished uploading and you will see a message saying that the upload of your video is complete. Write down the URL for the video for future reference. Click the *Embed* button. A small window will show the code highlighted in blue. Copy and paste the code into your web page. You may have to wait a few minutes before you can view the video.

Since early 2012 the YouTube code snippet has been simplified and it can be made to validate. The following is an example of the new <iframe> format of the YouTube downloadable code:

```
<iframe width="420" height="315" src="http://www.youtube.com/embed/xxxxxxxxxxx?rel=0" ↵
frameborder="0" allowfullscreen>
</iframe>
You will appreciate the simplicity of the <iframe> method which has replaced the former
<object> <embed> method.
```

Figure 6-4 shows a typical YouTube-hosted video.

Figure 6-4. A typical YouTube-hosted video. Note the YouTube logo.

Listings 6-4a and 6-4b are included in this chapter's downloadable files, but the YouTube video will not play for security reasons. The identity number has been replaced in the listing with xxxxxxxxxxx. However, you can still view the video in any browser other than IE 7 and IE 8. Also, if you insert your own YouTube-hosted video into the file, you will be able to view the result in any browser including IE 7 and IE 8; just make sure the code snippet is in the <iframe> format.

You can use a YouTube clip on its own, or you can use a YouTube clip as a fallback in a page that uses the HTML5 <video> tag.

To use the YouTube clip alone, simply delete the code shown bold in Listing 6-4a. Either way, when using your own YouTube-hosted video, it will display in all browsers, including IE 7 and IE 8.

Listing 6-4a. Creating a Page with HTML5 Videos and an Embedded YouTube Video (wagon-YT.html)

```
<!doctype html>
<html lang=en>
<head>
<title>An embedded video stored on YouTube plus video tag</title>
<meta charset=utf-8>
meta details go here
</head>
<body>
<video width="400" height="300" controls="controls">
<source src=" video/wagon3.mp4" type="video/mp4">
<source src=" video/wagon3.webm" type="video/webm">
<source src=" video/wagon3.ogv" type="video/ogg">
<iframe width="420" height="315" src=http://www.youtube.com/embed/xxxxxxxxxx?rel=0 ↵
  frameborder="0" allowfullscreen></iframe>
</video>
</body>
</html>
```

Although this works in all browsers, something odd happens when you try to validate it; the W3C HTML5 validator finds errors that will horrify strict HTML4 and XHTML aficionados. If you want the code to validate, you must remove some items as shown next. When I commented-out those items to make it validate, it still worked in all browsers.

The amended Listing 6-4b has some items (shown bold) commented-out to make the file validate.

Listing 6-4b. An Embedded YouTube Video that Validates (wagon-YT-validated.html)

```
<!doctype html>
<html lang=en>
<head>
<title>Wagon embedded YouTube video validated</title>
<meta charset=utf-8>
<!--<meta details go here>-->
<!--</head>-->
<body>
<video width="400" height="300" controls="controls">
<source src=" video/wagon3.mp4" type="video/mp4">
<source src=" video/wagon3.webm" type="video/webm">
<source src=" video/wagon3.ogv" type="video/ogg">
<iframe width="420" height="315" src="http://www.youtube.com/embed/xxxxxxxxxx?rel=0"> ↵
<!--frameborder="0" allowfullscreen--></iframe>
<!--</body>-->
</html>
```

Using Vimeo

The Vimeo interface is easier to understand and use than the new You Tube interface. For both online services, the code is easy to download and embed into a page. There appears to be no difference in their performance.

The basic version of Vimeo video is free, but it cannot be used for commercial advertisements, such as selling products or services. Personal use, non-commercial, and small scale production units are permitted. For commercial use, the pro version costs $60 per year or $9.95 a month.

Whichever you sign up for, Vimeo provides an easy uploader. First read the three rules on the web site, then click Upload Item on the top menu. You will see a window that will enable you to navigate your hard drive to find the video. Embedding your code is simple, just hover over the video or click it, then click the Embed button (second one down on the right) on the opening frame of the video. The code will then appear. Copy and paste the code into your web page. You can choose the player's colors and size. Vimeo is probably the easiest service to use and customize.

Clear advice is found at `http://vimeo.com/faq#what_is_embedding`.

■ **Note** Just as I finished writing this book, Vimeo released an updated web site. The web site was not quite complete in all details, but the signup and uploading procedure appear to be similar to the previous instructions.

Figure 6-5 shows a Vimeo-hosted butterfly movie embedded using Listing 6-5.

html5 video tag with vimeo fallback

Butterfly and orange from Fred Bloggs on Vimeo

Figure 6-5. A Vimeo-hosted video. Note the Vimeo logo.

The embedded Vimeo code for Figure 6-5 can be found in Listing 6-5 (I have changed some detail for security). As with YouTube, a video page can be incredibly simple when using the Vimeo code alone without a semantic video tag or a fallback. This is an easy way of putting a video on a web site because it avoids the need to convert the video file to the three file formats .mp4, .webm, and .ogg.

The file won't validate in the HTML5 validator because some deprecated attributes such as webkitallowfullscreen are not allowed with the <iframe> tag. However, your clients will probably not care whether the video validates as long as it plays.

Listing 6-5 is included in this chapter's downloadable files, but the video will not play in IE 7 or IE 8. For security, the Vimeo identity number has been replaced in the listing with xxxxxxxx. However, using the version that includes the <video> tag, you can still view the video in any browser other than IE 7 and IE 8. Also, if you insert your own Vimeo-hosted video into the file, you will be able to experiment and view the result in any browser.

You can use the Vimeo clip on its own, or you can use the Vimeo clip as a fallback in a page that uses the HTML5 <video> tag.

To use the Vimeo clip alone, simply delete the code shown in bold in Listing 6-5. Either way, using your own Vimeo-hosted video, the video will display in all browsers, including IE 7 and IE 8.

Listing 6-5. Using the HTML5 Video Tag with an Embedded Vimeo Video (video-tag-and-vimeo.html)

```
<!doctype html>
<html lang=en>
<head>
<title>HTML5 video tag with Vimeo fallback code</title>
<meta charset=utf-8>
<style type="text/css">
body { text-align: center; font-family:Arial; font-size:100%; font-weight:bold;
}
</style>
</head>
<body><br><p>html5 video tag with vimeo fallback</p>
<video width="400" height="300" controls="controls">
<source src=" video/butterfly-movie.mp4" type="video/mp4">
<source src=" video/butterfly-movie.webm" type="video/webm">
<source src=" video/butterfly-movie.ogv" type="video/ogg">
<iframe src="http://player.vimeo.com/video/xxxxxxxx?title=0&amp;byline=0&amp;portrait=0"
width="400" height="300" frameborder="0" webkitAllowFullScreen mozallowfullscreen
allowFullScreen></iframe><p><a href="http://vimeo.com/33108823">Butterfly and orange</a> from
<a href="http://vimeo.com/userxxxxxxx">Fred Bloggs</a> on <a href="http://vimeo.com">
Vimeo</a></p>
</video>
</body>
</html>
```

The next section describes two, simple JavaScript methods for allowing videos to be viewed in any browser, including IE 7 and IE 8. They both need a small JavaScript file or two and these can be downloaded from the book's page at www.apress.com

The Flowplayer and the OS FLV Fallbacks for IE 7 and IE 8

If your client does not wish to use YouTube or Vimeo, two other solutions are described next. These use the HTML5 video tag and a small piece of JavaScript:

- Adobe Shockwave Flash plays `.mp4` video files with a little help from Flowplayer and the Video for Everybody technique.

- The free JavaScript player OS FLV (with or without the `<video>` tag).

Adobe claims that 98 percent of Windows computers have the Adobe Flash video player installed. Therefore, a Shockwave Flash file can be used as the fallback for IE 7 and IE 8. The Flash video player will be activated only if the browser cannot play any of the HTML5 source files. IE 7 and IE 8 do not understand the HTML5 video tag; therefore, they will ignore the HTML5 source elements and play the fallback video.

Using the Video for Everybody (VfE) Solution

The fallback file for IE 7 and IE 8 is an .mp4 file enabled in the Shockwave Player with the help of a JavaScript snippet from Flowplayer. This solution was devised by Kroc Camen, who named it Video for Everybody. He invented VfE to encourage developers to use HTML5 and a fallback for IE 7 and IE 8, and to discourage them from relying on Flash and from wrapping `.mp4` (aka H.264) in a Flash container. To quote Camen: "It's shocking to think that so many web sites already have H.264 video files that they want to show you, yet insist on wrapping them in a crashy, unreliable, and slow Flash shell without any kind of fallback."

His second reason for inventing VfE was the advent of iPhones and iPads, which do not use Flash. He also urged developers to provide links as a last resort for downloading the video files. VfE has been remarkably successful, but as Kroc Camen says, "Video for Everybody is a vanishing mediator. It exists to bridge the gap between the disparity of Flash and HTML5."

Unfortunately, at the time of writing his web site shows only the HTML code and not the web pages. His URL is `http://camendesign.co.uk/code/video_for_everybody.html`.

The video will appear as shown in Figure 6-6.

Figure 6-6. The video as it appears in IE 7 and IE 8. Note the downloadable video files listed beneath the picture.

Jonathan Neal produced an online code generator for Video for Everybody that is fun and informative. It is at http://sandbox.thewikies.com/vfe-generator/

The following are the requirements for the Kroc Camen solution:

- *A poster*: Create a picture or title page as an opening screen for the video. To use a still from the video, run the video and stop it at a suitable point. Right-click it and save the picture as a .jpg file.

- *Three video files*: Using your file converters, make three versions of your video to produce files with the formats .mp4, .ogv, and .webm. Listing 6-5 assumes that the poster and the three video files are located in a folder named video.

- *The Flowplayer files*: Go to the Flowplayer web site at

    http://flowplayer.org/download/index.html

    Or download the free version of Flowplayer from the companion web site at the book's page at http://www.apress.com. The free version is available for commercial use. More comprehensive commercial versions are also available.
    Place the two files, flowplayer-3.2.7.swf and flowplayer.controls-3.2.5.swf, in the folder that will eventually contain the web page. (The FlowPlayer version number may have changed by the time you read this).

The web page: Listing 6-6 is an adaptation of Kroc Camen's Video for Everybody. It creates a typical web page, but for clarity, the page contains only the video. The page validates in the W3C HTML5 validator.

Listing 6-6. Creating a Page with Embedded Video Using VfE (camen-flowplayer-wagon.html)

```
<!doctype html>
<html>
<head>
<title>Camen-flowplayer-wagon</title>
<meta charset=utf-8>
</head>
<body>
<!-- "Video For Everybody" http://camendesign.com/code/video_for_everybody-->
<video controls="controls" poster="video/wagon-poster.jpg" width="640" height="480">
    <source src="video/wagon3.mp4" type="video/mp4">
    <source src="video/wagon3.webm" type="video/webm">
    <source src="video/wagon3.ogv" type="video/ogg">
        <object type="application/x-shockwave-flash" data="flowplayer-3.2.7.swf" ↵
        width="640" height="480">
        <param name="movie" value="flowplayer-3.2.7.swf">
        <param name="allowFullScreen" value="true">
        <param name="wmode" value="transparent">
        <param name="flashVars" value="config={'playlist': ↵
        ['video/wagon-poster.jpg',{'url':'video/wagon3.mp4','autoPlay':false}]}">
        <img alt="Colyton Wagon Wanderer" src="video/wagon-poster.jpg" width="640"
        height="480" title="No video playback capabilities, please download the video ↵
        below">
        </object>
</video>
<p>
<strong>Download video:</strong> <a href="video/wagon3.mp4">MP4 format</a> | <a
href="video/wagon3.ogv">Ogg format</a> | <a href="video/wagon3.webm">WebM format</a>
```

```
</p>
</body>
</html>
```

■ **Caution** Video for Everybody works in IE 7 and IE 8, as well as all the modern browsers. However, I have sometimes experienced a problem in IE 7 and IE 8 when Adobe updates the security settings for the Flash Player. This can result in an error message saying that it cannot find the .mp4 file and it suggests that you should try "loosening the security settings." This means accessing:

http://www.macromedia.com/support/documentation/en/flashplayer/help/settings_manager04.html#117502
There you will find an online security manager panel. Select the Always Allow radio button, then click Edit Location. Add a location (i.e., the folder where your video files are held), then wait until a green circle with a white tick appears in the lower window. This means your security settings are reset. This is one of the reasons why I will be glad to say goodbye to Flash Player.

We will now look at another JavaScript solution to the problem of allowing IE 7 and IE 8 users to enjoy your videos. This method can be used with or without the semantic video tag.

The OS FLV Free Video Player

The free, open-source player OS FLV was produced and sponsored by Jambo Media. This came complete with a code generator. The generated code could be easily embedded into the web page. This worked without any hassle and showed no brand mark. But my euphoria was short-lived as I eventually found some bugs. Also, it seemed that the site administrator was no longer answering queries. Being a free program and open source, the producers were under no obligation to maintain their forums beyond the point where the feedback had solved most of the bugs.

The most annoying bug caused the Replay button to remain on the video after it was clicked. The other bug was that the volume control needed a double-click to close it. Also, the progress indicator stopped short before reaching the end of its slot.

Eureka! Then I stumbled across an RSS feed from the Italian web designer Gianluca Guarini. He had fixed the bugs and was offering the revised code to anyone for free. This solution worked out-of-the-box. It also worked in any browser and in versions 4 and 5 of HTML.

Gianluca Guarini has kindly given me permission to include the OS FLV files in the companion web site for this book's page at http://www.apress.com The files will be included when you download this chapter's zip file. Gianluca Guarini's web site can be found at http://www.gianlucaguarini.com The original OS FLV project can be found at: http://www.osflv.com

---

■ **Note** Gianluca Guarini does not provide any support for his code; nor does this book's companion web site. This should not be a problem, however, because the code is easy to apply and works without any snags.

Figures 6-7a and 6-7b show this player in action. It has a Chrome-like set of controls.

Figure 6-7a. The OS FLV player's opening screen   *Figure 6-7b. Showing the progress bar*

Procedure

For this video player you will need to insert a few script files into the folder for the HTML page that contains your video code. They are the JavaScript files for OS FLV that will power your video and make it available to everyone including users of IE 7 and IE 8. Following these steps will not be difficult, but you do need to download this chapter's files from the companion web site at the book's page on http://www.apress.com

1. Create a folder called osflv-folder in the root folder of your web site.

2. In the download for this chapter, you will find a folder called osflv-player.

3. Open the folder named osflv-player and copy its files into your osflv-folder.

4. The contents of the osflv-folder should now be as follows:

    -   Two JavaScript files: AC_RunActiveContent.js and rac.js

    -   Three OSplayer files: Osplayer.as, Osplayer.fla, Osplayer.swf

    -   The code generator: firefox_codegen.html

5. Convert your video file into the .flv format and place it in the osflv-folder.

6. Create and place a poster in a folder named images and place that folder in the osflv-folder (optional). The poster is butterfly.jpg in my listing.

7. Use Mozilla Firefox to view firefox_codegen.html. Fill out the form to generate the code.

8. Or, a quicker method would be to download my code from the companion web site and insert your own file names to replace the items shown in bold type in Listing 6-7a. Only two file names need replacing.

9. Embed the generated (or downloaded) code into your web page.

10. Add your web page and its CSS file to the osflv-folder.

Listing 6-7a shows the generated code embedded into an HTML5 page. I have moved the first bit of generated script to the <head> section (the generator placed it in the <body> section). Listing 6-7a provides identical controls in every browser.

Listing 6-7a. Using The OS FLV Script to Play a Video (osflv-butterfly-identical-controls.html)

```
<!doctype html>
<html lang=en>
<head>
<title>osflv-butterfly-identical-controls</title>
<meta charset=utf-8>
<script src='AC_RunActiveContent.js' type="text/javascript">
</script>
</head>
<body>
<script type="text/javascript">
 AC_FL_RunContent('codebase', 'http://download.macromedia.com/pub/shockwave/cabs/flash/↵
swflash.cab#version=9,0,0,0', 'width', '320', 'height', '265', 'src', ↵
 ((!DetectFlashVer(9, 0, 0) && DetectFlashVer(8, 0, 0)) ? 'OSplayer' : 'OSplayer'), ↵
'pluginspage', 'http://www.macromedia.com/go/getflashplayer', 'id', 'flvPlayer', ↵
'allowFullScreen', 'true', 'movie', ((!DetectFlashVer(9, 0, 0) && DetectFlashVer(8, 0, 0)) ↵
? 'OSplayer' : 'OSplayer'), 'FlashVars', 'movie=video/butterfly-movie.flv↵
&btncolor=0x333333&accentcolor=0x20b3f7&txtcolor=0xffffff&volume=70&previewimage=images↵
/butterfly.jpg&autoload=on');
</script>
<!--<noscript>
 <object width='320' height='265' id='flvPlayer'>
  <param name='allowFullScreen' value='true' />
  <param name='movie' value='OSplayer.swf?movie=video/butterfly-movie.flv&↵
btncolor=0x333333&accentcolor=0x20b3f7&txtcolor=0xffffff&volume=70&↵
previewimage=previewimageurl&autoload=on'>
   <embed src='OSplayer.swf?movie=video/butterfly-movie.flv&btncolor=0x333333&↵
accentcolor=0x20b3f7&txtcolor=0xffffff&volume=70&previewimage=previewimageurl&↵
autoload=on' width='320' height='265' allowFullScreen='true' ↵
type='application/x-shockwave-flash'>
 </embed>
 </object>
</noscript>-->
 </body>
 </html>
```

▓ **Caution** I have placed all the relevant files in one folder for convenience. Set the menu button that connects to the video page so that it links to the correct folder.

The OS FLV player overrides the player incorporated within each browser. This results in identical controls in every browser. Some web site designers prefer this; *but some users may not.* Some users would prefer to see the controls they are accustomed to when using their preferred browser. IE 7 and IE 8 show the OS FLV player controls, but to ensure that the users' traditional controls are displayed in other browsers, use the generated code in an HTML5 page like this.

Listing 6-7b preserves the browser's native controls using IE 9, Mozilla Firefox, Chrome, Safari, and Opera. In IE 7 and IE 8, the appearance will be identical to Figures 6-7a and 6-7b. Place the .mp4, .webm, and .ogg versions of the video in a folder called video and put that folder inside your osflv-folder.

Listing 6-7b. Using the OS FLV script as a Fallback with the Video Tag (osflv-butterfly-native.html)

```
<!doctype html>
<html lang=en>
<head>
<title>osflv-butterfly-native-controls</title>
<meta charset=utf-8>
<script src='AC_RunActiveContent.js' type="text/javascript">
</script>
<link type="text/css" rel="stylesheet" href="position-video.css">
</head>
<body>
<div id="position-video">
<video width="320" height="240" controls="controls">
            <source src=video/butterfly-movie.mp4 type="video/mp4">
            <source src=video/butterfly-movie.ogv  type="video/ogg">
            <source src=video/butterfly-movie.webm type="video/webm">
<script type="text/javascript">
 AC_FL_RunContent('codebase',
 'http://download.macromedia.com/pub/shockwave/cabs/flash/swflash.cab#version=9,0,0,0', ↵
 'width', '320', 'height', '265', 'src', ((!DetectFlashVer(9, 0, 0) && ↵
DetectFlashVer(8, 0, 0)) ? 'OSplayer' : 'OSplayer'), 'pluginspage', ↵
 'http://www.macromedia.com/go/getflashplayer', 'id', 'flvPlayer', ↵
 'allowFullScreen', 'true', 'movie', ((!DetectFlashVer(9, 0, 0) && ↵
DetectFlashVer(8, 0, 0)) ? 'OSplayer' : 'OSplayer'), 'FlashVars', ↵
 'movie=video/butterfly-movie.flv&btncolor=0x333333&accentcolor=0x20b3f7&↵
txtcolor=0xffffff&volume=70&previewimage=images/butterfly.jpg&autoload=on');
</script>
<noscript>
 <object width='320' height='265' id='flvPlayer'>
  <param name='allowFullScreen' value='true'>
  <param name='movie' value='OSplayer.swf?movie=video/butterfly-movie.flv&btncolor=0x333333&↵
accentcolor=0x20b3f7&txtcolor=0xffffff&volume=70&previewimage=previewimageurl&autoload=on'>
   <embed src='OSplayer.swf?movie=video/butterfly-movie.flv&btncolor=0x333333&accent↵
   color=0x20b3f7&txtcolor=0xffffff&volume=70&previewimage=previewimageurl&autoload=on' ↵
   width='320' height='265' allowFullScreen='true' type='application/x-shockwave-flash'>
   </embed>
  </object>
 </noscript>
</video>
</div>
</body>
</html>
```

Using Listing 6-7b in an HTML5 page, the video will play in all the major browsers, including Internet Explorer 7 and 8. Opera 11 had a bug that prevents the controls from working, but this has been fixed in version 11.5. It will also play on iPhones and iPads. Users of Mozilla Firefox, Chrome, and Safari no longer need to have Flash installed. Eventually, when users have stopped using IE 7 and IE 8, we can dispense with the fallback element (Oh, happy day!).

▨ **Tip**   There are several other free players that are available, including Kaltura (`http://www.kaltura.org`)
JWPlayer (`http://www.longtailvideo.com/players/jw-flv-player/`), and
SWFObject.JS (`http://hubpages.com/hub/Embed-SWF-FLV-MP4-Flash-Video`).

Testing Your Video and MIME Types

When testing your video, ensure that your Flash Player and QuickTime player are functioning properly and that the appropriate MIME types are set on your server.

MIME types? It means Multipurpose Internet Mail Extension. Aren't you glad you asked?

Although it started as a mailing item, MIME types have developed into a method for transferring non-HTML formatted files across the internet. They are used by browsers to determine media content types. Videos won't play unless the correct MIME type is set in the server.

Every computer manual I have read emphasized the importance of MIME types, but they omit to tell the reader how to apply MIME types. Do MIME types go into the page markup? Or are they added to the server somehow? Or is it both? After a great deal of searching, I discovered that the answer varies. It depends on the category of the MIME type.

▨ **Caution** When providing HTML5 video for a web site, be sure to contact your host server and request that the MIME types are set for `.ogv`, `.mp4`, `.flv`, and `.webm` videos files. Your videos won't play in some browsers if you neglect to do this. Some enlightened hosts allow the web designer to add MIME type permissions to a server. For more information on MIME types, see the Appendix.

The following notes were extracted from a treasure trove of `.htaccess` and MIME data (see `http://tomraftery.com/2005/01/15/creating-an-htaccess-file/`).

The MIME type is a snippet of code that most hosts use to set the MIME types on their server. It lives in a file called `.htaccess`, which can contain some or all of the following AddTypes:

```
AddType video/ogg .ogv
AddType video/mp4 .mp4
AddType video/webm .webm
AddType video/x-flv .flv
AddType application/x-shockwave-flash swf
```

Editing a Client's Video

What should you do if the client's video needs editing? For instance, it might be too long and needs to be shortened. It might include clips that must be removed because you would not wish to see them on one of your web sites. Some of the clips might need removing because they are poor quality, such as blurred or shaky. The client may want sound added or removed. The client may even pass the video camera to you and ask you to download and edit the contents. The client might want you to add a still with an overlaid title, or to add a rolling list of credits to close the video.

If you have edited a video before, you will be able to accept the client's video clips and edit them. Of course, you would provide an estimate of the cost and explain what you need to do to make the video acceptable.

If you have never edited a video before, you have the following choices:

- Ask the client to have the video edited by someone else.

- Explain that you have not edited a video before, but you are willing to give it a try.

The latter requires that you get a video editor and become reasonably proficient at using it. You will need plenty of space on your hard disk (or you could attach an external hard drive). The free Windows Live Movie Maker (WLMM) is excellent and the Help files are not too obscure. WLMM came installed with Windows XP and Vista in the root start-up menu. It must be downloaded for Windows 7 (http://www.microsoft.com/downloads). However, be warned that any video-editing program is not like any other piece of software and it takes some learning—but it is creative and great fun. WLMM is naturally based on the real life movie editing process where you have a collection of film clips that must be trimmed, assembled in the correct order, and then combined. Some of the clips need to be blended into the next clip using fades and dissolves.

Adding sound and titles is not too difficult, and rolling credits can be added at the end of a video. Beware of using loud sound. In particular, do not use background sound if someone is speaking. This irritating gimmick beloved of advertisers and documentary films, will ruin your video. Presenters often have their commentaries made inaudible by a cacophony of inappropriate background "music".

In Windows Live Movie Maker, a video loaded into the program appears as a series of clips or short pieces laid out in the main pane. Each clip can be previewed (played) in the preview pane and paused to allow you to trim the clip. The two main features are the time line and the story board. You can rearrange the order of the clips in either, but use the time line to trim clips or to add/remove sound. The Help button is a white question mark in a blue circle located on the top right. You must be online to see the Help files.

Because this book is about web design, I will spend no more time on video editing. Try reading *Getting Started with Windows Live Movie Maker* by James Floyd Kelly (Friends of ED, 2010).

Create a Slide Show

Slide shows are sometimes more informative than videos because the user is in total control of what they see. A slide show can be paused to enable a particular slide to be examined for as long as the user wishes. This section gives four methods for creating slide shows that can be embedded in web pages.

This section describes the following four popular methods for creating web embedded slide shows:

- Using a snippet of JavaScript from BarelyFitz Designs (see Figure 6-8).

- Using the Animoto online slide show creator (see Figure 6-9).

- Converting a PowerPoint slide show into a video.

- Using Windows Live Movie Maker.

The BarelyFitz Designs Slide Show

Patrick Fitzgerald of BarelyFitz Designs produced an excellent piece of free, open-source JavaScript for slide shows. He also provides a very useful tutorial on his web site :

http://www.barelyfitz.com/projects/slideshow/

Figure 6-8 shows a screenshot of a slide show created using the BarelyFitz technique.

Figure 6-8. *A slide show with controls*

In the next section, you'll learn how to create the slide show depicted in Figure 6-8.

Creating a BarelyFitz Slide Show

This technique is easy to understand and implement. No knowledge of JavaScript is required; just amend the listing to insert your own slides.

1. Access the BarelyFitz web site (http://www.barelyfitz.com), click the Download & Examples tab, and download the JavaScript script slideshow.js. Place the script file in the folder containing the web page, and upload a copy to the server folder where the page will be hosted.

2. Prepare a blank web page and place it in the same folder as the JavaScript code.

3. Collect the pictures for your slide show and place them in a subfolder within the folder containing your web page. For the easiest solution, make your slides all the same size. If you want to use different sizes, remove any mention of

width and height from the markup; but be warned, you will have a slide show that jumps around to accommodate the various sizes. To minimize the jumping, make the pictures the same height.

4. The markup for Figure 6-8 is adequate for most purposes. Adapt it to support your own slides. Replace the items in bold italics with your own pictures; add any number of pictures. Then upload the page to your server. This example assumes that the slides are in a folder called slides.

Using the HTML5 code in Listing 6-8, the slide show works in all browsers, including IE 7 and IE 8.

Listing 6-8. *(slide-show.html)*

```
<!doctype html>
<html lang=en>
<head>
<title>Slide show for Figure 6-8 based on BarelyFitz Designs</title>
<meta charset=utf-8>
<script type="text/javascript" src="slideshow.js">
</script>
<script type="text/javascript">
SLIDES = new slideshow("SLIDES");
s = new slide();
s.src = "slides/Mitzi1.jpg";
s.text = "Open link in same window";
SLIDES.add_slide(s);

s = new slide();
s.src = "slides/Mitzi2.jpg";
s.text = "Open link in same window";
SLIDES.add_slide(s);

s = new slide();
s.src = "slides/Mitzi3.jpg";
s.text = "Open link in same window";
SLIDES.add_slide(s);

s = new slide();
s.src = "slides/Mitzi4.jpg";
s.text = "Open link in same window";
SLIDES.add_slide(s);

</script>
</head>
<body onLoad="SLIDES.pause()">
<a href="javascript:SLIDES.hotlink()">
<img name="SLIDESIMG" src="slides/Mitzi1.jpg"
 width="300" height="229" border="1" title="Mitzi" alt="Mitzi">
</a>
<!--The control buttons can be arranged in a different order by changing the ↵
order of the items in the form-->
        <form>
        <input type=button value="Next" onClick="SLIDES.next()">
        <input type=button value="Previous" onClick="SLIDES.previous()">
```

```
        <input type=button value="Play" onClick="SLIDES.play()">
        <input type=button value="Pause" onClick="SLIDES.pause()">
        </form>
<script type="text/javascript">
if (document.images)
{
  SLIDES.set_image(document.images.SLIDESIMG);
  SLIDES.update();
  SLIDES.play(); //optional
}
</script>
</body>
</html>
```

To alter this interval between continuously playing slides, open the JavaScript file slideshow.js with Notepad and find the "timeout" section. You will see that the default is 3,000 milliseconds (3 seconds). Change the figure to speed up or slow down the interval between slides.

Explore the BarelyFitz web site and then select the Tutorial tab for more detail on embedding and configuring the code in a web page. The web site has several worked examples; from these you could discover how to add additional features, such as descriptive text that alters with each slide change, or a drop-down list of slides, or different button controls.

The Animoto Slide Show Creator

The Animoto Lite version is only suitable for testing because it has limited facilities and cannot be used for commercial purposes. If after trying it you wish to buy it, the Pro versions have few restrictions and various levels of licensing are available depending on your needs. It also offers an iPhone app. You will find Animoto at http://animoto.com.

The program offers a wide range of opening screens and music, but it forces you to choose some music. Unfortunately, the one choice of music that is missing is "none." You must choose a theme, some music, and bits of text or it won't move on to the next step. Most of the music is not at all pleasant, but I did find some good items in the classical section. When you have uploaded your slides and selected the themes and music, click the Create Video button. Eventually you will receive an email telling you the video of the slide show is available for viewing. You can view it and download its code for embedding in a web page.

An Animoto slide show is shown in Figure 6-9.

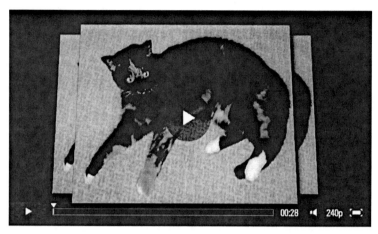

Figure 6-9. *An Animoto slide show*

The Animoto downloaded code snippet uses Shockwave Flash and looks like the following:

```
<object id="vp13vUA9" width="432" height="240" classid=↵
"clsid:d27cdb6e-ae6d-11cf-96b8-444553540000">
<param name="movie" value="http://static.animoto.com/swf/w.swf?w=swf/vp1&e=1323028467↵
&f=3vUA9wXxd8zgGDF87fQJqw&d=28&m=b&r=240p&volume=100&start_res=240p&i=m&options=">
</param>
<param name="allowFullScreen" value="true">
</param>
<param name="allowscriptaccess" value="always">
</param>
<embed id="vp13vUA9" src="http://static.animoto.com/swf/w.swf?w=swf/vp1&↵
e=1323028467&f=3vUA9wXxd8zgGDF87fQJqw&d=28&m=b&r=240p&volume=100&↵
start_res=240p&i=m&options=" type="application/x-shockwave-flash" ↵
allowscriptaccess="always" allowfullscreen="true" width="432" height="240">
</embed>
</object>
```

Convert a PowerPoint Slide Show into a Video

This is an effective way of creating a slide show and it is very versatile. It will import many types of input, even animated .gifs. The free version will convert the video to MP4, WMV, and AVI video with no watermark. If you convert to any other file types, the slide show will have a watermark in the top-left corner.

Download the freeware version of the E.M. PowerPoint converter from http://www.effectmatrix.com/PowerPoint-Video-Converter/Free-PowerPoint-Video-Converter.htm
The web site banner is Etinysoft, so don't think you have arrived at the wrong source.

166

Using Windows Live Movie Maker to Create a Slide Show

Pictures can be imported into Windows Live Movie Maker and then arranged in the required sequence. The slide show will then be saved as a `.wmv` file. The procedure for using Windows Live Movie Maker to create a slide show as a video is as follows:

1. Put the slides into a folder so that you can locate them easily.

2. Open Windows Live Movie Maker and click Add Videos and Photos. Navigate to the folder containing the slides.

3. Open each slide until they are all shown in the right-hand pane.

4. Click Edit on the menu and adjust the time interval between slides to, let's say, 3 seconds.

5. Options are available for various transitions and fades.

6. Click Home on the menu and click the Save Movie button on the toolbar.

7. Select For Computer and then give the file a name. Click Save.

The resulting `.wmv` file can be viewed in any player, such as the Windows Media Player or QuickTime. To add it to a web page, the created file could then be uploaded to YouTube so that you can embed the downloadable code. The resulting video can be viewed in any browser. Figure 6-10 shows the YouTube version of the slide show.

Figure 6-10. The slide show as created in Windows Live Movie Maker and then stored on YouTube. Note that the appearance of the YouTube frame has recently changed a little.

Listing 6-10 shows how the downloadable YouTube version of the `.wmv` file is embedded in an HTML5 web page. The markup is extremely simple, but if your client does not want to use YouTube, then the `.wmv` file could be converted to other formats for use in one of the previously described methods of embedding a video.

Listing 6-10. Embed a YouTube Video of a Windows Live Movie Maker File (slides-video-YT.html)

```
<!doctype html>
<html lang=en>
<head>
<title>Embedded YouTube video of an .wmv slide show </title>
<meta charset=utf-8>
<meta details go here>
</head>
<body>
<iframe width="420" height="315" src="http://www.youtube.com/embed/xxxxxxxxxxx?rel=0" ↵
frameborder="0" allowfullscreen></iframe>
</body>
</html>
```

Summary

In this chapter, you learned that the new HTML5 `<audio>` and `<video>` tags allow AV to play without plug-ins, but the `<audio>` and `<video>` tags will not work in IE 7 and IE 8. The good news is that IE 9 promises to support the `<audio>` and `<video>` tags. However, IE 9 will only work on computers using Vista or Windows 7.

You were alerted to the fact that you would need some file converters, and several tried and tested converters were recommended. You were shown several fallback methods for solving the problem of displaying videos in IE 7 and IE 8. Alternative video solutions were provided, such as YouTube and Vimeo. Then you learned how to use two, simple JavaScript solutions to ensure that videos would be seen in any browser. The chapter ended describing four ways of creating and embedding slide shows into a web page.

In the next chapter, you will discover how to give rounded corners to boxes, web pages, and tab menus. The new CSS3 method of rounding corners is described with many, fully worked projects.

CHAPTER 7

Rounded Corners

CSS3 will enable web designers to produce rounded corners (rounded borders in CSS3 speak) without using JavaScript. Currently, only the latest versions of Mozilla Firefox, Chrome, IE 9 and Safari support this feature; therefore, an interim JavaScript method must be used for older browsers including IE 7 and IE 8.

The chapter covers:

- A simple JavaScript solution for creating rounded corners for basic rectangles and also complex pages
- A description of the new CSS3 Rounded Corners module
- A summary of the shorthand code for CSS3 rounded corners
- CSS3 rounded corners applied to tab menus

A Simple JavaScript Solution

Alessandro Fulciniti produced a simple JavaScript solution, which is free under a GNU GPL license (please acknowledge the author if you use the script). It works in all browsers including IE 6. Full details can be found on his web site at http://www.html.it/articoli/niftycube/index.html.

In Figure 7-1, the two panels have rounded corners applied by using JavaScript.

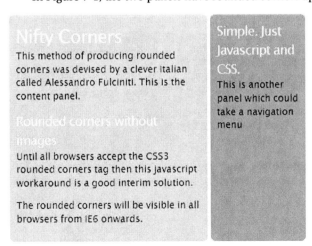

Figure 7-1. Rounded corners applied by JavaScript

WYSIWYG design programs may not display the corners properly. View the pages in browsers to see the rounded corners.

■ **Note** The files `niftyCube.js` and `niftyCorners.css` must be downloaded from the Nifty Corners web site or from this book's web page. Include the files in the folder containing your web page. The HTML does not link to the file `niftyCorners.css`, but the JavaScript file refers to it. The files for this chapter can be downloaded from the book's web page. All the files have internal styles for instructional purposes only.

Listing 7-1 contains an internal style sheet for illustrative purposes only.

Listing 7-1. *Creating Rounded Corners on Panels Using Nifty Corners (fig1-nifty.html)*

```
<!doctype html>
<html lang=en>
<head>
<title>Nifty Corners: Javascript and CSS</title>
<meta charset=utf-8>
<head>
<style type="text/css">
body { padding: 20px;background: #FFF;color: #3C0012; text-align: center; ↵
    font:85%/1.45 "Arial";
}
h1,h2 { margin: 0;padding: 0 10px;letter-spacing: -1px;font-weight:100;color: #FFF;
}
h1 { font-size: 200%;
}
h2 { font-size: 140%;
}
p { margin:0;padding: 0 10px 1em;
}
div#container { width:450px;margin: 0 auto;padding:10px 0;text-align:left;
}
div#content { float:left;width:300px;padding:10px 0;background: #FFBD00;
}
div#navpanel { float:right;width:145px;padding:10px 0;background:#42B4AC
}
</style>
        <script type="text/javascript" src="niftycube.js"></script>
        <script type="text/javascript">
        window.onload=function(){
        Nifty("div#content,div#navpanel","same-height big" );
        }
</script>
</head>
<body>
<div id="container">
<div id="content">
<h1>Nifty Corners</h1>
```

```
<p>This method of producing rounded corners was devised by a clever Italian ↵
called Alessandro Fulciniti. This is the content panel. </p>
<h2>Rounded corners without images</h2>
<p>Until all browsers accept the CSS3 rounded corners tag then this javascript ↵
workaround is a good interim solution.</p>
<p>The rounded corners will be visible in all browsers from IE6 onwards.</p>
</div>
<div id="navpanel">
<h2>Simple. Just Javascript and CSS.</h2>
<p>This is another panel which could take a navigation menu</p>
</div>
</div>
</body>
</html>
```

▧ **Caution** Each element to be given rounded corners must be a `<div>` with an id, for example, `<div id="leftcol">`. You will not be able to round the corners of items that have semantic tags. Because HTML5 does not care whether you use semantic tags or `<div>`s, this is not a problem, just use `<div>`s. The good news is that you can also easily give rounded corners to your existing HTML4 and XHTML web pages.

Before moving on to the more complex examples of using Nifty Corners, some basic rules will be provided as follows:

General Rules

The link to the JavaScript file (shown in bold) is inserted within the `<head></head>` tags.

The elements to be given rounded corners are listed as follows:

```
Nifty ("#leftcol, #rightcol");
```

To give two columns the same height, use the attribute "same-height" as follows:

```
Nifty("#leftcol, #rightcol","same-height");
```

If the "same height" parameter is omitted, the columns will have heights that match their individual content.

Radius of the rounded corners: The size of the corner radius is specified by either small, normal, or big. The default is normal when no size is specified.

For a big radius and the same height columns, the attributes would be as follows:

```
Nifty("#leftcol, #rightcol","same-height big");
```

For big radii on all corners but a sharp top-right corner

```
Nifty("#leftcol", "tl bottom big");
```

This means give a big radius to the top-left corner and to both bottom corners. The top-right corner is not mentioned, so it does not get a radius.

For big radii on all corners except the top-left corner

```
Nifty("#leftcol", "tr bottom big");
```

This means give a big radius to the top-right corner and to both bottom corners. The top-left corner is not mentioned, so it does not get a radius.

For big radii on all corners except the bottom-right corner

```
Nifty("#leftcol", "bl top big");
```

This means give a big radius to the bottom-left corner and to both top corners. The bottom-right corner is not mentioned, so it does not get a radius.

A Web Page with Rounded Borders

Rounded borders on a web page give a modern appearance that clients are increasingly requesting. Nifty Corners provides a neat solution that is easy to implement. Rounded corners on the white frame and on some corners inside the frame are shown in Figure 7-2.

Figure 7-2. A full page showing element borders with rounded corners

---

■ **Note** The height of the `<h1>` box must be equal to the height of the header image, minus any top and bottom padding. The middle panel (`midcol`) must be slightly taller than the side columns. Do not add rounded corners to the middle panel, because this causes the middle panel to drop below the outer columns in Internet Explorer 8.

Listing 7-2 applies Nifty Corners to a complex page with columns and borders.

Listing 7-2. Creating Rounded Corners in a Complex Page (fig2-nifty.html)

```
<!doctype html>
<html lang=en>
<head>
<title>A whole page with rounded corners</title>
<meta charset=utf-8>
<style type="text/css">
body { width:100%; margin:auto; margin-top:0; padding: 10px; background: #bbd999; ↵
color: #000; text-align: center; font: medium Arial,sans-serif
}
h1,h2,p { margin: 0; padding: 0 10px; font-weight:normal;
}
p { padding: 0
}
h1 { font-size: 300%;color: #FFF; letter-spacing: 1px; height:164px;
}
h2 { font-size: 180%;line-height:1;color:#002455; margin-top:0;
}
#container { width:960px; margin: 0 auto 10px auto; padding:10px;text-align:left; ↵
background:#FFF; position:relative; clear:both;
}
#mainpanel { width:960px; margin:auto; margin-bottom:0; margin-top:-25px; ↵
background-color:#cee1ba; text-align:center;
}
#hdr { padding-top:10px; width:100%; text-align:center; margin:auto; ↵
background-image:url('images/banner.jpg'); background-repeat:no-repeat; ↵
background-position:65;
}
#leftcol { float:left; width:140px; background: #FFD154; margin-left:10px;
}
#rightcol { float:right; width:140px;background: #FFD154; padding:5px; margin-right:10px;
}
#rightcol h2 { font-size: 120%; color: #9E4A24;
}
#midcol { margin-left:160px; margin-right:160px; margin-top:0; padding:0 10px 10px 0;
}
#mid-left-col { width:47%; float:left;
}
#mid-right-col { width:47%; float:right;
}
#ftr { clear:both;width:950px; background: #C4E786;padding:5px; margin-top:10px; ↵
text-align:center;
```

```
}
ul.nav { list-style-type:none; padding-left:0; margin-left:0;
}
ul.nav a { display:block; width:90px; background:#cee1ba;; margin:0 auto 2px auto; ↵
padding:4px;
}
a.navbtn:link { color: navy; background-color:#cee1ba; text-decoration:none; ↵
font-weight:normal;
}
a.navbtn:visited { color: navy; background-color:#cee1ba; text-decoration: none; ↵
font-weight:normal;
}
a.navbtn:active { color: navy; background-color:#cee1ba; text-decoration: none; ↵
font-weight:normal;
}
a.navbtn:hover { color: red; background-color:#ffd154; text-decoration: none; ↵
font-weight:normal;
}
</style>
        <script type="text/javascript" src="niftycube.js"></script>
        <script type="text/javascript">
        window.onload=function(){
        Nifty("#container","big");
        Nifty("#mainpanel","same-height normal");
        Nifty("#leftcol,#rightcol", "same-height big");
        Nifty("#hdr,#ftr","normal");
        }
        </script>
</head>
<body>
<div id="container">
<div id="hdr"><br><h1>Rounded Corners</h1>
</div><br>
<div id="mainpanel"><br>
<div id="leftcol"><br>Menu column<br>
        <ul class="nav">
                <li><a class="navbtn" href="#">page 2</a></li>
                <li><a class="navbtn" href="#">page 3</a></li>
                <li><a class="navbtn" href="#">page 4</a></li>
                <li><a class="navbtn" href="#">page 5</a></li>
                <li><a class="navbtn" href="#">page 6</a></li>
                <li><a class="navbtn" href="#">page 7</a></li>
</ul><br>
</div>
<div id="rightcol">
<h2>Auxiliary Panel</h2>
<p>This panel can be used for adverts, additional information, or items like ↵
validation certificates.</p>
</div>
<div id="midcol">
<h2>Middle panel for content</h2>
<div id="mid-left-col"><br>
</div><br>
```

```
<div id="mid-right-col">
<p>This method uses CSS and Javascript.<br>If Javascript is turned off in the ↵
users computer, the page differs only in that the corners are not rounded.  </p>
A clever Italian called Alessandro Fulciniti produced this simple ↵
Javascript/CSS solution.<br><br>Full details can be found on his website
<a href="http://www.html.it/articoli/niftycube/index.html">↵
        www.html.it/articoli/niftycube/index.html</a>
</div>
<img alt="Coly River" height="196" src="images/colrivblu.jpg" width="298"></div><br>
</div>
<div id="ftr">Footer goes here
</div>
</div>
</body>
</html>
```

■ **Note** The menu links are shown as href="#". These must, of course, be changed to link to your pages.

A Web Page with Rounded Border and Rounded Panels

The rounded borders can be extended to items within the page border to give a consistent feel to the page's design. Figure 7-3 is a screenshot of a page with rounded border and rounded internal panels.

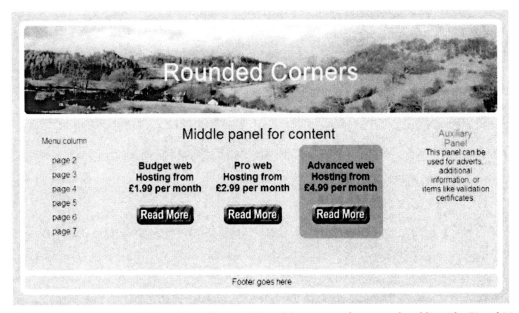

Figure 7-3. *A page containing three offers positioned by means of an unordered list. The "Read More" buttons are images with hyperlinks targeting the appropriate pages.*

Listing 7-3 applies Nifty Corners to a page giving rounded borders and three rounded internal panels.

Listing 7-3. *Creating Rounded Corners on Internal Panels (fig3-nifty.html)*

```
<!doctype html>
<html lang=en>
<head>
<title>A whole page with rounded corners and rounded panels</title>
<meta charset=utf-8>
<style type="text/css">
body { width:100%; margin:auto; margin-top:0; padding: 10px; background: #bbd999; ↵
color: #000; text-align: center; font: medium Arial;
}
h1,h2,p { margin: 0; padding: 0 10px; font-weight:normal;
}
p { padding:0;
}
h1 { font-size: 300%;color: #FFF; letter-spacing: 1px; height:164px;
}
h2 { font-size: 180%; line-height:1; color:#002455; margin-top:0;
}
img { border:0;
}
div#container { width:950px; margin: 0 auto 10px auto; padding:10px;text-align:left; ↵
background:#FFF; position:relative; clear:both;
}
div#mainpanel { width:950px; margin:auto; margin-bottom:0; margin-top:-10px; ↵
background-color:#cee1ba; text-align:center;
}
#hdr { padding-top:10px; width:100%; text-align:center; margin:auto; ↵
background-image:url('images/banner.jpg'); background-repeat:no-repeat; ↵
background-position:65;
}
#leftcol { float:left; width:140px; background: #FFD154; margin-left:10px;
}
#rightcol { float:right; width:140px;background: #FFD154; padding:5px; margin-right:10px;
}
#rightcol h2 { font-size: 120%; color: #9E4A24;
}
#midcol { margin-left:160px; margin-right:160px; margin-top:0; padding:0 10px 10px 0;
}
#mid-left-col { width:47%; float:left;
}
#mid-right-col { width:47%; float:right;
}
#ftr { clear:both; width:940px; background: #C4E786; padding:5px; margin-top:10px; ↵
text-align:center;
}
ul#nav { list-style-type:none; padding-left:0; margin-left:0;
}
ul#nav a { display:block; width:90px; background:#cee1ba;; margin:0 auto 2px auto; ↵
padding:4px; text-decoration:none;
}
```

```
a.navbtn:link { color: navy; background-color:#cee1ba; text-decoration:none; ↵
font-weight:normal;
}
a.navbtn:visited { color: navy; background-color:#cee1ba; text-decoration: none; ↵
font-weight:normal;
}
a.navbtn:active { color: navy; background-color:#cee1ba; text-decoration: none; ↵
font-weight:normal;
}
a.navbtn:hover { color: red; background-color:#FFD154; text-decoration: none; ↵
font-weight:normal;
}
ul#about,ul#about li { list-style-type:none; margin:auto; padding:0;
}
ul#about { width: 550px; margin:auto; text-align:center;
}
ul#about li { float:left;width: 150px; height:150px; padding:10px; margin:8px 8px 0 0;
}
li#adv1 { background: #FC0;
}
li#adv2 { background: #9F3;
}
li#adv3 { background: #39F;
}
.clear { clear:both;
}
</style>
        <script type="text/javascript" src="niftycube.js"></script>
        <script type="text/javascript">
        window.onload=function(){
        Nifty("#container","big");
        Nifty("#mainpanel","same-height normal");
        Nifty("#leftcol,#rightcol", "same-height big");
        Nifty("#hdr,#ftr","normal");
        Nifty("#about li","top bottom big fixed-height");
        }
        </script>
</head>
<body>
<div id="container">
<div id="hdr"><h1><br>Rounded Corners</h1>
</div><br>
<div id="mainpanel"><br>
<div id="leftcol">
        <br>Menu column<br>
        <ul id="nav">
                <li><a class="navbtn" href="page2.html">page 2</a></li>
                <li><a class="navbtn" href="page3.html">page 3</a></li>
                <li><a class="navbtn" href="page4.html">page 4</a></li>
                <li><a class="navbtn" href="page5.html">page 5</a></li>
                <li><a class="navbtn" href="page6.html">page 6</a></li>
                <li><a class="navbtn" href="page7.html">page 7</a></li>
        </ul><br>
```

```
</div>
<div id="rightcol">
<h2>Auxiliary Panel</h2>
<p>This panel can be used for adverts, additional information, or items like ↵
validation certificates.</p>
</div>
<div id="midcol">
<h2>Middle panel for content</h2>
<ul id="about">
    <li id="adv1"><h3>Budget web Hosting from &pound;1.99 per month</h3><br>↵
    <a href="budget.html"><img alt="£1.99 per month. Read More" title="£1.99 per month. ↵
    Read More"height="39" src="images/read-more.gif" width="117" ></a><br></li>
    <li id="adv2"><h3>Pro web Hosting from &pound;2.99 per month</h3><br>↵
    <a href="proweb.html"><img alt="£2.99 per month. Read More" title="£2.99 per month. ↵
    Read More"height="39" src="images/read-more.gif" width="117" ></a></li>
    <li id="adv3"><h3>Advanced web Hosting from &pound;4.99 per month</h3><br>
    <a href="advanced.html"><img alt="£4.99 per month. Read More" title="£4.99 per month. ↵
    Read More"height="39" src="images/read-more.gif" width="117" ></a></li>
</ul>
<br style="clear:both;">
</div>
<br class="clear">
</div><div id="ftr">Footer goes here</div>
</div>
</body>
</html>
```

Nifty Corners on Tab Menus

Rounded menu tabs are extremely popular and were formerly tricky to implement as they required several images with transparent corners. The simple solution provided by Nifty Corners is shown in Figure 7-4. I placed the listings and a full explanation in Chapter 4 (on rollover menus) where I felt it rightly belonged.

Figure 7-4. *Rounded tabs using Nifty Corners*

The following section looks at the new CSS3 rounded corners module, this requires no JavaScript but rounded elements will default to square corners in IE 7 and IE 8.

The CSS3 Rounded Corners Module

The CSS3 border-radius module creates rounded corners on block elements (including images) and it removes the need for JavaScript. It also eliminates the need for images and multiple <div> tags. See the W3C for the latest details of this module at http://www.css3.info/preview.

As of November 2011, the following browsers support CSS3 rounded corners:- Opera, Safari, and Chrome. New versions of Mozilla Firefox support the CSS3 border-radius; older versions required the -moz- prefix. Internet Explorer 9 supports the CSS3 border-radius markup. IE 9 is only available for Vista and Windows 7. The corners will not be rounded in Windows XP, IE 6, IE 7, and IE 8. The JavaScript solution is available for IE 6, IE 7, and IE 8.

Figure 7-5 shows the result of using CSS3 rounded corners on each corner of a colored panel.

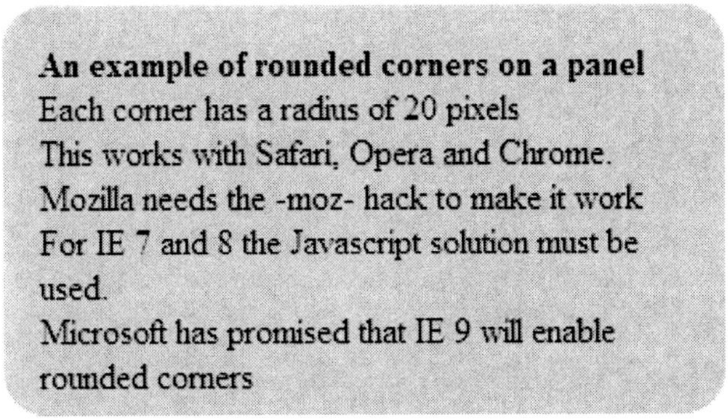

An example of rounded corners on a panel
Each corner has a radius of 20 pixels
This works with Safari, Opera and Chrome.
Mozilla needs the -moz- hack to make it work
For IE 7 and 8 the Javascript solution must be used.
Microsoft has promised that IE 9 will enable rounded corners

Figure 7-5. Rounded corners on a colored panel

This is the simplest box model and it works in all browsers except IE 6, IE 7, and IE 8. The item -moz-border-radius:20px; is only required to support versions of Mozilla Firefox prior to version 5. In this project, the colored panel has all four corners rounded with the same radius (the internal style sheet is for demonstration only; it would normally be an external style sheet). In Listing 7-5, the code for rounded corners is shown bold. Some padding will be necessary to prevent the content protruding from the corners.

Listing 7-5. Creating Rounded Corners on a Rectangle (fig5-four-identical-on-panel.html)

```
<!doctype html>
<html lang=en>
<head>
<title>Four identical corners on a coloured panel Fig. 5</title>
<meta charset=utf-8>
        meta content goes here
<style type="text/css">
#box-1 { margin:auto; text-align:left; background-color:#F90;
        width:300px; height:150px; padding:15px;
        border-radius: 20px; -moz-border-radius:20px;
        }
</style>
</head>
<body>
<p> </p>
<p id="box-1"><strong>An example of rounded corners on a panel</strong><br>
Each corner has a radius of 20 pixels<br>This works with Safari, Opera and Chrome. Mozilla
currently requires the -moz- hack to make it work<br>For IE 7 and 8 the Nifty Corners
Javascript solution must be used. <br>Microsoft has promised that IE 9 will enable ↵
rounded corners
</p>
```

```
</body>
</html>
```

Figure 7-6 shows a black border around a colored panel with rounded corners.

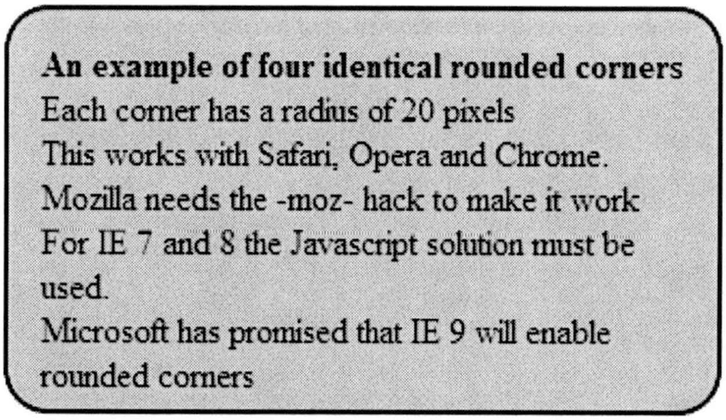

An example of four identical rounded corners
Each corner has a radius of 20 pixels
This works with Safari, Opera and Chrome.
Mozilla needs the -moz- hack to make it work
For IE 7 and 8 the Javascript solution must be used.
Microsoft has promised that IE 9 will enable rounded corners

Figure 7-6. *A colored panel with a black border*

In Listing 7-6, the black border is added using the code shown bold. . The item -moz-border-radius:20px; is only required to support versions of Mozilla Firefox prior to version 5.

Listing 7-6. *Rounding the Corners of a Rectangle with a Black Border (fig6-panel-blackbdr.html)*

```
<!doctype html>
<html lang=en>
<head>
<title>Coloured panel with black border Fig. 7-6</title>
<meta charset=utf-8>
        meta content goes here
<style type="text/css">
#box-1 { margin:auto; text-align:left; border:2px #000 solid;
        width:300px; height:150px; padding:15px; background-color:#F90;
        border-radius: 20px; -moz-border-radius:20px;
}
</style>
</head>
<body>
<p> </p>
<p id="box-1"><strong>An example of four identical rounded corners</strong><br>
Each corner has a radius of 20 pixels<br>This works with Safari, Opera and Chrome.
Mozilla needs the -moz- hack to make it work<br>For IE 7 and 8 the Nifty Corners Javascript
solution must be used.
<br>Microsoft has promised that IE 9 will enable rounded corners</p>
</body>
</html>
```

Figure 7-7 shows a black border around a block of text.

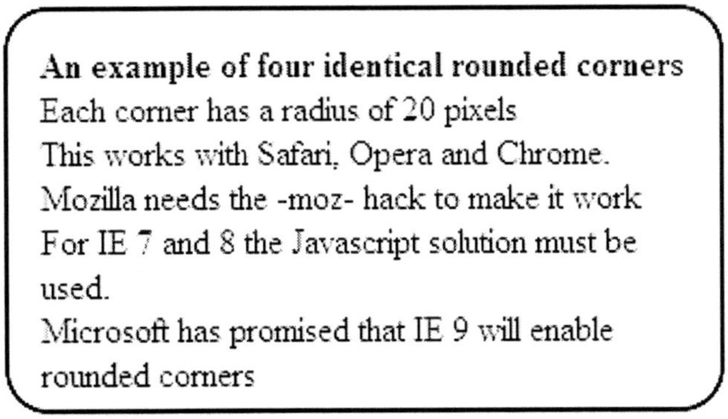

Figure 7-7. *Rounded corners on a block of text*

Listing 7-7 rounds all four corners with the same radius on a block of text (the internal style sheet is for demonstration only and it would normally be external). The item `-moz-border-radius:20px;` is only required to support versions of Mozilla Firefox prior to version 5.

Listing 7-7. *Applying CSS3 Rounded Corners to a Block of Text (fig7-four-rounded-text.html)*

```
<!doctype html>
<html lang=en>
<head>
<title>Text box with four rounded corners</title>
<meta charset=utf-8>
meta content goes here
<style type="text/css">
#box-1 { margin:auto; text-align:left; border:2px #000 solid;width:300px; height:150px; ↵
padding:15px; border-radius: 20px; -moz-border-radius:20px;
}
</style>
</head>
<body>
<p> </p>
<p id="box-1"><strong>An example of four identical rounded corners</strong><br>
Each corner has a radius of 20 pixels<br>This works with Safari, Opera and Chrome. ↵
Mozilla needs the -moz- hack to make it work<br>For IE 7 and 8 the Javascript solution ↵
must be used. <br>IE 9 has promised it will work with rounded corners</p>
</body>
</html>
```

■ **Note** The next CSS3 border radius projects have -moz hacks. As time passes, Mozilla Firefox will not require the -moz hacks. Try commenting-out the hacks and test the code with Mozilla Firefox occasionally. The hacks will allow support for older versions of Firefox and should be ignored by modern versions.

The CSS3 markup can specify a different radius for each corner. The CSS3 specification gives two methods for creating different radii on each corner. The first method is as follows:

Method 1.

```
#box-1 { border: size color solid;
border-top-left-radius: size;
border-top-right-radius: size;
border-bottom-right-radius: size;
border-bottom-left-radius: size;
}
```

Replace the word *size* with pixels or a percentage. Percentages relate to the corresponding dimensions of the box; in other words, on a box that is 200 pixels square, a 10 percent radius would give a corner radius of 20 pixels.

However, Mozilla Firefox does not currently understand this, even with the -moz- hack. Mozilla does understand a variation of this as indicated next in bold.

```
#box-1 { border: size color solid;
      border-top-left-radius: size; -moz-border-radius-topleft: size;
      border-top-right-radius: size; -moz-border-radius-topright: size;
      border-bottom-right-radius: size; -moz-border-radius-bottomleft: size;
      border-bottom-left-radius: size; -moz-border-radius-bottomright: size;
      }
```

However, Mozilla, Safari, and Chrome do understand the shorthand method (the second method), which is as follows:

Method 2.

```
#box-1 { border: size color solid;
border-radius: size size size size;
}
```

The markup specifies the box corner radii in clockwise order starting with the top-left corner, as follows:

```
top left, top right, bottom right, bottom left
```

Each corner can have a different radius. Figure 7-8 shows a panel with a two-pixel wide black border. The panel has a 30-pixel radius at the top-left corner, a 20-pixel radius at the top-right, a zero radius on the bottom-right corner, and a corner radius of 10 pixels at the bottom-left corner.

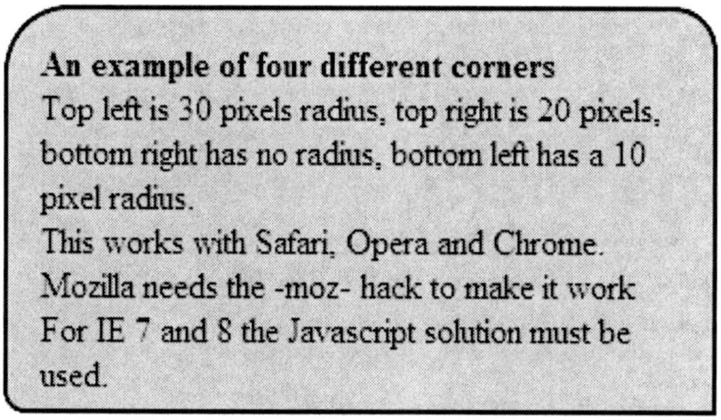

An example of four different corners

Top left is 30 pixels radius, top right is 20 pixels, bottom right has no radius, bottom left has a 10 pixel radius.

This works with Safari, Opera and Chrome.

Mozilla needs the -moz- hack to make it work

For IE 7 and 8 the Javascript solution must be used.

Figure 7-8. Four different corners using shorthand code

Listing 7-8 uses CSS3 to apply a selection of roundings to a colored panel. When viewed in IE 7 and IE 8 the rectangle will have sharp corners.

Listing 7-8. Applying a Variety of Corners with CSS3 Rounding (fig8-panel-4diff.html)

```
<!doctype html>
<html lang=en>
<head>
<title>Fig. 8 Panel with four different rounded corners</title>
<meta charset=utf-8>
        meta content goes here
<style type="text/css">
#box-1 { margin:auto; text-align:left; padding:15px; border:2px black solid; ↵
width:300px; height:150px; background-color:#F90; ↵
border-radius: 30px 20px 0 10px ; ↵
-moz-border-radius: 30px 20px 0 10px ;
}
</style>
</head>
<body>
<p> </p>
<p id="box-1"><strong>An example of four different corners</strong><br>↵
Top left is 30 pixels radius, top right is 20 pixels, bottom right has no radius, ↵
bottom left has a 10 pixel radius.<br>This works with Safari, Opera and Chrome. Mozilla ↵
needs the -moz- hack to make it work<br>For IE 7 and 8 the Nifty Corners Javascript ↵
solution must be used. <br></p>
</body>
</html>
```

Elliptical Corners with CSS3

Elliptical corners can be created by using two size values. To create an elliptical corner requires two radii. In the code snippet below, the first size fixes the vertical radius (30 pixels) and the second (15 pixels) fixes the horizontal radius. To remember the order, I use the mnemonic Valuable Hint (vertical then horizontal).

```
#box-1 { border-top-left-radius: 30px 15px; }
#identifier { border-top/bottom-left/right-radius: vertical size  horizontal size; }
```

Figure 7-9 shows various elliptical corners.

Figure 7-9. Four different elliptical corners

Listing 7-9 introduces you to CSS3 elliptical corners as applied to a panel with a black border. The panel will have sharp corners when viewed in IE 7 and IE 8.

Listing 7-9. Applying a Selection of CSS3 Elliptical Corners (fig9-elliptical-corners.html)

```
<!doctype html>
<html lang=en>
<head>
<title>Box with a different ellipse on each corner</title>
<meta charset=utf-8>
        meta content goes here
<style type="text/css">
#box-1 { margin:auto; text-align:center; border:2px black solid; width:300px; height:150px;
border-top-left-radius: 30px 15px; -moz-border-radius-topleft:30px 15px;
border-top-right-radius: 25px 10px; -moz-border-radius-topright:25px 10px;
border-bottom-right-radius: 10px 25px; -moz-border-radius-bottomright:10px 25px;
border-bottom-left-radius:15px 30px; -moz-border-radius-bottomleft:15px 30px;
}
</style>
</head>
<body>
<p> </p>
<p id="box-1"></p>
</body>
</html>
```

Summary of Shorthand Rules for CSS3 Rounded Corners

CSS3 rounded corners provide a shorthand version for rapid markup, the rules for shortening the markup are as follows:

Rule A: If a value is zero, the corner will be square, not round.

Rule B: The shorthand property can be used to define all four corners simultaneously. The property accepts either one or two sets of values separated by a forward slash, each consisting of one, two, three, or four lengths or percentages. If all four values are supplied, the order will be top-left, top-right, bottom-right, and bottom-left.

Rule C: The first set of values (before the forward slash) defines the vertical radii of the four corners.

Rule D: The second (optional) set of values, after the forward slash, defines the horizontal radii for all four corners.

Rule E: If there is only one set of values, these determine both the vertical and horizontal radii equally.

Rule F: If values are omitted, they follow this rule: if a dimension for bottom-left is omitted, it will be the same as top-right; if a dimension for bottom-right is omitted, it will be the same as top-left.

Rule G: If only one value is supplied, it is used to set all four radii equally.

The following are examples:

```
#box-1 { border-radius: 10px 15px 10px 15px / 15px 10px 15px 10px;  (four elliptical corners)
```

```
#box-1 { border-radius: 10px;  (four identical rounded corners)
```

Now for a real brain bender:

```
#box-1 { margin:auto; text-align:center; border:30px #FFCC66 solid; width:250px; ↵
height:150px; border-radius: 10px 20px/20px;
}
```

In the "brain bender" code the corner radii can be translated as follows: all corners have a horizontal radius of 20 pixels dictated by the single size after the forward slash (shown bold). The top-left corner is modified by a vertical radius of 10 pixels, it is, therefore, elliptical.

The second dimension (20 pixels) gives the top-right corner a horizontal radius of 20 pixels, as it already has a vertical radius of 20 pixels it is not an ellipse, but the corner has a simple radius of 20 pixels.

Rule F kicks in because only two dimensions are given to the left of the forward slash,. This makes the bottom-right corner the same as the top-left corner. Rule F also makes the bottom-left corner the same as the top-right corner. The result looks like Figure 7-10.

Figure 7-10. Rounded and elliptical corners created with the briefest possible shorthand markup

Listing 7-10 uses CSS3 to apply a selection of roundings and ellipses to a panel. When viewed in IE 7 and IE 8, the rectangle will have sharp corners.

Listing 7-10. Applying CSS3 Rounded Corners and Ellipses Using Shorthand (fig10-brain-bender.html)

```
<!doctype html>
<html lang=en>
<head>
<title>Fig. 10 Brain bender shorthand</title>
<meta charset=utf-8>
       meta content goes here
<style type="text/css">
#box-1 { margin:auto; text-align:center; border:2px #000 solid; width:300px; height:150px;
         border-radius: 10px 20px/20px; -moz-border-radius: 10px 20px/20px;
}
</style>
</head>
<body>
<p> </p>
<p id="box-1"></p>
</body>
</html>
```

We will now demonstrate the application of CSS3 rounded corners to a tab menu

Tabs with Rounded Corners Using CSS3

Menus with rounded tabs are very popular and were formerly tricky to implement. The simple solution provided by the CSS3 rounded borders module is listed next and the end result is shown in Figure 7-11. This module does not work in IE 7 and IE 8, but it falls back gracefully as shown in Figure 7-12.

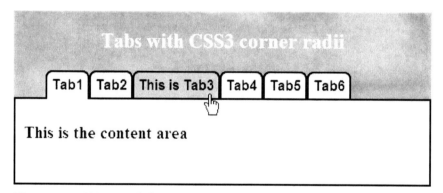

Figure 7-11. CSS3 rounded corners on a tab menu

The CSS3 rounded tabs in Figure 7-11 work in Mozilla Firefox, Safari, Opera, and Chrome, but not in IE 6, IE 7, or IE 8. Later we will use a conditional IE style sheet as a fallback to square corners (see Figure 7-13). IE 9 should show rounded corners. In Figure 7-11, page one's tab has been selected, it turns white and merges with the content panel. When the mouse hovers over a tab, the tab changes color. The cursor is shown hovering over Tab 3.

Note Tab 3 is longer than the others. The tabs grow or shrink automatically to accommodate the text.

The active element is changed from page to page to match the active page, the active element is shown bold in Listing 7-11a. The HTML Listing 7-11a is the markup for Figures 7-11, 7-12 and 7-13. A conditional fall back link (shown bold) will allow an acceptable display using IE 7 and IE 8, but the tab corners will be sharp.

Listing 7-11a. Creating Rounded Tabs with CSS3 (fig11-css3-tabs-rounded.html)

```
<!doctype html>
<html lang=en>
<head>
<title>CSS3 rounded tabs</title>
<meta charset=utf-8>
        meta content goes here
<link href="css3-tabs.css" rel="stylesheet" type="text/css">
        <!--[if lte IE 8]>
        <link href="css3-tabs-ie.css" rel="stylesheet" type="text/css">
        <![endif]-->
</head>
<body>
<div id="header">
<h1>Tabs with CSS3 corner radii</h1>
</div>
<div id="nav">
        <ul>
        <li><a class="tab" id="activelink" href="#">Tab1</a></li>
        <li><a class="tab" href="#">Tab2</a></li>
        <li><a class="tab" href="#">This is Tab3</a></li>
        <li><a class="tab" href="#">Tab4</a></li>
        <li><a class="tab" href="#">Tab5</a></li>
        <li><a class="tab" href="#">Tab6</a></li>
        </ul>
</div>
<div id="content">
<h2>This is the content area</h2>
<br>
</div>
</body>
</html>
```

Note Each `href="#"` must of course be replaced by the URL for your page. The `id` for the active link must be changed on each page to match the page. For instance on page 5 the id for the active link will appear alongside the link for page 5, i.e., `<li><a class="tab" id="activelink" href="#">Tab5</a></li>` and on that page the first tab will become `<li><a class="tab" href="#">Tab1</a></li>`. Figure 7-13 shows the result.

Listing 7-11b is the CSS3 style sheet for the rounded tab menu illustrated in Figure 7-11.

Listing 7-11b. Creating the CSS markup for Listing 7-11a (css3-tabs.css)

```
#header { width:500px; height:100px; background-image:url('images/bluepan.jpg'); ↵
background-repeat:no-repeat; background-position:center; color:white; text-align:center;↵
margin-bottom:-27px;
}
h1 { font-size:150%; font-weight:bold; padding-top:20px;
}
h2 { font-size:125%;
}
#nav ul {width:400px; position:relative; top:-14px;
}
ul li { text-decoration:none; display:inline;
}
ul li a.tab { font-family:Arial; color:black; font-size :medium; font-weight:bold; ↵
background-color:#ffff00; ↵
/*-moz-border-radius-topleft:8px;É-moz-border-radius-topright:8px;*/
border-top-left-radius:8px; border-top-right-radius:8px; border:2px solid black; ↵
padding:5px; padding-bottom:5px;margin :-2px; text-decoration:none; border-bottom:none;
}
.tab:hover { background-color:lime; color:black;
}
#activelink {background-color:white; border-bottom:0; padding-bottom:7px;
}
#content {margin-top:-25px; padding:10px; width:476px; border:2px solid black;
}
```

■ **Note** The commented-out lines shown bold in the CSS style sheet Listing 7-11b are not required for versions of Mozilla Firefox later than 5. The item in bold text can now be omitted, but if you wish to also cater for earlier versions of Firefox, remove the comment symbols.

Figure 7-12 shows the menu when tab5 is selected.

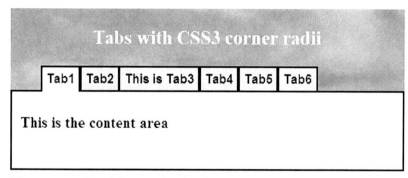

Figure 7-12. The tab for page five has been selected

Figure 7-13 shows how the tab menu will appear in IE 7 and IE 8.

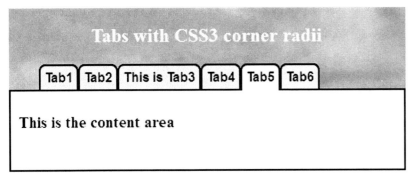

Figure 7-13. *The tabs have square corners in IE 7 and IE 8*

Because of the inclusion of the IE conditional in Listing 7-11a, the conditional CSS markup Listing 7-13 gives an acceptable display in IE 7 and IE 8 as shown in Figure 7-13. However, the tabs will have square corners.

The conditional CSS in Listing 7-13 applies an adjustment to the margins of some elements.

Listing 7-13 shows the IE conditional CSS.

Listing 7-13. *The Conditional CSS to Allow an Acceptable Tab Menu for IE 7 and IE 8 (css3-tabs-ie.css)*

```
#header { margin-bottom:-25px;
}
#content {margin-top:-25px;
}
```

Summary

In this chapter, you learned how to create rounded corners on boxes (panels) using Alessandro Fulciniti's simple JavaScript solution. This technique was then applied to the borders and panels in a full web page. You were then introduced to CSS3 rounded corners applied to boxes; the whole range of possibilities of this technique was presented. Finally, you learned how to apply CSS3 rounded corners to a tab menu.

In the next chapter, you will discover how to apply drop shadows to images and text blocks so that they appear to float above the page surface. You will also be shown how to surround a web page with shadow. You will then be introduced to projects applying CSS3 drop shadows to images, text boxes, and text.

Drop Shadows

Drop shadows can turn pictures and text blocks into eye-catching illustrations that seem to hover above the surface of the page. The CSS3 recommendations include a new drop shadow facility and this is described first in this chapter. Internet Explorer 7 and 8 do not support CSS3; therefore the rest of the chapter gives instructions for CSS2 workarounds that will enable IE 7 and IE 8 users to see the shadows. Drop shadows for images and text boxes can be achieved by the following three methods:

- Use the new CSS3 drop shadow (this does not work in IE 7 or IE 8).

- Use a graphics package for drop shadows applied directly to the image or text. This chapter gives instructions for producing drop shadows quickly and easily using the free and open source program GIMP (previously known as The Gimp in versions prior to 2.6).

- Use CSS2 and a .png background image of a shadow that extends or contracts to match the size of the picture (this is Big John's method; more on this later in the chapter). The shadows can be viewed in all browsers including IE 8. This method will create two- or four-sided shadows by using a shadow background image (or images). The chapter gives instructions for creating the shadow images in the free GIMP graphics program.

CSS3 Drop Shadows do not Need Shadow Images

The CSS3 *box shadow* module is a new feature for creating drop shadows. It can be applied to any box, such as an image or a paragraph. This module provides a much easier way of creating drop shadows *because no shadow images are needed*. This feature is supported by all browsers except IE 7 and IE 8.

Tip For more information on CSS3 box shadows see `http://www.css3.info/preview/box-shadow/`

The attributes specified in the new box shadow module consist of three dimensions (four for a four-sided shadow). Additional optional dimensions are available for the attributes *spread*, and *color*. The attributes and dimensions are as follows:

1. **The shadow's horizontal offset.** Positive offset puts the shadow on the right of the box; a negative offset puts the shadow on the left of the box.

2. **The shadow's vertical offset.** A positive offset puts the shadow below the box. A negative offset puts the shadow above the box.

3. **The shadow's blur radius.** The higher the number, the more blurred the shadow will be. If set to zero, the shadow will be sharp cornered.

4. The shadow will follow rounded corners when the rounded corner feature of CSS3 is used.

5. Optional attributes are available for example, *spread* (the size of the shadow) and *inset* (creates an inner shadow). See the web site at http://www.css3.info/preview/box-shadow/ for details.

■ **Caution** Be sure to put the dimensions of an image in the style sheet. For instance, an image 296 pixels wide and 196 pixels high would require a CSS statement like this:

```
#shadow { box-shadow: 6px 6px 6px #888; width: 296px; height:196px; }
```

The CSS3 drop shadow for a colored paragraph is shown in Figure 8-1.

This is a paragraph with CSS3 drop shadow

Figure 8-1. The CSS3 drop shadow added to a colored paragraph

Listing 8-1a creates a simple colored paragraph with a drop shadow on two sides.

Listing 8-1a. Creating a Colored Paragraph with a Shadow on Two Sides (css3-para-shadow.html)

```
<!doctype html>
<html lang=en>
<head>
<title>This is a colored paragraph with CSS3 drop shadow</title>
<meta charset=utf-8>
<link rel="stylesheet" type="text/css" href="css3-para-shadow.css">
</head>
<body>
<div id="para-shadow">
<p>This is a paragraph with CSS3 drop shadow</p>
</div>
</body>
</html>
```

The CSS code in Listing 8-1b creates a drop shadow with a blur radius of 4 pixels, positioned 6 pixels to the right, and 6 pixels below the paragraph.

Listing 8-1b. The CSS Style Sheet for Listing 8-1a (css3-para-shadow.css)

```
#para-shadow p { box-shadow: 6px 6px 8px #888; padding: 5px 5px 5px 15px; width:300px; ↵
background-color:#66FF99; color:black; font-weight:bold;
}
```

Figure 8-2 shows a CSS3 drop shadow for an image. The Coly River photographs used in this chapter are by kind permission of Colin Haynes.

Figure 8-2. The CSS3 for this example gives a drop shadow with a blur radius of 5 pixels, positioned 6 pixels to the right, and 6 pixels below the image.

Internet Explorer 9, Mozilla Firefox, Safari, and Opera support this CSS3 box shadow. In Listing 8-2a, the CSS3 targets the **<div id="shadow">** to add the drop shadow to the picture.

Listing 8-2a. Creating a Drop Shadow with a Blur Radius of 5 Pixels (css3-image2.html)

```
<!doctype html>
<html lang=en>
<head>
<title>An image with a CSS3 drop shadow</title>
<meta charset=utf-8>
<link rel="stylesheet" type="text/css" href="css3-image1.css">
</head>
<body>
<div id="shadow">
<img alt="Coly River" title="Coly River" height="196" src="images/colrivblu.jpg" width="298">
</div>
<br><br>
</body>
</html>
```

Listing 8-2b targets the <div> containing the shadow id.

Listing 8-2b. The CSS Style Sheet for Listing 8-2a (css3-image1.css)

```
body { color: #fff;
}
#shadow { box-shadow: 6px 6px 6px #888; width: 296px; height:196px;
}
```

The CSS3 drop shadow can also produce a white border, as shown in Figure 8-3.

Figure 8-3. *The CSS3 code gives an image with a white frame and a drop shadow with a blur radius of 6 pixels, positioned 6 pixels to the right, and 6 pixels below the image.*

A background color has been added so that you can see the top of the white frame clearly. The shadow color may need tweaking to match the background color. In Listing 8-3a, the `<div>` shown in bold type is targeted by the CSS style sheet to produce the shadow.

Listing 8-3a. *Creating a Shadow and a White Border Around an Image (css3-image-whitebdr.html)*

```
<!doctype html>
<html lang=en>
<head>
<title>Image with CSS3 drop shadow and white border</title>
<meta charset=utf-8>
<link rel="stylesheet" type="text/css" href="css3-image-whitebdr.css">
</head>
<body>
<div id="shadow-bdr">
<img alt="Coly River" title="Coly River" height="196" src="images/colrivblu.jpg" width=298>
</div>
</body>
</html>
```

In Listing 8-3b, the white border is created by the markup shown bold; the rest of that line creates the shadow.

Listing 8-3b. *The CSS Style Sheet for Listing 8-3a (css3-image-whitebdr.css)*

```
body { background-color:#99CCFF;
}
#shadow-bdr { background-color:#fff; padding:10px; box-shadow: 6px 6px 6px #78b; ↵
            width: 296px;
}
```

CSS3 Four-Sided Shadow

The CSS3 box-shadow module can provide four-sided drop shadows by means of a zero offset and one extra attribute. A typical example is shown in Figure 8-4. The related code is shown in Listings 8-4a and 8-4b.

Figure 8-4. A CSS3 four-sided drop shadow

Listing 8-4a. Placing a Shadow Around Four Sides of an Image (css3-image-4sides)

```
<!doctype html>
<html lang=en>
<head>
<title>Image with a 4 sided CSS3 drop shadow</title>
<meta charset=utf-8>
<link rel="stylesheet" type="text/css" href="css3-image-4side.css">
</head>
<body>
<div id="shadow">
<img alt="Coly River" title="Coly River" width="298" height="196" src="images/colrivblu.jpg">
</div>
<br><br>
</body>
</html>
```

In Listing 8-4b, compare the styling shown bold (note the two zeros) with the styling of the previous two-sided example.

Listing 8-4b. The CSS Style Sheet for Listing 8-4a (css3-image-4sides.css)

```
body { color: #fff;
}
#shadow { margin:20px auto 0 auto;
}
#shadow { box-shadow: 0 0 6px 6px #888; width: 298px; height:196px;
}
```

CSS3 Drop Shadow for Text

This works with all the current browsers except IE 6, IE 7, IE 8, IE 9, and IE 10 beta. In Internet Explorer the shadow code will be ignored and the text will appear as Figure 8-5. Never use a pale color on an equally pale background because, without the shadow, Internet Explorer will not show the text distinctly.

Figure 8-5. The text when viewed in IE 6, 7, 8, 9 and 10 (beta) does not display the drop shadow

The effect in browsers other than IE 6, IE 7, IE 8, and IE 9 is shown in Figure 8-5b.

Figure 8-6. The CSS3 drop shadow as it appears in Mozilla, Opera, Safari, and Chrome

Listings 5a and 5b show the HTML and CSS code for Figures 8-5 and 8-6. In the CSS Listing 8-5b, the <div> shown in bold type in Listing 8-5a is targeted by the CSS style sheet to produce the drop shadow.

Listing 8-5a. Applying a Drop Shadow to Text (css3-text-shadow.html)

```
<!doctype html>
<html lang=en>
<head>
<title>This gives text with a CSS3 drop shadow</title>
<meta charset=utf-8>
<link rel="stylesheet" type="text/css" href="css3-text-shadow.css">
</head>
<body>
<div id="banner">
<h1>This is a CSS3 drop shadow on text</h1>
</div>
</body>
</html>
```

In Listing 8-5b, the drop shadow is created by the markup shown bold.

Listing 8-5b. The CSS Style Sheet for Listing 8-5a (css3-text-shadow.css)

```
body {background-color:#99CCFF;
}
#banner h1 { color: #fff; padding: 50px 0 0 20px; margin: 0; font-size: 2.6em; ↵
text-shadow: 0.1em 0.1em 0.2em black;
}
```

This translates as: shadow offset 0.1 em to the right, shadow offset 0.1 em below the image, blur radius 0.2 em, the shadow color is black.

Creating Drop Shadows for IE 7 and IE 8

Because IE 7 and IE 8 cannot support CSS3 drop shadows, an interim technique must be used. There are two possibilities:

1. Use a graphics package to add a drop shadow to the image or text.

2. Use shadow background images in the background.

Use a Graphics Package

Until recently, creating drop shadows in graphics packages has been a veritable obstacle course. The following describes a typical procedure for some former packages.

1. Load an image into the program.

2. Add 30-pixels-wide borders all round.

3. Select Layers ➤ New Raster Layer.

4. Return to Layer 1.

5. Click the new border with the magic wand and fill it with white.

6. Click Selections and invert the selection.

7. Select Effects ➤ 3D Effects ➤ Drop Shadows.

8. Set the dimensions and the opacity in the next dialog box.

9. Move the image over the shadow until you are satisfied with the appearance.

10. Choose Select ➤ Select None.

11. Select Layers ➤ Merge Layers (flatten).

12. Crop the top and left white borders.

13. Save the image.

Phew! The result was a nice drop shadow that could be seen in IE 7, IE 8, and all newer browsers, as shown in Figure 8-7.

Figure 8-7. A drop shadow produced by a typical graphics package

Most packages involved messing with *Layers* and the *Select* feature. Fortunately, the majority of programs are now simplifying the procedure and providing better instructions.

I use GIMP to create drop shadows quickly and easily. This free package is crammed with advanced features and is easy to download and install. The latest release at the time of writing was GIMP 2.6. You can also download an excellent fully illustrated manual. The web site is at
http://www.gimp.org/downloads

Compare the following steps using GIMP with the procedure previously described:

1. Load an image into GIMP.

2. Select Filters ➤ Light and Shadow.

3. Click Drop Shadow.

That's it! No fiddling with layers, no selections. Figure 8-8 shows the result of adding a drop shadow with GIMP 2.6 and earlier versions.

Figure 8-8. A drop shadow created using GIMP

If you use a different graphics program, explore the Help files for the instructions on drop shadows. The 500-page manual that came with my other graphics package contained one unhelpful sentence on drop shadows. If your program has a similar manual, you may find useful advice by visiting forums related to your graphics program.

Figure 8-9 shows the result of using GIMP to create a drop shadow on text.

THIS IS A DROP SHADOW ON TEXT

Figure 8-9. GIMP can create a drop shadow on text.

Try the following exercise:

1. Open GIMP and Click File ➤ New.

2. Click the landscape icon; set the width to 500 pixels and the height to 35 pixels.

3. Click the **A** icon in the Toolbox.

4. In the Toolbox, click the icon next to Font. From the drop-down list, choose sans bold italic.

5. Choose the size and color of the font; let's try 24pt black. A text box will appear in the edit window.

6. Enter your text and then click Filters on the menu.

7. Select Light and Shadow then choose Drop Shadow.

8. On the next dialog, try the following settings:

    - Offset x: 2

    - Offset y: 2

    - Blur radius: 2

    - Leave the color as the default black; set the Opacity to 70 percent.

9. Click OK.

10. To save the file, choose Save As in the File menu item and save it as a .jpg or a .png image.

Using Background Images and CSS2 to Create Drop Shadows

Background shadow images can automatically expand and contract to accommodate various image sizes. I am most grateful to Big John for publishing this CSS2 technique for drop shadows. Examples 8-10 to 8-15 follow his technique. Be sure to visit Big John's excellent web site (note the .net domain) at *http://*www.positioniseverything.net.

This web site has a most helpful explanation of how the method works. The web site is also a treasure trove of practical information on CSS.

By surrounding a block such as a paragraph or an image with <div>s containing shadow images, this method can provide shadows on two sides or four sides. We will start with shadows on two sides.

Two-Sided Shadows Using CSS2 Background Shadow Images

Figure 8-10 shows a drop shadow on two sides of an image. It's two, associated code examples are shown in Listings 8-10a and 8-10b.

Figure 8-10. A simple image with shadows on two sides

Three <div>s in Listing 8-10a hold parts of three shadow images. These consist of two corner shadow images and the main shadow image. The fourth <div> holds the picture. These <div>s are shown in bold.

Listing 8-10a. Surrounding an Image with a Shadow on Two Sides. (two-shadowfig10.html)

```
<!doctype html>
<html lang=en>
<head>
<title>2 sided drop shadow Fig 8-10</title>
<meta charset=utf-8>
      meta details go here
```

```
<link  rel="stylesheet" type="text/css" href="two-shadowfig10.css">
</head>
<body>
        <div class="top-right-corner">
        <div class="bottom-left-corner">
        <div class="shadowbox">
        <div class="innerbox">
        <img title="Coly River" alt="Coly River" width="298" height="196" src="colrivblu.jpg">
        </div>
</div>
</div>
</div>
</body>
</html>
```

The CSS Listing 8-10b for Figure 8-10 uses three background images, top-rightcorner.png, bottom-leftcorner.png, and main-shadow.png . Figures 8-10, 8-11, and 8-12 all use the same shadow images. These can be downloaded from the book's web page. The picture is located within the background shadows by using position:relative; in the CSS.

Listing 8-10b. The CSS Style Sheet for Listing 8-10a (two-shadowfig10.css)

```
.top-right-corner { background:url(top-rightcorner.png) right top no-repeat; width: 305px;
}
.bottom-left-corner { background:url(bottom-leftcorner.png) left bottom no-repeat; ↵
padding-top:8px; padding-left:8px;
}
.shadowbox { background:url(main-shadow.png) bottom right;
}
.innerbox { position: relative; left:-8px; top:-3px;
}
```

You may have to tweak the .innerbox position a little to ensure that no white edge appears; for instance, at first I had this setting: .innerbox { position:relative; left:-8px; top:-8px; }, but a one-pixel, white edge appeared at the bottom of the picture. By changing to top:-7px;, the white edge was removed.

Placing a shadow around an image that has a white frame is shown in Figure 8-11.

Figure 8-11. An image with a shadow on two sides and a white border

This example has been given a colored background so that the top and left side of the white border can be clearly seen. See the next Listings 8-11a through 8-11d for the associated code.

Method 1: Add the White Frame

The image must first be given a white border. In this example, a 10-pixel, white border was added using a graphics program. The image was then saved with the new name, colrivblu-whitebdr.jpg. These borders increased the dimensions of the image by 20 pixels; the new size is 318 pixels × 216 pixels, and these figures were carefully noted, ready for the next step—Listing 8-11a.

Listing 8-11a. Adding a Drop Shadow and White Border (twoshad-whitebdr1.html)

```
<!doctype html>
<html lang=en>
<head>
<title>Figure8-11. Two sided drop shadow. Pic has whiteborder</title>
<meta charset=utf-8>
        meta details go here
<link  rel="stylesheet" type="text/css" href="twoshad-whitebdr1.css">
</head>
<body>
        <div class="top-right-corner">
        <div class="bottom-left-corner">
        <div class="shadowbox">
        <div class="innerbox">
<!--set the new image dimensions for the new image-->
<img title="Coly River" alt="Coly River" width="318" height="216" ↵
src="images/colrivblu-whitebdr.jpg">
</div>
</div>
</div>
</div>
```

```
<p>Two sided shadow with white border</p>
</body>
</html>
```

Listing 8-11b. The CSS Style Sheet for Listing 8-11a (twoshad-whitebdr1.css)

```
body { background-color:#CCFFCC; font:black arial medium;
}
.top-right-corner { background:url('images/top-rightcorner.png') no-repeat right top; ⏎
                    width: 326px;
}
.bottom-left-corner { background:url('images/bottom-leftcorner.png') no-repeat left bottom; ⏎
                      padding-top:8px; padding-left:8px;
}
.shadowbox { background:url('images/main-shadow.png') right bottom;
}
.innerbox { position: relative; left:-8px; top:-4px;
}
```

Method 2: Use CSS to Add the White Frame

An image with a ready-made border provides a solution, but CSS can be used to add a white border. The CSS method is preferable as it loads faster and avoids the hassle of having to use your paint program to add a border. However, it may need some fiddling with the style sheet to get it just right.

Listing 8-11c gives the same appearance as Figure 8-11. A class named .frame is added to the image so that the white border can be added; this is shown in bold.

Listing 8-11c. Using a Class to Provide a White Border (twoshad-whitebdr2.html)

```
<!doctype html>
<html lang=en>
<head>
<title>Two sided drop shadow and CSS white border</title>
<meta charset=utf-8>
<link  rel="stylesheet" type="text/css" href="twoshad-whitebdr2.css">
</head>
<body>
<div class="top-right-corner">
<div class="bottom-left-corner">
<div class="shadowbox">
<div class="innerbox">
<img class="frame" title="Coly River" alt="Coly River" width="298" height="196" ⏎
src="images/colrivblu.jpg">
</div>
</div>
</div>
</div>
<p>Two sided shadow with white border</p>
</body>
</html>
```

The class .frame was used in the HTML to target the image in order to add the white border. This new line, img.frame { border:10px white solid; }, is added to the CSS Listing 8-11d (shown in bold).

Listing 8-11d. The CSS Style Sheet that Defines the Class .innerbox (twoshad-whitebdr2.css)

```
body { background-color:#CCFFCC; font:black arial medium;
}
.top-right-corner { background:url('images/top-rightcorner.png') no-repeat right top; ⏎
width: 326px;
}
.bottom-left-corner { background:url('images/bottom-leftcorner.png') no-repeat left bottom; ⏎
                      padding-top:8px; padding-left:8px;
}
.shadowbox { background:url('images/main-shadow.png') right bottom;
}
.innerbox { width:298px; height:216px; position: relative; left:-8px; top:-8px;
}
img.frame { border:10px white solid;
}
```

CSS2 Two-Sided Drop Shadow for Text

Figure 8-12 shows the effect of adding a drop shadow to a block of text.

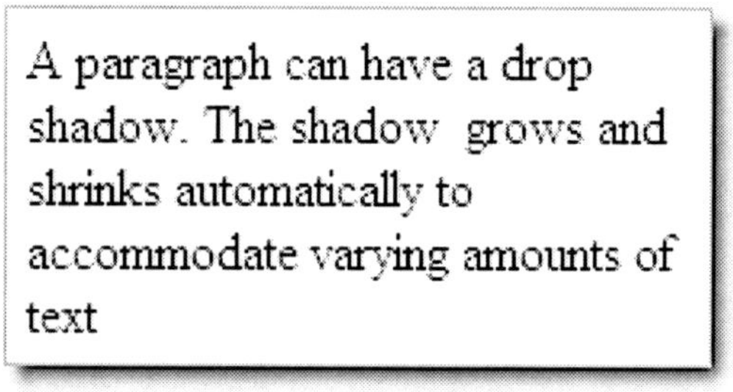

Figure 8-12. A two-sided drop shadow on a paragraph can be achieved using the same technique that was used for images.

The HTML in Listing 8-12a is almost the same as the previous projects, except that a block of text is used instead of a picture.

Listing 8-12a. Placing a Two-sided Drop Shadow Around a Block of Text (two-shadowtext.html)

```
<!doctype html>
<html lang=en>
<head>
<title>Paragraph with 2 sided drop shadow</title>
<meta charset=utf-8>
<link rel="stylesheet" type="text/css" href="two-shadowtext.css">
</head>
<body>
<div class="top-right-corner">
<div class="bottom-left-corner">
<div class="shadowbox">
<div class="innerbox">
<p>A paragraph can have a drop shadow. The shadow grows and shrinks ⏎
automatically to accommodate varying amounts of text</p>
```

```
</div>
</div>
</div>
</div>
</body>
</html>
```

Figure 8-12 has 5 pixels of padding between the text and the sides of the paragraph content box. This is shown in bold in the next Listing. The 200 pixels wide content plus the left and right padding gives a total width of 220 pixels, this is added into the style of the top-right-corner (shown in bold in Listing 8-12b). The text block was given a thin silver border so that the top and left edges were clearly visible.

Listing 8-12b. The CSS Style Sheet for Listing 8-12a (two-shadowtext.css)

```
body { background-color:#FFF; font:black arial medium;
}
.top-right-corner { background:url('images/top-rightcorner.png') no-repeat right top; ↵
                    width:220px;
}
.bottom-left-corner { background:url('images/bottom-leftcorner.png') no-repeat left bottom; ↵
                      padding-top:8px; padding-left:8px;
}
.shadowbox { background:url('images/main-shadow.png') right bottom;
}
.innerbox { position: relative; left:-8px; top:-8px;
}
.innerbox p { margin:0; padding:5px; width:200px; border:1px silver solid;
}
```

CSS2 Four-Sided Drop Shadow

A drop shadow can be placed around all four sides of an image using a CSS background image. Wider background shadows may appear less realistic because the radii of the shadow at the corners may appear too big for the shadow of a sharp-cornered picture.

Figures 8-13 and 8-14 show the effect of two different shadows widths.

Figure 8-13. Narrow drop shadow on four sides

Figure 8-14. Wide drop shadow on four sides

Figures 8-13, 8-14, and 8-15 use only one, rectangular shadow image.

■ **Tip** A limited number of drop shadow images can be downloaded from the book's web page or you can create your own using a graphics manipulation package. The drop shadow image must be a transparent .png file.

Listing 8-13a has four <div>s and again uses the CSS background image property. The positioning of the <div>s and their closing </div>s is extremely important. This example with a 10-pixel shadow works best with an XHTML listing. The shadow works in all modern browsers, but it does not display correctly in IE 6 or IE 7.

■ **Note** In the listing, corner a is the top-right corner, corner b is the bottom-left corner.

Listing 8-13a. *Surrounding an Image with Four 10 Pixel wide Shadows (fourside-drop10px.html)*

```
<!DOCTYPE html PUBLIC "-//W3C//DTD XHTML 1.0 Transitional//EN"
"http://www.w3.org/TR/xhtml1/DTD/xhtml1-transitional.dtd">
<html xmlns="http://www.w3.org/1999/xhtml">
<head>
<meta content="text/html; charset=utf-8" http-equiv="Content-Type" />

<title>A 10 pixel wide drop shadow on 4 sides</title>
        meta content goes here…
<link  rel="stylesheet" type="text/css" href="fourside-drop10px.css">
</head>
<body>
        <div class="shadow-one">
                <div class="corner-a"></div>
                <div class="corner-b"></div>
        <div class="shadow-two">
        <div class="shadow-three">
        <div class="shadow-four">
<img title="River Coly" alt="River Coly" height="197" src="images/colriv.jpg"↵
width="301" margin="0" padding="0">
        </div>
        </div>
        </div>
        </div>
</body>
</html>
```

Listing 8-13b uses a single, rectangular shadow image, shadow10p.png, and CSS positioning.

Listing 8-13b. *The CSS Style Sheet for Listing 8-13a (fourside-drop10px.css)*

```
.shadow-one { position:absolute; padding-top:20px; padding-left:20px;
}
```

```
.corner-a { position:absolute; right:0; top:0; width:20px; height:20px; ↵
            background:url('images/shadow10p.png') right top no-repeat;
}
.corner-b { position:absolute; left:0; bottom:0; width:20px; height:20px; ↵
            background:url('images/shadow10p.png') left bottom no-repeat;
}
.shadow-two { position:relative; background :url('images/shadow10p.png') ↵
              right bottom no-repeat;
}
.shadow-three { position:relative; left:-20px; top:-20px; ↵
                background:url('images/shadow10p.png') left top no-repeat;
}
.shadow-four { position:relative; left:10px; top:10px;
}
```

■ **Note** In Figure 8-13, the width of the shadow areas on the .png image is 10 pixels. The 20 pixels dimensions in the CSS listing are twice the .png shadow width. Shadow-four is the same width (10 pixels) as the .png shadow areas.

A wider drop shadow was shown in Figure 8-14. Listing 8-14a has four <div>s and again uses the CSS background image property. The positioning of the <div>s and their closing </div>s is extremely important. The shadow works best using XHTML instead of HTML5. The shadow can be viewed in all modern browsers, including IE 8, but it does not display correctly in IE 6 or IE 7.

Listing 8-14a. Placing a 30 Pixel wide Drop Shadow on Four Sides (fourside-drop30px.html)

```
<!DOCTYPE html PUBLIC "-//W3C//DTD XHTML 1.0 Transitional//EN"
"http://www.w3.org/TR/xhtml1/DTD/xhtml1-transitional.dtd">
<html xmlns="http://www.w3.org/1999/xhtml">
<head>
<meta content="text/html; charset=utf-8" http-equiv="Content-Type" />
<title>Wider drop shadow on 4 sides</title>
<link rel="stylesheet" type="text/css" href="fourside-drop30px.css" />
</head>
<body>
        <div class="shadow-one">
                <div class="corner-a"></div>
                <div class="corner-b"></div>
        <div class="shadow-two">
        <div class="shadow-three">
        <div class="shadow-four">
<img title="River Coly" alt="River Coly" height="197" src="images/colriv.jpg" ↵
width="301" margin="0" padding="0" >
        </div>
        </div>
        </div>
        </div>
</body>
</html>
```

CSS Listing 8-14b uses a single rectangular shadow image, shadow30p.png, and CSS positioning.

Listing 8-14b. The CSS Style Sheet for Listing 8-14a (fourside-drop30px.css)

```
.shadow-one { position:absolute; padding-top:60px; padding-left:60px;
}
.corner-a { position:absolute; right:0; top:0; width:60px; height:60px; ↵
        background:url('images/shadow30px.png') right top no-repeat;
}
.corner-b { position:absolute; left:0; bottom:0; width:60px; height:60px; ↵
        background:url('images/shadow30px.png') left bottom no-repeat;
}
.shadow-two { position:relative; background :url('images/shadow30px.png') ↵
        right bottom no-repeat;
}
.shadow-three { position:relative; left:-60px; top:-60px; ↵
            background:url('images/shadow30px.png') left top no-repeat;
}
.shadow-four { position:relative; left:30px; top:30px;
}
```

■ **Note** In Figure 8-14, the width of the shadow areas on the .png image is 30 pixels. The 60 pixels dimensions are twice the .png shadow width. Shadow four is the same width (30 pixels) as the .png shadow areas.

Four-Sided Drop Shadows Around Paragraphs

Paragraphs can be made to appear as if they are floating above the page surface by using a drop shadow. Figure 8-15 shows a paragraph with no border but it is surrounded by shadows.

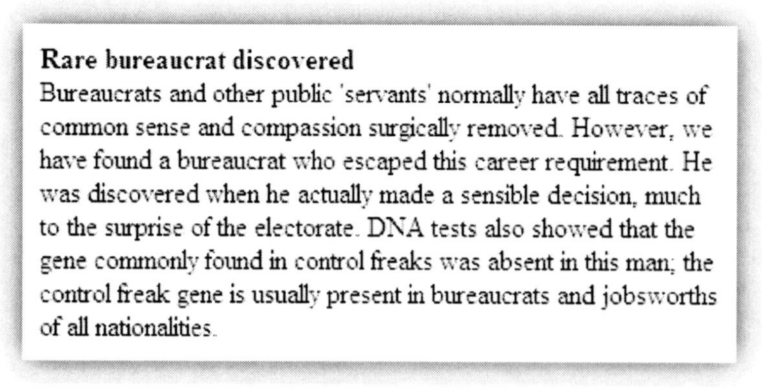

Rare bureaucrat discovered
Bureaucrats and other public 'servants' normally have all traces of common sense and compassion surgically removed. However, we have found a bureaucrat who escaped this career requirement. He was discovered when he actually made a sensible decision, much to the surprise of the electorate. DNA tests also showed that the gene commonly found in control freaks was absent in this man; the control freak gene is usually present in bureaucrats and jobsworths of all nationalities.

Figure 8-15. When placing a four-sided shadow around a piece of text, use a paragraph and give the paragraph a width so that the shadows have something to attach themselves to.

The process is exactly the same as the previous projects but a paragraph is use instead of a picture (see Listings 8-15a and 8-15b).

Listing 8-15a. Apply a Drop Shadow to Four Sides of a Block of Text (shadow-paragraph.html)

```
<!doctype html>
<html lang=en>
<head>
<title>Paragraph with shadow round all four sides</title>
<meta charset=utf-8>

<link rel="stylesheet" type="text/css" href="shadow-paragraph.css">

</head>
<body>
<div id="wrapper">
        <div class="shadow-one">
                <div class="corner-a"></div>
                <div class="corner-b"></div>
        <div class="shadow-two">
        <div class="shadow-three">
        <div class="shadow-four">
<p><b>Rare bureaucrat discovered</b><br>Bureaucrats and other public &#39;servants&#39; ↵
        …some text has been ommitted from this markup to save space…
present in bureaucrats and jobsworths of all nationalities.</p><!-- close paragraph-->
        </div>
        </div>
        </div>
        </div>
</div>
</body>
</html>
```

Listing 8-15b. The CSS Style Sheet for Listing 8-15a (shadow-paragraph.css)

```
/*SET 4 SIDED SHADOW*/
.shadow-one { position:absolute; padding-top:60px; padding-left:60px;
}
.corner-a { position:absolute; right:0; top:16px; width:60px; height:60px; ↵
background:url('images/shadow30px.png') right top no-repeat;
}
.corner-b { position:absolute; left:0; bottom:16px; width:60px; height:60px; ↵
background:url('images/shadow30px.png') left bottom no-repeat;
}
.shadow-two { position:relative; ↵
background :url('images/shadow30px.png') right bottom no-repeat;}
.shadow-three { position:relative; left:-60px; top:-60px; ↵
background:url( 'images/shadow30px.png' ) left top no-repeat; }
.shadow-four {position:relative; left:30px; top:30px; }
#wrapper { width:420px;
}
p {width:400px; padding:10px;
}
```

Troubleshooting the Shadows in Listings 8-13 through 8-15

If you have any problems with the shadows just discussed, the information in this section should help you out. For starters, always begin with the height for corner *a* and corner *b* set to zero, as follows:

```
.corner-a {position:absolute; right:0; top:0; width:60px; height:60px; ↵
background:url('images/shadow30px.png') right top no-repeat;
}
.corner-b {position:absolute; left:0; bottom:0; width:60px; height:60px; ↵
background:url('images/shadow30px.png') left bottom no-repeat;
}
```

Corner *a* is the top-right corner of a box; corner *b* is bottom-left corner of a box.
The zero settings resulted in a problem with corners *a* and *b*, as shown in Figure 8-16.

```
.corner-a { position:absolute; right:0; top:16px; width:60px; height:60px; ↵
background:url('images/shadow30px.png') right top no-repeat;
}
.corner-b { position:absolute; left:0; bottom:16px; width:60px; height:60px; ↵
background:url('images/shadow30px.png') left bottom no-repeat;
}
```

Figure 8-16 shows faulty corners *a* and *b*.

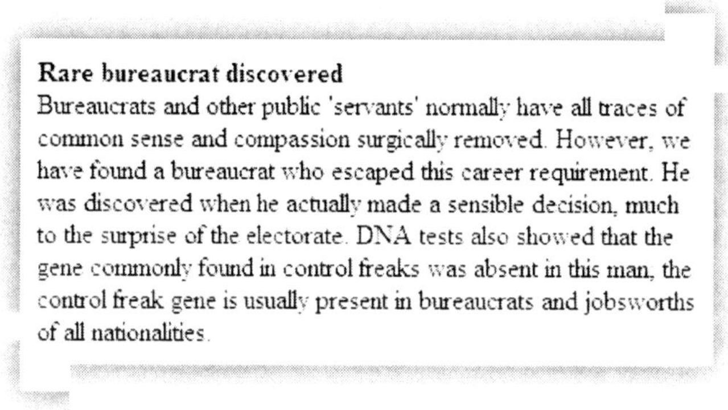

> **Rare bureaucrat discovered**
> Bureaucrats and other public 'servants' normally have all traces of common sense and compassion surgically removed. However, we have found a bureaucrat who escaped this career requirement. He was discovered when he actually made a sensible decision, much to the surprise of the electorate. DNA tests also showed that the gene commonly found in control freaks was absent in this man, the control freak gene is usually present in bureaucrats and jobsworths of all nationalities.

Figure 8-16. A problem with corners a and b

Correcting the Fault

By trial and error, change the top and bottom pixels for corners *a* and *b*. In this example, the solution was to change the zeros to 16 pixels.

```
.corner-a { position:absolute; right:0; top:16px; width:60px; height:60px; ↵
background:url('images/shadow30px.png') right top no-repeat;
}
.corner-b { position:absolute; left:0; bottom:16px; width:60px; height:60px; ↵
background:url('images/shadow30px.png') left bottom no-repeat;
}
```

The .png Shadow Images

Where can you obtain .png shadow images? A small number can be downloaded from Big John's web site (www.positioniseverything.net). I have included a few shadows in the download package available from the book's web page. You can design your own .png shadow images using the free GIMP graphics program. The instructions are rather complicated, but you will not need the plug-ins that are necessary when using some other packages. Information on GIMP is available at http://www.gimp.org/ and you can also download the program and the help files from the GIMP web site.

Creating .png Shadow Images in GIMP

The aim this section is to produce a four-sided drop shadow surrounding an empty rectangle.

1. Open Gimp and click File ➤ New.

2. In the next dialog box, click Advanced Options.

3. Click the left icon (located below the Height option) to select Portrait. Specify the size of your required shadow (for instance 640 pixels wide × 400 pixels high). In the Color Space field, select Greyscale (it has the UK English spelling).

4. Select Fill With ➤ Transparency, then click OK. The empty image is created; it is covered with a checkerboard pattern that denotes transparency. Figure 8-17 shows the GIMP's Toolbox window.

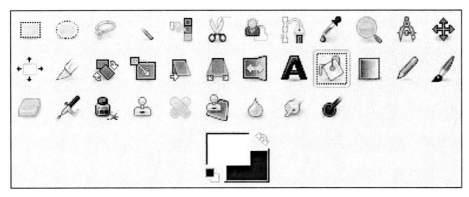

Figure 8-17. The GIMP's Toolbox window. The white swatch overlaps the black swatch.

5. Now select the color white, click the curved double-headed arrow to ensure that the white square overlaps the black square. The top color represents the fill color, whereas the black (on the lower color selected) is the background color. In the Toolbox window, click the Bucket Fill icon. Click the white square then go back to the checkerboard image and left click it to turn it white.

6. Click Layer ➤ New Layer. Ensure the Transparency radio button is selected, accept all the default settings, and click OK.

7. In the menu, click Windows ➤ Dockable Dialogs ➤ Layers Dialog. This will place a dialog box on the screen showing the layers.

8. Ensure that the layer with the checkerboard pattern is always selected (it will have a pale-colored background when it is selected; the unselected layer will be white).

Now we will decide on the width of the shadow image, let's say it will be 20 pixels.

1. Click Select ➤ All. You will now see the dashed outline moving like a line of marching ants.

2. Click Select ➤ Shrink. A dialog box will allow you to choose the amount by which the image is shrunk; let's say 30 pixels.

3. Ensure the box labeled Shrink from Image Border is ticked. Click OK.

4. Now you will see that the inner and outer images have dashed borders. Only the inner image will have marching ants. Click Filters ➤ Light and Shadow ➤ Drop Shadow.

5. On the dialog box, set the offsets to zero, the blur radius as 20 pixels, and the opacity as 70.

6. Make sure the box labeled Allow Resizing is unchecked. Click OK. You will see a third layer, called Drop Shadow, has appeared; just ignore it. The docked Layers window is illustrated in Figure 8-18.

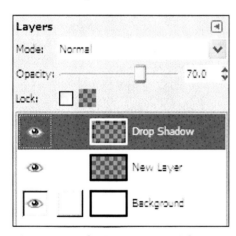

Figure 8-18. *The GIMP Layers Dialog*

7. **Do not save it yet,** but look at the layers dialog box and click the eyeball relating to the Background layer. Now you can see the drop shadow in the edit pane as the checkerboard is revealed once more.

8. Click File ➤ Save As and choose where to save it. *At the top* of the dialog box, name the file and be sure to include the file type by adding .png to the file name (example: mydropshadow.png).

9. Click the *Save* button. A dialog box labeled Export File will pop up. Ensure that the radio button labeled Merge Visible Layers is selected. Then click the Export button. Accept the default settings on the next dialog box and click the Save button.

The shadow image that this creates can be used in the previous background shadow image examples and it can be sliced to give the image required later in this section for images 8-21a, 8-21b, and 8-21c. Experiment with the various dimensions but always include the two zeros for the offsets. Eventually you could create a library of shadow sizes; remember that large shadow sizes can be used for smaller images as the shadow contracts or expands to fill the <div>s. However, if you use a shadow too small for the image it surrounds, it will be hidden behind the image. The shadow we just created is shown in Figure 8-19.

Figure 8-19. The shadow created using GIMP

Adding a Shadow Around the Main Panel of a Web Page

The technique in this example is best used for fixed-width layouts, but semi liquid pages are possible with a little extra hassle using .png shadow images that grow or shrink to match the box element. Figure 8-20 shows a full page with drop shadows on all four sides of a fixed-width page.

Figure 8-20. *The shadow wraps around the entire page's white border. This works in all browsers.*

■ **Note** A drop shadow was added to the white lettering in the header panel by using the new CSS3 module. The CSS3 text shadow in Listings 8-20, 8-22, and 8-23 does not work in Internet Explorer 6, 7, 8, and 9. The .png shadows are not transparent in IE 6.

Listing 8-20a is for a fixed-width of 960 pixels and a screen with a horizontal resolution of 1024 pixels. The shadow used is 1024 pixels wide and deep.

Listing 8-20a. *Creating a shadow around the Border of a Web Page (shadow-fullpage.html)*

```
<!DOCTYPE html>
<html lang=en>
<head>
<title>Complete page with shadow around wrapper</title>
<meta charset=utf-8>
<link rel="stylesheet" type="text/css" href="shadow-fullpage.css" />
        <!--Add conditional Javascript for IE 7 and 8-->
        <!--[if lte IE 8]><script src="html5.js">
        </script>
        <![endif]-->
</head>
<body>
        <div class="shadow-one">
                <div class="corner-a"></div>
                <div class="corner-b"></div>
```

```
        <div class="shadow-two">
        <div class="shadow-three">
        <div class="shadow-four">
<div id="wrapper">
<header><h1>Shadow all around main white frame</h1></header><!-- close banner-->
<div id="mainContent"><!--this panel will contain two columns-->
<h2>Latest News
</h2>
<article>
        <h3>Rare bureaucrat discovered</h3>
        <p>Bureaucrats and other public &#39;servants&#39; normally have all traces of common
                Some of the text has been omitted here to save space
        and jobsworths of all nationalities.</p>
</article><!--close left col-->
<article>
        <h3>Man bites dog</h3>
        <p>Cedric Sidebottam age 46, mistook his Yorkshire terrier for a hamburger; he
        spread mustard on the dog and then bit it.  The dog recovered but Cedric
        was admitted to hospital suffering from shock and food poisoning.</p>
        <p> </p>
</article><!-- close right col-->
<nav>
        <h2>Menu</h2>
        <ul>
        <li><a href="#">Page 2</a></li>
        <li><a href="#">Page 3</a></li>
        <li><a href="#">Page 4</a></li>
        <li><a href="#">Page 5</a></li>
        <li><a href="#">Page 6</a></li>
        <li><a href="#">Home page</a></li>
        </ul>
</nav><!-- close menupanel-->
</div><!-- close mainContent-->
<footer>This is the footer
</footer>
        </div><!-- close wrapper -->
<!--close the four shadow divs-->
        </div>
        </div>
        </div>
        </div>
</body>
</html>
```

Listing 8-20b. CSS Style Sheet for Listing 8-20a (shadow-fullpage.css)

```
body { text-align: center; background: #e6e6e6;
}
/*add display attributes for the semantic tags*/
header, footer, section, article, nav { display:block;
}
#wrapper { margin: -20px auto 0 auto; width: 940px; border:10px white solid; padding:0;
}
```

```
header { width: 940px; height: 154px; margin: 0; border-bottom:10px white solid; ↵
background: url(images/bluepan.jpg);
}
article { margin-left:10px; width:40%; display:inline; float:left; text-align:left;
}
#mainContent {margin:0; width: 940px; float: left; background-color:#aac9f6;
}
nav { width: 120px; margin-right:10px; padding: 0 5px 5px 0; float: right;
}
footer { margin:0; text-align:center; clear: both; background-color:#aac9f6;
}
br.clear { clear:both;
}
body { font: 76%/1.6 "Lucida Grande", Geneva, Verdana, sans-serif;
}
a { font-weight: bold; color: navy; text-decoration: none; border-bottom: 1px solid navy;
}
a:hover {color:#906; border-bottom: 1px solid #906;
}
header h1 { color: #fff; padding: 50px 0 0 20px; margin: 0; font-size: 2.6em; ↵
                text-shadow: 0.1em 0.1em 0.2em black;
}
h2, h3, h4 { margin-top: 0; color: black; font-weight: bold;
}
h2 { font-size: 2.2em; margin-bottom:0;
}
h3, nav h2 { font-size: 1.6em; margin-bottom:0;
}
h4 { font-size: 1.2em; margin-bottom:0;
}
p { margin-top:0; margin-bottom:6px;
}
#mainContent p, #mainContent h2, #mainContent h3, #mainContent h4, #mainContent ul, ↵
{ margin-left: 10px; margin-right: 10px; background-color:#aac9f6;
}
nav ul, nav ul li { list-style: none; margin: 0 0 2px 10px; padding: 0;
}
/*SET 4 SIDED SHADOW STYLES*/
.shadow-one {position:absolute; padding-top:60px; padding-left:60px;
}
.corner-a {position:absolute; right:0; top:-20px; width:60px; height:60px; ↵
background:url('images/shadow30px.png') right top no-repeat;
}
.corner-b {position:absolute; left:0; bottom:0; width:60px; height:60px; ↵
background:url('images/shadow30px.png') left bottom no-repeat;
}
.shadow-two { position:relative; ↵
background:url('images/shadow30px.png') right bottom no-repeat;
}
.shadow-three { position:relative; left:-60px; top:-60px; ↵
background:url('images/shadow30px.png') left top no-repeat;
}
.shadow-four { position:relative; left:30px; top:30px;
}
```

░ **Caution** Although this method is effective, it has a big drawback. The vertical length of this page is restricted by your choice of the dimension of the shadow image. The 1024-pixel shadow used in Figure 8-7 restricts the page to a vertical height of 980 pixels and the content panel is restricted to a vertical height of 780 pixels. It would not be a problem on the home page, which should not exceed the height of the browser window; but it might be a severe handicap for subsequent pages.

Overcoming the Height Restriction

The following three solutions are available:

- Use a bigger shadow image. This would mean finding or creating a bigger shadow image; however, even though the vertical height is extended, it would still be restricted.

- Use a sliced shadow image.

- Use shadows on the sides; no top or bottom shadows.

Using a Sliced Shadow Image

This example is adapted from a template created by Andy Budd (http://www.andybudd.com) for the book *Blog Design Solutions* (Friends of ED, 2006). The example is for an 800 × 600 screen and, although too small for today's screens, it serves to demonstrate the technique. Using larger shadow files, it can be adapted for big screens and high resolutions.

Figures 8-22a through 8-22c show a shadow image sliced into three items using a paint program.

Figures 8-21a, 8-21b, and 8-21c. Labeled *top-shadow.png, middle-shadow.png,* and *bottom-shadow.png*

In this example, the heights of the slices are as follows: the top slice is 20 pixels, the middle slice is 64 pixels, and the bottom slice is 20 pixels. The worked example for an extendable shadow is illustrated by the screenshot shown in Figure 8-22.

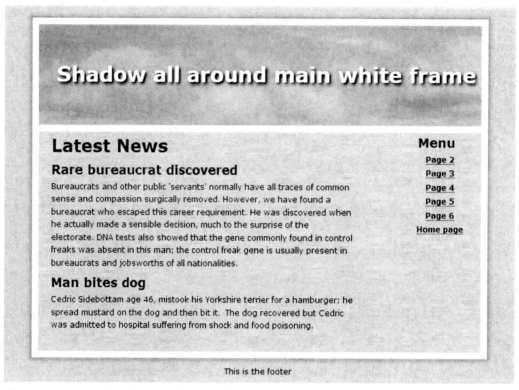

Figure 8-22. *A shadow that extends vertically to any height*

The top and bottom shadows are fixed. In Listing 8-22a, the CSS style sheet targets the wrapper to apply the side shadows.

Listing 8-22a. *Placing an Extendable Shadow Around the Border of Web Page (shadow-fullpage-extendable.html)*

```
<!doctype html>
<html lang=en>
<head>
<title>Complete page with extendable shadow around wrapper</title>
<meta charset=utf-8>
<link rel="stylesheet" type="text/css" href="shadow-fullpage-extendable.css">
        <!--Add conditional Javascript for IE7 and 8-->
        <!--[if lte IE 8]><script src="html5.js">
        </script>
        <![endif]-->
</head>
<body>
<div id="top"><!--place top shadow on page--></div><!-- close top -->
<div id="wrapper"><!--surrounds all elements below the top shadow-->
<header><h1>Shadow all around main white frame</h1></header><!-- close banner -->
```

```
<div id="mainContent"><!--this panel will contain two columns-->
<!--<div id="content">-->
<div id="leftcol">
<h2>Latest News</h2>
<h3>Rare bureaucrat discovered</h3>
<p>Bureaucrats and other public &#39;servants&#39; normally have all traces of common
                some text omitted here to save space
usually present in bureaucrats and jobsworths of all nationalities.</p>
<h3>Man bites dog</h3>
<p>Cedric Sidebottam age 46, mistook his Yorkshire terrier for a hamburger; he ↵
spread mustard on the dog and then bit it.  The dog recovered but Cedric ↵
was admitted to hospital suffering from shock and food poisoning.</p><p> </p>
</div><!-- close leftcol-->
<nav><br>
   <ul><h3>Menu</h3>
       <li><a href="#">Page 2</a></li>
       <li><a href="#">Page 3</a></li>
       <li><a href="#">Page 4</a></li>
       <li><a href="#">Page 5</a></li>
       <li><a href="#">Page 6</a></li>
       <li><a href="#">Home page</a></li>
   </ul><!-- close links-->
</nav><!-- close menupanel-->
</div><!-- close mainContent -->
<br class="clear">
</div><!-- close wrapper -->
<div id="bottom"></div><!-- open and close bottom shadow-->
<footer>This is the footer</footer><!--open and close footer -->
</body>
```

The side shadow slice is repeated vertically to match the length of the wrapper; this is achieved in Listing 8-22b by targeting the wrapper.

Listing 8-22b. The CSS Style Sheet for the Listing 8-22a (shadow-fullpage-extendable.css)

```
/*This css template is derived from a template created by Andy Budd (www.andybudd.com) ↵
for the book "Blog Design Solutions", and is released under a Creative Commons ↵
Attribution-NonCommercial-ShareAlike 2.5 License*/
body { margin: 0; padding: 0; text-align: center; background: #e6e6e6; ↵
font: 76%/1.6 "Lucida Grande", Geneva, Verdana, sans-serif;
}
/*add display attributes for the semantic tags*/
header, footer, section, article, nav { display:block;
}
#wrapper, #top, #bottom { margin: 0 auto; padding: 0 10px; width: 720px;
}
/*apply shadows*/
#wrapper { background: url(images/middle.png) repeat-y;
}
#top { height: 20px; margin-top: 20px; background: url(images/top.png) no-repeat;
}
#bottom { height: 20px; background: url(images/bottom.png) no-repeat;
}
```

```
header { width: 700px; height: 154px; margin: 0; margin-left:10px; ↵
border-bottom:10px white solid; background: url(images/bluepan.jpg);
}
#leftcol { margin: 0 10px; display:inline; /* fix IE double margin float bug */↵
float: left; width: 500px; text-align:left;
}
#mainContent {margin:0 0 0 10px; border:0 10px 0 10px white solid; width: 700px; ↵
float: left; background-color:#aac9f6;
}
nav { width: 140px; margin-right:10px; padding: 0 5px 5px 0; float: right;
}
footer { margin:0; text-align:center; clear: both;
}
br.clear { clear:both;
}
a { font-weight: bold; color: navy; text-decoration: none; border-bottom: 1px solid navy;
}
a:hover {color:#906; border-bottom: 1px solid #906;
}
header h1 { color: #fff; padding: 50px 0 0 20px; margin: 0; font-size: 2.6em; ↵
         text-shadow: 0.1em 0.1em 0.2em black;
}
h2, h3, h4 { margin-top: 0; color: navy; font-weight: bold;
}
h2 { font-size: 2.2em; margin-bottom:0;
}
h3, nav h2 { font-size: 1.6em; margin-bottom:0;
}
p { margin-top:0; margin-bottom:6px;
}
#mainContent p, #mainContent h2, #mainContent h3, #mainContent h4, #mainContent ul, ↵
#mainContent ol { margin-left: 10px; margin-right: 10px
}
nav ul li { list-style: none; margin:0; padding: 0;
}
</html>
```

Using Shadows Only on the Sides of a Wrapper

For this technique, the wrapper must touch the top of the browser window. If possible, try to make the bottom of the wrapper touch the bottom of the browser window.

Figure 8-23 shows a page with side shadows.

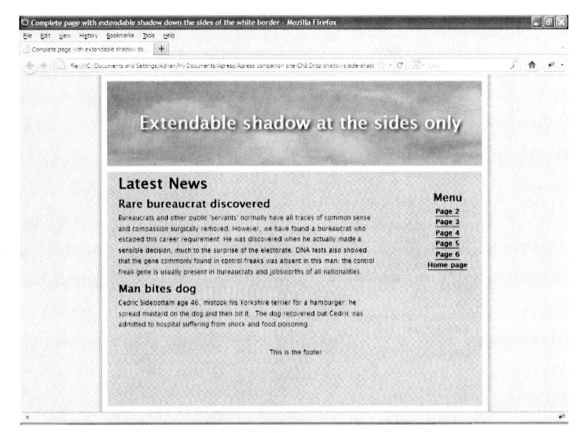

Figure 8-23. *A shadow added only to the sides of a web page*

In Listing 8-23a, the top and bottom shadow locations are omitted and the wrapper is moved to the top of the page by means of the top margin in the CSS sheet. In Listing 8-23b, the CSS targets the wrapper to place the side shadows as a vertically repeated tile.

Listing 8-23a. Adding a Shadow Only to the Sides of a Web Page (side-shadow-fullpage-extendable.html)

```
<!doctype html>
<html lang=en>
<head>
<title>Complete page with extendable shadow down the sides of the white border</title>
<meta charset=utf-8>
<link rel="stylesheet" type="text/css" href="side-shadow-fullpage-extendable.css">
        <!--Add conditional Javascript-->
        <!--[if lte IE 8]><script src="html5.js">
        </script>
        <![endif]-->
</head>
<body>
<div id="wrapper">
```

```
<header><h1>Extendable shadow at the sides only</h1></header><!-- close banner-->
<div id="mainContent">
<div id="leftcol"><h2>Latest News</h2>
<h3>Rare bureaucrat discovered</h3>
<p>Bureaucrats and other public &#39;servants&#39;
        some text has been omitted to save space
 usually present in bureaucrats and jobsworths of all nationalities.</p>
<h3>Man bites dog</h3>
<p>Cedric Sidebottam age 46, mistook his Yorkshire terrier for a hamburger; he
spread mustard on the dog and then bit it.  The dog recovered but Cedric
was admitted to hospital suffering from shock and food poisoning.</p>
<p> </p>
</div><!-- close leftcol-->
<nav><br>
   <ul><h3>Menu</h3>
        <li><a href="#">Page 2</a></li>
        <li><a href="#">Page 3</a></li>
        <li><a href="#">Page 4</a></li>
        <li><a href="#">Page 5</a></li>
        <li><a href="#">Page 6</a></li>
        <li><a href="#">Home page</a></li>
   </ul><!-- close links-->
</nav><!-- close menupanel-->
<footer>This is the footer</footer><!-- close footer -->
</div><!-- close mainContent -->
<br class="clear">
</div><!-- close wrapper -->
</div>
</body>
</html>
```

Listing 8-23b. The CSS Style Sheet for Listing 8-23a (side-shadow-fullpage-extendable.css)

```
/*This css template is adapted from a template created by Andy Budd (www.andybudd.com) ↵
for the book"Blog Design Solutions", and is released under a Creative Commons Licence*/
body { margin: 0; padding: 0; text-align: center; background: #e6e6e6; ↵
font: 76%/1.6 "Lucida Grande", Geneva, Verdana, sans-serif;
}
/*add display attributes for the semantic tags*/
header, footer, section, article, nav { display:block;
}
#wrapper{ margin: 0 auto -20px auto; padding: 0 10px; width: 720px; clear:both;
}
/*apply drop shadows to sides*/
#wrapper { background: url(images/middle.png) repeat-y;
}
header { width: 700px; height: 154px; margin: 0; margin-left:10px; ↵
background: url(images/bluepan.jpg); border-top:10px white solid;
}
#leftcol { margin: 0 10px; display:inline; /* fix IE double margin float bug */↵
                float: left; width: 500px; text-align:left;
}
```

```
#mainContent {margin:0; width: 700px; float: left; background-color:#aac9f6; ⏎
border:10px white solid; min-height:425px;
}
nav { width: 140px; margin-right:10px; padding: 0 5px 5px 0; float: right;
}
footer { margin:0; text-align:center; clear: both; background-color:#aac9f6;
}
br.clear { clear:both;
}
a { font-weight: bold; color: navy; text-decoration: none; border-bottom: 1px solid navy;
}
a:hover {color:#906; border-bottom: 1px solid #906;
}
header h1 { color: #fff; padding: 50px 0 0 20px; margin: 0; font-size: 2.6em; ⏎
            text-shadow: 0.1em 0.1em 0.2em black;
}
h2, h3, h4 { margin-top: 0; color: navy; font-weight: bold;
}
h2 { font-size: 2.2em; margin-bottom:0;
}
h3, nav h2 { font-size: 1.6em; margin-bottom:0;
}
p { margin-top:0; margin-bottom:6px;
}
#mainContent p, #mainContent h2, #mainContent h3, #mainContent h4, #mainContent ul, ⏎
#mainContent ol {margin-left: 10px; margin-right: 10px
}
nav ul li { list-style: none; margin:0; padding: 0;
}
```

Using the Shape Collage Software

This software can produce good borders and shadows, as shown in Figure 8-24.

Figure 8-24. A drop shadow and white border created in Shape Collage

A free trial version of Shape Collage can be downloaded from *http://*www.shapecollage.com. It can produce the drop shadow with or without a white frame, as shown in Figure 8-25 on the left.

If, after exploring it, you think it might be useful, you can buy it for about $29 (£26 UK), and then you will be able to produce images without the watermark, as well as unlocking several extra features. The program can also create collages, as its name implies.

I found Shape Collage tricky to use at first. The following are basic guidelines for testing the free trial version.

1. Before opening Shape Collage, write down the following information:

   • The size of the image requiring a drop shadow.

   • The location of the image on your hard drive.

   • The background color of the web page that you intend to place the finished image.

2. Open Shape Collage and then close the nag screen.

3. On the next panel, under Shape select Rectangle, set the collage size to about 50 percent wider than the image width and set the height to about 50 percent greater than the image height.

4. In the example shown, the image was 296 pixels wide and the height was 196 pixels. I set the collage size to 450 × 300.

5. Under Photo Size, click Manual, and set the actual image size to 296 pixels.

6. Under Photos, change the quantity to one.

7. Click the Appearance tab.

8. In the Background field, click the white field. You are presented with a color picker. Select the background color of your web page.

9. Select the Border color in the same way. Leave the default border width at 3.3 percent. Change it to zero if you do not want a frame around the picture.

10. Click the Advanced tab and choose Rotation as None and 0, 0.

11. For the Shadow offset, choose 1.

12. Click File ➤ Add File.

13. Navigate to the file's location and select it, then click OK.

14. You will be back at the main screen. At the bottom of the center panel, click the Create button.

15. On the next screen, you can choose a folder and you can name the file. You will be given a choice of three file formats .jpg, .png, or .psd (Photoshop file).

16. Click Save.

17. A small pop-up will appear asking what quality you want. The default is fine, so click Save.

Summary

In this chapter, you learned several ways of creating drop shadows to make your pictures and text blocks seem to float above the page. The chapter first described the new CSS3 box-shadow module and you learned how to apply CSS3 shadows to images and text. Then, because IE 7 and IE 8 do not support CSS3 box-shadows, it was suggested that a graphics package could be used to apply drop shadows. In particular, GIMP 2.6 was recommended as a free comprehensive program with an extremely simple drop shadow facility. An alternative method was then demonstrated; it used shadow background images for drop shadows that could be viewed in all modern browsers and in IE 8.

In the next chapter, you will learn several ways of creating collages and how to construct a picture gallery with captions.

CHAPTER 9

Create Collages and Galleries

Static collages and galleries are popular ways of displaying several images (in addition to the rollover gallery described in Chapter 2). Collages are more decorative and normally have no captions. Gallery images usually require captions; these can be added using CSS or by using the new HTML5 `<figure>` tag. However, this last method requires the use of some JavaScript to enable IE 7 and IE 8 to understand the `<figure>` tag.

Prior to the launch of CSS in 1998, groups of pictures were arranged in a table. This resulted in a great deal of HTML markup. Tables are now deprecated and CSS is used to easily create rows and columns of pictures with much less HTML markup. Web designers naturally tend to think immediately in terms of code or graphics software for creating a collage. Some low-tech methods are available and they can be useful on some occasions. The chapter begins with two of these alternative approaches.

Make a Paper-and-Paste Collage and Scan it

Some clients have presented me with a bunch of cuttings from their trade brochures and asked me to make a collage from them for their home page.

This can be rather messy as it involves paper, scissors, and paste. This method allows images to be arranged in interesting ways compared with other techniques that have rather rigid layouts.

When the messy bit is complete, the scissors-and-paste collage is then scanned and the resulting image saved in your web site folder. Use an image manipulation package to fill empty corner spaces with color to match the background color of your web page. Alternatively, you could save it as a `.gif` or a `.png` file with a transparent background.

Use a Word Processor

Clients sometimes design a collage on a word processor and then present me with the file. I could ask them for the original images and then create the collage from those, but they might be offended, as this implies that their handiwork is not good enough.

A word processor might seem to be an unlikely way of producing a collage; however, the process is easy if you are familiar with inserting images and arranging them on a page. Avoid using a table if you can; but if you should use a table, select None in the Borders and Shading options.

Figure 9-1 illustrates the fact that collages created using a word processor need not be confined to a rectangle. The church photographs used in this chapter are by kind permission of William Llewellyn.

Figure 9-1. A collage created using MS Word

The word processor method is as follows:

1. Insert the images into a word processor document and arrange them into a collage.

2. Select the **group** of pictures using Shift+Click.

3. Copy and paste the group into Microsoft Paint or some other paint program.

4. Save the group as a .tif file and edit it as necessary.

5. Export it as a compressed .jpg file or a .png file.

This works best on a white background. If placed on a solid color background, the rectangular spaces forming the four corners of the collage in Figure 9-1 must be filled with the background color before it is inserted into a web page.

You can download an MS Word collage template, but I personally find these templates a little too restrictive. Try the templates at http://www.microsoft.com/canada/home/memories-and-crafts/articles /create-a-digital-photo-collage.aspx.

Use CSS to Position Separate Images on a Page

A collage can be constructed using HTML and CSS to position the images (see Figure 9-2).

Figure 9-2. A collage with small gaps between the images

Most collage software will only produce a rectangular collage. To produce a layout like Figure 9-2, the best method is to use CSS2 and some <div>s (see Listings 9-2a and 9-2b). This project has small gaps and some owners prefer this as each image is then clearly defined.

Listing 9-2a. Creating a Collage with Default Gaps Between the Images (collage-churches-gaps.html)

```
<!doctype html>
<html lang=en>
<head>
<title>Collage of five churches-with gaps</title>
<meta charset=utf-8>
        meta details go here
<link rel="stylesheet" type="text/css" href="churches-style1.css">
</head>
<body>
<div id="container">
 <div id="collage">
    <img title="Church 1" src="images/church1.jpg" alt="Church 1" width="220" height="165">
    <img title="Church 2" src="images/church2.jpg" alt="Church 2" width="158" height="182">
    <img title="Church 3" src="images/church3.jpg" alt="Church 3" width="220" height="172">
    <br>
    <img title="Church 4" src="images/church4.jpg" alt="Church 4" width="213" height="170">
    <img title="Church 5" src="images/church5.jpg" alt="Church 5" width="220" height="170">
</div>
</div>
</body>
</html>
```

The images line up well and consistently in all the main browsers except Opera; the bottom row of images overlaps the top row in Opera by about three pixels. Note the line break <br>; it is inserted to push two of the images down to create a second row of images.

Listing 9-2b. The CSS Style Sheet for Listing 9-2a (collage-churches-gaps.html)

```
body { width:960px; min-width:780px; margin:auto;
}
img { border:0; margin:0; padding:0;
}
#container { text-align:center; margin:10px auto 0 auto;
}
#collage { margin:0 auto 0 auto; text-align:center;
}
```

Eliminate the Gaps

Despite there being no border or margins, a two-pixel gap is apparent between each image in Figure 9-2. Some clients prefer this, but what about the client who wants the images to butt up against one another? Using negative margins the gaps close up nicely in IE 6, IE 7, and IE 8, and in all other browsers except Opera. The next project, Listing 9-3, demonstrates the use of negative margins as a way of positioning the images accurately, and so eliminating the gaps.

Figure 9-3 shows the same collage with the gaps closed by using CSS markup.

Figure 9-3. Using negative margins eliminates the gaps between the images

This links to a different style sheet (churches-style2.css), which contains the negative margins that close the gaps (shown in bold). The markup also contains an IE conditional (see Listing 9-3a).

Listing 9-3a. Eliminating the Gaps by Using Negative Margins (collage-churches.html)

```
<!doctype html>
<html lang=en>
<head>
<title>Collage of five churches-with no gaps</title>
<meta charset=utf-8>
        meta details go here
<link rel="stylesheet" type="text/css" href="churches-style2.css">
        <!--[if IE]>
        <link rel="stylesheet" type="text/css" href="collage-ie.css">
        <![endif]-->
</head>
<body>
<div id="container">
 <div id="collage">
    <img title="Church 1" src="images/church1.jpg" alt="Church 1" width="220" height="165">
    <img title="Church 2" src="images/church2.jpg" alt="Church 2" width="158" height="182">
    <img title="Church 3" src="images/church3.jpg" alt="Church 3" width="220" height="172">
<br>
    <img title="Church 4" src="images/church4.jpg" alt="Church 4" width="213" height="170">
    <img title="Church 5" src="images/church5.jpg" alt="Church 5" width="220" height="170">
</div>
</div>
</body>
</html>
```

Listing 9-3b. The Style Sheet for Listing 9-3a (churches-style2.css)

```
/*position body and table at horizontal centre of screen*/
body {width:960px; font-family:"times new roman"; font-size:medium; ↵
color:navy; margin:auto; min-width:780px;
}

img { border:0; margin:0; padding:0;
}

#container { text-align:center; margin:10px auto 0 auto;
}

#collage { margin:0 auto 0 auto; text-align:center;
}

#collage img { margin-top: -3px; margin-bottom:-2px; margin-left:-2px; ↵
margin-right:-2px;
}
```

In IE 6, IE 7, and IE 8, the bottom row of images now overlaps the top row by one pixel, hence the IE conditional in the head of the HTML5 markup. The conditional style sheet for IE would be collage-ie.css, and it contains just one line, as follows:

```
#collage img { margin:-2px; }
```

231

IE 6, IE 7, IE 8, Mozilla Firefox, Safari, and Chrome now butt together without overlap. In Opera, the bottom row overlaps the top row by three pixels. Because Opera has a very small share of the browser market, this solution is a reasonable compromise.

Merged Images

A client might ask me to blur the edges of the individual images to produce a collage with pictures that merge into one another. I feel that this gives an overall muddled appearance, but the customer is always right. Spending hours feathering the edges and trying to overlap them is not my idea of fun, especially as the end result may disappoint the client. If the client insists on merged images, there are three solutions:

1. If the client wishes to use a merged collage from her sales brochure, scan the brochure image and use that on the web page.

2. Use paper and paste, and then scan the result. This never looks very professional, however; examples are shown in Figures 9-4 and 9-5.

3. Use proprietary software.

Figure 9-4. Cut out the images larger than the final image should be. Lay them out roughly in position.

Where the edges overlap, cut the edge of one of the images into curved shapes or make a saw tooth edge, as shown in Figure 9-4. Paste all the images together and scan the assembled collage. Then, using the clone brush (or the blur tool) in a paint program, soften the edges of the saw teeth or the curves.
The end result should look something like Figure 9-5.

Figure 9-5. Merged images using paper, paste, and scanning

Figure 9-5 is a poor example because of the complicated images and garish colors. Merged images will not be so messy if you use less-cluttered photographs and choose images with pastel colors.

Using Proprietary Software

Some paint/photo manipulation programs allow several images to be combined into one large image; however, I find the process more time-consuming and restrictive than the MS Word method or the CSS method.

The programs that I cover in this section are not intuitive, so be prepared to spend some time exploring them. All the programs produce a rectangular collage. If you require a non-rectangular image like Figures 9-3, 9-4, and 9-5, use the MS Word method or the CSS method, and abandon all hope of blurring the abutting areas.

Microsoft AutoCollage

The Microsoft AutoCollage program produces merged collages like the one shown in Figure 9-6. For Windows XP, Vista, and Windows 7, the 30-day free-trial version is useful but it is watermarked. It costs $20 (UK £18).

Figure 9-6. *A collage using Microsoft AutoCollage*

The program is good for collage-style banner headings, but the software has the following two drawbacks:

1. The minimum number of pictures used in a collage is seven. This might be acceptable for a printed collage, but on a computer screen, more than six pictures look like an explosion in a vegetable store.

2. Positioning the pictures involves a fair amount of trial and error.

To download Microsoft AutoCollage, go to http://explore.live.com/windows-live-photo-gallery. Select a language, and then click the Download Now button. Double-click the downloaded file wlsetup-web.exe to install the program. Open the program and find the item labeled Extras on the right of the menu bar. Click the little down arrow and select AutoCollage 2008. A web page will open; click Download Now. On the left-hand panel, click Download 30 Day Trial. A video on the home page explains how to use the software, but the commentary is not very distinct.

▪ **Tip** Before using any of these programs or projects, prepare by placing copies of the images in a new folder so that you can locate them easily.

Shape Collage

The free-trial version of Shape Collage has limitations, but you might wish to investigate it. If you master the trial version and find it useful, the full version is available for a reasonable price. The web site is at http://www.shapecollage.com.

▦ **Tip** The free-trial version of Shape Collage is heavily watermarked. At the time of writing, the non-watermarked, Pro version costs about $75. Shape Collage is also available for iPhone and iPad.

Picasa 3.0

Picasa 3.0 is free software that produces various collage formats; but it does not support merged pictures like that shown in Figure 9-6. The program's toolbar is unusual because it sits at the bottom of the screen. On the toolbar, you find the collage icon.

The big mystery with Picasa is how to save the finished collage. Strangely, you don't have to save the image. When you click Create Collage, it automatically saves it in the Picasa Projects folder. Picasa 3.0 only produces collages for an even number of photos, and the finished collage is always a rectangle.

Other Resources

The following programs offer similar capabilities:

- Photovisi (http://www.photovisi.com): Free. Some color changes can occur when using this program.

- Smilebox (http://smilebox.com): Free. Mute your speakers before accessing this to avoid the disco-style cacophony.

- iFoxSoft Photo Collage http://www.ifoxsoft.com): Free trial, then $26 (£23.50 UK).

- PhotoMix (http://www.photomix.com): Free trial, then $29 (£26 UK).

- Picture Collage Maker (http://www.picturecollagesoftware.com): Free trial, then $30 (£27 UK).

Using a Graphics Program to Create a Collage

Most graphics packages can create a collage, but the instructions can be hard to find and the process can sometimes take longer than using HTML5 or CSS (such as Listings 9-3a and b). However, more subtle effects can often be achieved by using a graphics package; images can be moved behind or in front of other images, allowing overlaps. Also, by making each layer less opaque, the overlapping images can blend into each other and each image can have blurred edges to enhance the blending. The next project tells you how to make basic collage with GIMP, a free graphics program. The finished result is shown in Figure 9-7.

Figure 9-7. *A collage created with GIMP*

Creating a Collage with GIMP

For this project, prepare the pictures and put them in a new folder so that you can get at them easily. For Figure 9-7, the five pictures were resized so that they were all 200 pixels wide. The three pictures in the top row would give a horizontal total of 600 pixels. Therefore, the collage needed a background layer at least 600 pixels wide (3 × 200) and about 400 high (2 × 200). Note that in GIMP, the "word dialogue" is spelled the European way. The stages are as follows:

1. Open GIMP and click Windows ➤ Dockable Dialogues ➤ Layers. This puts the Layers Dialogue panel on the screen. Click File ➤ New.

2. On the next dialogue click the Landscape icon and select 640 pixels wide × 400 pixels high, and then click OK. On the Toolbox panel, click the crossed, double-headed arrows to select Move.

3. On the menu, click File ➤ Open ➤ Open as New Layers. Navigate to the folder and select the images by holding down Ctrl while you click them all. Then click the Open button to automatically copy them all to new layers.

4. You will now see the layers listed in the Layers Dialogue panel. The first image will be visible in the Image Window. You will be able to move the image to the left and top of the pane. Click the next layer in the Layers dialogue. A dotted box will appear on top of the first image. Slide the dotted rectangle to the right and you will see the next image appear.

5. Click the next layer in the Layers Dialogue and move the resulting dotted rectangle away from the previous image. You will now have three visible images in the top row. Repeat this for the remaining two images and move them into position below the top row.

6. From now on, to slide an image around, first you need to click its layer in the Layers Dialogue panel. You will be able to slide them and choose whether to overlap them or keep them adjacent to each other. If they overlap and you wish to switch the overlapped image so that it lies above the other image, click the image's layer in the Layers Dialogue. In the Layers Dialogue, click the green up arrow (or the green down arrow if you wish to move it underneath another image).

7. You are now ready to save the collage. Click File ➤ Save As In the Save As dialogue panel, enter a file name at the very top of the panel. Be sure to give it a suffix such as .png.

8. Navigate to the folder where you want the collage to be stored, and then click the Save button. An Export dialogue box will appear; ensure that the Merge Visible Layers radio button is selected. Click the Export button.

9. On the next PNG dialogue box, accept the default settings and click Save.

▓ **Tip** You can download GIMP and its illustrated manual at www.gimp.org/downloads/. I also recommend reading the book *Beginning GIMP: From Novice to Professional* by Akkana Peck (Apress, 2008).

A Picture Gallery with Captions

Captions can greatly enhance a gallery of pictures; the added text can provide useful information about the picture and provide a more interesting web page. Figure 9-8 shows a page set out as a gallery. Each picture has a caption. Although the captions are minimal and not very informative, they serve to demonstrate the technique.

Figure 9-8. A gallery of pictures using CSS2 to attach captions to pictures

My thanks go to portrait artist Ann Roe Jones, who kindly gave me permission to use the photographs of her impressive portraits, as well as part of a web page that I designed for her. Visit her web site at http://www.annroejones-artist.co.uk.

Chapter 1 described how HTML5 allows pictures to have captions that cling to the pictures no matter where they are moved. This can also be achieved using CSS2 in an HTML5 page with no semantic tags, as demonstrated in this next project. This means that users of IE 7 and IE 8 can view the gallery, and web designers do not have to insert the Remy Sharp JavaScript snippet into the code, as demonstrated in Listing 9-8a.

■ **Tip** At this point, the HTML5 purist will be gasping in horror. Fear not. I present a purely HTML5 version in Listing 9-8c. The appearance of the collage is identical whether using Listings 9-8a and 9-8b or Listings 9-8c and 9-8d.

Listing 9-8a. Displaying a Gallery of Images with Captions (portraits.html)

```
<!doctype html>
<html lang=en>
<head>
<title>Gallery pictures with attached captions</title>
<meta charset=utf-8>
        meta details go here
<head>
<link rel="stylesheet" type="text/css" href="portraits.css" />
</head>
<body>
<div id="hdr">
  <h1>Ann L Roe <span class="swac"> SWAc</span></h1>
</div>
<div id="leftcol"><!--start of left column-->
  <ul id="menu">
    <li class="btn"><a title="Portrait Paintings" href="portraits.html">Portraits</a></li>
    <li class="btn"><a title="Commissions" href="commissions.html" >Commissions</a></li>
    <li class="btn"><a title="Prints" href="prints.html">Prints</a></li>
    <li class="btn"><a title="Latest" href="latest.html">Latest News</a></li>
    <li class="btn"><a title="About Ann" href="about.html">About Ann</a></li>
    <li class="btn"><a title="Return to Home Page" href="index.html">Home Page</a></li>
  </ul>
</div>
<div id="midcol-portraits">
        <h3><b>SOME PORTRAITS BY ANN ROE (JONES) SWAc</b></h3>
<div id="gallery">
  <div class="figure">
    <img alt="Professor Clemments OBE" height="307" src="images/prof-h307.jpg" width="224">
    <p>Professor Robert Clements OBE</p>
  </div>
  <div class="figure">
    <img title="Dr Alan Cotton" src="images/doctor.jpg" alt="Dr Alan Cotton" ↵
    width="250" height="307">
    <p>Dr Alan Cotton</p>
  </div>
  <div class="figure">
   <img title="Reuben" src="images/reuben225.jpg" alt="Reuben" width="225" height="308">
   <p>Reuben</p>
  </div><p> </p>
  <div class="figure">
   <img alt="Xanthe Mosely" height="300" src="images/xanthe.jpg" width="222">
   <p>Xanthe Mosely</p>
  </div>
```

```
     <div class="figure">
      <img alt="Megan" height="300" src="images/megan.jpg" width="213">
      <p>Megan</p>
     </div>
<div id="aside"><p > </p>
<p ><b>All of Ann&#39;s portraits are painted <br />in oils on canvas.</b></p>
<p >For information on commissioning a portrait, click the &#39;Commissions↵
&#39; button </p>
<p >Click the &#39;Contact Ann&#39; button to request more detailed information.</p>
</div>
</div><br><br>
<div id="ftr"><br>
     Footer goes here
</div>
</div>
</body>
</html>
```

Listing 9-8b. *The CSS Style Sheet for Listing 9-8a (portraits.css)*

```
body { min-width:980px; font-family:"times new roman"; font-size:medium; ↵
color:black; margin:auto; max-width:1000px;
}
#hdr { width:100%; margin:auto; height:60px; text-align:center;
}
/* use display:inline to remove IE6 double margin bug from side menu*/
#leftcol { float:left; margin-left:0; width :135px; display:inline; padding:0; zoom:1;
}
img { border:none;
}
#midcol-portraits {margin-left:175px; margin-right:15px; zoom:1;
}
div .figure { float:left; margin-right:5px; display:inline;
}
.figure p { font-size:80%; height: 15px; margin:0 auto 0 auto; text-align:center; ↵
width:200px;
}
#gallery img { margin-right:20px; margin-top:5px;
}
#aside { float:left; width:260px;
}
#ftr {clear:both; text-align:center;
}
/* set side menu position */
ul#menu { float:left; margin-left:0; width:120px;
}
/* set general side button styles */
li.btn { margin-bottom: 4px; text-align: center; list-style:none;
}
/* set general anchor styles */
li.btn a { display: block; color: white; background:#D20B0D; font-weight: bold; ↵
text-decoration: none
}
```

240

```
/* specify state styles */
/* mouseout (default) */
li.btn a { background: #D20B0D;  border: 4px outset #FFAAAA;
}
/* mouseover */
li.btn a:hover  { background: maroon;   border: 4px outset maroon;
}
/* onmousedown */
li.btn a:active { background:#AECBFF;  border: 4px inset #AECBFF;
}
h1 {font-size:300%; font-weight:bold; color:#D20B0D; margin-top:0; margin-bottom:0; ↵
font-family:"Calligraph421 BT"; font-style:italic; text-align:center;
}
span.swac {font-size:x-large; font-weight:bold; color:#D20B0D; font-style:italic; ↵
text-align:center;
}
h3,h4 { margin-top:0; margin-bottom:0;
}
h2 {font-size:x-large; font-weight:bold; margin-top:0; margin-bottom:0;
}
```

For HTML5 Purists

Now for the pure HTML5. Listing 9-8c uses semantic tags and a JavaScript snippet that allows users of IE 8 to view the page. The HTML5 captions are included; these use the tags <figure> and <figcaption>.

Listing 9-8c. Display a Gallery of Images with Captions Using HTML5 Tags (portraits-html5-captions)

```
<!doctype html>
<html lang=en>
<head>
<title>Gallery pictures with HTML5 attached captions</title>
<meta charset=utf-8>
        meta details go here
<link rel="stylesheet" type="text/css" href="portraits-html5-captions.css">
        <!--Add conditional Javascript-->
        <!--[if lte IE 8]><script src="html5.js">
        </script>
        <![endif]-->
</head>
<body>
<div id="wrapper">
<header>
  <h1>Ann L Roe <span class="swac"> SWAc</span></h1>
</header>
<!--start of left column-->
<nav>
  <ul>
        <li><a title="Portrait Paintings" href="portraits.html">Portraits</a></li>
        <li><a title="Commissions" href="commissions.html" >Commissions</a></li>
        <li><a title="Prints" href="prints.html">Prints</a></li>
        <li><a title="Latest" href="latest.html">Latest News</a></li>
        <li><a title="About Ann" href="about.html">About Ann</a></li>
        <li><a title="Return to Home Page" href="index.html">Home Page</a></li>
```

```
            </ul>
        </nav>
        <div id="midcol-portraits">
                <h3><b>SOME PORTRAITS BY ANN ROE (JONES) SWAc</b></h3>
        <div id="gallery">
                <div class="figure">
                <figure>
                <img alt="Professor Clemments OBE" height="307" src="images/prof-h307.jpg" ↵
                width="224">
                <figcaption><br><p>Professor Robert Clements OBE</p></figcaption>
                </figure>
                </div>
                <div class="figure">
                <figure>
                <img title="Dr Alan Cotton" src="images/doctor.jpg" alt="Dr Alan Cotton" ↵
                width="250" height="307">
                <figcaption><br><p>Dr Alan Cotton</p></figcaption>
                </figure>
                </div>
                <div class="figure">
                <figure>
                <img title="Reuben" src="images/reuben225.jpg" alt="Reuben" width="225" height="308">
                <figcaption><br><p>Reuben</p></figcaption>
                </figure>
                </div>
                        <p> </p>
                <div class="figure">
                <figure>
                <img alt="Xanthe Mosely" height="300" src="images/xanthe.jpg" width="222">
                <figcaption><br><p>Xanthe Mosely</p></figcaption>
                </figure>
                </div>
                <div class="figure">
                <figure>
                <img alt="Megan" height="300" src="images/megan.jpg" width="213">
                <figcaption><br><p>Megan</p></figcaption>
                </figure>
                </div>
        <aside>
                <p> </p>
                <p><b>All of Ann&#39;s portraits are painted <br>in oils on canvas.</b></p>
                <p>For information on commissioning a portrait, click the &#39; ↵
                Commissions&#39; button </p>
                <p>Click the &#39;Contact Ann&#39; button to request more detailed information.</p>
        </aside>
        </div>
        </div><br><br>
        <footer><br>Footer goes here
        </footer>
        </div>
        </body>
        </html>
```

Listing 9-8d shows the CSS for the HTML5 gallery.

Listing 9-8d. *The CSS Style Sheet for Listing 9-8c (portraits-css3-captions)*

```
/*set attributes for consistent appearance in all browsers*/
p, ul, li, h1, h2 { margin:0; padding:0;
}
img { border:0;
}
/*add display attributes for the semantic tags*/
header, footer, section, article, nav { display:block;
}
#wrapper{min-width:980px; font-family:"times new roman"; font-size:medium; color:black; ⏎
margin:auto; max-width:1000px;
}
header {width:100%; margin:auto; height:60px; text-align:center;
}
#midcol-portraits {margin-left:165px; margin-right:15px; zoom:1;
}
div .figure { float:left; margin-right:5px; display:inline;
}
.figure p { font-size:80%; height: 15px; margin:0 auto 0 auto; text-align:center; width:200px;
}
#gallery img { margin-right:20px; margin-top:5px;
}
aside { float:left; width:260px;
}
footer {clear:both; text-align:center;}
/* set side menu position */
nav {float:left; margin-left:0; width :135px; padding:0; zoom:1;}
/* set general side button styles */
nav ul li{ margin-bottom: 4px; text-align: center; list-style:none;  }
/* set general anchor styles */
nav ul li a { color: white; background:#D20B0D; font-weight: bold; text-decoration: none }
/* specify state styles */
/* mouseout (default) */
nav li a { background: #D20B0D;  border: 4px outset #FFAAAA; display:block; }
/* mouseover */
nav li a:hover  { background: maroon;    border: 4px outset maroon;}
/* onmousedown */
nav li a:active { background:#AECBFF;  border: 4px inset #AECBFF }
h1 {font-size:300%; font-weight:bold; color:#D20B0D; margin-top:0; margin-bottom:0; ⏎
font-family:"Calligraph421 BT"; font-style:italic; text-align:center;
}
span.swac {font-size:x-large; font-weight:bold; color:#D20B0D; ⏎
font-family:"Calligraph421 BT"; font-style:italic; text-align:center;
}
h3,h4 { margin-top:0; margin-bottom:0;}
h2 {font-size:x-large; font-weight:bold; margin-top:0; margin-bottom:0;}
```

Summary

In this chapter, you discovered several ways of creating collages and two methods of producing a picture gallery with captions. You might like to explore the possibility of adding drop shadows to the gallery images, a technique you learned in Chapter 8. Or perhaps you might try experimenting with the rollover gallery of images described in Chapter 2. You now have several ways of presenting a collection of images.
In the next chapter, you will learn how to add the PayPal payment system to a web site.

CHAPTER 10

Add PayPal

The PayPal system of payment for goods and services is extremely popular, very secure, and trusted by most users. Since PayPal added the ability to use credit/debit cards, the service has boomed and it is now one of the most accepted methods of sending and receiving payments, subscriptions, or donations.

The PayPal payment system can be easily integrated into web pages so that people can pay for goods and services offered on commercial web sites. At first you may feel nervous about setting up a PayPal account because you are dealing with money, and in particular you may be dealing with your client's money. However, PayPal has made the process such that you can easily backtrack or even cancel and start again. Almost everything you enter into the PayPal forms can be changed later.

How Does PayPal Work?

Is PayPal a bank? Although PayPal is not a traditional bank, it is an internet bank. In fact, it is a bank that only operates online; it has no branches. Having no branch premises or branch staff, PayPal can offer a very economical cash-handling service to web site owners and web site users. PayPal even handles currency conversion, which can be very helpful when dealing with international commerce. Also, with PayPal, a merchant can accept many forms of payment, including all the major credit cards.

PayPal makes a small charge for every transaction. This applies only to the web owner, not to customers. A typical charge at the time of writing was $0.32 (£0.20 in the United Kingdom), plus 3 percent of the transaction cost. For instance, if you sell something for $16 (£10), the total charge might be $0.80 (£0.50). These costs may be out-of-date now, but they do indicate that PayPal's fees are very affordable. Also, fees vary depending on the country, the type of account, and the transaction; in the United States, this ranges from 1.9 percent to 2.9 percent of the total, plus $0.30.

A fee is charged for currency conversion. It ranges from 3.4 percent of the monthly sales for a small amount to 1.4 percent for amounts over $93,000 (£55,000).

PayPal deducts a very small fee for transferring money from your PayPal account to your personal bank account.

OK, PayPal is virtually free, so how does it survive? Two hundred and twenty million PayPal account owners have money deposited in PayPal accounts. The money is mostly deposited there by paying customers. This money earns interest for PayPal. Also, advertisers pay PayPal to send you an occasional advertisement.

To transfer money from your PayPal account into your personal bank account, you must access your PayPal account and instruct PayPal the amount of money to transfer (see the section "Managing a PayPal Account" near the end of this chapter).

> ⬛ **Caution** PayPal is very safe, but beware of emails purporting to come from PayPal. When PayPal sends you an email it states *your full name* and it will *never* ask for your PayPal personal details. Bogus PayPal e-mails are addressed to "Dear member" or "Dear PayPal member" and they are phishing for your account details. Forward bogus emails to `spoof@paypal.com` to help track down these criminals.

Setting up a PayPal Account

> ⬛ **Note** Because the interface and the set-up procedure can vary a little from country to country, this chapter only gives hints on what to look for and what to do on the PayPal sign-up forms. A little common sense will guide you safely through the sign-up and configuration steps once you know what to look for. Also, PayPal has a Help Center web site at `https://www.paypal.com/help`. The steps for setting up a business account and downloading payment buttons are described briefly at `https://www.paypal.com/webapps/mpp/merchant`. There you will find the five types of payment buttons available for download. The best starting point for UK readers is probably a PDF document at `https://www.paypal-business.co.uk/pdf/website-payments-standard.pdf`.

The procedure assumes that your client requires a business account. Make a careful note of all the details you enter, including the Merchant Account ID. File the details carefully so that you can always find them quickly and easily. The initial step consists of setting up a PayPal account for the web site owner. This section will guide you through this process.

1. US readers should go to `https://www.paypal.com/webapps/mpp/merchant`.

2. UK readers should access `www.paypal.co.uk/uk` and click the Sign Up button. On the home page choose PayPal for Your Business and click the Get Started button.

3. US readers should then click the Get Started button. On the next screen you are offered upgrades; either select an upgrade or click the No Thanks button.

4. On the next screen, US readers see an explanation of the next three steps. Click the Create New Account button.

5. On the next screen, both US and UK readers can sign up for a business account. Click the Get Started button.

6. After clicking the appropriate Get Started button in the sign-up screen, you come to another sign-up screen, that shows the three steps once more. Here you choose the country and the language from the drop-down menu, and then click the Create New Account button. Use the drop-down list to select a Business Type. During the next three steps, you add your client's preliminary information for setting up an account and confirm your client's email address. PayPal will send your client an email containing simple instructions.

7. On the next screen you will find a drop-down menu where you must choose a Payment Solution. No advice is provided by PayPal, but the choices are explained at the

HomeBusinessWiz.com web site at http://www.homebusinesswiz.com/2010/04/paypal-business-accounts-standard-or-pro.html

The web site recommends that you choose Website Payments Standard. With this type of Payment Solution, customers can pay by PayPal or debit/credit card. When customers pay, they come to the PayPal-hosted payment page. The Standard payment scheme is free but the Pro scheme has a monthly fee. After choosing your payment solution, click Continue.

8. Fill out the next form and click Continue. Provide the next items of required information to complete the sign up. You will receive an email giving final instructions. You will then have a PayPal account.

9. To link to your bank account, access your PayPal account and set up your personal banking information. As a method of account verification, PayPal will place a small amount of money into your bank account, and then ask you to verify that the money was deposited.

Now that the account is set up, the next step is to log in to the account and tweak your client's PayPal profile to reflect the client's preferences.

Adjust Your Client's Account Details Using Profile

Profile is where you fine-tune the client's personal and payment details. The PayPal account has a default profile set up. You will probably need to tweak this. For instance, you may wish to add VAT/sales tax details. To amend your profile, access the PayPal home page and log in to your account or your client's account.

1. Just below the row of blue tabs, find Profile and click it.

2. With US accounts, click Profile and then find Sales Tax and click the Update link on the far right of the screen. The sales tax options allow you to create sales taxes by state as well as for international transactions by country. Click Add New Sales Tax, select the territory, and enter the percentage for the sales tax. Use the International Sales tax option for the United States, and enter the zip code and select the state. If the postage is also subject to sales tax, tick the box labeled Apply Rate to Postage Amount.

3. In the UK, look for VAT, and click the Update link on the far right of the screen. In the next screen, enter the percentage for the VAT. If the postage is also subject to VAT, tick the box labeled Apply Rate to Postage Amount.

4. Click the yellow Continue button and log out.

Now that you have an account and set the client's Profile preferences, you can select and download secure payment buttons.

Download Encrypted PayPal Buttons

At one time, rogue buyers could hack into the PayPal payment button code and enter reduced prices. PayPal provided an encryption method, but it was very complex and impossible to edit. Now PayPal has an encrypting process for buttons that is very straightforward and easily edited by the account holder. The code for buttons is now hosted safely on the PayPal site instead of on the web page. The prices are no longer accessible to hackers. If your web site has the old, vulnerable buttons, they will need to be re-created.

PayPal provides two methods of downloading hosted secure buttons:

- New buttons for a new web site page.

- Adding new buttons to a web page that has one or more buttons already saved and hosted.

Step 1: Accessing the PayPal Button Factory

To access the PayPal Button Factory, follow these steps:

1. Access `http://www.paypal.co.uk` (in the United Kingdom) or `www.paypal.com` (in the United States).

2. Log in to your PayPal account.

3. Click Profile in UK accounts. For USA accounts go to Merchant Services tab and My Saved Buttons.

4. Look for PayPal Buttons ➤ Manage My Payment Buttons. Click the relevant Update link on the far right.

5. On the next screen, click Create New Button in the Related Items box on the right.

6. On the next screen, choose a button type from the drop-down menu. As you choose a button, the image will appear in the box titled Your Customer's View. The buttons list includes Buy Now, Shopping Cart, Gift Vouchers, Donations, Subscription, Automatic Billing, and Installment Plan. If you click the item Which Button Shall I Choose, you will see an illustration of each one with an explanation of its purpose. Be sure to select Use My Secure Merchant Account ID under the heading Merchant Account IDs. This masks your client's email address to prevent spammers from finding it.

7. In the box labeled Customize Button, you will be able to modify the button or even add your own image.

8. Fill out the remaining details. When you are satisfied, click Create Button, and then you will be able to copy and paste the code into your web page.

If you are satisfied with the button, you can generate the HTML code for it by clicking Create Button at the bottom of the page.

Step 2: Tracking and Inventory, Profit, and Loss (Optional)

You will find this optional item near the bottom of the screen. It provides tracking and inventory options for a button. To use this feature, tick the box labeled Track Inventory, Profit and Loss.

- You now choose whether to track the stock level By Item or By Option. In both cases, you must enter the item ID that you entered previously.

- For Qty in Stock, enter the number of the items that you currently have in stock. If you select the option for a stock level under Alert Quantity, it will trigger an email from PayPal to inform you that your stock in that item is low.

You will be asked to specify whether or not to allow customers to purchase something that is out of stock. If you choose Yes, customers can purchase the out-of-stock item as usual. If you select No, they cannot purchase the item. You have the option to redirect customers to a web page that informs them that the item is out of stock; this occurs when a user clicks Continue Shopping.

On this screen, PayPal also offers a reporting system for tracking the profits and losses.

Step 3: Customize Advanced Features of the Button

In this step you can do the following:

- Allow your customers to add a message with the order.

- Allow you to acquire the customer's postal address.

- Set a web page for your customer to return to after completing or canceling the checkout procedure.

- Experienced designers can add other advanced variables to the button. The advanced variables offer many features that could be useful for more complex ordering processes, including passing information back to your web site if you wish to have a special post-sales page.

Copy and Save the Buttons

Once you have completed the previous steps, you can click Create Button at the bottom of the page.

The code appears in the next window. Click the Select Code button. Then use Ctrl+C to copy the code to memory. Alternatively, click the Go Back to Edit This Button link if you wish to make some changes.

■ **Caution** Paste the code for each button into a text editor such as NotePad. Save with easily recognizable names. This is a safety precaution in case you mess up the web page and have to start again. You won't want the hassle of downloading all the buttons again from scratch.

Embedding the PayPal Buttons in a Page

■ **Tip** I recommend that you first practice using the default buttons. Experiment with the more complex buttons as you become familiar with the PayPal interface. Remember that you can practice by creating buttons, embedding them, and then deleting them.

Embedding the PayPal buttons is just a matter of downloading the generated code from the PayPal web site and pasting it into your page.

1. Design your PayPal order page and save it. This will be a page based on the style of the other pages on your web site. Leave blank areas where you will eventually paste the PayPal buttons when you have downloaded them.

2. Load the page into your web design program in code view. Then copy and paste the button codes into the page code.

3. If you have Add to Cart buttons, you also need to download a View Cart button. Select its code and copy it to the web page HTML. You can do this after adding the first button on a page and it will work for all subsequently added buttons on that page. You only need one View Cart button on a page. The View Cart button may not be very obvious on the interface for your country; it may not be available from the main menu. In this case, to create a View Cart button, you go to the code page after clicking Create Button for the Shopping Cart button. You are offered the option to create a View Cart button (the second item below the code window).

Note The screenshot in Figure 10-1 was created offline; therefore, the PayPal buttons are not yet visible.

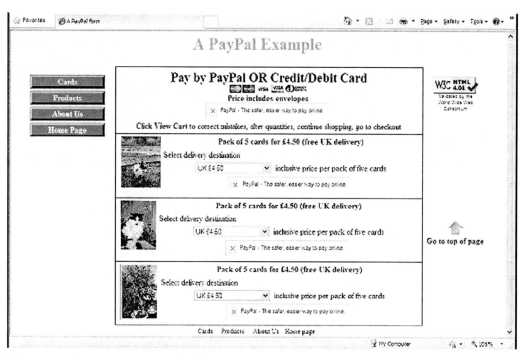

Figure 10-1. A page not connected to the internet

The PayPal buttons are not visible in Figure10-1 because these are loaded dynamically by PayPal. In a WYSIWYG program running offline, your page will appear like Figure 10-1. When you go online, the buttons appear, as shown in Figure 10-2.

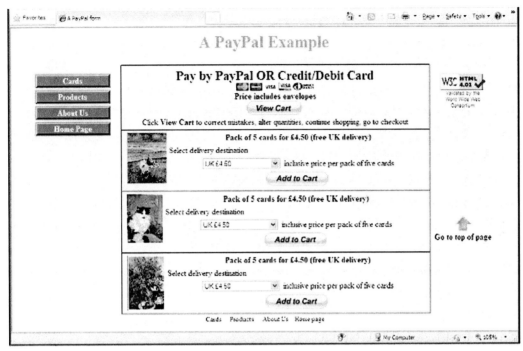

Figure 10-2. The page when connected to the internet. The buttons have been dynamically inserted by PayPal.

I am most grateful to the artist Ann Roe Jones for giving permission to use the pictures shown in Figures 10-1 and 10-2. The page can be seen on the web site that I designed and produced for her

(http://www.annroejones-artist.co.uk).

Note The blocks of PayPal code in this example were deliberately altered for security reasons. The downloaded PayPal code is shown in bold font.

Listing 10-1a creates the pages shown in Figures 10-1 and 10-2. This listing shows four PayPal buttons pasted into the page. They are indicated by bold type. The first button is the View Cart button and the next three are the Add to Cart buttons.

Listing 10-1a. Creating a Web Page with Encrypted PayPal Buttons (pay-cards.html)

```
<!doctype html>
<html lang=en>
<head>
<title>A PayPal payment page</title>
<meta charset=utf-8>
```

```
<link rel="stylesheet" type="text/css" href="pay-cards-html5.css">
        <!--conditional Javascript added for IE 7 and 8 users-->
        <!--[if lte IE 8]>
        <script src="html5.js">
        </script>
        <![endif]-->
        </head>
<body>
<div id="container">
<a id="top"></a>
  <h1>A PayPal Example</h1>
<nav><!--side menu column starts-->
   <ul>
        <li><a href="#" title="Greetings Cards">Cards</a></li>
        <li><a href="#" title="Products">Products</a></li>
        <li><a href="#" title="About Us">About Us</a></li>
        <li><a href="#" title="Return to Home Page">Home Page</a></li>
   </ul>
</nav><!--end of side menu column-->
<div id="rightcol"><!--Start of far right column-->
<p class="cntr"><br><img alt="" src="images/valid-html401.png" width="88" ↵
height="31"><br><span class="tiny">Validated by the<br>World Wide Web<br>↵
Consortium</span></p>
<p class="cntr redarrow"><a href="#top"><img  title="Go to top of page" ↵
src="images/upred.gif" alt="Go to top of page" width="33" height="30"></a><br>↵
<b>Go to top of page</b></p>
</div><!--end of right column-->
<div class="box"><!--CREATE FIRST BOX-->
<h2 class="cntr">Pay by PayPal OR Credit/Debit Card</h2>
<img src="images/debitcards.gif" alt="Cards" title="Cards" width="149" height="16"><br>
<h2>Price includes envelopes</h2>
<!--Embed the view cart button code-->
<form target="paypal" action="https://www.paypal.com/cgi-bin/webscr" method="post">
        <input type="hidden" name="cmd0" value="_s-xclick" />
        <input type="hidden" name="encrypted0" value="-----BEGIN PKCS7-----
        The downloaded View Cart button has an enormous amount of code, a large chunk
        has been left out here to save space.
PZVCt3PZQ5JXw1vUx5LOCiOTFThe5bZV9/drVWjIpZDFBsq5fVzaZURC3m6xpgA==-----END PKCS7-----">
<input type="image" src="https://www.paypal.com/en_GB/i/btn/btn_viewcart_LG.gif"
name="submit0" alt="PayPal - The safer, easier way to pay online.">
<img alt="" src="https://www.paypal.com/en_GB/i/scr/pixel.gif" width="1" height="1">
        <br>Click <b>View Cart</b> to correct mistakes, alter quantities, continue ↵
        shopping, go to checkout
</form>
</div>
<div class="box"><!--CREATE SECOND BOX-->
<img title="Beach" alt="Beach" height="95" src="images/beach2thumb.jpg" style="float: left; ↵
margin-left: 5px; margin-right: 5px" width="77"><b>Pack of 5 cards for &pound;4.50 ↵
(free UK delivery)</b>
<form target="paypal" action="https://www.paypal.com/cgi-bin/webscr" method="post">
<input type="hidden" name="cmd" value="_s-xclick">
<input type="hidden" name="hosted_button_id" value="10350939">
```

```
<p><input type="hidden" name="on0" value="Delivery Destination"></p>
<p class="lft">Select delivery destination</p>
<p><select name="os0">
        <option value="UK">UK &pound;4.50</option>
        <option value="Europe">Europe &pound;6.20</option>
        <option value="Outside Europe">Outside Europe &pound;7.20</option>
</select>  inclusive price per pack of five cards</p>
<input type="hidden" name="currency_code" value="GBP">
<input type="image" src="https://www.paypal.com/en_GB/i/btn/btn_cart_LG.gif" ↵
name="submit" alt="PayPal - The safer, easier way to pay online.">
<img alt="" src="https://www.paypal.com/en_GB/i/scr/pixel.gif" width="1" height="1">
</form>
</div>
<div class="box"><!--THIRD BOX-->
<img title="Sir Patrick Moore's cat" alt="Sir Patrick Moore's cat" height="91"
src="images/catthumb.jpg" style="float: left; margin-left: 5px; margin-right: 5px" ↵
width="69" /><b>Pack of 5 cards for &pound;4.50 (free UK delivery)</b>↵
<form target="paypal" action="https://www.paypal.com/cgi-bin/webscr" method="post">
<input type="hidden" name="cmd" value="_s-xclick">
<input type="hidden" name="hosted_button_id" value="10350961">
<p><input type="hidden" name="on0" value="Delivery Destination"></p>
<p class="lft">Select delivery destination</p><p>
<select name="os0">
        <option value="UK">UK &pound;4.50</option>
        <option value="Europe">Europe &pound;6.20</option>
        <option value="Outside Europe">Outside Europe &pound;7.20</option>
</select>  inclusive price per pack of five cards</p>
<input type="hidden" name="currency_code" value="GBP">
<input type="image" src="https://www.paypal.com/en_GB/i/btn/btn_cart_LG.gif" ↵
name="submit" alt="PayPal - The safer, easier way to pay online.">
<img alt="" src="https://www.paypal.com/en_GB/i/scr/pixel.gif" width="1" height="1">
</form>
</div>
<div class="box-bottom"><!--FOURTH BOX-->
<img title="Ferns and Flowers" alt="Ferns and Flowers" height="103" ↵
src="images/fernsthumb.jpg" style="float: left; margin-left: 5px; margin-right: 5px" ↵
width="73">
<b>Pack of 5 cards for &pound;4.50 (free UK delivery)</b> ↵
<form target="paypal" action="https://www.paypal.com/cgi-bin/webscr" method="post">
<input type="hidden" name="cmd" value="_s-xclick">
<input type="hidden" name="hosted_button_id" value="10351323">
<p class="lft"><input type="hidden" name="on0" value="Delivery Destination"></p>
<p class="lft">Select delivery destination</p>
<p><select name="os0">
        <option value="UK">UK &pound;4.50</option>
        <option value="Europe">Europe &pound;6.20</option>
        <option value="Outside Europe">Outside Europe &pound;7.20</option>
</select>  inclusive price per pack of five cards</p>
<input type="hidden" name="currency_code" value="GBP" />
```

```
<input type="image" src="https://www.paypal.com/en_GB/i/btn/btn_cart_LG.gif" ⏎
name="submit" alt="PayPal - The safer, easier way to pay online.">
<img alt="" src="https://www.paypal.com/en_GB/i/scr/pixel.gif" width="1" height="1">
</form>
</div>
</div>
<footer><p class="cntr">Footer goes here</p></footer>
</body>
</html>
```

▓ **Note** The PayPal code for each button usually contains the attribute border="0". This border is best removed by CSS markup; therefore, delete border attributes from the listing so that your page will validate.

This Listing 10-1b is the CSS style sheet for Listing 10-1a. It creates boxes for the images and the PayPal buttons without using deprecated tables.

Listing 10-1b. The CSS Style Sheet For Listing 10-1a (pay-cards.css)

```
/*add display attributes for the semantic tags*/
header, footer, section, article, nav { display:block;
}
body {font-family:"times new roman"; font-size:medium; color:black; ⏎
background:white url('images/yellowgradient2.gif') repeat-x;
}
#container {min-width:960px;  max-width:1100px; padding:0; margin:auto;
}
header {width:100%; margin:auto; height:60px; text-align:center;
}
nav { float:left; margin:0; width :125px; display:block; padding:0; border:0 zoom:1;
}
#rightcol {float:right; width:120px; text-align: left; display:inline; margin:0; border:0
}
/* set general side button styles */
nav ul { margin-left:30px; padding-left:0;width:120px; list-style-type:none;
}
nav ul li { margin-bottom: 4px; text-align: center;
}
/* set general anchor styles */
nav li a { display: block; color: white; background:#D20B0D; font-weight: bold;
text-align:center;
}
/* specify state styles. */
/* mouseout (default) */
nav li a { background: #D20B0D;  border: 4px outset #FFAAAA; text-decoration: none;
}
/* mouseover */
nav li a:hover { background: maroon; border: 4px outset maroon;
}
```

```
/* onmousedown */
nav li a:active { background:#AECBFF; border: 4px inset #AECBFF
}
p.redarrow {text-align:center; padding-top: 250px;
}
.box { margin:0 150px 0 190px; padding:5px; text-align:center; border:1px solid black; ↵
border-bottom:0;
}
.box-bottom { margin:0 150px 0 190px; padding:5px; text-align:center; border:1px solid black;
}
img { border:0;
}
footer {clear:both; text-align:center;
}
h1 {font-size:xx-large; color:red; margin-top:10px; margin-bottom:5px; text-align:center;
}
h2 {font-size:x-large; font-weight bold; margin-top:5px; margin-bottom:5px; ↵
font-weight:bold;
}
span.tiny {text-align: center; font-family: Arial; font-size: xx-small; color: #000;
}
p {margin-top:5px; margin-bottom:5px;
}
p.cntr {text-align:center;
}
p.lft {text-align:left;
}
```

Add a Donation Button

A donation button allows users to contribute to your organization. In this case, the users specify the amount they wish to donate. The button code is downloaded from the PayPal web site; and like the Buy Now button, it is enciphered and completely secure. Use the instructions given earlier under the heading To Access the PayPal Button Factory. Follow Those Steps, but select the Donations button. Fill out the form and make sure that the box is ticked next to Save Button at PayPal (this will protect the button from fraudulent changes). Click Create Button.

The PayPal Donations button code will appear; copy and paste it into your text editor and save it with a memorable name. Then paste the code into your web page where you want the button to appear.

▓ **Tip** Using the same process, a Subscription button can be downloaded and various options set, such as the amount and the renewal date.

A secure donation button is shown in Figure 10-3.

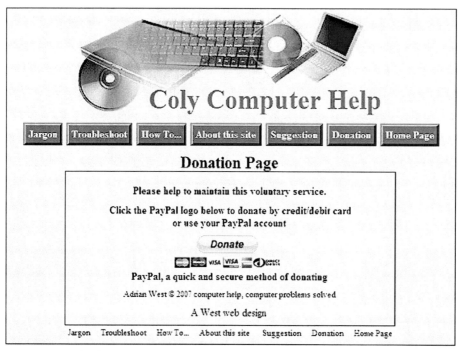

Figure 10-3. *The donation page on my free, computer-help web site. The PayPal Donation button is encrypted to prevent tampering by hackers.*

For Figure 10-3, the PayPal code was downloaded and inserted in the HTML code. When the page is viewed online, it dynamically loads a yellow button and also the debit/credit card logos.

The downloaded code for the button looks something like the following (the value has been changed to 1234567ABC for security):

```
<form action="https://www.paypal.com/cgi-bin/webscr" method="post">
<input type="hidden" name="cmd" value="_s-xclick">
<input type="hidden" name="hosted_button_id" value="1234567ABC ">
<input type="image" src="https://www.paypal.com/en_US/GB/i/btn/btn_donateCC_LG.gif" ↵
border="0" name="submit" alt="PayPal - The safer, easier way to pay online.">
<img alt="" border="0" src="https://www.paypal.com/en_GB/i/scr/pixel.gif" width="1"
height="1">
</form>
```

The Please Pay Button

The donation button can be adapted to use when the customer needs to obtain a quotation on goods before proceeding with an order. If the quotation is acceptable, the customer can then send payment via the donation button. The donation button can be customized using your own image and text.

The Please Pay button shown in Figure 10-4 was customized using a graphics program; the code was downloaded from PayPal.

```
┌────────────────────────────────────────────┐
│                                              │
│   Thank you for accepting our quotation     │
│                                              │
│     You can pay by one of two methods:-     │
│                                              │
│    1. Click CHECK. A form will appear. Please│
│        fill it out and mail it with your check│
│                                              │
│                    OR                        │
│                                              │
│    2. By PayPal or Debit/Credit card,       │
│        click the Please Pay button           │
│                                              │
│          Please Pay                          │
│                                              │
└────────────────────────────────────────────┘
```

Figure 10-4. Paying for an amount that matches a quotation

Design a customized button as follows:

1. Design a Please Pay button in .gif format in a graphics program and place it in the images folder on your web site's root folder. Make a note of the URL for the button image.

2. Log in to the client's account and for UK, click My Selling Preferences in the Profile. For USA accounts go to My Selling Tools, then PayPal buttons update. Or more easily, try the Merchant Services tab.

3. Click Create a New Button and select the Donations button from the drop-down list.

4. Fill in the fields.

5. Under the heading Customize Button, click Use Your Own Button Image.

6. Enter the URL for the button that you designed.

7. Click Create Button, then copy and paste the code into your web page.

When the customer agrees to the vendor's quotation, the customer enters the amount after clicking the Please Pay button. In Listing 10-4, the code for the customized downloaded payment button is shown in bold text (for security the PayPal reference number has been changed to 12345ABC).
    (A downloadable file is not available for this listing)

Listing 10-4. Adding a Customized PayPal Button to a Web Page

```
<!doctype html>
<html lang=en>
<head>
<title>Please Pay</title>
<meta charset=utf-8>
<style type="text/css">
body {font-size:medium; text-align:center;
}
```

```
#container { width:400px; padding-top:10px; border:1px black solid;
}
h1 { font-size:120%;
}
</style>
</head>
<body>
<div id="container">
<h1>Thank you for accepting our quotation</h1>
You can pay by one of two methods:-
<p>1. Click <b><a href="#check">CHECK</a></b>.  A form will appear. Please
<br>fill it out and mail it with your check</p>
<p>OR</p>
2. By PayPal or Debit/Credit card, <br>click the <b>Please Pay</b> button
<form action="https://www.paypal.com/cgi-bin/webscr" method="post">
<input type="hidden" name="cmd" value="_s-xclick">
<input type="hidden" name="hosted_button_id" value="12345ABC">
<input type="image" src="please-pay.gif" border="0" name="submit" alt="PayPal - The safer,
easier way to pay online.">
<img alt="" border="0" src="pixel.gif" width="1" height="1">
</form>
</div>
</body>
</html>
```

Test Your PayPal Buttons

Once the downloaded code has been added to your web site, some of the payment process can be tested. However, the full payment flow cannot be tested with a single account because PayPal does not allow members to make a payment to themselves.

■ **Note** Members are permitted to have both a Personal account and a Business/Premier account. For testing purposes, a member may want to open a separate Personal PayPal account.

Go to your web site and locate the PayPal payment button page that you wish to test.

1. Click on the button.

2. If the button is functioning correctly, you are taken to a PayPal Payment page. Your computer will have cookies enabled, so you see your own PayPal username. However, when your buyer clicks Buy Now, they see their own PayPal username if they have a PayPal Account.

3. If the customer is not a PayPal member, they can click on the Click Here button where it says If You Do Not Have a PayPal Account, Click Here.

Customers Can Use PayPal or a Debit/Credit Card

If customers have no PayPal account, they use the alternative payment link to enter their name and delivery address. They will then be prompted for details such as payment amount, debit/credit card type and number, email address, and phone number. They can choose to save the information by creating a PayPal account to simplify future transactions.

Customers are fully protected by PayPal's fraud prevention feature. Premier and business account holders can turn the feature on or off by logging in to PayPal, going to Profile, clicking Website Payment Preferences under the Selling Preferences column, and ticking the yes/no box under PayPal Account Options.

Managing a PayPal Account

To access the account so that the owner can manage it, go to http://www.paypal.co.uk (in the United Kingdom) or www.paypal.com (in the United States). Then follow these steps:

1. Log in using the button on the left.

2. Your email address is shown. Enter your password and click the Login button.

3. Click History for an overview of what has happened in your account.

4. When you have finished, click Logout.

5. To transfer money from your PayPal account into your personal bank account, you must access your PayPal account and then instruct PayPal the amount to transfer.

6. Access your PayPal account and click Withdraw.

7. Click Withdraw funds to your bank account.

8. Enter the amount to be transferred.

9. Below the Amount field, ensure that your personal bank account is shown.

10. Click Continue.

11. On the next page, confirm that the details are correct and click the Submit button.

12. The transaction will take about three days to complete.

13. Request Money allows you to receive or request money from anyone with an email address in 190 countries and regions that accept PayPal. To request money for an auctioned item, request payment from a customer, or send a personal payment request by entering the recipient's email address and the amount you are requesting.

Tip PayPal offers a full API for even further control of your shopping cart and other buttons. Try experimenting with the useful Website Payments Standard Overview page at https://cms.paypal.com/us/cgi-bin/?cmd=_render-content&content_ID=developer/. It goes through many of the advanced features that developers can use to work with PayPal, including a reference to all of the PayPal variables. PayPal also has a shipping calculator that may prove useful to you.

Summary

This chapter has shown you that the step-by-step process of adding PayPal to a web site is not mysterious, but relatively simple and logical. You have learned how to embed the downloaded code for various PayPal buttons and you have been reassured about security. You have also learned how the web site owner can transfer money and view a PayPal account's balance.

In the next chapter, you will learn more about security and how it affects email addresses and feedback forms. Safe solutions will be provided and although a little JavaScript is used and a PHP form filter is described, no knowledge of either script language is needed.

CHAPTER 11

Secure Feedback Methods

Emails and feedback forms are the most popular contact methods allowing users to communicate easily with web site owners. Unfortunately, both contact methods can be abused. Hackers can hijack a form and use it to send malware to the site owner. E-mail addresses are harvested and sold to spammers. Both actions cause distress and an influx of spam to the site owner; and they don't enhance the reputation of the web designer. This chapter discusses some options to prevent these risks.

Enciphering Email Addresses to Prevent Spam

Escrambler is a free, anti-spam device. It was originally produced as a plain, clickable link, and was later enhanced by the addition of an image of the email address by InnerPeace.org. Their web page at `http://innerpeace.org/escrambler.shtml` will quickly generate the code for you. Or you can adapt the JavaScript snippet that follows.

Insert the following JavaScript snippet into the <body> section where you want the email address to appear. The JavaScript also places a picture of the email address on the page so that the user can click it or make note of it for future use. However, the email address image is no help if the user has disabled JavaScript; therefore the picture (with no link) should also be shown somewhere on the page in the usual way.

The JavaScript will disguise the email address so that spam spiders can't read it. The JavaScript breaks down the traditional email address into little bits and then reassembles it. Spam spiders have great difficulty reading JavaScript and images; even if they could read JavaScript, the email address is so fragmented that they would not make sense of it. For your own email scrambler, just change the items in bold.

The following example hides the address fredbloggs@aol.com

```
<p>
<script type="text/javascript">
<!--
        function escramble(){
        var a,b,c,d,e,f,g,h,i
        a='<a href=\"mai'
        b='fredbloggs'
        c='\">'
        a+='lto:'
        b+='@'
        b+='aol.com'
        e='</a>'
        f=''
```

```
g='<img src=\"'
h='images/bloggs-email.jpg'
i='\" alt="Email Me" border="0">'
if(f) d=f
else if(h) d=g+h+i
else d=b
document.write(a+b+c+d+e)
}
escramble()
//-->
</script></p>
```

▓ **Caution** The variable f is followed by two single quotes, not a double quote. The line `g='<img src=\"'` ends in a double quote followed by a single quote.

The JavaScript code allows for the following two conditions:

- The full e-mail address appears on the screen in the form of an image that is clickable, but invisible to spam spiders.

- If no image is available, a link having the words Email Me appears on the web page.

Clicking either the image or the words "Email Me" causes the user's default email program to open with the email address already filled in. Users may need to be told that the email may go into their Outbox and, therefore, needs to be sent by clicking the Send/Receive button.

Creating an Image of the email Address

Most paint programs can create a `.png` or `.gif` image containing the mail address. Make the background transparent so that the background color of the page shows through. However, creating text with a paint program may not give a satisfactory result. It can also be time-consuming and sometimes downright frustrating, especially if you need to match a page's colored background. The following is a method that always gives a good result and can be less complicated than adding text with a paint program:

1. In your WYSIWYG web page editor, make a copy of a web page containing the appropriate background color.

2. In a clear space on that page, type the email address using the preferred font size and color.

3. Make a screen capture of the page using the Alt+ Print Screen keys (or use the Snipping tool in Windows 7).

4. Open your paint program and paste into it the screenshot.

5. Crop the picture and save the result as a `.jpg` or a `.png` file (see Figure 11-1).

Figure 11-1. Example image for a colored background using this method

A Minor Problem Solved

Your client may decide not to put her email address on the web site. Instead she may prefer to use a feedback form. However, there is nothing to prevent someone from ignoring the form and contacting her directly by guessing her e-mail address. This very rarely happens, and the sender is not a spammer, so tell your client to not be alarmed. I have personally received only a handful of these emails in a decade. This is a minor problem and can be ignored.

So how does he know your client's email address? He knows because he found her web site. Why does he try to contact her? He wants to establish a reciprocal link from her web site to his web site. Her secure feedback form (described in the next section) prevents the sender from supplying his URL details. He must use a normal email so he makes an intelligent guess. He tries info@clientswebsite.co.uk or sales@clientswebsite.co.uk, and so on. If your client has a "catchall" email address, the person could also type something like postmaster@clientswebsite.co.uk and it might reach your client. His email would then be able to include his genuine URL. He won't include a dodgy URL because he could be traced through his email.

By establishing a reciprocal link, he is hoping to improve his search engine ranking by having as many external links as possible to his site. Your client should look at the person's web site(s); she will usually find that his content is in no way related to her web site, so she should *not* agree to a reciprocal link. Also, she will most likely find that his link page has between 40 and 100 links on it. If she agrees to a reciprocal link, search engines will assume she is using a link farm and as a consequence they may penalize her web site.

If your client is receiving this type of email, the simplest solution is to use a different email address in the handler, such as her home broadband address, clientsemailaddress@herisp.co.uk. No one will be able to guess her home email address, but the downside is that her business replies won't be distinguished from her personal emails.

Secure Feedback Forms

When designing feedback forms, we need to consider the following three points:

1. Because layout tables are deprecated, CSS must be used to align the input fields neatly.

2. Blind and severely visually-impaired users can use their screen readers to read and reply to forms. Accessibility rules must be observed; these are covered in Chapter 14.

3. Filters must be built into the form handler to prevent the form being hijacked for nefarious purposes.

Bogus Replies

Concerning the third point, when I first began to design web sites, I added feedback forms to many of my clients' web sites and all of them were plagued by people who used the form to send bogus replies to the site owners. The replies contained gobbledygook and dodgy URLs. The hijackers used robots to send bogus replies once or twice a week. The site owners were naturally disappointed and puzzled because they thought they had received an order. Fortunately, they did not click a link on these bogus replies, but they contacted me immediately for a solution.

What do bogus replies look like? A typical bogus reply is shown in the box that follows. For security, I have altered the URLs and the email address. The replies contain gobbledygook as well as live links that lead to dodgy web sites. A web site owner unfamiliar with the weird behavior of hackers might be tempted to click a link, which could lead to all sorts of mayhem.

```
     Content-type: text/html;charset="iso-8859-1"
From: ezrxsk@xyzvjox.com
X-Antivirus: AVG for E-mail 8.0.100 [270.4.1/1510]
From: Damon Rosario
superobligation hobbledehoyish foreread minaway wips taenioid chancellorism unsocket
3Sy6Rl  <a href=\"http://qmuxlytwkukt.com/\">qmuclytwkuxt</a>,
[url=http://iqdqouydsqzn.com/]iqdqouydsqzn[/url],
[link=http://lvcukrrfrlpj.com/]lvkuckrrfrlsj[/link], http://uiaopyzucuiyba.com/
     <a href= http://www.axtemplate.com/ >Axtemplate.com</a>
 http://www.moley.co.jp/
```

The following is a genuine email received from the secure form:

```
     This message was sent from:
http://www.theowners-website.co.uk/form.html
-----------------------------------------------------------
Name of sender: Andrew Eastman
Email of sender: aeastman@myisp.co.uk
Telephone No: 01390 5233726
W98,ME,2000?: No
XP?: No
Vista?: No
Windows7?: Yes
Laptop?: Yes
Desktop?; No
----------------------- MESSAGE -----------------------------------
How can I persuade my computer to make a decent cup of coffee?
-----------------------------------------------------------------------
```

An Example of a Hack-Proof Feedback Form

Bogus feedback can be stopped by means of a PHP, ASP.NET, or other server-side handlers. In this chapter, I have chosen to use a PHP handler because the language is a little easier to understand and implement. The handler causes an error message to pop up if a URL is entered into any text field. This stops bogus replies completely in every case. Hackers do not hijack a form to send advertisements for Viagra; they are hoping the site owner will click the URL link and fire up the sender's dodgy web site(s). The web sites could be pornographic or more likely, contain malware such as a Trojan that would take control of the site owner's computer. Figure 11-2 shows the form used in this project.

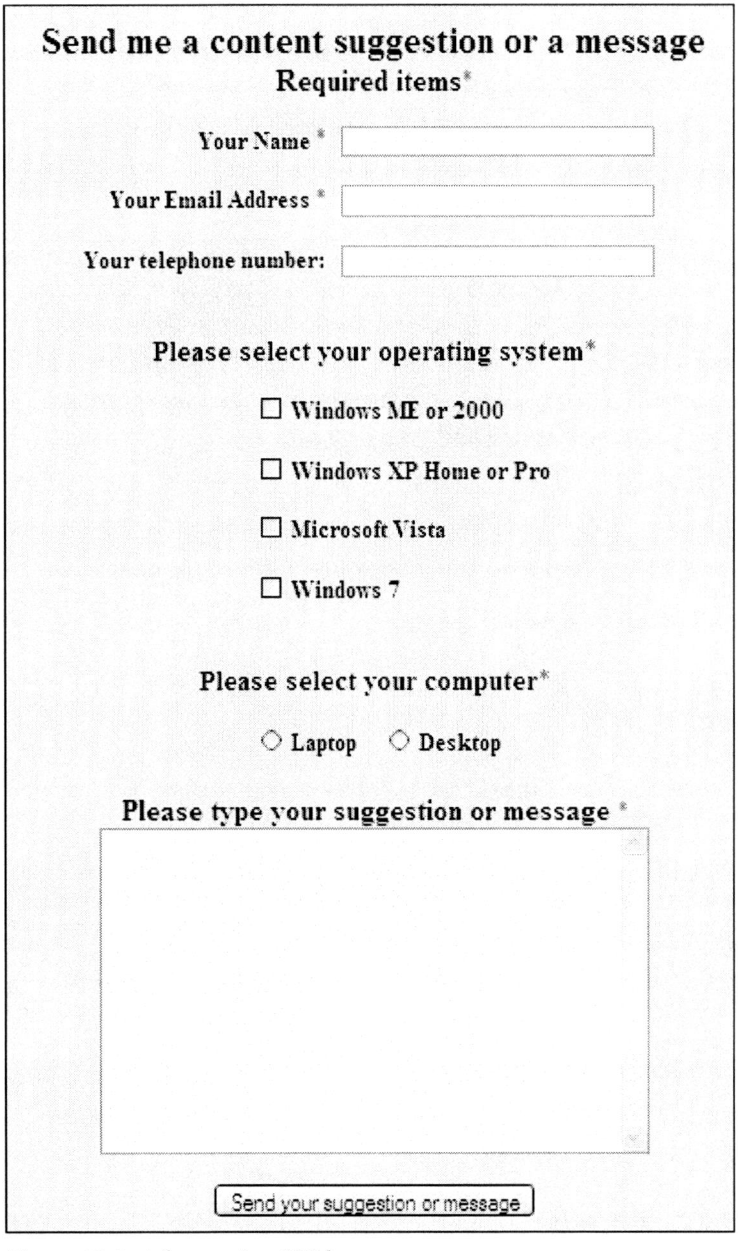

Figure 11-2. A form using CSS layout

You can download the example form, the handler, and the associated files from the companion web site at http://www.apress.com. Insert your own details in place of the items shown in bold text in Listings 11-2a, 11-2b, and 11-2c.

■ **Note** HTML5 has new tags and attributes for forms. These will be mentioned later in this chapter. Meanwhile, this example uses HTML4 tags because the HTML5 recommendations for forms are still being developed. Also, browser support is currently patchy, and unfortunately, the new controls do not prevent the entry of URLs.

■ **Tip** An internal CSS style sheet may be used if no other page needs the form styling instructions. Or you could have a separate external style sheet to specify only the layout of the form elements. The link statement for this would have to be the last of a series of link statements in the <head> section. This would be in addition to a link to an external style sheet for styling the rest of the page (such as navigation buttons). If you don't want navigation buttons on the form, you should at least put a Go Back button on the form (see Chapter 20).

Determine the widths and padding in the style sheet by trial and error. As some web design programs are not true WYSIWYG, always test the layout in various browsers. The next groups of code describe the elements of a typical form.

The code snippet for a typical text field takes the following form:

```
<div id="name">
        <label for="username"><b>Your Name:</b></label>
        <input id="username" name="username" size="30">
</div>
```

For every text field on the form, <label>…</label> and <input>…</input>, tags must be used with the two attributes for and id, as shown in the code snippet. This is very important for persons using a screen reader.

For text fields and text areas, the <label> tag must come first before the <input> tag so that the label sits to the left of the field.

For checkboxes and radio buttons, the opposite order must be used; the <input> tag must come first before the <label> tag so that the label sits to the right of the field.

The following is *the code snippet for CSS for checkboxes* (by using CSS, the checkboxes have been lined up nicely with the same class/identifier on each):

```
/*The CSS for positioning the checkboxes on the page*/
.chk1 {text-align:left; padding-left:30%;

}
```

The *code snippet for the HTML for check boxes* follows:

```
<div class="chk1">
  <input id="chkbox1" name="w98me2000" value="Yes" type="checkbox">
  <label for="chkbox1"><b>Windows ME or 2000</b></label>
</div><br>
<div class="chk1">
  <input id="chkbox2" name="xp" value="Yes" type="checkbox">
  <label for="chkbox2"><b>Windows XP Home or Pro</b></label>
</div> <br>
```

…and so on.

The two radio buttons are positioned on the page by CSS a style that targets the id named rad.

```
/*Position the radio buttons on the page*/
#rad {text-align:left; padding-left :30%;
}
```

The following is the *code snippet for the HTML for the radio buttons*:

```
<div id="rad">
<input id="radio1" name="laptop" value="Yes" type="radio">
<label for="radio1"><b>Laptop</b></label>    
<input id="radio2" name="desktop" value="Yes" type="radio">
<label for="radio2"><b>Desktop<br></b></label>
</div>
```

Semantic tags are not used in Listing11-2a to avoid the need to add JavaScript for IE 7 and IE 8 users, the form then works in all browsers, including IE 7 and IE 8.

Listing 11-2a. Creating a Secure Form as Shown in Figure 11-2 (feedback-form.html)

```
<!doctype html>
<html lang=en>
<head>
<title>Send a suggestion to my computer help and advice service</title>
<meta charset=utf-8>
<!--<meta details go here>-->
<link rel="stylesheet" type="text/css" href="feedback.css" media="screen">
</head>
<body>
<a id="top"></a>
 <br><div>
<h2>Send me a content suggestion or a message</h2>
<h3>Required items <span class="red">*</span></h3>
<!--start of form-->
<div id="form">
<form action="form-handler.php" method="post">
<div>
        <label class="label" for="username"><strong>Your Name</strong>↵
        <span class="red">*</span>
        <input id="username" name="username" size="30"></label>
</div><br><br>
<div>
        <label class="label" for="useremail"><strong>Your Email Address</strong>
        <span class="red">*</span>
        <input id="useremail" name="useremail" size="30"></label>
</div><br><br>
<div>
        <label class="label" for="phone"><strong>Your Telephone Number </strong>
        <input id="phone" name="phone" size="30"></label>
</div><br><br>
<div>
  <h3>Please select your operating system <span class="red">*</span></h3>
</div>
```

267

```
<div class="chk1">
        <input id="chkbox1" name="w98me2000" value="Yes" type="checkbox">
        <label for="chkbox1"><strong>Windows ME or 2000</strong></label>
</div><br>
<div class="chk1">
        <input id="chkbox2" name="xp" value="Yes" type="checkbox">
        <label for="chkbox2"><strong>Windows XP Home or Pro</strong></label>
</div><br>
<div class="chk1">
        <input id="chkbox3" name="vista" value="Yes" type="checkbox">
        <label for="chkbox3"><strong>Microsoft Vista</strong></label>
</div><br>
<div class="chk1">
        <input id="chkbox4" name="windows7" value="Yes" type="checkbox">
        <label for="chkbox4"><strong>Windows 7</strong></label>
</div><br>
<div>
<h3>Please select your computer<span class="red">*</span></h3>
</div>
<div id="rad">
        <input id="laptop" name="computer" value="Laptop" type="radio">
        <label for="laptop"><strong>Laptop</strong></label>    
        <input id="desktop" name="computer" value="Desktop" type="radio">
        <label for="desktop"><strong>Desktop</strong></label></div>
<div id="sug"><br>
        <label for="suggest"><strong>
          Please type your suggestion or message</strong><span class="red">*</span></label>
          <br><br>
        <textarea id="suggest" name="suggestion" rows="12" cols="40"></textarea><br><br>
</div>
<div id="submit">
        <input id="sb" value="Send your suggestion or message" title="Send suggestion ↵
        or message" type="submit">
</div>
</form>
</div>
<!--end of form-->
</div>
</body>
</html>
```

▓ **Note** When the Submit button is clicked, the items in bold type in Listing 11-2a will be sent to the form handler (Listing 11-2c) for processing.

The form in Listing 11-2a is linked to the following style sheet, Listing 11-2b. This creates the layout of the various form fields.

Listing 11-2b. Creating the CSS Style Sheet for Listing 11-2a (feedback.css)

```
/*FEEDBACK.CSS*/
/*reset browsers for cross-client consistency*/
html,body,h1,h2,h3,h4,h4,h5,h6,p {margin:0; padding:0
}
img {border-style: none; float: none; margin-left: 0; margin-right: 0;
}
body {text-align:center; background-color:#D7FFEB; color:black; ⏎
font-family: "times new roman"; max-width:1024px; min-width:800px;font-size: medium; ⏎
color: #000; margin: auto; width:95%;
}
/*The h1 heading is not used on the form shown; its inclusion is for a probable h1 ⏎
heading on your own form*/
h1 {padding: 110px 0 0 12%; font-family :"times new roman";  font-size: 250%; ⏎
color: #000; font-weight:bold;}
h2 { margin-top:15px; }
span.red { font-size:medium; color:red; font-weight:bold;
}
/*center the back button on the thankyou page*/
#back-button { margin:auto; text-align:center; width:200px; height:25px; padding:5px; ⏎
background-color:brown; color:white; font-size:110%; font-weight:bold;
}
#back-button a { text-decoration:none; color:white;
}
#back-button a:hover { color:red;
}
/*set heading details*/
h1,h2 , h3, h4, h5 { margin-top:0; margin-bottom:10px;
}
h2 { font-size:130%; font-weight:bold;
}
h3 { font-size:110%; font-weight:bold; text-align:center;
}
/*PARAGRAPHS*/
p {margin-bottom:10px; margin-top:0;
}
/*FORM. Position the form elements on the page*/
#form {width :500px; margin:auto; text-align:center;
}
.label { float:left; width: 400px; text-align:right; clear:left;
}
.chk1 { text-align:left; padding-left :30%;
}
#rad { text-align:left; padding-left :30%;
}
#sug { text-align:center; margin:auto;
}
#submit { text-align:center;
}
```

As previously stated, when the Submit button on the form is clicked, the user's details are sent to the form handler. The form handler is described next in Listing 11-2c.

269

The Form Handler and Its Anti-Hack Filters

You can download the form, the style sheets, and the form handler from the companion web site at http://www.apress.com. The handler is a piece of PHP code, but you do not need to learn PHP to use it. The handler contains logical operators that will filter out errors and URLs. The URL filters will exasperate and stop a human hijacker, and will cause a robotic device to have a nervous breakdown.

⬛ **Note** To begin testing , set your own email address so that you are the recipient, then test the form. When you are satisfied that the form is sending test emails to you, and the resulting email is satisfactory, then comment-out your own email address and remove the comment slashes from the client's email address so that the client (the web owner) receives the emails instead of you. Of course, this does not apply if the web site is your own.

Note that in Listing 11-2c, single line comments are preceded by a double slash // and multi-line comments use /*......*/ just like CSS comments. Also, a PHP document begins with <?php and ends with ?> and these tags must not include spaces.

For the curious, the weirder bits of code are explained at the end of this section.

⬛ **Caution** The handler must be saved as a PHP document, and after uploading the handler, right-click it in the server pane of your FTP client, there you will be able to set the CHMOD to 644. This will stop unauthorised persons accessing it. If they try using the handler's file name to open it, they will not see the handler; they will be directed instantly to the form. Make sure your server has PHP enabled, if it is not enabled, contact the host and instruct them to enable the server.

Substitute your own details for the items shown in ***bold italics*** in the handler Listing 11-2c Because the person sending the message will be entering his own details (name, email address, and phone number); they are not shown in bold italics.

Listing 11-2c. Creating the PHP Form Handler (form-handler.php)

```php
<?php
/* FORM-HANDLER.PHP Feedback Form PHP Script Ver 5.0 */
// set the email address for the recipient, this setting sends it to your client for example
//$mailto = "webmasters-mailaddress@your-isp.com" ;
$mailto = "yourclient@clients-isp.com" ;
//choose the subject so that you can recognize emails sent from this form
$subject = "Help query" ;
/*The next block of code tells the handler where to find the various documents ⬏
associated with it. In this case the documents and the form are all in the same root ⬏
folder.*/
// list the pages to be displayed,
```

```php
$formurl = "http://www.clients-website.com/feedback-form.html" ;
$errorurl = "http://www.clients-website.com/error.html" ;
$thankyouurl = "http://www. clients-website.com /thankyou.html" ;
$emailerrurl = "http://www. clients-website.com /emailerr.html" ;
$errorphoneurl = "http://www. clients-website.com /phonerror.html" ;
$errorsuggesturl = "http://www. clients-website.com /suggesterror.html" ;
$errorboxurl = "http://www. clients-website.com /error.html" ;
$uself = 0;
// ------- Set the information received from the form as $ values ---------------
$headersep = (!isset( $uself ) || ($uself == 0)) ? "\r\n" : "\n" ;
/*The following code receives the items from the HTML form and converts them to formats ↵
 that can be used by the handler, for example, username is converted to $username.*/
$username = $_POST['username'] ;
$useremail = $_POST['useremail'] ;
$phone = $_POST['phone'];
$w98me2000 = $_POST['w98me2000'];
$xp = $_POST['xp'];
$vista = $_POST['vista'];
$w7=$_POST['windows7'];
$computer=$_POST['computer'];
$suggestion = $_POST['suggestion'] ;
$http_referrer = getenv( "HTTP_REFERER" );
if (!isset($_POST['useremail'])) {
        header( "Location: $formurl" );
        exit ;}
//Check that all three essential fields are filled in
if (empty($username) || empty($useremail) || empty($suggestion)) {
header( "Location: $errorurl" );
        exit ; }
//Check that at least one box has been ticked
if ((!$w98me2000 and !$xp and !$vista and !$w7)) {
        header( "Location: $errorboxurl" );
        exit ; }
//check that no urls have been inserted in the username text area
if (strpos ($username, '://')||strpos($username, 'www') !==false){
        header( "Location: $errorsuggesturl" );
        exit ; }
//Check that no urls  haves been entered in the phone field
if (strpos ($phone, '://')||strpos($phone, 'www') !==false){
        header( "Location: $errorphoneurl" );
        exit ; }
//check that no urls have been inserted in the suggestion text area
if (strpos ($suggestion, '://')||strpos($suggestion, 'www') !==false){
        header( "Location: $errorsuggesturl" );
        exit ; }
        if ( ereg( "[\r\n]", $username ) || ereg( "[\r\n]", $useremail )) {
        header( "Location: $errorurl" );
        exit ; }
#remove any spaces from beginning and end of email address
$useremail = trim($useremail);
#Check for permitted email address patterns
```

```php
$_name = "/^[-!#$%&\'*+\\.\/0-9=?A-Z^_`{|}~]+";
$_host = "([-0-9A-Z]+\.)+";
$_tlds = "([0-9A-Z]){2,4}$/i";
if(!preg_match($_name."@".$_host.$_tlds,$useremail)) {
        header( "Location: $emailerrurl" );
        exit ; }
if (get_magic_quotes_gpc()) {
        $message = stripslashes( $message ); }
if(!$w98me2000) {$w98me2000 = "No";}
if(!$xp) {$xp = "No";}
if(!$vista) {$vista = "No";}
if(!$w7) {$w7 = "No";}
if($computer !=null) {$computer = $computer;}
//-- SET UP THE EMAIL'S CONTENT, FORMAT IT, SEND IT. THEN SHOW A THANK YOU PAGE --
$messageproper =
        "This message was sent from:\n" .
        "$http_referrer\n" .
        "------------------------------------------------------------\n" .
        "Name of sender: $username\n" .
        "Email of sender: $useremail\n" .
        "Telephone No: $phone\n" .
        "W98,ME,2000?: $w98me2000\n" .
        "XP?: $xp\n" .
        "Vista?: $vista\n" .
        "Windows7?: $w7\n" .
        "Computer?:$laptop\n" .
        "Computer?;$desktop\n" .
        "----------------------- MESSAGE ------------------------\n\n" .
        $suggestion .
        "\n\n------------------------------------------------------------\n" ;
mail($mailto, $subject, $messageproper, "From: \"$username\" <$useremail>" . $headersep .
"Reply-To: \"$username\" <$useremail>" .
$headersep . "X-Mailer: feedback4.php 5.0" ); header( "Location: $thankyouurl" ); exit ;
?>
```

For the Curious: An Explanation of Some of the PHP Code

(Skip this section if you are too busy or not interested.)

The **!isset function** checks to ensure the value for the sender's email has been set in the $_POST array. The exclamation mark (!) means NOT.

```php
if (!isset($_POST['useremail'])) {
        header( "Location: $formurl" );
        exit ;
}
```

if(!preg.match completes the test to see if the email address is in the correct format. The **reg** part stands for *regular expression* (this the US translation, where regular = standard, not the UK meaning, in which regular means "at equal intervals"). If the email address does not conform to the accepted standard, then an error message is displayed.

magic_quotes is a PHP filter which, if turned on, will insert an escape slash to preserve any single or double quote marks in the message entered by the user.

```
if (get_magic_quotes_gpc()) { $message = stripslashes( $message );
}
```

When checking that the essential fields have been filled in, double vertical lines (||) means OR.

The next piece of code translates like this: if the username field is empty or the useremail field is empty or the suggestion field is empty, then show an error message called errorurl, which says that an essential field has not been filled in.

```
if (empty($username) || empty($useremail) || empty($suggestion)) { header( "Location:
$errorurl" ); exit;
}
```

In the HTML form, the default for the check boxes and radio buttons was set to Yes.

If a box or radio button is not clicked, then the value can be changed to "No" by the handler, as follows:

```
if(!$xp) {$xp = "No";}
```

This means if $xp has not been selected, then assign the value "No" to $xp.

Test to ensure that at least one check box has been ticked (note the use of and in this statement).

```
if ((!$w98me2000 and !$xp and !$vista and !$w7)) {
header( "Location: $errorboxurl" );
exit ;
}
```

The user needs to be notified if the message has been sent successfully. He also needs to know if he has made an error when filling in the form. The following section gives suggested feedback pages that will inform the user, and also offer help if he has provided faulty or unacceptable data.

The "Thank You" Page and the Error Messages

The "thank you" page confirms to the user that the email was sent successfully. For consistency, the "thank you" page should look like all the other pages on your web site. Try to include your navigation menu in the "thank you" page (or at least a Go Back button). It would be a pity to lose the visitor. It would also be helpful to add a Go Back button to each error page. The "thank you" page is shown in Figure 11-3 and the code is Listing 11-3. The page has a Go Back button with the text—"Return to Home Page"—but you can replace this button with your main navigation menu. The styling for the button is incorporated in the style sheet feedback.css.

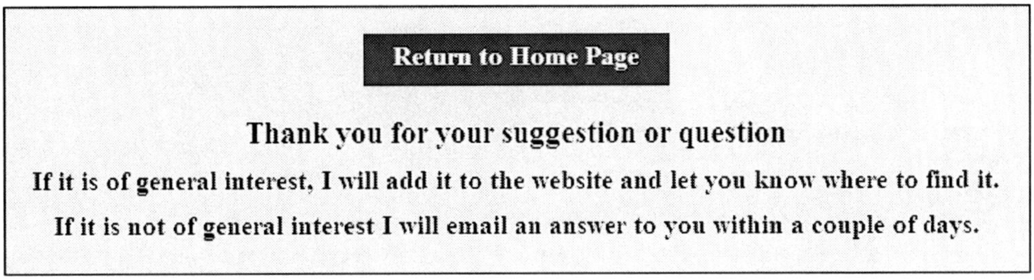

Return to Home Page

Thank you for your suggestion or question

If it is of general interest, I will add it to the website and let you know where to find it.

If it is not of general interest I will email an answer to you within a couple of days.

Figure 11-3. A "thank you" page

Listing 11-3. *Creating the Thank You Page (thankyou.html)*

```
<!doctype html>
<html lang=en>
<head>
<title>Thank you for your message</title>
<meta charset=utf-8>
<!--<meta details go here>-->
<link rel="stylesheet" type="text/css" href="feedback.css" media="screen">
</head>
<body>
<a id="top"></a><br>
<div id="back-button"><a title="Return to the Home page" href="index.php">Return to Home
Page</a>
</div>
<div><br>
<h2>
Thank you for your suggestion or question</h2>
<h3> If it is of general interest, I will add it to the website and let you know where
to find it.</h3>
<h3>If it is not of general interest I will email an answer to
you within a couple of days.</h3>
</div>
</body>
</html>
```

If the email message was not sent successfully, an explanatory error message will appear.

Why use error pages instead of echoing a piece of text to the screen? My clients prefer the distinct message and the help that a page provides, rather than the usual, small, error messages in red that can be overlooked or that are so often too brief.

The style sheet in Listing 11-4 is used for all five error messages (Listings 11-5 through 11-9).

Listing 11-4. *(error.css)*

```
body { text-align:center; font-size: large; font-weight:bold;
}
span.red {color:red; font-size:xlarge; font-weight:bold;
}
```

Listing 11-5 provides the code for the Missing Essentials Error Message.

Listing 11-5. *(error.html)*

```
<!doctype html>
<html lang=en>
<head>
<title>Error message. Missing essentials</title>
<meta charset=utf-8>
        meta details go here
<link rel="stylesheet" type="text/css" href="error.css">
</head>
<body>
```

```
<p>One or more of the essential items in the form has not been filled in.</p>
<p>Essential items have a red asterisk like this <span class="red">*</span></p>
<p>Please click the Back button on your internet browser and then supply the ↵
missing information.</p>
</body>
</html>
```

Listing 11-6 shows the code for the email error message.

Listing 11-6. (emailerr.html)

```
<!doctype html>
<html lang=en>
<head>
<title>Email error message</title>
<meta charset=utf-8>
<meta details go here>
<link rel="stylesheet" type="text/css" href="error.css">
</head>
<body>
<p>Your email address has an incorrect format.</p>
<p>Please click the Back button on your internet browser<br> and then correct your ↵
email address.</p>
</body>
</html>
```

Listing 11-7 provides the code for the phone error message.

Listing 11-7. (phonerror.html)

```
<!doctype html>
<html lang=en>
<head>
<title>Phone error message</title>
<meta charset=utf-8>
        meta details go here
<link rel="stylesheet" type="text/css" href="error.css">
</head>
<body>
<p> </p><p> </p>
<p>The telephone number must be numbers and spaces only, with no letters or punctuation></p>
<p>Please click the Back button on your internet browser<br> and then correct your ↵
telephone number.</p>
</body>
</html>
```

Listing 11-8 provides the code for the tick box error message.

Listing 11-8. (boxerror.html)

```
<!doctype html>
<html lang=en>
<head>
<title>Box error</title>
<meta charset=utf-8>
```

```
        meta details go here
<link rel="stylesheet" type="text/css" href="error.css">
</head>
<body>
<p> </p><p>Please tick one of the boxes to say which Operating System your ↵
have on your computer.</p>
<p>Essential items have a red asterisk like this<span class="red">*</span></p>
<p>Please click the Back button on your Internet browser and then supply the ↵
missing information.</p>
</body>
</html>
```

Listing 11-9 provides the code for the message forbidding the entry of URLs.

Listing 11-9. (suggesterror.html)

```
<!doctype html>
<html lang=en>
<head>
<title>Error message. Do not enter URLs</title>
<meta charset=utf-8>
        meta details go here
<link rel="stylesheet" type="text/css" href="error.css">
</head>
<body>
Sorry, but website addresses are not allowed<br><br>This is to prevent low-life ↵
scumbags from inserting links which lead to dodgy websites.
<p>Please click the Back button on your internet browser<br>and then remove any ↵
website addresses from the form.</p>
</body>
</html>
```

The new HTML5 form controls were explained in Chapter 1. We now need to consider whether these controls will eventually replace the input filters in the PHP form handler provided in this chapter.

The New HTML5 Form Controls

The HTML5 recommendations for forms are almost complete, but various browsers interpret them differently. HTML5 forms are not straightforward because other factors affect them.

- A hack-proof form needs a handler in PHP, ASP.NET, or Perl server-side code. The handler must match the new HTML5 form tags.

- Accessibility will be compromised unless great care is taken to integrate the new HTML5 elements with the requirements of screen readers.

- For some time, IE conditionals and alternative style sheets will have to be used so that surfers with the most-used browser can see and use your forms.

- At the time of writing, IE 9 does not support HTML5 forms. IE 10 will most likely support them.

■ **Note** Only Opera 9.5 + supports all the new form elements at the time of writing. Other new browsers support some of the form features. To see which browsers currently support HTML5 form controls, visit http://wufoo.com/html5/

Even though HTML5 controls are built-in to the HTML5 forms, robots and humans can still enter dodgy URLs. Therefore, you will still need the protection of an anti-hack form handler for some fields.

You could add further protection against robots when using the PHP feedback handler described earlier; for instance, you might place an image of some text on the page so that the text must be entered correctly, or you could ask a question that must be answered before the form handler will send the email. An alternative solution would be to use CAPTCHA, as described next.

Using CAPTCHA

CAPTCHA is one way of making a feedback form more secure. We are all familiar with the wiggly script of a CAPTCHA image, like the one shown in Figure 11-4.

Figure 11-4. A CAPTCHA image

It is designed to stop robots using the form. Unfortunately, it won't stop an unscrupulous human from sending your client a feedback message containing an unpleasant or dangerous link or a dodgy web address. The PHP handler is the only way to do that. Perhaps the safest solution is to use CAPTCHA in conjunction with the secure feedback form and its PHP handler.

When using CAPTCHA, each time the form is accessed, a different image appears. This can be actioned by the organization supplying the CAPTCHA service or a random generator can be programmed and called up on the form. Some CAPTCHA methods incorporate spoken versions of the characters so that blind or partially-sighted persons can use the form.

The CAPTCHA code is downloaded and embedded in the page containing the form. CAPTCHA can be a free service and it can be used on commercial sites. Visit http://captchas.net (note the letter "s" after CAPTCHA in the URL) to learn more and download the code.

The simplest code version for downloading is PHP. It can be embedded directly into an HTML5 page. Three files have to be downloaded and installed on your server. This solution needs knowledge of JavaScript and PHP. To see if you are skilled enough to use the captchas.net method, have a look at the sample code at http://captchas.net/sample/php/

■ **Tip** Several other CAPTCHA suppliers exist; some require payment and some are easier to embed and understand than others. Try exploring http://hellocaptcha.com and http://www.google.com/recaptcha.

Summary

In this chapter, you learned how to use a little JavaScript to stop spam spiders from collecting your client's email address. By using this script, your clients will not be deluged with spam. You also learned the reason for using a hack-proof feedback form. The chapter and the companion web site provide you with a template for a form and its hack-proof handler. Although the handler is written in PHP, no knowledge of PHP is required to implement it. Just download the template and enter your own information where the listings in this chapter show items in bold type.

Some information about CAPTCHA was provided, although I would rather use the feedback form-handler because it is a little safer than CAPTCHA for preventing access by human rogues. No safeguards are 100 percent secure and CAPTCHA has been bypassed by determined criminals using optical character recognition (OCR). For more information, see the Wikipedia article on CAPTCHA at http://en.wikipedia.org/wiki/CAPTCHA.

In the next chapter, we will examine the problems presented by the large variations in monitor color rendition, screen size, and display resolution. Several solutions will be offered and their advantages and drawbacks will be explained.

Monitor Mayhem

Will your web site colors be the same on all monitors? Which type and size of monitor should you design for? Is it possible for a web site to look attractive on a wide range of screen sizes and resolutions? This chapter describes the problems and explores the possible solutions. The following topics will be presented and discussed:

- Monitors and the problem of color rendition
- Monitor sizes and resolutions
- Monitors and the problem with fixed-width layouts
- Monitors and the problem with liquid layouts
- Monitors and semi-liquid layouts—the best solution
- Other monitor-related considerations

Monitors and the Problem of Color Rendition

Cathode ray tube (CRT) monitors generally gave strong vibrant colors, and they were set to a fairly consistent standard by each manufacturer. The situation has changed since the introduction of TFT monitors (thin, flat-screen monitors; TFT stands for thin-film transistor). The overwhelming majority of TFT monitors bundled with computers are low-fidelity, twisted nematic (TN) screens; some of these are incapable of reproducing a wide and faithful range of colors.

In addition, they are often factory-set to maximum brilliance so that colors are washed-out pale pastels, sometimes with a distinct blue cast. Although TFT screens have adjustment buttons, users rarely notice these; if they do spot them, they are usually too timid to use them.

Rich web page colors designed on a CRT monitor can look very pale and muddy when viewed on a TFT screen. One of my sites had a background that was a lemon-yellow gradient; a few TFT screens rendered this color as a muddy, gray-green. I experimented with variations of lemon yellow and eventually the poorest screens showed a sort of lemon yellow; not as bright as I would have liked, but it was acceptable.

As most users have low-fidelity, twisted nematic (TN) screens, the best strategy is to design web sites on a similar screen. When designing web sites, you might even connect a low-fidelity screen in parallel with your expensive, high-quality TFT screen to ensure that your web pages look reasonable on poor screens. Set the screen to be slightly brighter (washed out) than you would personally prefer. Then design for colors that look reasonable on that screen. Use your graphics package to make pictures slightly darker than you would for a CRT monitor.

If you have been requested to alter an older web site so that it looks reasonable on a TFT screen, you may have to darken the pictures using your graphics program. Then darken the text and menu buttons using CSS. If you use hexadecimal code in your CSS to describe colors, you can darken them by reducing the numbers and letters; for instance

- Mid blue is #0000FF; when FF is decreased to 80, it becomes #000080, which is navy blue.

- Hexadecimal numbers are (from darkest to lightest) 0, 1, 2, 3, 4, 5, 6, 7, 8, 9, A, B, C, D, E, F.

- To make a color lighter, increase the hexadecimal characters. For instance, royal blue is #0000FF; a paler version of the blue could be #7070FF.

- To avoid spending too much time on trial and error when determining suitable colors, download the zip file CCA-2.2.zip from http://www.paciellogroup.com/resources/contrast-analyser.html

Scroll down the home page of The Paciello Group web site until you see Download and a list of language versions. Click the appropriate language version to download the zip file. Unzip it into a new folder, and then create a desktop shortcut to the file CCA-2.2.exe.

Figure 12-1 shows the Color Contrast Analyser (CCA-2.2) interface.

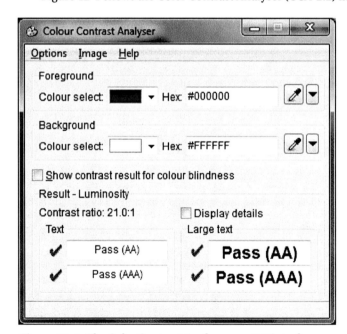

Figure 12-1. The Color Contrast Analyser ver. 2.2 interface

The Color Contrast Analyser can be used in two ways; if you click Options on the menu you can adjust colors by means of sliders, or you can see what happens to a color when you change the hexadecimal numbers.

1. Double-click the shortcut (the spelling of "color" in the CCA interface is the UK and Australian *colour*).

2. Type the color's hexadecimal number in the Foreground Colour Select Hex field. You will see the color in the corresponding Colour Select field.

3. Change the hexadecimal code a little at a time until you achieve the required color.

4. Make a note of the hexadecimal color code and use it to amend your CSS style sheet.

■ **Tip** Originally, only 17 colors could be specified by a name such as red or blue. Now, you can name 147 colors, such as `color: mediumpurple;` for example. For more information, visit `www.w3schools.com/cssref/css_colornames.asp` and `http://somacon.com/p142.php`.

One other problem will be encountered: compared with Internet Explorer, Mozilla Firefox displays paler border colors on menu buttons styled by the CSS dynamic pseudo-class method. In most cases, this is acceptable, but if not, you could experiment with the border colors to provide a compromise that looked reasonable in both IE and Mozilla Firefox. As an alternative, the CSS style sheet for IE could be made a conditional style sheet; the main style sheet would then provide the border colors for the other browsers.

Monitor Sizes and Screen Resolutions

No matter which resolution you design for (see Table 12-1), there will be drawbacks. You cannot possibly know the size of the users' monitors or how the resolution is set up. Elderly folk with fading eyesight may set a 19-inch screen to 800 × 600, preferring big, blurred icons and fonts to sharp but small icons and fonts.

■ **Tip** For an interesting page on various screen and color resolutions statistics, visit `http://www.w3schools.com/browsers/browsers_display.asp`.

Table 12-1. The resolutions currently available (pixels horizontal × vertical)

4:3 ratio of width to height	800 × 600	1024 × 768	1152 × 864	1600 × 1200
Other ratios of width to height	1024 × 600	1280 × 720	1280 × 800	1280 × 1024
	1366 × 768	1440 × 900	1680 × 1050	1920 × 1080

Non-normal ratios can slightly distort the appearance of a web site; items are stretched vertically. Some wide screen ratios can introduce a horizontal distortion; for example, a soccer ball becomes oval like a rugby ball.

Some users have a Favorites panel permanently pinned on the browser window so that the usable width of the browser window is reduced, causing the user to scroll horizontally.

Most sites have both long and short pages. On short pages, no vertical scroll bar is displayed. On long pages, the vertical scroll bar appears and the page can move sideways a little so that items appear to jump around as the user moves from short pages to long pages. CSS absolute positioning can partly overcome this.

The real screen area is less than the stated number of pixels because of the following:

- People lose vertical screen space by adding extra and unnecessary toolbars, such as those provided by Google or Yahoo.

- The Windows vertical scroll bar takes up some of the width, allow at least 24 pixels for this when setting the width of your pages. For example, use a fixed width of around 980 pixels for the most common horizontal monitor resolution of 1024. Use 1200 pixels for a monitor with a horizontal resolution of 1280 pixels.

- There are slight differences in the way that Internet Explorer and Mozilla Firefox render pages; however, most of these can be smoothed out by a reset at the beginning of the style sheet.

Web designers must accept the fact that they can't win. Whatever size and resolution they design for, the result for different screens sizes will always be a compromise. The rest of this chapter will help you to find the best compromise for your web site or your clients' web sites.

The next section discusses the three types of layout: fixed, liquid, and semi liquid. It describes their problems, limitations, and possible solutions.

▓ **Note** The markup for the next three examples is identical except for the content of the `<title>` tags and attributes shown bold in the CSS files. Heights are included in the CSS sheets to produce short screenshots, but heights should not normally be specified because you will need different heights for each page, depending on the amount of content. For instructional purposes, positional `ids` are used to indicate column positions.

Monitors and the Problem with Fixed-Width Layouts

I am sometimes requested to take over an older, fixed-width web site that was designed for screens with a resolution of 800 pixels × 600 pixels. The owner was disturbed by the fact that on modern screens (above 1024 × 768 resolution), the web site pages looked too small. With the advent of even larger resolutions and huge screens, the pages began to resemble postage stamps.

I might redesign the web site with a fixed width of 1024 × 800 and accept the fact that it will cause users to scroll horizontally on an 800 × 600 screen. Fixed-width web sites are the easiest to design and control, and because most web sites are fixed width, users currently accept their limitations on bigger screens. At some future date, the 1024-pixel fixed width will need to be increased to match the ever-increasing screen sizes and resolutions.

Figure 12-2 shows a fixed-width layout on a 19-inch screen.

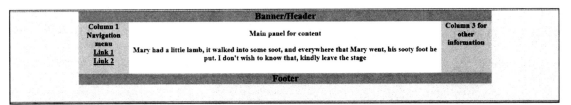

Figure 12-2. Example of a simple, three-column, 980-pixel, fixed-width layout on a 19–inch screen. This page would almost fill a screen that was set to 1024 pixels horizontal resolution.

The web page in Figure 12-2 has a fixed width of 980 pixels and is shown here on a 19-inch screen at its natural resolution. The fixed width (980 pixels) is the most popular at the moment. It is used by web sites such as www.bbc.co.uk. If the horizontal dimension is shrunk by using the cursor to drag the right-hand edge to the left, the edge slides over the content like drawing a curtain across it. This is good practice because the content layout is not disturbed by shrinking the width. On smaller or lower resolution screens or when the screen is shrunk by the user, the elements on a page may slide over each other. This can be prevented by using CSS positioning or by having a container set to a fixed width as in the Listing 12-2b.

Download the code files for this chapter from the book's page at http://www.apress.com. View the three files in a browser on a 19-inch screen set to its native resolution, then try shrinking the width of the browser window to test that the layout does not collapse when the horizontal width is reduced.

The Listing 12-2a produces the screen display shown in Figure 12-2.

▪ **Note** Semantic tags have not been used in the next three examples in order to keep the markup simple for instructional purposes.

Listing 12-2a. Creating a Fixed Width Page (fixed-3col.html)

```
<!doctype html>
<html lang=en>
<head>
<title>Fixed width layout with three columns</title>
<meta charset=utf-8>
        meta details go here
<link rel = "stylesheet" type = "text/css" href = "fixed.css">
</head>
<body>
<div id="container">
<div id = "hdr" >Banner/Header</div>
        <ul>Column 1 Navigation menu
                <li>Link 1</li>
                <li>Link 2</li>
        </ul>
<div id = "col-3">Column 3 for other information>
</div>
<div id = "main-panel"><p>
<strong>Main panel for content</strong></p><p>Mary had a little lamb, it walked into ↵
some soot, and everywhere that Mary went, his sooty foot he put. I don't wish to ↵
know that, kindly leave the stage</p>
```

```
</div>
<div id = "ftr">Footer
</div>
</div>
</body>
</html>
```

The width is fixed in the CSS (fixed.css) by simply inserting width:980px;. This is shown in bold in Listing 12-2b.

Listing 12-2b. The CSS Style Sheet for Listing 12-2a (fixed.css)

```
Width:100%; body { text-align: center;background-color:yellow; font-family:"times new roman";
font-size:large; font-weight:bold;
}
#container { width:980px; padding: 0; text-align: center; margin:auto;  ↵
background-color:white;
}
/* set widths and float on nav col and col 3*/
ul { float: left; padding:0; margin:0; width: 100px; height:120px;
}
li { padding-left:0; margin-left:0; list-style-type:none; text-decoration:underline;
}
#col-3 { float: right; width: 100px; height:120px;
}
/* set main-panel margins 5px greater than ul column and col-3 widths*/
#main-panel { margin-left: 105px; margin-right:105px;
}
#hdr { font-size:x-large; font-weight:bold;
}
/* force footer to stay at the bottom */
#ftr { clear: both; font-size:x-large; font-weight:bold;
}
/* show boundaries by using colors - for clarity only */
#hdr, #ftr { background: fuchsia;
}
ul, #col-3 { background: aqua;
}
#main-panel { background: white;
}
```

We next examine the liquid layout, which was developed to cope with the variations in screen width. It was a reasonable solution for a while, but as screens became wider and screen resolutions increased, it became clear that the liquid layout had its own problems. These will be explained next.

Monitors and the Problem with Liquid Layouts

On smaller screens, the liquid web site can go to pieces due to *float drop*. This means that an element on a page, such as an image, drops down below the other elements. See Chapter 19 for troubleshooting float drop.

Liquid sites have another problem: text can stretch across a high resolution wide screen, making reading difficult; the reader's head waves too and fro like a windshield wiper. You should always present text in columns to solve this problem. On high-resolution wide screens, liquid layouts result in large, unsightly gaps between in-line pictures. This can be can be partly overcome by placing pictures one above the other on a page with the text to the side of the pictures.

If you have problems with liquid pages and you have a deadline to meet, don't spend too much time on it, but change to a fixed width (let's say 980 pixels). Then return to the problem after the launch date.

A CSS background pattern can be liquid if it is a repeating pattern. This can give the impression of continuity by repeating the background so that it spans the entire width and height of the screen.

A liquid layout page is shown filling the width of a 19-inch screen in Figure 12-3.

Figure 12-3. A simple, liquid, three-column layout. This example fills 100 percent of any screen width. Note the wide span of the central text. This effect would worsen on screens with high resolutions.

A liquid layout designed on a screen with 1024 horizontal resolution will look messy on screens with smaller resolutions. Listing 12-3a and its CSS Listing 12-3b provide a liquid layout by setting the container to a width of 100 percent. This is shown in bold type.

Listing 12-3a. Creating a Liquid Page that will Fill any Screen Width (liquid-3col.html)

```
<!doctype html>
<html lang=en>
<head>
<title>Liquid 3 column layout.</title>
<meta charset=utf-8>
        meta details go here
<link rel = "stylesheet" type = "text/css" href = "liquid.css">
</head>
<body>
<div id="container">
<div id = "hdr" >Banner/Header</div>
<ul>Column 1 Navigation menu
                <li>Link 1</li>
                <li>Link 2</li>
</ul>
<div id = "col-3">Column 3 for other information
</div>
<div id = "main-panel"><p><strong>Main panel for content</strong></p>
<p>Mary had a little lamb, it walked ↵
into some soot, and everywhere that Mary went, his sooty foot he put. ↵
I don't wish to know that, kindly leave the stage</p>
</div>
<div id = "ftr">Footer
</div>
</div>
</body>
 </html>
```

In Listing 12-3b (the CSS style), the liquid layout uses a width of 100 percent, but liquid layouts can have a smaller percentage figure. The key to liquid layouts is that a percentage is used to define the width instead of pixels.

Listing 12-3b. The CSS Style Sheet for Listing 12-3a (liquid.css)

```
/* flood the background with yellow */
body { text-align: center; background-color:yellow; font-family:"times new roman"; ↵
font-size:large; font-weight:bold;
}
#container { width:100%; padding: 0; text-align: center; margin:auto; background-color:white;
}
ul { float: left;  padding:0; margin:0; width: 100px; height:120px;
}
li  { padding-left:0; margin-left:0; list-style-type:none; text-decoration:underline;
}
#col-3 { float: right; width: 100px; height:120px;
}
/* set panel margins 5px greater than ul and col-3 widths*/
#main-panel { margin-left: 105px; margin-right:105px; font-weight:bold;
}
#hdr { font-size:x-large;font-weight:bold;
}
/* force footer to stay at the bottom */
#ftr { clear: both; font-size:x-large; font-weight:bold;
}
/* show boundaries and set colors - for clarity only */
#hdr, #ftr { background: fuchsia;
}
ul, #col-3 { background: aqua;
}
#main-panel { background: white;
}
```

We have seen that both fixed and liquid layouts have their problems. In the next example, we will examine an acceptable solution using semi-liquid layouts.

Monitors and Semi-Liquid Layouts

A semi-liquid layout is a variation on the liquid layout that uses two special attributes namely, min-width and max-width. A page using a semi-liquid layout is shown in Figure 12-4.

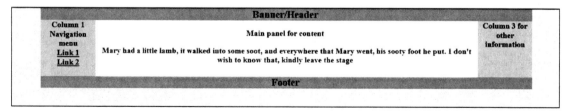

Figure 12-4. A semi-liquid layout with restricted max- and min-widths. This is the best compromise.

Figure12-4 is shown on a 19-inch screen set to its native resolution. The page is designed to never exceed 1200-pixels horizontal width; therefore, the content in the white panel does not stretch excessively. Viewed on a screen with a resolution less than 960 pixels, the viewer will have to scroll to see some of the right-hand column. It is a good idea to put non-essential information in the right-hand column, such as credits and advertisements. This leaves the main content exactly as the designer intended, no matter what resolution or size is used to view it. Listing 12-4a and its associated CSS Listing 12-4b provide the semi-liquid layout shown in Figure 12-4.

Listing 12-4a. Creating a Semi-liquid Page (liquid-3col-max-min.html)

```
<!doctype html>
<html lang=en>
<head>
<title>Liquid layout with restricted max and min width</title>
<meta charset=utf-8>
        meta details go here
<head>
<link rel = "stylesheet" type = "text/css" href = "liquid-maxmin.css">
</head>
<body>
<div id="container">
<div id = "hdr">Header/Banner<br></div>
<ul>Column 1<br>Navigation menu
<li>Link 1</li>
<li>Link 2</li>
</ul>
<div id = "col-3">Column 3<br>for other information
</div>
<div id = "main-panel"><p><strong>Main panel for content</strong></p>
<p>Mary had a little lamb, it walked into ↵
some soot, and everywhere that Mary went,<br>his sooty foot he put. I don't ↵
wish to know that, kindly leave the stage</p>
</div>
<div id = "ftr">Footer
</div>
</div>
</body>
</html>
```

The CSS Listing 12-4b provides a neat solution for the problem of variations in screen width. The attributes max-width and min-width limit the display so that it does not become too wide and cannot be shrunk to the extent that the layout falls apart. The width is a percentage, like the liquid layout, and limits are set by the code shown in bold.

Listing 12-4b. The CSS Style Sheet for Listing 12-4a (liquid-maxmin.css)

```
/* flood the screen with yellow*/
body { text-align: center; background-color:yellow; font-family:"times new roman"; ↵
font-size:large; font-weight:bold;
}
#container { width:95%; margin:auto; background-color:white; text-align: center; ↵
max-width:1200px; min-width:960px;
}
#hdr {  font-size:x-large;font-weight:bold;
```

```
}
/* set widths and float on nav col and col 3*/
ul { float: left;  padding:0; margin:0; width: 100px; height:120px;
}
li  { padding-left:0; margin-left:0; list-style-type:none; text-decoration:underline;
}
#col-3 { float: right; width: 100px; height:120px;
}
/* set panel margins 5px greater than col-1 & col-3 widths */
#main-panel { margin-left: 105px; margin-right:105px; background-color:white;
}
/* force footer to stay at the bottom */
#ftr { clear: both;
}
/* color the elements - for clarity only */
#hdr, #ftr { background: fuchsia;
}
ul, #col-3 { background: aqua;
}
#main-panel { background: white;
}
```

By combining the two techniques—a full-width body background color and a semi-liquid layout—an acceptable solution can be applied to the problem of variations in screen width and resolution.

An Acceptable Compromise

Use a semi-liquid web site container or wrapper. Give the body a background color or gradient to fill any screen size and resolution. Define this color in the CSS, as follows:

```
/* Flood the whole screen with yellow*/
body { background-color:yellow; }
#container { width:95%; min-width:960px; max-width:1200px; margin:auto; }
```

This gives the *impression* of a page that fills the screen (the body's background) while leaving the content (the #container) well laid-out in the center of the screen. Making the header/banner fill the width of the screen can reinforce this impression, but this is not always attractive. The semi-liquid container with minimum width prevents a layout going to pieces on smaller resolutions. The maximum width limit ensures that the content will not sprawl across a big screen showing huge gaps between elements.

Other considerations can determine the layout of a web site. You will need to consult your client about the equipment he is using and his future intentions concerning that equipment. Also the advent of handheld devices complicates the problem of choosing suitable layouts.

Other Monitor-Related Considerations

When designing a web site for an office or a factory's internal use, you will need to visit the premises to determine the screen sizes and resolutions. The employees will not be pleased if they have to continually scroll horizontally to access items on the page. Should the company invest in new equipment with bigger screens, you will need to change the container width to match. You may have to put the text into two columns for ease of reading.

> ▓ **Note** The employment of two columns for text is essential for wide layouts and particularly for liquid layouts. See Chapter 13 for methods of designing two or more columns of text.

Other types of users and devices will increasingly need special consideration. The advent of new handheld devices with different operating systems and browsers complicates and increases the difficulty of the tasks confronting the web site designer.

Will the Web Site Work on a Handheld Device?

Handheld is a term describing mobile phones and tablets. Designing for handheld devices is a big manual unto itself and, therefore, will only have a brief mention in this book. Many web sites designed for desktop computers already work reasonably well on larger mobiles and tablets (provided that they validate, and do not contain frames or table layout).

> ▓ **Tip** *Programming the Mobile Web* by Maximiliano Firtman (O'Reilly Media, 2010) is a book on the subject.

The Problem

The advent of handheld devices that can view web sites is the web designers' latest nightmare. The screen resolution can vary from 176 × 220 pixels to 1280 × 800 pixels. Mobile phones generally have portrait-style screens taller than their width, and screens vary from 2.8 inches to 4 inches. Tablet screens vary from 3.2 inches to 10 inches. The Samsung Galaxy Tab 10.1 has a 10.1-inch display with a resolution of 1280 × 800. The Apple iPad has a 9.7-inch display with 1024 × 768 pixels. Some mobiles and most tablets have the ability to flip the screen view from portrait to landscape. The higher resolution is possible on handheld touchscreen devices because they don't have to provide room for a keyboard. Originally, handheld devices were either mobile phones or tablets; now the distinction is blurred because tablets incorporate phones and cameras.

At the Consumer Electronics Show in 2011, no less than 80 tablets were on display. As for operating systems, the battle is between several platforms/browsers at the moment and this seems set to increase. Among these are iOS4 OS6 4, Android, Opera, Windows 7, Windows 8, WebOS, Blackberry OS, Simbian, and QNX Neutrino.

At first, browsers for handheld devices were adaptations of desktop browsers. They are now more likely to be designed specifically for handheld devices. The browsers have to be more compact than desktop browsers because handhelds have less RAM and no hard disk to swap memory with.

Browsers for handheld devices are more compact; that means they have dispensed with much of the code that compensates for markup errors. Because they are less tolerant, validation of the pages becomes absolutely essential.

Web designers sometimes produce alternative style sheets to match the miniature screens, to the various mobile browsers, lower resolutions, and various operating systems. Handheld users are familiar with using a zoom facility to explore a web page. If you create special style sheets for handhelds, try to reduce the need for horizontal scrolling. When providing these alternative style sheets, place a link to them before any other link, as follows:

```
<link rel="stylesheet" type="text/css;" href="md-sheet.css" media="handheld" />
<link rel="stylesheet" type="text/css;" href="stylesheet.css" media="screen" />
```

Creating the alternative styles for a web site requires a great deal of trial and error followed by a series of tests on mobile devices. With 80 different handheld devices and a multitude of platforms and browsers, the task is truly daunting. No web designer can hope to ensure that the style sheets will be suitable for the entire range of devices.

Therefore, the designer's first task is to decide which of her web sites are most likely to be viewed on handheld devices. She should then concentrate on making them handheld-friendly.

Web designers are faced with difficult choices. They could decide to

1. Ignore handheld devices.

2. Design for desktops, laptops, netbooks, tablets, and mobiles with screens larger than (let's say) 6 inches.

3. Design for desktops, laptops, netbooks, tablets, and mobiles with screens larger than (let's say) 6 inches, as well as two or three of the smaller, most popular handhelds.

4. Try to accommodate everything.

Choices one and two are manageable. The third solution requires that you wrestle with some testing methods. The fourth solution has a learning curve the size of Mount Everest. Larger companies can afford the time and manpower to create completely separate sites for handhelds and tablets. For some general guidance on how to set up and create alternative style sheets for solutions two and three, visit http://www.opera.com/developer/tools.

The Opera site contains useful tools, including a tablet and phone simulator.

Producing an Alternative Style Sheet for Handhelds

One solution would be to have a special style sheet for handhelds that makes the display acceptable. Although, you will probably discover that you also need modified HTML markup. This can be kept to a minimum with careful planning. The following are some hints on modifying the markup so that you can use two style sheets with HTML pages that support both desktops and handhelds.

- Reduce the size and quantity of images.

- Simplify the home page, making it a container for the links to the other pages. The links should be a simple, vertical, unordered list.

- Text should be in one column with a restricted maximum width if possible to avoid horizontal scrolling.

- Keep banners and logos to a basic minimum or hide them.

- The quantity of text should be condensed to the absolute minimum.

- Be sure to examine lots of web sites on handheld devices so that you can see the difference between good and bad adaptations of web sites.

Testing a Web Site for Handheld Compatibility

Individual web designers or small teams will have problems affording equipment for testing handhelds. This is because of the huge range of devices and their several operating systems and browsers. The following is a list of possibilities:

- Ask children, grandchildren, or friends with handheld devices to view your web site and ask them to comment on any problems.

- Download some handheld emulators for testing web sites.

- Buy some handhelds or pay monthly subscriptions for a selection of the most popular models.

- Enter "Remote device access" into a search engine and examine the results for possible remote-testing facilities.

- W3C has a validator for mobile markup at `http://validator.w3.org/mobile`. Upload your file or URL to see if the markup is suitable for handheld devices.

Emulators

I found several downloadable emulators on the internet, but they were very difficult to set up and master. I needed a PhD in gobbledygook to follow the instructions; however, I did have some success with the Opera Mini emulator. Once installed, it has a launcher that enables you to choose various screen sizes, resolutions, and orientations (landscape or portrait).

You can download the Opera emulator from `http://www.opera.com/developer/tools/`.

The emulator was tricky to operate, but the help files on the Opera developer web site explained the non-intuitive controls. For the help files, visit `http://dev.opera.com/articles/view/opera-mobile-emulator/`.

Summary

This chapter discussed the problem of the wide variations in color, size, and resolution of desktop and laptop monitors. Compromise solutions were covered; these can be downloaded and tried on various screens. Fortunately, the physical size of monitors imposes its own limit; few users have room for anything wider than a 23-inch screen. You also learned how the `max-width` and `min-width` attributes offer the best solution to the problem of screen size variation.

Handheld devices can now receive and view web sites. We briefly covered the problems posed by these devices. Handhelds vary widely in size and have many different operating systems. New ones are being launched every month and their browsers are upgraded frequently. Manuals for designing web sites for handhelds will quickly date.

The next chapter is closely related to this chapter and deals with the appearance of a web site on the screen. You will learn what makes a page attractive to the user and how to keep the user interested enough to explore the site, rather than wandering away to another site. You will also discover how the site's usefulness contributes to this aim.

CHAPTER 13

Appearance and Usefulness

Visitors will only explore a web site if it is attractive and useful. Some web site owners ask for a site that pleases them, without considering what will please their site's visitors. Such a site makes the owner happy, but it may do nothing for the visitor or for the owner's business. Site owners should ask themselves what the site will do for visitors. They should ask several people what they would hope to find if they accessed the site.

When talking to potential clients, explain that the web site design process starts not by thinking of text and pictures, but with planning. First and foremost, determine the general goal of the site. Is it for sharing information? Or is it expected to generate sales? Starting with a goal makes it easier to design the site and helps everyone concerned to focus on the purpose of the web site. Concentrate on making the web site's message appear quickly, clearly, and directly.

Consider the navigation and how your secondary content interacts with your goal. Plan the pages or sections. Each page should cover one topic only. List the topics and use the list to plan the navigation menu. Plan the navigation menu and structure *before* starting to compose pages; this will save many hours of tedious revision later.

Appearance

This section on web site appearance begins with a brief discussion about the use and abuse of text; the manner in which the textual content is displayed can enhance or ruin a web page. Next, you will learn about the importance of the home page; how its appearance can either tempt users to explore further or drive them away from your web site. This is followed by a discussion on the effect of colors, and finally some useful tips are provided to help you create more attractive pages.

The Use and Abuse of Text

The guidelines in this section are just plain common sense, but be sure to use them as a checklist to improve your work in case the heart overrules the head. When I began designing web sites, some clients presented me with reams of text guaranteed to drive users away from their web site. I then had the tedious task of condensing the text and this occasionally annoyed the client, which was understandable. I demonstrated that it was possible to condense the text and still retain every bit of the message that the client wished to convey.

I also presented them with this little piece of advice: verbose text may be acceptable in a book, a magazine, or a brochure, but lots of text, especially if it is on the home page, will kill a web site stone dead.

Tests show that, when presented with a large quantity of text, a web site visitor will groan and switch to another web site. This is because reading text on a screen is very tiring compared to a printed page. Visitors do not visit web sites for a read; they surf to find particular information, and they want to find it quickly.

Condensing the text applies chiefly to the main pages, but if you are describing a product or a service, or giving information, don't leave out important details for the sake of brevity; just eliminate the words that add nothing to the message.

That All Important Home Page Must Be Like a Venus Flytrap

All sites start with a home page. The design of the home page is especially important because it is the visitor's first impression and it communicates the tone of the site. Make it an attractive magazine cover (see Figure 13-1). Use it to stimulate the visitor's interest. This is easily done by revealing just enough and no more; this arouses curiosity.

Figure 13-1. The Venus flytrap. Photo courtesy of http://aboutfacts.net

The home page should be like a Venus Flytrap, an attractive landing place that draws the visitors in deeper and keeps them from going to another web site. Each page must clearly focus on one topic and one topic only. This particularly applies to the home page. The focus will be on a brief description of what the web site is about. This must be amplified by the wording on the buttons or links on the navigation menu.

What destroys the focus on a home page? Nothing could be worse than a home page plastered with RSS feeds, commendations, badges, links to irrelevant sites, flashing advertisements, marquees, and running videos. Badges, commendations, and certificates of accreditation have a part to play, but these are best located on an About Us page. W3C validation logos can be placed in a sidebar or in the footer because clients are often keen to show that they employed a competent designer. A yard-long home page and huge blocks of text are focus killers. A page without a clear focal point turns visitors away.

Figures 13-2 and 13-3 show a focused and an unfocused home page.

Figure 13-2. A clean, uncluttered home page

Figure 13-3. Yuck!

The home page must be very brief and uncluttered. Too much information on the home page is bad. It makes subsequent pages redundant. Why should visitors bother to click the menu items if the home page says it all?

The home page must clearly indicate what the site is about.

If you are The Haven Retirement Complex, don't just show the heading "The Haven" with a picture of the building or some happy residents. *Briefly* shout out what is offered; something like the following:

Sheltered Retirement Accommodation

Rented accommodation for older people who want

independence with companionship and support in a caring environment

That says it all in a nutshell; don't add any more text. Let the menu buttons tempt the user to discover the rest of the story.

Pictures can explain things quicker than words. But large pictures (or too many pictures) can make the home page load slowly. Visitors will then turn away to find a web site that loads faster.

White space is essential for focus. Use plenty of white space on each page to focus attention on the important bit. White space means space with no text or pictures. If you have a pale turquoise background, then the white space will be pale turquoise, but it is still classed as white space. White space focuses the attention on the essentials. Poor designers feel tempted to fill every available area of a page. A crowded page is a turn off.

Keep the home page short. Make the height of the home page no greater than the screen window height. Don't make visitors scroll down the home page. If they have to scroll down, you have put too much on the home page. Scrolling down may mean that the menu will no longer be there to tempt them. Of course, subsequent pages can be longer. A short home page ensures that the visitor will look at the menu buttons for more information.

Choose colors carefully. The best text color for clarity and ease of reading is black text on a white background. Sharp background colors such as bright red are irritating if they cover large areas of the page. If your site is selling something, use bright but not garish colors, and use them sparingly (just for the products or the menu buttons). A garish color mix indicates a tasteless and amateurish web site. If you are not selling something but you are providing information, use backgrounds of pale pastel colors to create calm; the visitor will linger longer on a calm web site. Dark background colors are sinister and off-putting (especially black, which is really only suitable for a funeral parlor). Avoid full-page background graphics (watermarks or textures); they can result in a fussy page that makes text difficult to read. Ensure that the text and background color have enough contrast to enable partially-sighted persons to read your web site easily (see Chapter 14 for details on color contrast).

If the client has a house style with a color scheme, or a brochure, or a colored logo, any of these would make a good starting point for a color scheme. Showing a color palette to clients can also help them to choose a theme.

Originally, only 17 colors could be specified by a name such as red or blue. Now, 147 colors can be named like this example: `color: mediumpurple;`. For more information on this, see `www.w3schools.com/css/css_colornames.asp` and `http://somacon.com/p142.php`.

▦ **Tip** Need ideas for colors? Try the following web sites: `http://colorschemedesigner.com` or `http://colorschemer.com` or `http:www.elizabethcastro.com/html/colors/backflapcolors.html` or `www.december.com/html/spec/color.html`.

Every graphic on your site should have a `title` and an `alt` so that even if your visitors have graphics turned off, they can discover what the pictures are about. More importantly, this allows partially-sighted and blind persons to hear a spoken description of the pictures. If a page has pictures without an `alt`, it will not validate. Logos should have empty `alt`s and `title`s like this: `alt=" "` and `title=" "`, which will not hinder the disabled, but will validate. Mozilla will not show a tool tip unless the `title` tag is present.

Every hyperlink must have a `title` like this: `<a href="Page-two.html" title="Page Two">Page Two</a></li>`.

Avoid scrolling text (marquees), autostarting videos, and anything that moves. These gimmicks are the best way to drive people away from your web site. Gimmicks can be intensely irritating or they can become the main focus of attention—to the degree that the rest of the page is ignored. The only exception would be a moving picture (not on the home page) that shows how something works. Whether it runs or not should be under the control of the user; it should not autostart. If it is an animated `.gif`, it must have a limited number of cycles; let's say between five and ten cycles. Video, audio, and slideshows are acceptable if they are not on the home page and users are given the choice as to whether they want to watch/hear it or not (the media files must not autostart).

Autostart means that the sound or video automatically begins when the page is loaded. It's a bad idea because it is bound to irritate. The sudden burst of sound can cause users to jump out of their skins, especially blind users. Users will either immediately switch away from your web site or frantically search for a way to turn off the AV clip. They will probably never return to your site again. Make sure the AV can only begin at the user's request. Autostart might just be acceptable for audio if it loads a short but quiet arpeggio. Perhaps a quiet, soothing piece of background music might be tolerable if it is brief and does not repeat in a never ending loop.

Frames: This was the design method that allowed the content to scroll up and down behind a fixed banner and menu. Frames are no longer acceptable; search engines refuse to penetrate frames in order to locate subsequent pages. Frames do not work on mobile devices and they make screen reading virtually impossible for the blind and partially sighted.

Pages Other Than the Home Page

Printed matter, audio, and film communicate in a linear manner. Viewers start at the beginning and work their way through to the end. *A web site is quite different*; it is non-linear. Users explore by jumping around on the site. Web sites are more like a telephone directory; to find Fred Blogg's telephone number, you pick up the directory (equivalent to the home page), jump to the Bs (for Blogg), skipping past all the other pages. You then skip the B entries until you come to Blo—. After locating the correct phone number, you probably don't explore other pages. The directory has served its purpose. If a visitor to a web site can jump straight to the information he is seeking, then the web site has served its purpose.

Suppose John Smith and his wife decide to take the children on a farm-based holiday in Devon, UK, between July 25 and August 25. John types "farm holiday Devon" into a search engine. He selects the first farm holiday on the results page. On the web site, he sees a menu button labeled Vacancies. He clicks it and is taken to a page that shows him that there are no vacancies on the dates he wants. Using the next search result, the home page is a horrible amateurish mess, so he skips to the next web site on the list. This site gives no indication on how to find out about vacancy dates, so he skips to the next search result. The next web site has no menu button for available dates; instead, the home page tells him to telephone for dates. He can't be bothered with the hassle of telephoning, so off he goes to the next web site. This one has a menu button leading to available dates, which he clicks and sees that there is a suitable date. Good! He will now click the menu button for prices and finds it is far too expensive. So he continues his search until he finds the perfect fit.

Let's analyze this.

1. He visited the home page on six web sites.

2. He abandoned two sites immediately.

3. He explored one other page beyond the home page on three sites.

4. Then he explored two other pages beyond the home page on the last site.

Web site owners find it hard to believe that users don't read every one of their carefully crafted pages.

However, if John finds the right vacancy at the right price, he will then explore the other pages on that web site to find out what the accommodation is like, where it is located, what the local attractions are, who the owners are (in the About Us page), and finally, he will use the order form to book a holiday.

Visitors regard content on their computer screen as being directed only at them. Your tone and writing style should be casual and very concise. This gives a personal touch, as if you are speaking one-to-one. Verbose formal prose may demonstrate how articulate and learned you are, but it will irritate your busy visitors; they will go elsewhere.

Always use headings and subheadings. Use h1, h2, h3, h4, h5, and h6 headings. Visitors rarely read text; they bounce from heading to heading looking for specific topics that interest them. Blind and partially-sighted visitors can hop from heading to heading with a screen reader by tapping the H key. Headings were once neglected because of the big line spaces above and below them. The spaces and font sizes of headings are now easily adjusted using CSS (see Chapter 14).

Never spread text right across a page. When the eye has reached the end of a long line of text, the visitor turns his head back to the beginning of the line and is usually lost (and he eventually gives up the struggle). Use two columns instead. The accepted maximum width of a column is 5.25 inches (133 mm) on a resolution of 1024 × 768. A web site for children should have even smaller column widths.

Small fonts are not user-friendly. The text in the main body should never be smaller than 100 percent for Times New Roman and never less than 80 percent for Arial or Verdana. Nobody will bother to fetch a magnifying glass to peer at a web site set in 8 pt.

Try not to use more than two fonts on a page. Arial and Verdana are the preferred sans serif fonts because they were designed for easy reading on web sites. Times New Roman is the best serif font because it was specifically designed and tested for good readability, especially for printed matter.

Text should be split into bite-size chunks, use bullets or headings where appropriate. Selling points are best highlighted by bullets. If possible, let the text be interspersed with pictures. Once visitors have located a site that offers what they are looking for, they will be eager to explore more pages. Finally, when they are hooked, they will want to know more about the people offering the product. The About Us page is usually the last to be visited, but it can clinch a sale.

Do not use justified paragraphs. Justified text is a killer and must be avoided at all costs. The brain has to struggle to overcome the wild variation in gaps between the words. Also, justified text looks boring compared with the liveliness of ragged, right-justified text. Compare the two styles in magazines to see how interesting a ragged-right style looks. Justified text can be a problem to the dyslexic and to anyone using screen magnification software because the varying gaps between words are also magnified. Justified text has distracting rivers of white space running through it.

Small italic fonts never look good on a web site. Small italic font appears on a computer screen as a series of what typographical designers call "jaggies." The text has a rough, sawtooth appearance; therefore, italics should be avoided except for larger fonts.

Helping Your Clients Choose a Design

If your clients have no experience of web site design, they will want to know how to proceed. Always be as helpful as possible because they will need to learn the basics; this calls for a great deal of patience. The more they learn from you, the less likely they are to ask for daft things. Strongly resist the temptation to demonstrate your expertise; it will contribute nothing to discovering what your client wants.

New clients sometimes present you with a printed page from a ghastly web site and say, "That is how I would like my web site to look." The best approach is to agree at first then say something like "Let's see how we can go one better than that. We need some input from both of us to tidy it up a little." I gently point out why some of the ghastly bits in the client's sample would detract from the proposed site.

As previously mentioned, any of the client's existing marketing materials or logos make a great starting point. The client may have reached the point where he wants to change his house style; not only does this help you work with your client to create a completely new look and feel, but it provides an opportunity to generate more work for you or your team.

When talking to prospective clients who have no idea what they want or who have no knowledge of web site design, I sit them beside me in front of my computer screen to do each of the following:

- I show them a page of templates to help them choose a color and a page layout (see Figure 13-4).

- I ask them to list the topics they wish to include. I then explain that one topic equals one page and that one topic is one button or link on the navigation menu.

- I explain approximately how much each page will cost so that they are absolutely certain about their commitment if they agree to proceed.

- I explain how much hosting and domain registration will cost.

- I explain how much each image will cost to process and insert into a page.

- I ask how they intend to provide me with images.

- I ask what on-going maintenance they might require and I give them an estimate of the cost of updating the web site.

- I make sure the prospective client understands the size and time limitations of hosting videos (see Chapter 6 for details).

- I suggest they carefully consider everything we discussed before committing to the project.

Figure 13-4. A typical page of samples to help a client choose a color and a design

The point of all this is that prospective clients should feel reassured and go away feeling that they know something about the process and are no longer dummies. If you make a prospective client feel foolish or ignorant, you deserve to lose him or her.

Make the project a fully cooperative venture. Using my own web site host, I create a folder called "hidden," then I let the client know the URL to this folder. I upload the client's draft pages one by one into that folder so that he or she can see the latest page and view any progress on earlier pages. The client can then contribute and comment every step of the way.

Arrange the registration and hosting of the web site with your clients. I have mine sit next to me and register the site in their names. Then I give the clients all the FTP details in case they should wish to switch to another webmaster at some time in the future. I explain that the web site will be registered and hosted in the client's name and that he or she will own the copyright for the web site. Some despicable web designers will lock a client into an endless contract so that the client can never transfer the site to someone else. Having trapped the client, these loathsome web site designers will then charge an extortionate annual maintenance fee.

A Show/Hide Text Technique Giving a Compact Page

In this chapter's "Use and Abuse of Text" section, I explained that too much text drives people away from a web site. A news page can be made more compact and easier to use by displaying only the headlines. Users can expand the headline to read the news item of their choice (see Figures 13-5 and 13-6). For this you will need to download the JavaScript file jquery.js and put it in the root folder of your web site. jQuery is a cross-browser library designed to simplify client-side scripting.

The following hide/show technique was perfected and published by Karl Swedberg. For the download, go to http://jquery.com. For more information, see http://www.learningjquery.com/2006/09/basic-show-and-hide and also http://www.learningjquery.com/2007/02/more-showing-more-hiding

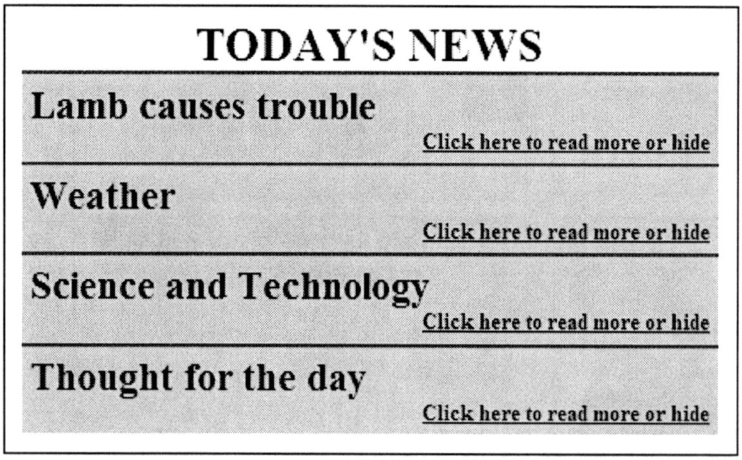

TODAY'S NEWS

Lamb causes trouble

Click here to read more or hide

Weather

Click here to read more or hide

Science and Technology

Click here to read more or hide

Thought for the day

Click here to read more or hide

Figure 13-5. I have taken the simplest version of Karl Swedberg's technique and added a few, user-friendly embellishments.

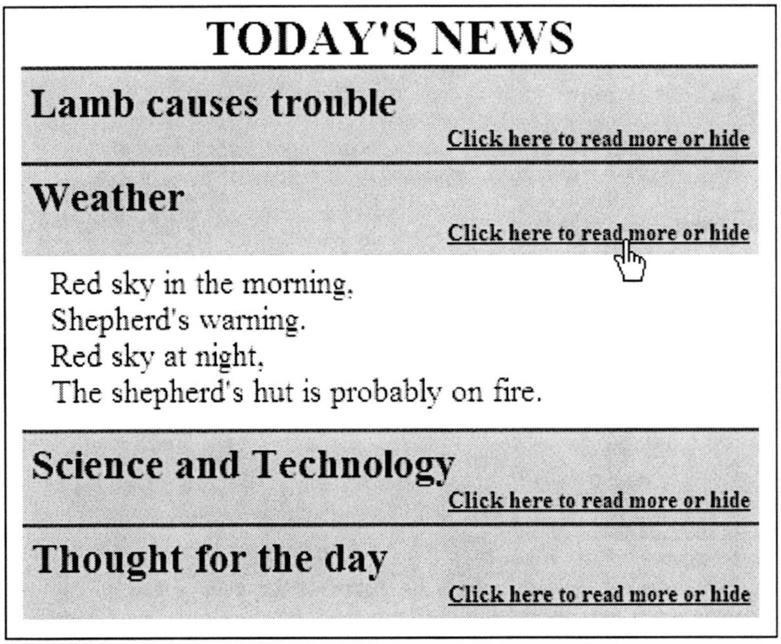

TODAY'S NEWS

Lamb causes trouble

Click here to read more or hide

Weather

Click here to read more or hide

Red sky in the morning.
Shepherd's warning.
Red sky at night,
The shepherd's hut is probably on fire.

Science and Technology

Click here to read more or hide

Thought for the day

Click here to read more or hide

Figure 13-6. The news item is expanded when clicked.

The code for creating a page of headlines with a show/hide facility in Figures 13-5 and 13-6 is shown in Listing 13-5.

Listing 13-5. Creating a Show/Hide Page with jquery (show-hide.html)

```
<!doctype html>
<html lang=en>
<head>
<title> Show/hide text from learningjquery.com</title>
<meta charset=utf-8>
        meta details go here
<script src="jquery.js" type="text/JavaScript">
</script>
<script type="text/JavaScript">
$(document).ready(function() {
$('div.demo-show:eq(0)> div').hide();
$('div.demo-show:eq(0)> h3').click(function() {
$(this).next().slideToggle('fast');
});
});
</script>
<style type="text/css">
body { font-size:110%;
}
.demo-show { width: 400px; margin:0 auto 0 auto; text-align:left;
}
```

```
h1 { font-size:150%; font-weight:bold; margin:5px 0 0 0;
}
.demo-show h2 { font-size:130%; margin:0; background: #bfcd93; ↵
border-top: 2px solid #386785; border-bottom:0; padding:5px 0 0 5px;
}
.demo-show h3 { font-size:small; margin: 0; color:blue; text-decoration:underline; ↵
cursor:pointer; background: #bfcd93; text-align:right; padding:0 5px 5px 0;
}
.demo-show div { margin:0 0 5px 10px; padding:5px;
}
span.link { font-size:small; color:blue; text-decoration:underline; text-align:right;
}
#container { width:450px; margin:auto; text-align:center;
}
</style>
</head>
<body>
<div id="container">
<h1>TODAY&#39;S NEWS</h1>
        <div class="demo-show">
                <h2>Lamb causes trouble</h2>
                <h3>Click here to read more or hide</h3>
        <div>Mary had a little lamb<br>that walked into some soot<br>And everywhere ↵
        that Mary went<br>His sooty foot he put
        </div>
        <h2>Weather</h2>
                <h3>Click here to read more   or hide</h3>
        <div>Red sky in the morning,<br>Shepherd&#39;s warning.<br>
                Red sky at night,<br>The shepherd&#39;s hut is probably on fire.
        </div>
                <h2>Science and Technology</h2>
                <h3>Click here to read more or hide</h3>
        <div>Scintillate, Scintillate globule ethereal<br>How I contemplate your ↵
        structure and material.<br>(with apologies to twinkle twinkle little star)
        </div>
                <h2>Thought for the day</h2>
                <h3>Click here to read more or hide</h3>
        <div>&quot;Give me golf clubs, fresh air and a beautiful woman partner,<br>↵
        and you can keep your clubs and the fresh air.&quot;<br>Jack Benny
        </div>
        </div>
        </div>
</body>
</html>
```

An internal style was used in Listing 13-5 for convenience only. The second block of JavaScript code is shown, but it would normally be extracted into an external file and named show-hide.js. The markup would then call the JavaScript file like this:

```
script src="show-hide.js" type="text/JavaScript">
</script>
```

The first piece of JavaScript calls the file jquery.js; this is the engine that drives this technique.

```
<script src="jquery.js" type="text/JavaScript">
</script>
```

The first line of the next block of JavaScript is `$(document).ready(function() {`
It is saying, "When the page is loaded, execute the next JavaScript lines."
In the HTML markup all the news items are enclosed by a `<div>` with the class demo-show.

```
<div class="demo-show">
        News snippets go here
</div>
```

Each news item is written within a markup group like the following (shown in bold):

```
<h2>Lamb causes trouble</h2>
<h3>Click here to read more or hide</h3>
<div>Mary had a little lamb<br>that walked into some soot<br>And everywhere ⏎
that Mary went<br>His sooty foot he put
</div>
```

The second line of JavaScript interacts with the user. The line `$('div.demo-show:eq(0)>
div').hide();` targets each `<div>` within the demo-show class and hides the content of the `<div>`.
The next two lines target the `<h3>` tags within the demo-show group:

```
$('div.demo-show:eq(0)> h3').click(function() {
$(this).next().slideToggle('fast');
);
```

They trigger a fast, toggle action that makes the content of the `<h3>` tags into links. These links show
or hide the divs containing the expanded news item.

The CSS styles make these links blue and underlined to indicate that they are live links.

Finally, a cursor is added to the links in the CSS relating to the `<h3>` targets. The link and cursor
styles are shown in bold type.

```
.demo-show h3 {  font-size:small; margin: 0; color:blue; ⏎
text-decoration:underline; cursor:pointer; background: #bfcd93; ⏎
text-align:right; padding:0 5px 5px 0;
}
```

■ **Note** The cursor name `pointer` is a misnomer; you would expect it to be an arrow, but it is actually a hand.

The new HTML5 `<details>` and `<summary>` tags provide a show/hide feature but at the time of
writing only Chrome them. As a result, I have been unable to test the proposed markup properly
without a reasonable range of browser support. When this feature is used, the `<summary>` element will be
clickable to expand or shrink the details.

Show/Hide in HTML5

The markup for the new HTML5 show/hide feature will be something like this:

```
<details>
<summary>Was the Mona Lisa a paint by numbers kit?</summary>
<p>No, Leonardo used a graphics program on the world's first computer, Colossus </p>
</details>
```

Usefulness

A useful web site will become a popular web site. For example, a manufacturer of quiz-buzzers could become more popular than other quiz buzzer manufacturers if his web site contained useful things such as quiz questions and instructions on a variety of alternative quiz games. A web site is useful if it has a recognizable branding, an easily understood navigation system, and a simple means of searching the web site.

Boost the Site's Image with a Favicon

The word *favicon* stands for favorites icon. Such icons can add a touch of importance to a web site simply because all the big names have a favicon. They are also useful for site recognition and branding. More importantly, it is useful, it helps the user to quickly identify a particular site in the Favorites list (bookmarks list) and on a browser tab. Figure 13-7 shows the the favicon on my computer-help web site.

Figure 13-7. *The "C" in the Address field and in the tab is the favicon for http://www.colycomputerhelp.co.uk*

The favorites that stand out in a Favorites or History list, are the ones that have a favicon as shown in Figure 13-8.

Figure 13-8. The "C" favicon stands out in the Favorites list.

Creating the Favicon

A favicon must be a 16-pixel square, which means that, because it is so small, you can forget about fine detail. In Figure 13-9 the Coly Computer Help favicon is shown enlarged; it demonstrates that favicons cannot show sharp detail. However, this does not matter as long as you simplify the content.

Figure 13-9. The Coly Computer Help favicon

      Use some ingenuity and choose a meaningful icon. For my web site (http://www.colycomputerhelp.co.uk), I chose the first letter of the URL; that is, "C" in a distinctive uppercase font in blue. Use a color if you can; it will make it stand out in the Favorite's list and on browser tabs. Shrink the image down to 16 × 16 pixels and save it as a .gif or .png file. It is important to save it as a 16-color image; otherwise it will become very blurred. Now it must be converted to an .ico file and renamed favicon.ico.

> ■ **Tip** Many paint programs are unable to save an image in the .ico format. Adobe Photoshop needs a plug-in and Paint Shop Pro 7 to 9 will not save in the .ico format. The free programs GIMP and IrfanView save .ico files. IcoFX is a free program for producing icons. It is available for download from http://www.icofx.ro. Although it is rather tricky to use, once mastered, it is a useful utility. As you would expect, it takes .png and .gif image files and saves the resulting icon as an *.ico* file.

Upload the favicon icon to your root directory at the host, it must be named favicon.ico. You do not have to add anything to the HTML code. However, if you wish to play safe, or the favicon does not show on a particular browser, you can add a link in the <head> section of the page like this:

<link rel="shortcut icon" href="favicon.ico">

All the browsers except Chrome will show the favicon on the left of the address bar. All except Chrome will show it on browser tabs and in the Favorites list (bookmarks).

> ■ **Caution** If you have several web sites and each one has a favicon, *they must all be named* favicon.ico. Clearly, to avoid confusion you must take great care to store them apart in folders relating to each web site.

There is a potential problem. After uploading the favicon, you may find it does not show up in the address bar although it might appear on a browser tab. This means that a copy of the previous non-favicon version of your page is stored in your browser's cache, the old version is being displayed. You will need to empty the browser's cache. Alternatively, look at that web site on another person's computer or on one of your other computers. If you can see the favicon in another computer or in a different browser, then you know it was successfully loaded even though you can't see it in your usual browser while the old page is in your cache.

Usefulness for Visitors and Owners

A web site is most useful if it contains everything the visitor need to know. It is less useful if the information is not easily accessed, not clear, or missing. It is useful if it is frequently updated and contains items that cause the visitor to return again and again. A page printer button also makes a web page more useful and it will save ink and paper (see Chapter 17 for the page printer button).

On the home page and all other pages of a commercial site, **make it easy for visitors to contact the owner of the web site.** The information could be included in the footer of each page. This way, no matter which pages are saved or printed, visitors will retain that important information. However, this could create a maintenance problem—if you change one of the items, every page will have to be changed. Or if you prefer to have the information on one page, use the Contact Us page or the About Us page. These pages should include an enciphered email address or a link to a feedback form so that visitors can readily email the owner; the owner's phone number; and the owner's postal address. Contact details—postal address and telephone number—are essential to instill confidence and to meet legal requirements. Sensible visitors do not order from sites that have no postal address or telephone number. Also include business registration numbers and links with appropriate trade associations so that the customer can check the reputation of the business.

If the site owner wants people to order items online, give the user all the information necessary to order immediately and with confidence. **You must display prices**: a sale will most probably be lost if the visitor has to stop and telephone for prices. Don't hide information such as sales tax and delivery costs. A potential order will probably be abandoned if extra costs are suddenly tacked on at the end of the order process. Warn the customer in advance about the additional costs.

Don't Baffle the User

The navigation system (the menu) must be crystal clear. The clearer the navigation, the more useful the site. To decide what to put in the menu, ask the question, "What might the visitor want to learn from this web site?" Better still, ask other people what information they would wish to find on the web site. For example, the menu buttons for a bed-and-breakfast web site might include Any Vacancies?, Prices, Location, Accommodations, Booking Form, About Us, and Contact Us.

Make it easy for the visitors to do two things:

- Get the information they are seeking quickly and easily.

- Be able to move easily and logically from one page to another.

Information is useless if users can't find it easily and quickly.

The best navigational menu buttons are colored, non-pictorial buttons with contrasting text. Do not to use wordless pictures for menu buttons because navigation then needs to be explained; that is, you will have to tell people to click the picture for more information. Visitors expect a straightforward, horizontal or vertical menu that needs no explanation. If you have a large number of menu items, then use both horizontal and vertical menus on the page. Make the horizontal buttons bigger than the vertical buttons. Make sure site visitors do not feel bewildered or trapped. Test the web site with people who are not expert surfers. You have failed if your "guinea pig" says, "What do I do next?"

Avoid JavaScript drop-down menus. These hide the information the visitor is searching for (most unfriendly). Try not to use too many pages of sub-menus. Search engines are unable to penetrate JavaScript menus, that means that your home page will be the only page indexed by the search engines. This ensures that your site will have a very low ranking unless your site is about a unique topic. Also, a JavaScript menu can be difficult, if not impossible, to use on mobile and tablet browsers.

Don't confuse visitors with lots of bits and pieces scattered randomly over the page. Make only one main point or topic per page. Layout each page so that the user can focus on your main point. A busy page fails to direct the user to the key feature. Show things in related groups.

Practice consistency. Use the same navigation buttons in the same position on every page. Use the same background color and font on every page. This is easily achieved by making a template from your home page. The style sheet should also ensure consistency.

Ensure that visitors know which page they are on and what each page will do for them. If visitors cannot work it out immediately, they will go elsewhere. Put a brief, explanatory heading at the top of the page so that people can see what the page is about without scrolling down. People *will* scroll down, but only if they are reasonably sure that there is something of interest to them on the rest of the page.

Avoid underlined words or phrases. Visitors will think these items are hyperlinks. And an underline can hide an underscore. Designers who underline text are revealing their age; underlining is a throwback to the days of ancient mechanical typewriters. Underlining is completely unnecessary now that you can use bold or a bigger font or color to emphasize a word or phrase.

Adding a Search Field to a Web Site

A search field can increase a web site's usefulness or it can draw people away from your site, depending on how it is implemented. If you choose to provide search capability on *only* your own web site, this presents no problem. The searches concentrate on your web site, but occasionally one or two other web sites might show up on the search results. If you choose the code for searching the entire internet, then users will be tempted to explore some of the search results and abandon your web site; not a good idea. Next, I describe the web site search-box code provided by the three dominant search engines: Bing, Yahoo!, and Google.

Bing Search Box

Add a Bing search box that will only search *your* web site, as shown in Figure 13-10.

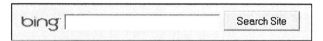

Figure 13-10. Add a Bing search field

The main search engines provide code snippets. Bing is the easiest to install. Listing 13-10 shows how to include a Bing search box in a web page.

Listing 13-10. Including a Bing Search Box in a Web Page (bing-search.html)

```
<!doctype html>
<html lang=en>
<head>
<title>Bing search box</title>
        <style type="text/css">
        #bingbox img { margin-bottom:-7px; border:none;
        }
        </style>
</head>
<body>
<div id="bingbox"><br>
<p>
<form method="get" action="http://www.bing.com/search">
        <input type="hidden" name="cp" value="1252">
        <input type="hidden" name="FORM" value="FREESS">
        <a href="http://www.bing.com/">
        <img rc="http://www.microsoft.com/presspass/_resources/images/↵
        img_windowsBingLogo.png" alt="Bing" ></a>
        <input type="text" name="q" size="30">
        <input type="submit" value="Search Site">
        <input type="hidden" name="q1" value="site:www.yourweb site.com">
</form>
</p>
</div>
</body>
</html>
```

The following notes refer to the bold items in Listing 13-10:

- The internal style removes the border from the Bing logo and pushes it down in line with the field.

- **<p>** Bing uses a table here but because tables are deprecated, I changed the markup to a paragraph.

- Change the figure **1252** to match the code page number of the `charset` your web site is written in. For example, the number will be 1252 if your web site has `<charset:windows-1252>` in the head section. The number will be `utf-8` if your web site has `<charset:utf-8>` in the head section.

- The URL is not `<input type="hidden" name="q1" value="http://www.yourweb site.com">` as you would expect, but it must include the word "site" as follows:

`<input type="hidden" name="q1" value="http://`**site**`:www.your-web-site.com">`

Don't forget to replace `www.your-web-site.com` with your own web site address.

Yahoo! Search Box

Although Yahoo! has united with Bing, some large organizations use Yahoo! as the default search engine on their web sites. Since many users are familiar with the Yahoo! interface, it is included in this section. For the Yahoo! search box code, go to Yahoo! at `http://search.yahoo.com/info/ysearchbox_instructions.html` or use Listing 13-11.

Figure 13-11 shows an enlarged view of one of the four available Yahoo! search boxes.

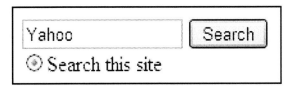

Figure 13-11. The Yahoo! search box

Four formats are available, but the instructions are rather confusing. I have simplified the Yahoo! code, as shown in Listing 13-11.

Listing 13-11. Include Yahoo! Search Box on a Web Page(yahoo-search.html)

```
<p class="search">
        <form method=get action="http://search.yahoo.com/search">
        <a href="http://search.yahoo.com/"></a>
        <input type="text" name="p" value="Yahoo" size=15>
        <input type="hidden" name="fr" value="yscpb">
        <input type="submit" value="Search"><br>
        <input type="radio" name="vs" value="http://www.your-web-site.com" ↵
        checked="checked">Search this site
        </form>
</p>
```

Insert your own web site URL in place of `www.`*`your-web-site.com`*.

Google Search Box

Figure 13-12 shows one version of the various downloadable Google search boxes suitable for a web site.

Figure 13-12. Add a Google search field

Google requires that you sign up to an account and then it presents you with a rather baffling form to fill. To avoid all this hassle, Dave Taylor has simplified and improved the Google code. See his web site at www.askdavetaylor.com/how_can_i_add_a_google_search_box_to_ my_website.html.

Listing 13-12 is an adaptation of Dave Taylor's code. An internal style sheet is used for illustration purposes only. No Google account is needed. It shows how to install a Google search box in a web page.

Listing 13-12. Inserting a Google Search Box in a Web Page (google-search-1.html)

```
<!doctype html>
<html lang=en>
<head>
<title>Google search field by Ask Dave Taylor</title>
<meta charset=utf-8>
        <style type="text/css">
        #outerbox { border:1px solid black; padding:4px; width:300px; height:40px; ↵
        text-align:center; font-size:75%;
        }
        .googlebox { display:inline;
        }
        .hidden { display:none;
        }
        </style>
</head>
<body>
<div id="outerbox">
<p class="googlebox">
        <form method="get" action="http://www.google.com/search" >
        <input type="text" name="q" size="25" maxlength="255" value="">
        <input type="submit" value="Google Search"><br>
        <input class="hidden" type="checkbox" name="sitesearch"
         value="my-web-site.com" checked="checked">Search this web site
        </form>
</p>
</div>
</body>
</html>
```

For your own web site, change the URL shown in bold type in Listing 13-12.

Figure 13-13 shows the header on my web site. It contains the Google search box using my simplified version of Dave Taylor's code (see Listing 13-13).

Figure 13-13. I have simplified the Google search for the web site; no Google account is needed for this.

In Listing 13-13a, I have embedded the Google search box in a page heading and I have further simplified Dave Taylor's code. As previously mentioned, no Google account is needed.

Listing 13-13a. Embedding a Google Search Box in a Web Page (google-search-2.html)

```
<!doctype html>
<html lang=en>
<head>
<title>A page with a search field using Google</title>
<meta charset=utf-8>
<link rel="stylesheet" type="text/css" href="search.css">
</head>
<body >
<div id="hdr">
<h1 >Coly Computer Help</h1>
<div class="search">
        <form method="get" action="http://www.google.com/search">
        <input type="text"   name="q" size="15" maxlength="255" value="">
        <input type="submit" value="Find">
        <input type="hidden" name="sitesearch" value="http://www.your-web-site.co.uk"><br>
        Search this web site
</form>
</div>
</div>
</body>
</html>
```

For your own web site, change the URL shown in bold type.
Listing 13-13b is the CSS style sheet for HTML in Listing 13-13a.

Listing 13-13b. The CSS Style Sheet for Listing 13-13a (search.css)

```
/*reset browsers for cross-client consistency*/
html,body,h1,h2,h3,h4,h4,h5,h6,p {margin:0; padding:0
}
img { border-style: none; float: none; margin-left: 0px; margin-right: 0px;
}
body { text-align:center; background-color:#D7FFEB; color:black; ⏎
font-family: "times new roman"; max-width:1024px; min-width:800px; font-size: medium; ⏎
color: #000000; margin: auto; width:95%;
}
```

```
/* set header height and background image */
#hdr{ margin-top:0; margin-bottom:0; background-position:45% top; background-
image:url('images/compbkgcrop.jpg'); background-repeat:no-repeat; height:160px; padding-
bottom:0;
}
h1 { padding: 110px  0 0 12%; margin-bottom:0; font-family :"times new roman";
font-size: 250%; color: #0080a0;; font-weight:bold;
}
#hdr {  position:relative;
}
.search { position:absolute; top:10px; right:40px; height: 56px;
}
```

Summary

This chapter described the features that make a web site attractive to visitors. It also showed ways to tempt visitors to explore beyond the home page. A section on usefulness emphasized that even an attractive site will be abandoned or never revisited if it is not useful. Tips for creating useful features were provided. Consult this chapter frequently and apply its advice as you try other projects in the book.

In the next chapter, you will learn the basic requirements for making web sites accessible to the disabled user, in particular to the blind and partially sighted. Many countries including the United States and the United Kingdom have either made recommendations or have passed laws regarding web site accessibility, and you will be made aware of the main points of these. Apart from the legal aspect, the chapter also explains that accessibility also offers advantages to able-bodied users.

CHAPTER 14

Accessibility

In the United States and the United Kingdom, one in three adults is over the age of 50 and some of these will have visual problems. It would be folly to prevent these people from accessing your web site. Many e-commerce sites have seen a marked increase in sales after making their web sites accessible to the blind and partially sighted. This chapter mainly deals with methods of helping partially sighted and blind persons to explore web sites. The severely visually handicapped and the blind can use a screen reader (speaking browser) that turns the textual content of a web site into speech. Screen readers can also explain the layout of a web page to the user as well as describing the nature of each element in the markup. Later in the chapter you will learn more about screen readers and how to design web sites that these devices can understand. We will first refer briefly to the current laws and guidelines on accessibility.

Laws and Guidelines

Australia and the United Kingdom have laws regarding accessibility of web sites for the visually impaired; other countries such as Sweden, Ireland, and Japan have produced guidelines.

In the United States, some states have issued guidelines, and at the time of writing, the US Department of Justice Civil Rights Division is considering Federal regulations for web site accessibility. Meanwhile W3CAG2 and WAI are the main forces behind the implementing of accessibility recommendations. WCAG2 is the acronym for Web Content Accessibility Guidelines (http://www.w3.org/TR/WCAG/). WAI is the Web Accessibility Initiative (http://www.w3.org/WAI/).

United Kingdom law states that it should be possible or reasonably possible for disabled persons to use a web site. The law is known as the DDA which stands for Disability Discrimination Act. Australia has adopted the DDA as the basis of its own law

There is no need to panic and start re-designing all your web sites to conform to the law, but make an effort to amend those web sites that are most likely to be explored by the partially sighted or by blind persons, especially those using screen readers. This will demonstrate that you have tried to make those sites *reasonably* accessible. When designing a new web site you should bear in mind the lessons to be learned from this chapter.

Most countries including UK and Australia have adopted the WCAG2 guidelines as a basis for their own laws or guidelines.

The WCAG2 Guide has three standards.

A: Minimal (but absolutely essential) conformance to the WCAG2 guidelines

AA: Medium conformance to the WCAG2 guidelines

AAA: Full conformance to the WCAG2 guidelines

Web sites must at least conform to both **A** and **AA**. If possible, try to conform to **AAA**. The W3 and WAI status on accessibility specifications can be found at `http://www.w3.org/WAI/intro/components.php`. A list of check points is available from `http://www.w3.org/TR/WAI-WEBCONTENT/checkpoint-list.html`.

▓ **Note** The W3 WAI guidelines and the United Kingdom guidelines are similar. The following web sites give good advice on accessibility: `http://www.w3.org/WAI/PF/aria/`; `http://www.w3.org/WAI/intro/aria.php`; `http://www.webcredible.co.uk/user-friendly-resources/web-accessibility/uk-website-legal-requirements.shtml`; and `http://dev.opera.com/articles/view/introduction-to-wai-aria/`.

We will now discuss the help that web designers can provide for users with partial sight or color blindness. These users will not have reached the stage where they need screen readers. Web designers can make the web site more legible for the partially sighted by applying a few basic rules, and these will be described in the next section.

Help for the Partially Sighted and Color Blind

This section deals with factors that assist the partially sighted and color blind, but the able bodied will also benefit from the section's recommendations. It covers color contrast, text style/size, ease of navigation, and testing.

Color contrast ratios for text and background colors must meet certain standards.

- Hyperlink color should always be in a high-contrast color that is different from the normal text color.

- Text and background should have a contrast ratio of at least 4.5:1 at AA level, and 5:1 at AAA level. For specific recommendations, see `http://www.w3.org/TR/WCAG/`.

- Large text (extra-large normal or large bold) should have a contrast ratio of at least 3:1.

▓ **Caution** Ensure that your CSS style code contains both background color and foreground (text) color. For example, { …color:black; background-color:white; }. Do not split text and background colors between CSS and HTML. Be sure to define them both in one place.

Tip The Juicy Studio web site http://www.juicystudio.com/services/luminositycontrastratio.php has an excellent online contrast ratio tester, just enter the hex codes for your background and foreground (text) colors. Or try the Snook.ca's Colour Contrast Check at

http://www.snook.ca/technical/colour_contrast/colour.html.

My favorite analyzer, CCA-2.2 (see Figure 14-1), is available for downloading to your hard drive.

Download the zip file CCA-2.2.zip from http://www.paciellogroup.com/resources/contrast-analyser.html

You my have already downloaded CCA-2.2 when following Chapter 12. The instructions to do so are as follows: Scroll down the home page of the Paciello Group web site until you see Download and a list of language versions. Click the appropriate language version to download the zip file. Unzip it into a new folder then create a desktop short cut to access the file CCA-2.2.exe.

Figure 14-1 shows the Color Contrast Analyser (CCA-2.2) interface.

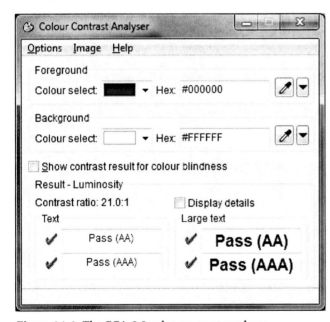

Figure 14-1. The CCA-2.2 color contrast analyser

To use the color contrast analyzer, follow these steps:

1. Double-click the short cut on the Desktop (note that the spelling of color in the CCA interface is the UK and Australian *colour*).

2. Select the foreground color (text color) either by using the drop-down arrow or by typing in the hexadecimal number.

3. Select the background color in the same way.

4. In the bottom panel, you will see the contrast ratio and you will be informed whether the contrast meets the AA or the AAA standard.

5. Change the hexadecimal code a little at a time until you achieve the required color contrast.

6. Make a note of the hexadecimal color code and use it to amend your CSS style sheet.

7. Try this experiment for color blindness: choose the most common form of color blindness using a green foreground and a red background. Now tick the box labeled "Show contrast result for color blindness." The bottom panel will expand to show the effect of those colors on three different forms of color blindness.

8. If you click Options on the menu you can adjust the colors by means of sliders.

To put things in perspective, let's look at an example of a color contrast change. A client asked me to use red menu buttons with white labels. The contrast ratio for white on red is 4:1. An almost identical red #D20B0D gave a much better contrast ratio of 5.4:1. Using this new red I was able to please the client and also make the text on the menu buttons visible to the partially sighted. Color contrast is not the whole story; we must also consider the size of the text.

Allow partially-sighted users to change the text size by using their own CSS style sheet. Even without a special style sheet the user can change the text size; for instance in IE under Tools, select Internet Options, then select Accessibility to choose the font size. When designing the web site, do not use fixed sizes such as pt or px; always specify *named* font sizes or percentages according to Table 14-1. For example, the following code selects the named font size medium:

```
body { background-color:#d7ffeb; font-family: Arial; font-size: medium; color: #000; }
```

Table 14-1. Font Sizes

Named size	xx-small	x-small	small	medium	large	x-large	xx-large
Percentage	58%	63%	88%	100%	112%	142%	200%
Point size	7 pt	7.5 pt	10.5 pt	12 pt	13.5 pt	17 pt	24 pt

▨ **Caution** Do not use a color selection for navigation. An example of a bad piece of navigation would be "Click the green button to go to next page. Click the red button to return to previous page." Such instructions are useless to the severely visually-impaired and to the user who is red/green color blind.

Avoid entire sentences and paragraphs in uppercase letters or italics. The shapes of lowercase letters are easier for everyone to read, including partially-sighted persons.

Also avoid justified text because it difficult to read, even for able-bodied users. This is because of the large variations in the gaps between words. The large gaps can particularly cause problems for those using screen readers and magnifiers. Users half way through a line of text can be fooled into thinking they have reached the end of the line, causing them to move down to the start of the next line.

General Advice

The following tips will greatly assist the visually handicapped:

- You could create alternative pages that use a different style sheet, giving high contrast. For an excellent example, see `http://www.juicystudio.com/services/luminositycontrastratio.php`.

  The second button on the Juicy Studio menu loads high-contrast pages. This is not a suitable solution if you have several pages because both versions of each page would have to be updated. Also, search engines do not like duplicate pages.

- Organize pages so they can be read in a logical sequence when the style sheet is turned off.

- Avoid JavaScript for navigation and functions other than buttons such as Print this Page, Bookmark this Page, and Return to Previous Page. These are acceptable only because they duplicate functions that are available in all the browsers.

- When providing information in PDF format, provide the same information in an alternative, accessible format (e.g., HTML or text) or provide links to the tools provided on the Adobe web site. Adobe is improving the PDF format so that it may soon be possible for screen readers to read PDF files.

- Ensure that links and page elements are keyboard navigable; create a logical tab key order for them.

- Do not cause pop-ups or other windows to appear without first warning the user.

- Give each page a unique `<title>` so that users know where they are within the site.

- Do not use tables for page layout. Use CSS for positioning items on your page. Table-based layouts are not suitable for disabled users. Most automated compliance scanners reject them because they cannot differentiate between data and layout tables.

- Avoid the use of ASCII art such as the "less than" (<) and "greater than" (>) symbols for pointing to something. Screen readers will read out its meaning, which is "less than" or "greater than." Use a Webding arrow or some text instead.

- Add a duplicate menu and Back to Top links at intervals on long pages.

- Do not use too many radio buttons and checkboxes because they make the form harder to complete.

- To assist people with hand tremors, ensure adequate space between fields, checkboxes, menu buttons, and radio buttons.

- Graphical menu buttons are accessible as long as the title/alt text describes the purpose of each button.

- JavaScript drop-down menus are inaccessible to screen reader users. Drop-down menus in PHP or ASP are accessible.

- Ensure that the `<html>` tag contains a language specification so that the screen reader can interpret the page correctly. For example, `<html lang=en>` for English.

- All images that convey useful information must contain tool tips by using `alt` and `title`. Images that are purely decorative convey no useful information; therefore, the correct alt/title for those images would be an empty alt (`alt=" "`) and any empty title would be (`title=" "`). Screen readers do not read out empty `alt` or `title` strings.

- Ensure that videos have subtitles so that the deaf can understand and enjoy them.

- The Tab key should provide a logical sequence for the benefit of disabled users who are unable to use a mouse. The default tabbing order is logical, so do not change it.

- Use brief, simple language.

- Text depicted by means of an image is useless because screen readers cannot read it. If you use an image containing text, make sure you include an "alt" tooltip that provides the text for the screen reader.

- This tip is most important: make absolutely sure that audio and video clips are neither autostart nor onmouseover. The sudden noise can cause blind or partially-sighted users to jump out of their skins. Always use onmousedown to start an audio or video clip and give an explanation and a warning.

- Add a "Skip to main content" link at the start of each page (but not the home page) so that the screen reader user can skip straight to the content and does not have to repeatedly trawl through the navigation menus. Some designers do this by locating a normal link, or an image, or a 1-pixel GIF image (therefore, invisible) at the start of each page with the title text "Skip to main content." Be sure that the wording is not "Skip to content." Make the link jump to an anchor (bookmark) at the start of the page content.

```
<a href="#maincontent">
<img title="Skip to main content" src="onepx.gif" height="1" width="1" ↵
border="0"
alt="Skip to main content"></a>
navigation menu which is to be skipped goes here
<!--Start of main content-->
<a id="maincontent"></a>
main content goes here
```

A minor drawback to this method is that the sudden appearance of a previously invisible link could confuse the sighted user. You might find it better to use a visible link; the choice is yours.

░ **Tip** Valuable information can be gleaned from the Royal National Institute for the Blind web site. (http://www.rnib.org.uk/webaccesscentre and www.rnib.org.uk/seeitright). RNIB uses the free WAVE program to monitor accessibility. RNIB checks the validity of the HTML and CSS with the WC3 and WDG validators. It browses the web site using various graphical browsers and Lynx, and listens to how the web site speaks using Freedom Scientific's JAWS (Job Access with Speech).

Testing Your Web Sites for General Accessibility

Designers could ask a partially sighted or a blind person to act as a guinea pig to test a web site for accessibility. However, this may not be possible or practical, so here are some tests that you can carry out yourself. Use the following checklist to see if your web site is accessible:

- Validate the code on your web pages using the W3C online validator at `http://validator.w3.org`

- Rest the cursor on each image and each link to ensure that tool tips, alts, and titles show up.

- Turn the volume down to see whether any audio content has text equivalents.

- Use the browser to enlarge fonts and see if the page is still viable.

- Resize the browser window to see if the page content is satisfactory at smaller widths.

- Ensure that the user does not need to scroll horizontally to an unreasonable extent at low resolutions.

- Check that labels and title tags on menu links clearly indicate their destination.

- Make sure that the disabled can use the keyboard to navigate through the links and form fields. Use the tab key to check this.

- Use clear, brief, simple text, split it into bite-size chunks with informative headings.

- Use front-loading content so that each paragraph begins with the conclusion.

- Use ordered or unordered lists where appropriate.

- Remove all items that flash or flicker, including marquees.

- Make absolutely sure that audio and video are not set to autostart or `onmouseover`.

Screen Readers for the Blind and Severely Visually-Impaired

The blind and the severely visually-impaired can use computers with the aid of a screen reader, sometimes called a "speaking browser," or to use the stilted jargon beloved of techies, "assistive technology." Screen readers do not actually read the screen, they read the source code. For an interesting audio demonstration of a screen reader and tables visit `http://www.xstandard.com/en/articles/wysiwyg-editors-and-bad-markup/`

■ **Tip** A free, open-source screen reader with demonstration video is available at `www.nvda-project.org`. Preliminary reports suggest that NVDA's HTML5 support is more advanced than some commercial programs. NVDA is designed for use with Mozilla Firefox. It has a user's guide; further tips are available at

`http://www.marcozehe.de/articles/how-to-use-nvda-and-firefox-to-test-your-web-pages-for-accessibility/`.

Screen readers and search engines rely on heading tags <h1> to <h6>. When using a screen reader, the user taps the H key to jump from heading to heading. The heading is spoken by the screen reader so that the user can decide whether the headed section is what he is looking for. If your page has no <h1> to

<h6> headings, the screen reader says, "There are no headings on this page," and the user is left floundering.

In the early 1990s, headings were often wrongly regarded as a way of making text bolder, bigger, or smaller. This is not surprising because W3Schools.com has this rather vague instruction: "<h1> defines the largest heading and <h6> defines the smallest heading."

The correct definition is: "<h1> is the most important and <h6> is the least important."

You may have avoided using <h1> to <h6> in the past because of the big gaps above and below the text. This is now easily remedied using CSS. For screen readers, the important heading should be at the top of the page and the least important at the bottom. Headings that appear earlier in the code are more important (and search engines and screen readers will regard them as being more important).

- A heading should be brief and accurately describe the topic of the paragraph it introduces.

- Use CSS to make the headings any size and any format you wish (see Figure 14-3).

- Start with h1 and never skip a heading; for instance, don't jump from h2 to h5.

Figure 14-2 shows the default heading sizes and line spacing.

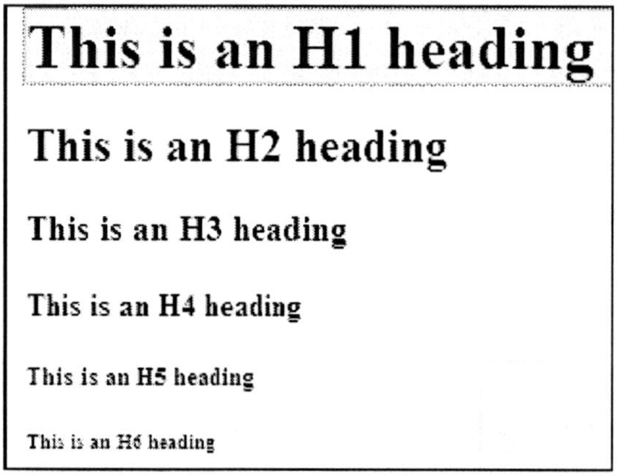

This is an H1 heading

This is an H2 heading

This is an H3 heading

This is an H4 heading

This is an H5 heading

This is an H6 heading

Figure 14-2. Unformatted headings (note the double-spacing between the lines of text)

Figure 14-2 shows the default heading styles. Figure 14-3 shows the headings when they are formatted using the CSS that is included in Listing 14-3. You would probably never change the font size in a real world page, this is simply a demonstration to prove that headings can be formatted. However, you could usefully change the line spacing for headings.

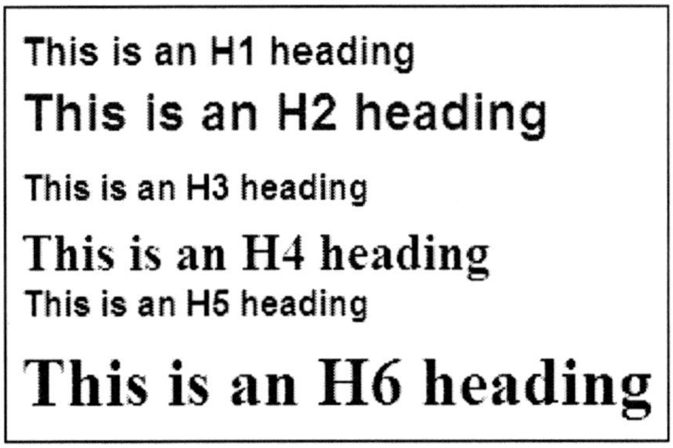

This is an H1 heading

This is an H2 heading

This is an H3 heading

This is an H4 heading

This is an H5 heading

This is an H6 heading

Figure 14-3. The appearance and size of each heading and the line spaces are changed by the use of CSS. Fortunately, screen readers will still recognize the headings as H1, H2, and so on.

Listing 14-3 shows the formatting applied to each heading. The heading size and line spacing can be changed to improve the appearance of a page for fully-sighted persons. A screen reader still accepts the hierarchy of the headings and it reads them out in order of importance. In other words, visually-impaired users understand the structure of the page because they hear the main heading (H1) spoken first, followed by H2, H3, and so on. Users move from heading to heading by pressing the H key.

Listing 14-3. Formatting the HTML Headings (hformatted.html)

```
<!doctype html>
<html lang=en>
<head>
<title>Formatted headings</title>
<meta charset=utf-8>
        <style type="text/css">
        h6 {font-size:200%; font-family:"Times New Roman"; margin-top:-20px;
        }
        h5 {font-size:medium; font-family: arial; margin-top:-10px;
        }
        h4 {font-size:150%; margin-top:-10px; margin-bottom:10px;
        }
        h3 {font-size:medium; font-family: arial; margin-top:-10px;
        }
        h2 {color:blue; font-family:arial; margin-top:-10px;
        }
        h1 {font-size:110%; font-family: arial;
        }
        </style>
</head>
<body>
<h1>This is an H1 heading</h1>
<h2>This is an H2 heading</h2>
<h3>This is an H3 heading</h3>
<h4>This is an H4 heading</h4>
<h5>This is an H5 heading</h5>
<h6>This is an H6 heading</h6>
</body>
</html>
```

Data Tables and Screen Readers

Data tables present a major problem for the visually impaired. If a table is not constructed to suit the way a screen reader works, a table with many columns is impossible to understand. The top row of headings will be spoken first, then the second row of cells will be spoken but with no reference to the headings, then the third row of cells, and so on. Unless the visually-impaired user is able to memorize all the headings, the rows will be unintelligible.

This section gives examples of tables varying from a simple, two-column table that needs no memorizing of headings, to tables with four columns with headings that would ordinarily have to be memorized. This section describes several methods of making the tables work with screen readers. Using these techniques, the column headings are linked to the cell content and spoken as the user moves along each row. The methods can be extended to more than four columns by adding extra columns to the markup.

■ **Note** Tables should only be used to present data. Accessible pages must never contain layout tables.

Data Table with Two Columns

Figure 14-4 shows a simple, two -column data table with content that is read easily by a screen reader and without the need for special tags. However, always use `<caption>` and `<table…summary="…">`. This enables screen readers to inform users that they have arrived at a table.

Events at St. Andrews Church	
Saturday 12th June	2.30pm Church Fête
Wednesday 16th June	7.00pm Concert in church
Saturday 19th June	10.30am to 5.00pm Flower Festival

Figure 14-4. Two-column data table

A plain, two-column table needs no headers. A screen reader will read across each row cell by cell and no column headings need to be memorized. Figure 14-4 was created using Listing 14-4, which has an internal style sheet for instructional purposes only.

Listing 14-4. Creating a Two Column Table (simple-2col.html)

```
<!doctype html>
<html lang=en>
<head>
<title>Two column table with no need for headers</title>
<meta charset=utf-8>
<style type="text/css">
table { width: 500px; border:1px black solid; border-collapse:collapse; ↵
font-family: "times new roman";
}
```

```
td { border:1px black solid;
}
th { border:1px black solid;
}
caption { font-weight:bold;
}
</style>
</head>
<body>
<table>
<caption>Events at St. Andrews Church</caption>
        <tr>
                <td>Saturday 12th June</td>
                <td>2.30pm Church F&ecirc;te</td>
        </tr>
        <tr>
                <td>Wednesday 16th June</td>
                <td>7.00pm Concert in church</td>
        </tr>
        <tr>
                <td>Saturday 19th June</td>
                <td>10.30am to 5.00pm Flower Festival</td>
        </tr>
</table>
</body>
</html>
```

With tables containing three or more columns, blind users and those with a severe sight problem would have to memorize the headings to make sense of the data. The next example is our first method for overcoming this problem. The difficulty can be avoided by replacing <td> with <th> in the top row of column headings. The tag <th> describes a cell that contains header information.

■ **Note** In order to hear the table cells spoken by a screen reader, a visually handicapped person would use the Ctrl+Alt keys and Right Arrow key to move along the rows.

Data Table with Three or More Columns

Figure 14-5 shows a more complex, three-column table. A person using a screen reader would first hear the top row of headings, and by using a method for linking cells to headings, the headings would not need to be memorized. The user would place the cursor in the first cell in the row beneath the Place heading. The user would then use Ctrl+Alt and the Right Arrow key to move along the row. The user would hear the following: "Place London, Hotel King Fisher, Cost £200."

Then tapping only the Down arrow would take the user to the start of the next row, the user would again use Ctrl+Alt and Right arrow to hear this: "Place Colyton, Hotel Leofric, Cost £30".

Hotel locations and prices per night per person		
Place	Hotel	Cost
London	King Fisher	£200
Colyton	Leofric	£30
Coventry	Ritz	£150

Figure 14-5. Three-column data table

■ **Caution** At the time of writing, a table in an HTML5 page could not be read properly by most older screen readers. This especially applied to JAWS (Job Access with Speech). Until the screen readers catch up with HTML5, you will need to use an XHTML 1.0 page to enable blind persons to read your data tables. Any pages in the web site that do not contain data tables can be in HTML5, but avoid using semantic tags until the screen readers are able to support them. Validate the XHTML 1.0 pages in `http://validator.w3.org`. See Chapter 18 for tips on validating XHTML 1.0 pages.

All the tables and Figures 14-5 through 14-9 can be read by current and older screen readers provided you use the XHTML DOCTYPE. When the screen readers catch up with HTML5, you could then change to the HTML5 DOCTYPE, but that will create a problem for users with older versions of JAWS. Listing 14-15 creates a table with three headings suitable for screen readers.

Listing 14-5. Creating an Accessible Table with Three Columns (three-col-hotels.html)

```
<!DOCTYPE html PUBLIC "-//W3C//DTD XHTML 1.0 Transitional//EN"
"http://www.w3.org/TR/xhtml1/DTD/xhtml1-transitional.dtd">
<html xmlns="http://www.w3.org/1999/xhtml">
<head>
<meta content="text/html; charset=utf-8" http-equiv="Content-Type" />
<title>Three column table with th headers</title>
        <style type="text/css">
        table { width: 330px; border:1px black solid; border-collapse:collapse; ↵
        font-family: "times new roman";
        }
        td { padding:0 5px 0 5px; border:1px black solid;
        }
        th { text-align:left; padding:0 5px 0 5px; border:1px black solid;
        }
        caption { font-weight:bold;
        }
        .right { text-align:right;
        }
        </style>
```

```
</head>
<body>
<table summary="Simple table with headers">
<caption>Hotel locations and prices per night per person</caption>
        <tr>
                <th>Place</th>
                <th>Hotel</th>
                <th class="right">Cost</th>
        </tr>
        <tr>
                <td>London</td>
                <td>King Fisher</td>
                <td class="right">&pound;200</td>
        </tr>
        <tr>
                <td>Colyton</td>
                <td>Leofric</td>
                <td class="right">&pound;30</td>
        </tr>
        <tr>
                <td>Coventry</td>
                <td>Ritz</td>
                <td class="right">&pound;150</td>
        </tr>
</table>
</body>
</html>
```

Our second method allows for a slightly more sophisticated table using the tags <thead> and <tbody>. Again, XHTML 1.0 must be used until older screen readers have been replaced by newer versions capable of reading a table in an HTML5 page.

Data Table Using the <thead> and <tbody>

To link data to headers for screen readers, it is necessary to use tags such as <thead>, <tbody>, <th>, <tr>, and <td>. The tag <thead> is the heading area for a table; <tbody> is the area in a table that contains the data (see Figure 14-6).

The price of lemons and pears		
	Lemons	Pears
Wholesale	$1.00	$1.50
Retail	$2.00	$2.50

Figure 14-6. A more advanced data table

In Listing 14-6, the <thead> and <tbody> items are shown in bold type.

Listing 14-6. Creating a More Complex Accessible Table (three-col-fruit.html)

```
<!DOCTYPE html PUBLIC "-//W3C//DTD XHTML 1.0 Transitional//EN"
"http://www.w3.org/TR/xhtml1/DTD/xhtml1-transitional.dtd">
<html xmlns="http://www.w3.org/1999/xhtml" xml:lang="en">
<head>
<meta content="text/html; charset=utf-8" http-equiv="Content-Type" />
<title>Three column table with thead and tbody</title>
<style type="text/css">
table { width: 500px; border:1px black solid; border-collapse:collapse; font-family:"times new
roman"; font-size:medium;
}
td { border:1px black solid;
}
th { border:1px black solid;
}
caption { font-weight:bold;
}
</style>
</head>
<body>
<table summary="The price of lemons and pears">
                <caption>The price of lemons and pears</caption>
                <thead>
                        <tr>
                                <td></td>
                                <th>Lemons</th>
                                <th>Pears</th>
                        </tr>
                </thead>
                <tbody>
                        <tr>
                                <th>Wholesale</th>
                                <td>$1.00</td>
                                <td>$1.50</td>
                        </tr>
                        <tr>
                                <th>Retail</th>
                                <td>$2.00</td>
                                <td>$2.50</td>
                        </tr>
                </tbody>
        </table><br />
</body>
</html>
```

Next, we will look at a third way of creating tables giving intelligible speech on screen readers. Cells will be linked to headings using identities (id).

Using id to Link Columns and Rows to Headers

Normally a screen reader reads the cells as if they were <div> tags; for instance, if the table in Figure 14-7 was coded as a straightforward table without ids or header tags, the bottom two rows would be read out by a screen reader as: "To Lisbon No Yes Yes. To Isle of Wight Yes Yes No."

Not very helpful. I am sure you will agree.

Instead, the table in Figure 14-7 uses id and header information to link the cells to the headings for screen readers.

Destination and method of travel			
Destination	**Coach**	**Boat**	**Air**
To Lisbon	No	Yes	Yes
To Isle of Wight	Yes	Yes	No

Figure 14-7. Linking columns and rows to headers with <id> and <th>

In the next method, the following code snippets show how each data cell is linked to its column heading and to the first item in its row by adding an <id> attribute to each <th> element. First, each heading is given an id that links it to its <th>. For example:

```
<tr>
<th id="th1">Destination</th>
<th id="th2">Coach</th>
<th id="th3">Boat</th>
<th id="th4">Air</th>
</tr>
```

Then the header id is linked to the data in each cell; for example:

```
<tr>
<td headers="th1">To Lisbon</td>
<td headers="th2">No</td>
<td headers="th3">Yes</td>
<td headers="th4">Yes</td>
</tr>
```

Each cell is linked to its heading so that a screen reader is able to state the relationship. As the user moves along the row below the headings, it reads the cell's heading and content like this: "Destination to Lisbon, Coach No, Boat Yes, Air Yes." Listing 14-7 includes the snippets as follows:

Listing 14-7. Creating an Accessible Table Using id and headers (four-col-travel.html)

```
<!DOCTYPE html PUBLIC "-//W3C//DTD XHTML 1.0 Transitional//EN"
"http://www.w3.org/TR/xhtml1/DTD/xhtml1-transitional.dtd">
<html xmlns="http://www.w3.org/1999/xhtml">
<head>
        <meta content="text/html; charset=utf-8" http-equiv="Content-Type" />
        <title>Four column table with id and th</title>
                <style type="text/css">
```

```
        table { width: 330px; border:1px black solid; border-collapse:collapse; ↵
        font-family: "times new roman";
        }
        td { padding:0 5px 0 5px; border:1px black solid;
        }
        th { text-align:left; padding:0 5px 0 5px; border:1px black solid;
        }
        caption { font-weight:bold;
        }
        .right { text-align:right;
        }
        </style>
</head>
<body>
<table summary="Destination and method of travel">
<caption>Destination and method of travel</caption>
<tr>
        <th id="th1">Destination</th>
        <th id="th2">Coach</th>
        <th id="th3">Boat</th>
        <th id="th4">Air</th>
</tr>
<tr>
        <td headers="th1">To Lisbon</td>
        <td headers="th2">No</td>
        <td headers="th3">Yes</td>
        <td headers="th4">Yes</td>
</tr>
<tr>
        <td headers="th1">To Isle of Wight</td>
        <td headers="th2">Yes</td>
        <td headers="th3">Yes</td>
        <td headers="th4">No</td>
</tr>
</table>
</body>
</html>
```

The following example uses a fourth method employing the scope attribute instead of the id attribute to associate cell data with its heading and to the first item in its row.

Using Scope to Link Cells and Headings

For tables such as the one shown in Figure 14-8, the id/headers pair can be replaced with the scope attribute. It's a pity that such a nondescript word was used; something like cell-linker would have explained its purpose better than scope.

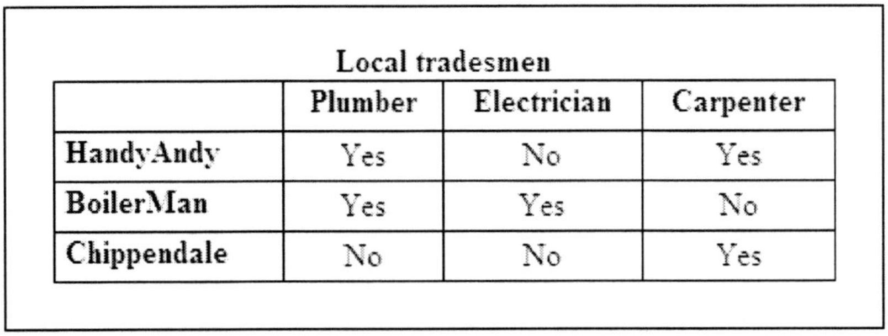

Local tradesmen			
	Plumber	Electrician	Carpenter
HandyAndy	Yes	No	Yes
BoilerMan	Yes	Yes	No
Chippendale	No	No	Yes

Figure 14-8. Linking cells and headings with scope

Listing 14-8. Creating an Accessible Table Using Scope (four-col-scope.html)

```
<!DOCTYPE html PUBLIC "-//W3C//DTD XHTML 1.0 Transitional//EN"
"http://www.w3.org/TR/xhtml1/DTD/xhtml1-transitional.dtd">
<html xmlns="http://www.w3.org/1999/xhtml">
<head>
<meta content="text/html; charset=utf-8" http-equiv="Content-Type" />
<title> Four column table using scope</title>
            <style type="text/css">
            table { width: 330px; border:1px black solid; border-collapse:collapse; ↵
            font-family: "times new roman";
            }
            td { padding:0 5px 0 5px; border:1px black solid;
            }
            th { text-align:left; padding:0 5px 0 5px; border:1px black solid;
            }
            caption { font-weight:bold;
            }
            </style>
</head>
<body>
<table summary="Linking cells to headers using scope">
<caption>Local tradesmen</caption>
<tr>
            <th></th><!--empty cell-->
            <th scope="col">Plumber</th>
            <th scope="col">Electrician</th>
            <th scope="col">Carpenter</th>
</tr>
<tr>
            <th scope="row" class="left">HandyAndy</th>
            <td>Yes</td>
            <td>No</td>
            <td>Yes</td>
</tr>
<tr>
            <th scope="row" class="left">BoilerMan</th>
            <td>Yes</td>
            <td>Yes</td>
            <td>No</td>
```

```
		</tr>
		<tr>
			<th scope="row" class="left">Chippendale</th>
			<td>No</td>
			<td>No</td>
			<td>Yes</td>
		</tr>
		</table>
		</body>
		</html>
```

We will now look at our fifth example, presenting the same table shown in Figure 14-7 and using a method we learned earlier.

A Further Exercise in Using <th> and id to Link Cells and Headings

In Listing 14-7, we learned how to use <th> with id and headers to link cells to the table headings. We will now use this method on the Local Tradesmen table as an alternative to using scope. The table's appearance will be identical to Figure 14-8 and for convenience, it is shown again as Figure 14-9 so that you can refer to it as you study the listing.

Local tradesmen			
	Plumber	**Electrician**	**Carpenter**
HandyAndy	Yes	No	Yes
BoilerMan	Yes	Yes	No
Chippendale	No	No	Yes

Figure 14-9. *This table is the same as Figure 14-8 but was achieved by using <th>, id and headers instead of scope.*

Listing 14-9 creates a four-column table with the same appearances as Figure 14-8 by using id instead of scope. Users of screen readers will hear each data cell related to its heading. The relevant tags and attributes are shown in bold type.

Listing 14-9. *Creating Accessible Table Figure 14-9 Without Using Scope (four-col-trade-id.html)*

```
<!DOCTYPE html PUBLIC "-//W3C//DTD XHTML 1.0 Transitional//EN"
"http://www.w3.org/TR/xhtml1/DTD/xhtml1-transitional.dtd">
<html xmlns="http://www.w3.org/1999/xhtml">
<head>
<meta content="text/html; charset=utf-8" http-equiv="Content-Type" />
<title>Four column table but using id instead of scope</title>
		<style type="text/css">
		table { width: 330px; border:1px black solid; border-collapse:collapse; ↵
		font-family: "times new roman";
		}
		td { padding:0 5px 0 5px; border:1px black solid; text-align:center;
```

```
}
th { text-align:left; padding:0 5px 0 5px; border:1px black solid;
}
caption { font-weight:bold;
}
.right { text-align:right;
}
</style>
</head>
<body>
<table summary="Table 14-6. As table 5 but not using scope">
<caption>Local Tradesmen</caption>
<tr> <th></th><!--empty cell-->
        <th id="plumber">Plumber</th>
        <th id="electrician">Electrician</th>
        <th id="carpenter">Carpenter</th>
</tr>
<tr>
        <th id="ha">HandyAndy</th>
        <td headers="ha plumber">Yes</td>
        <td headers="ha electrician">No</td>
        <td headers="ha carpenter">Yes</td>
</tr>
<tr>
        <th id="el">BoilerMan</th>
        <td headers="el plumber">Yes</td>
        <td headers="el electrician">Yes</td>
        <td headers="el carpenter">No</td>
</tr>
<tr>
        <th id="ca">Chippendale</th>
        <td headers="ca plumber">No</td>
        <td headers="ca electrician">No</td>
        <td headers="ca carpenter">Yes</td>
</tr>
</table>
</body>
</html>
```

▨ **Tip** Instructions for a complex table using `scope`, `colgroup`, `colspan`, and `rowgroup` are on Roger Hudson's web site at http://www.usability.com.au/resources.

We have seen that several different approaches are available for helping screen readers to speak the table cell data in a meaningful way; and they all work. So which method should you use?

Start by making the data table as simple as possible. Complex tables can usually be split into two or more simple tables. Having simplified a table, try the easiest of the methods we discussed first. If a screen reader such as JAWS can make sense of it, fine. If not, try one of the slightly more complex methods.

The next section deals with the way we can make feedback forms suitable for screen readers.

Screen Readers and Feedback Forms

The blind and the severely visually-impaired can use a screen reader to fill in forms. To make this possible, forms must follow these guidelines:

- Do not use table layout for forms. Use CSS and make the sequence of the form fields as logical as possible.

- Put plenty of space between form elements to help people who have difficulty placing the cursor due to hand tremor.

- Do not give instructions at the end of a form. Users with screen readers and screen magnification will not be aware of this information until they reach the end of the form.

A full listing for the layout of a form is not shown here because that topic is dealt with thoroughly in Chapter 11. Instead, the following list describes the most accessible format for individual form elements.

- **Position prompts for optimum accessibility.** Prompts are the texts explaining the purpose of the field; for example, Your Name, Your E-mail, and so forth.

- **The prompt text for input fields and text areas** should be to the *left* or *above* the field. To achieve this, the <label> statement must appear before the <input> statement.

- **For screen readers, the code must include for and id.** The id for the <input> element must be associated with the <label> element and must be unique for that page. The label is for an identified input field. In this example, the label is *for* an <input>, which is identified as id="username".

```
<label for="username">Your Name:</label>
<input id="username" name="username" size="30">
```

The form element would appear on the screen with its prompt where the blind user would expect to find it, like this:

Your Name:. [   ]

- To indicate that some form fields or text areas are essential or required items use a text asterisk together with the title="…" attribute within the input tag, as follows:

```
<label for="email"><strong>Your Email Address<span class="red"> * </span></strong />
<input id="email" name="email" size="30" title="Required information" ↵
alt="Required information">
```

W3C validation requires the 'alt' attribute. Mozilla Firefox only responds to 'title', therefore both are used.

- **Because not all of the check boxes or radio buttons need to be selected,** you cannot apply "required" or "optional" to the individual boxes or buttons. Apply the required or optional instruction to the *heading* of each group of boxes or buttons instead.

- **The prompt for check boxes and radio buttons must be to the right of the field** and it must be unique and unambiguous. Compared with the previous examples, the order of the label and input statements must be reversed (input appears before label). This puts the prompt to the right of the element. Forms should always use **for** and **id** for able-bodied and disabled users. This is essential for screen readers.

The listing for a checkbox will look like this:

```
<input type="checkbox" id="chkbox1" name="coffee" value="Yes">
<label for="chkbox1"><strong>Coffee</strong></label>
```

The code for a radio button will look like this:

```
<label for="laptop">
<input type="radio" name="computer" value="Laptop" id="laptop">Laptop
</label>   
<label for="desktop">
<input type="radio" name="computer" value="Desktop" id="desktop">Desktop
</label>
```

■ **Caution** When using radio buttons (to ensure that only one choice can be selected), each radio button in a group of radio buttons must have the same name but a different value. In the previous example, the same name is "computer" and the different values are "laptop" and "desktop."

The Code snippet for a textarea

The tag <textarea…> is used instead of <input…>. The label statement must precede the textarea statement, as follows:

```
<label for="suggest"><b>Please type your content suggestion or message</b></label>
<textarea id="suggest" name="suggestion" rows="12" cols="40">
</textarea><br><br>
```

- **Examine your form in a browser to test whether the prompt text has been correctly associated with the form item.** When you click on the prompt text, a flashing cursor should appear in the field (the form field has become focused). A checkbox is ticked or a radio button is selected.

- **In long forms, group information in related chunks.** This helps both visually impaired web users and fully sighted users. You can also use the HTML tags <fieldset> and <legend> tags, but not all browsers show fieldsets properly. The following is a code snippet for a fieldset:

```
<fieldset>
<legend>Personal details</legend>
--- Form items (eg title, name, age) ---
</fieldset>
<fieldset>
<legend>Contact information</legend>
--- Form items (eg address1, address2, town, postcode, phone) ---
</fieldset>
```

- **Label all date fields**, especially where separate input fields are placed in a row. A screen reader will only associate the Date text label with the first text input field. The recommendation is to use one field labeled DD/MM/YYYY or use three fields with label tags for each of the three fields Day, Month, and Year.

- **Place-holding text in a field is no longer necessary** and can be a nuisance to modern screen reader users.

- **Do not use drop-down field selections** that rely on JavaScript because they are inaccessible to screen reader users; although recent improvements have the latest screen readers able to cope with a certain amount of JavaScript.

- **A fully worked example of an accessible form with anti-spam filter** is provided in Chapter 11.

Screen Readers for HTML5, XHTML5, and CSS3

The creators of screen readers will need time to adapt their programs to the new recommendations. Until this occurs and until their behavior is known, web designers should use HTML4 or XHTML 1.0 for data tables.

The new <nav> tag for navigation menus will cause some head scratching until a standard for screen readers is decided; therefore, continue to use the "Skip to main content in HTML5" described earlier in the chapter.

The most problematic elements in an HTML5 page are multiple headings (h1 to h6) and <hgroup>. Until these are resolved, continue using HTML4 or XHTML.

What about "Skip to main content in HTML5"? In HTML5, you can specifically mark up all the "secondary" content on a page—such as navigation, branding, copyright notices—so it feels odd that you can't specifically markup the most important part of your page – the content. But what would be the purpose of marking it up specifically, anyway? If you need to style it, use a <div>.

■ **Tip** Many of the browsers that support HTML5 have not implemented accessibility support. To follow progress on this issue, see http://www.webaim.org/techniques/tables/data and http://www.accessibleculture.org/articles/2011/10/jaws-ie-and-headings-in-html5/.

Testing Your Web Site for Screen Reader Accessibility

The following are suggested steps to follow when testing your web site.

- Ask a partially-sighted person to look over the site while you take note of any problems found.

- Ask a severely visually-disabled user with a screen reader to listen to the site while you take note of any problems found.

- If possible, listen to your web site with a screen reader on your own computer. The most popular screen reader is JAWS for Windows (also the most expensive). You may be able to download a time-limited trial version of JAWS from http://www.freedomscientific.com or search for a time limited version of MS Windows-Eye. For a free screen reader, go to http://www.nvda-project.org

- Submit your amended site or page to a free, automated compliance scanner (ACS) such as WAVE at `http://wave.webaim.org`. WAVE provides a report that gives details of where your web site does not comply. WAVE's reports are reasonably easy to understand. WAVE concentrates on how a screen reader would respond to your page. It does it using colored icons that give a useful explanation when the cursor hovers over them. Unfortunately, WAVE does not currently cover color contrast ratio.

The AbilityNet ACS (`www.abilitynet.org.uk/`) reports on color contrast ratio. It uses the Compliance Sheriff scanner and only the initial scan is free. A Compliance Sheriff report can be baffling at first. It contains many boxes describing WCAG recommendations, but few hints on how to correct the non-compliances. Compliance Sheriff does not differentiate between layout tables and data tables. It incorrectly recommends that layout tables have captions, summaries, and even scope.

Be aware that although AbilityNet is an excellent charity, it has limited funds. It allows only one free scan of your web site. To progress past the first free scan costs of $170 (£120) per page. Remember, automated accessibility testing tools can't check whether the content is written in a helpful manner for the visually handicapped. Their remit is to check if the markup is suitable for screen readers to interpret intelligently. It is important to use front-loading content so that each paragraph begins with the conclusion. This simply means do not force the user to read a long paragraph to find out what it is about. Use the journalist's "headline" technique of telling what the paragraph is about in either the first line or the heading.

⬛ **Tip** The following screen readers and other resources are also available for download:
BrowseAloud `http://www.browsealoud.com` Thunder `http://www.screenreader.net` and WebbIE (free) `http://www.webbie.org.uk` If you use Firefox, take a look at `http://www.firevox.clcworld.net/about.html` Fire Vox is the screen reader for Mozilla Firefox.

The Royal National Institute for the Blind provides a very useful checklist for designing accessible webs sites. See `http://www.rnib.org.uk/professionals/Documents/WAC_See_it_Right_standard.doc`

⬛ **Tip** See `http://www.hassellinclusion.com/2011/01/web-accessibility-myths-2011-part2/` for stimulating and controversial thoughts on web site accessibility.

Summary

In this chapter, you learned about web accessibility problems experienced by the disabled, particularly the visually disabled. A brief reference to UK law and US guidance on this topic gave useful web site addresses for further reference. The chapter referred to the importance of color contrast and font sizes for partially-sighted persons.

A detailed checklist provided you with a way of assessing a web site for accessibility. The section on screen readers described how they function and the problems associated with data tables, especially with HTML5. The chapter described elements of forms that would work with screen readers. Try to keep these tips in mind when designing web sites, especially sites that might be useful to blind or partially-sighted persons.

The next chapter covers obsolete (deprecated) elements. You will learn how to replace these using CSS. HTML5 introduced new tags, which increased the number of deprecated elements. Worked examples will demonstrate how deprecated elements should be replaced.

CHAPTER 15

Dump Those Deprecated Items

The term "deprecated items" means that the World Wide Web Consortium (W3C) has phased out these items and you should not use them. A page containing deprecated tags and attributes will not validate, nor will it be suitable for handheld devices, screen readers, or search engines.

I sometimes take over the maintenance and redesign of a web site from another web master. Often the web site is old and full of deprecated items. My first task is to replace all the deprecated items with the modern equivalent. You may be required to do similar work. This chapter will help you to update a web site and also show you how to avoid including deprecated items in future web sites.

The chapter includes the following sections:

- Lists of deprecated items and their modern replacements

- The advantages of removing deprecated items

- Avoiding table layout for columns

- Avoiding table layout for an extendable content panel

- Using CSS instead of tables for multiple boxes with borders

- The CSS3 module for multiple columns

The Deprecated Items

Some tags and attributes were deprecated in the early years of HTML4. A few more are deprecated in HTML5; they are all listed together in Tables 15-1 and 15-2. When enhancing or updating a page on a web site you should grasp the opportunity to replace all deprecated items with CSS or with new tags. As previously mentioned, if someone transfers an old web site to you, the deprecated items will need to be replaced.

Table 15-1. Deprecated Tags

Deprecated tags	Replacement
`<acronym>`	`<abbr>`
`<applet>`	`<object>`
`<basefont>`	Use CSS font style sheet
`<big>`	Use CSS

Deprecated tags	Replacement
`<center>`	Use CSS code `text-align:centre` and `margin:auto;`
`<dir>`	Use `<ul>` to replace `<dir>` with an unordered list
`<embed>`	Was widely used even though deprecated; now reinstated in HTML5
`<fn>`	Locate footnotes with `<a href="#…">`
`<font>`	Define all fonts in a CSS style sheet
`<frame>`	None. Do not use frames
`<frameset>`	None. Don't confuse this with `<fieldset>`
`<marquee>`	None
`<menu>`	Replace with an unordered list (use `<ul>`)
`<strike>`	Use `<del>` or CSS
`<table>`	Deprecated if used to layout a page Reserve tables for tabular data only.
`<td width=" ">`	Use `<colgroup>` and `<col>` tags
`<u>`	Define underline by using CSS
`<xmp>`	Replace with `<pre>`

The attributes listed in Table 15-2 must all be replaced by CSS styling.

Table 15-2. *Deprecated Attributes*

In HTML markup	Replacement
align	Use a CSS style for all the attributes listed on the left
alink	
background	
bgcolor	
border	
cellpadding	
cellspacing	
clear	
color	

In HTML markup	Replacement
border	Use a CSS style for all the attributes listed on the left
height (except for images)	
hspace	
margin	
marginheight	
marginwidth	
size	
text	
width (except for images)	
vspace	
valign	

Replacing Deprecated Items

The amount of HTML markup will be reduced when deprecated items are replaced by CSS. However, the CSS sheet will then contain more markup. This gives a net saving because the CSS sheet is a single page, but many of the HTML pages linked to the style sheet will have less markup.

I usually place an up-arrow on lengthy pages like Figure 15-1. Clicking the arrow makes the cursor jump to the top of the page.

Go to top of page

Figure 15-1. An up-arrow and its text

Old HTML markup for the up-arrow would have included deprecated items shown here in bold type:

```
<p align="center"><b><font size="3" face="Times New Roman">Go to top of page</font></b>
<a href="#top">
    <img border="0" title="Go to top of page" src="images/bluearrow.gif" ↵
    align="middle" alt="Go to top of page" width="52" height="44"></a>
</p>
```

After removing the deprecated items and using a CSS style sheet, the markup becomes:

```
<p><b>Go to top of page</b>
<a href="#top">
    <img class="up-arrow" title="Go to top of page" src="images/bluearrow.gif" ↵
    alt="Go to top of page" width="52" height="44"></a>
</p>
```

The width and height tags are acceptable in the HTML markup when used with an image. The font family details and the class up-arrow would be defined in a CSS style sheet as follows:

```
.up-arrow { font-family: "times new roman"; font-size:100%; font-weight:bold; ↵
text-align:center; border:0; vertical-align:middle;
}
```

I use a class rather than an id because I need more than one up-arrow on very long pages. The markup was reduced from 241 characters to 172 characters and the markup will now validate. In a web site, this saving will be achieved in every page that contains up-arrows.

When more than one up-arrow is located in a side column, create an additional class of up-arrow called class="up-arrow-more".

In the CSS style sheet the additional class would be as follows:

```
.up-arrow-more { font-family:"times new roman"; font-size:100%; font-weight:bold; ↵
text-align:center; border:0; vertical-align:middle; margin-top:400px;
}
```

The additional arrows on the page are given the class up-arrow-more. The margin-top:400px forces the up-arrows apart vertically by a distance of 400 pixels. This avoids the need to insert lots of line breaks <br> or <p> tags between each up-arrow.

Anchors

In earlier times, the landing point at the top of a page was set by the HTML 4 markup as

```
<a name="top"></a>
```

The attribute name should now be replaced by id. The code becomes <a id="top"></a>. This is now general practice for all versions of HTML.

The same recommendation applies to anchors on other pages; for instance, to link from one page to a particular place on another page, the link might be

```
<a href="page3.html#colyton">Click for more information about Colyton</a>
```

When clicked, the link would take the user to a place on page3.html that would be labeled as

```
<a id="colyton"></a>
```

Validation: Pages containing deprecated items will not validate. Hand held devices and search engines can be hindered by pages that will not validate because they contain deprecated items.

The **‹embed›** tag was deprecated in HTML4 and it would not validate. However, it was so widely used (especially in videos) that it has been revived in HTML5. Its return is warmly welcomed.

Bold and Italic Text

Concerning deprecation, the following question often arises: should you now use <strong></strong> instead of <b></b> and <em></em> instead of <i></i>?

The <b></b> tag is not deprecated, the <strong></strong> tag gives a similar result, but a user's browser settings can override it. The CSS equivalent would be b { font-weight:bold; }.

The <i></i> tag is not deprecated, the <em> </em> tag gives a similar result but the user's browser settings can override it. The equivalent CSS code is i {font-style:italic;}.

I use them interchangeably when I am busy and I have deadlines to meet because I find the difference too subtle to worry about.

As a general rule, use <i> to italicize a word or phrase without changing its emphasis or mood; for example: "Don't miss *The Depraved Soap Opera* on TV channel 123 tonight."

Use <em> to emphasize a word or phrase; for example: "You mean actually *enjoy* that show?"

Data Tables Good, Layout Tables Bad

Tables should only be used to present data. Older web sites used tables for page layout and many still do. The World Wide Web Consortium (W3C) deprecated tables for page layout several years back. Mobile devices definitely do not like table layouts. Table layouts result in bloated pages. The HTML for a table layout can be three to four times bulkier than for CSS layout.

Once mastered, CSS layouts have much greater power and flexibility than table layouts. Table layouts can be a big problem for people using screen readers, speech output browsers, Braille browsers, and text browsers (see Chapter 14). Acceptable tables consisting of rows and columns of data like Table 15-3.

Table 15-3. Pub Quiz Scores

Position	Team	Points
1	Pig and Whistle	10
2	Dog and Duck	7
3	Bull and Butcher	4
4	Cat and Fiddle	0

■ **Note** Special rules apply to data tables for assisting the disabled. These are described in Chapter 14.

Multiple Columns Without Tables

CSS2-based, multiple columns can be designed quite easily without using tables. (This section of the chapter can be regarded as a supplement to the multiple column section of Chapter 12.) CSS3 can create columns of text, (see "The new CSS3 module for columns" later in this chapter), but currently, few browsers support this.

A Basic, Three-Column Page with Columns the Same Color

Semantic tags are not used in these examples so that IE 7 and IE 8 can display the results without having to resort to the complication of added JavaScript. If you wish to use semantic tags, be sure to add the JavaScript snippet and change the display instruction in the CSS as described in Chapter 1.

Figure 15-2 shows three columns created by CSS.

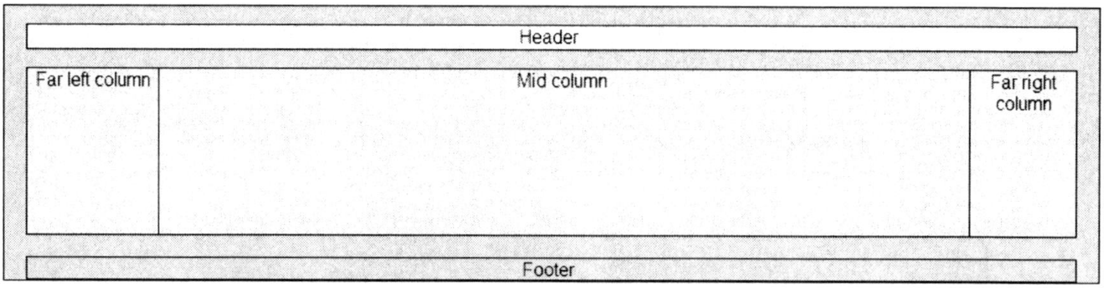

Figure 15-2. *A three column page with five sections or divisions*

This is achieved by creating five divisions (`<div>`s): one each for the header and footer and one for each column. Purists will be horrified by my use of presentational markup. Designers are discouraged from using identifiers like leftcol and rightcol; identifiers should indicate content not position. In this and subsequent examples, the presentational words leftcol, rightcol, and midcol are used for clarity. In a real web page, they could be replaced by something like menu-col, advert-col, and main-content.

Listing 15-2a uses CSS presentation to produce three columns instead using a deprecated table layout.

Listing 15-2a. *Creating Three Columns Without Using a Table (three-col-no-tables.html)*

```
<!doctype html>
<html lang=en>
<head>
<title>Three columns without tables</title>
<meta charset=utf-8>
        meta details go here
<link href="three-col-no-tables.css" rel="stylesheet" type="text/css" />
</head>
<body>
<div id="container">
        <div id="hdr">Header</div>
        <!--start of main panel that contains the menus and four columns of content-->
        <div id="mainpanel">
                <div id="leftcol">Far left column<!--the far left column starts-->
                </div><!--end of far left column>
                <div id="rightcol">Far right column<!--start of the far right column-->
                </div>
                <div id="midcol">Mid column<!--Start of the middle column-->
                </div><!-- midcol closed-->
        </div><!-- main panel closed--><br>
        <div id="ftr"><!-- start of footer-->
                Footer
        </div><!--footer closed-->
</div><!--container closed -->
</body>
</html>
```

The CSS layout is provided in Listing 15-2b.

Listing 15-2b. The CSS Style Sheet for the Layout of Figure 15-2 (three-col-no-tables.css)

```
body {background:white; font-family:arial; font-size:medium; color:black; ⏎
margin:auto; padding:7px;
}
#container { width:960px; border:1px black solid; margin:auto; text-align:center; ⏎
margin-top:0; background:#a5f400;
}
#hdr {width:920px;  height:20px; margin:15px auto 15px auto; background:yellow; ⏎
color:black; border:1px black solid;
}
/*THE MAIN PANEL CONTAINS THE THREE COLUMNS*/
#mainpanel {margin:auto; background:#d2ff81; text-align:center; width:920px; ⏎
height:140px; border:1px black solid;
}
#leftcol {float:left; width :115px; height: 140px; border-right:1px black solid;
}
#rightcol { float:right; width:92px; border-left:1px black solid; height:140px;
}
*SET MARGINS FOR MID COLUMN. THIS SITS BETWEEN THE FAR LEFT AND FAR RIGHT COLUMNS*/
#midcol { margin-left:120px; margin-right:105px; text-align:center; border:1px black solid;
}
#ftr {width:920px; margin:auto; text-align:center; clear:both; background: #a5f400; ⏎
border: 1px black solid;
}
```

A Basic, Four-Column Page with Columns the Same Color

Figure 15-3 shows the display produced by CSS markup for four columns.

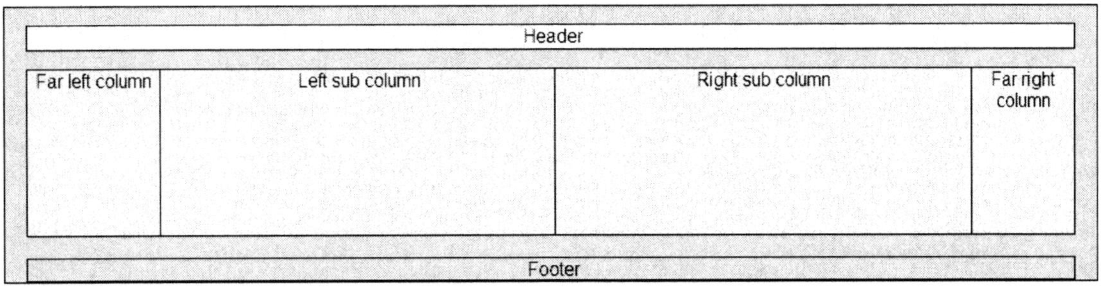

Figure 15-3. Four columns without using tables

Creating four columns is simply a matter of splitting the middle column into two sub-columns using <div>s . The Listings 15-3a and 15-3b identify these as subleft and subright.

Listing 15-3. Creating a Four Column Layout Without Tables (four-col-no-tables.html)

```
<!doctype html>
<html lang=en>
<head>
```

```
<title>Four columns with no tables</title>
<meta charset=utf-8>
<meta details go here>
<link href="four-col-no-tables.css" rel="stylesheet" type="text/css">
</head>
<body>
<div id="container">
        <div id="hdr">Header</div>
        <div id="mainpanel">
                <div id="leftcol">Far left column</div>
                <div id="rightcol">Far right column</div>
                <div id="midcol">
                        <div id="subleft">Left sub column</div>
                        <div id="subright">Right sub column</div>
                </div>
        </div><br>
                <div id="ftr">Footer</div>
</div>
</body>
</html>
```

The CSS layout for Figure 15-3 is provided by Listing 15-3b.

Listing 15-3b. Providing the CSS Layout for Four Columns (four-col-no-tables.css)

```
body {background:white; font-family:arial; font-size:medium; color:black; margin:auto; ↵
padding:7px;
}
#container { width:960px; border:1px black solid; margin:auto; text-align:center; ↵
margin-top:0; background:#a5f400;
}
#hdr {width:920px;  height:20px; margin:15px auto 15px auto; background:yellow; ↵
color:black; border:1px black solid;
}
#mainpanel {margin:auto; background:#d2ff81; text-align:center; width:920px; ↵
height:140px; border:1px black solid;
}
#leftcol {float:left; width :115px; height: 140px; border-right:1px black solid;
}
#rightcol { float:right; width:92px; border-left:1px black solid; height:140px;
}
#midcol { margin-left:120px; margin-right:105px; text-align:center;
}
#subleft { float:left; width: 49%; height: 140px; border-right:1px black solid;
}
#subright { float: right; width:49%; height: 140px; border:0;
}
#ftr {width:920px; margin:auto; text-align:center; clear:both; background: #a5f400; ↵
border: 1px black solid;
}
```

Four Columns with Differing Background Colors

Figure 15-4 shows four columns with different colors.

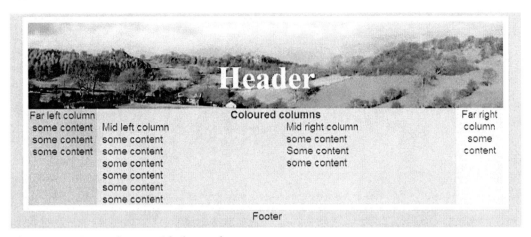

Figure 15-4. *Four columns with three colors*

Design becomes trickier if you require different colored columns as Figure 15-4. Personally, I much prefer columns to have the same color, it looks classy, concentrates the focus on the main topic, and presents designers with fewer problems. However, if you need columns with different colors, the least complicated method is described next. (Sources for other methods are provided at the end of this chapter.)

Listing 15-4a provides the content on the four column page.

Listing 15-4a. *Creating the Content for Four Columns With Three Colors (colour-columns1.html)*

```
<!doctype html>
<html lang=en>
<head>
<title>Colour columns</title>
<meta charset=utf-8>
        meta details go here
<link rel="stylesheet" type="text/css" href="style-colourcols1.css">
</head>
<body>
<div id="container">
        <div id="hdr"><h1>Header</h1>
        </div>
        <div id="leftcol">
                <p>Far left column</p><p>some content</p><p>some content</p>
                <p>some content</p><p> </p><p> </p><p> </p><p> </p>
        </div>
        <div id="rightcol">
                <p>Far right column</p><p>some content</p><p> </p><p> </p>
                <p> </p><p> </p>
        </div>
```

```
            <div id="midcol">
            <h2><b>Coloured columns</b></h2>
            <div id="mid-left-col">
                    <p>Mid left column</p>
                    <p>some content</p><p>some content</p><p>some content</p><p>some content</p>
                    <p>some content</p><p>some content </p>
            </div>
            <div id="mid-right-col">
                    <p>Mid right column</p>
                    <p>some content</p><p>Some content</p><p>some content</p>
            </div>
            </div>
                    <br class="clear"></div>
<div id="ftr">
<p>Footer</p>
</div>
</body>
</html>
```

The Listing 15-4b is the style sheet that presents the colored columns as in Figure 15-4.

Listing 15-4b. *The CSS Style Sheet for Colored Columns (style-colourcols1.css)*

```
/*SETTINGS FOR MAXIMUM CONFORMITY BETWEEN BROWSERS*/
html, body, h1, h2, h3, h4, h5, h6, p, ol, ul, li, form, fieldset, blockquote { ⏎
padding: 0; margin: 0; font-size: 100%; font-weight: normal;
}
img { border:0;
}
body { background:#BBD999; font-family:arial; font-size:120%; color:#4B6113; ⏎
margin:auto; padding:7px;
}
#container { width:900px; border: 10px white solid; margin:auto; text-align:center; ⏎
margin-top:0; background-color:#CEE1BA; color:#4B6113;
}
#hdr { padding-top:18px; height:141px; width:100%; margin:auto; ⏎
background-image:url('images/banner.jpg'); background-repeat:no-repeat; ⏎
background-position:65;
}
#hdr h1 { font-family: "times new roman"; text-align:center; color: white; ⏎
font-weight:bold; font-size: 300%; margin-top:50px;
}
#leftcol { float:left; width :130px; display:inline; background-color:#ACC;
}
#rightcol { float:right; width:92px; text-align:center; ⏎
background:url(images/yellow-square.gif) repeat-y right top;
}
/*SET MARGINS ON MID COLUMN*/
#midcol { margin-left:140px; margin-right:105px; text-align:center;
}
/*SET COLUMN WIDTHS FOR CONTENT. THESE SIT WITHIN THE MIDCOL*/
#mid-left-col {width:47%; float:left; text-align:left;
}
#mid-right-col {width:47%; float:right; text-align:left;
```

```
}
/*ENSURE DIVS AUTOMATICALLY STRETCH VERTICALLY TO ACCOMMODATE VARIOUS AMOUNTS OF CONTENT*/
br.clear { clear:both;
}
/*SET FOOTER TO CLEAR PRECEDING COLUMNS*/
#ftr {text-align:center; clear:both;
}
```

An Extendable, Colored, Central Panel with No Tables

For this next example, my thanks go to Mrs. Diana Board for giving me permission to use the home page that I designed for her web site (www.lowerfarmbandb.co.uk).

All the following examples use no tables. Figure 15-5 shows a four-column page. The pale green content panel with a white border needs a tweak to make it expand downwards to match the amount of content.

Figure 15-5. *The untweaked page*

Figure 15-6 shows the content panel extended downwards without resorting to a table layout.

347

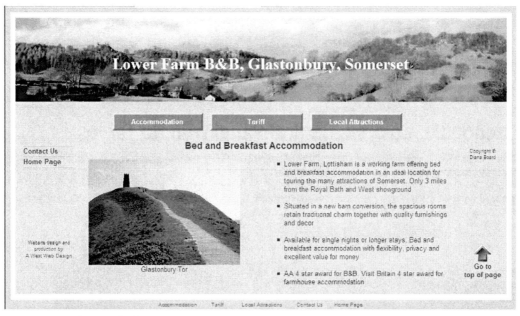

Figure 15-6. The tweaked page

The two photographs used in this home page Figure 15-6 are by kind permission of Walking Britain (www.walkingbritain.co.uk).

The item in bold type in Listing 15-6 is the tweak that pulls the frame down. In Listing 15-6 much of the content has been omitted as it is not relevant to the point being made. You can download the full listing from the companion web site, http://www.apress.com.

Listing 15-6. Creating the Structure for the Page Shown in Figure 15-6 (tweaked.html)

```
<!doctype html>
<html lang=en>
<head>
<title>Tweaked page</title>
<meta charset=utf-8>
        meta details go here
<link rel="stylesheet" type="text/css" href="style-fixed-sans.css" />
</head>
<body>
<a id="top"></a>
<div id="container">
<div id="hdr"><h1>Lower Farm B&amp;B, Glastonbury, Somerset</h1></div>
<div id="mainpanel"><!--start of main panel and horizonal buttons--><br>
<ul id="hmenew">
        The horizontal menu buttons go here
</ul><br>
<div id="leftcol"><!--side menu column starts-->
<ul id="menu">
        The two vertical menu buttons go here
```

```
</ul>
        Web design details and copyright notices go here
</div>
<div id="midcol" ><h2>Bed and Breakfast Accommodation</h2><p> </p>
<div id="mid-left-col" class="cntr">
<img alt="Glastonbury Tor" height="200" src="images/tor300.jpg" width="300"><br>↵
Glastonbury Tor<br>
</div>
<div id="mid-right-col">
<ul>
        <li>Lower Farm, Lottisham is a working farm offering bed and breakfast ↵
        accommodation in an ideal location for touring the many attractions of ↵
        Somerset. Only 3 miles from the Royal Bath and West showground<p> </p></li>
        <li>Situated in a new barn conversion, the spacious rooms retain traditional ↵
        charm together with quality furnishings and decor<p> </p></li>
        <li>Available for single nights or longer stays. Bed and
        breakfast accommodation with flexibility, privacy and excellent value for ↵
        money<p> </p></li>
        <li>AA 4 star award for B&amp;B. Visit Britain 4 star award for farmhouse ↵
        accommodation</li>
</ul>
</div>
</div>
<br class="clear"><br>
</div>
</div>
<div id="ftr">Footer links and photograph permissions go here</div>
</body>
</html>
```

The tweak for pulling the panel and border downwards is an additional item placed in the CSS style sheet. The code that was added is as follows:

```
/*ENSURE DIVS AUTOMATICALLY STRETCH VERTICALLY TO ACCOMMODATE VARIOUS AMOUNTS OF CONTENT*/
br.clear { clear:both;
}
```

Now we will look at boxes containing images and text. These were traditionally presented in a table. But because tables are deprecated, the next section shows you how to dispense with tables by using a CSS style sheet.

CSS Boxes and Borders

In the past, web designers would have used a table to construct Figure 15-7. Now that tables are deprecated, the boxes must be constructed using CSS. Figure 15-7 illustrates a set of boxes constructed entirely by means of CSS.

Borders and Boxes

Ann paints under her professional name of Ann L Roe (Jones)

She is an academician and trustee of the South West Academy of Fine and Applied Arts.

Ann studied painting, art and design in France, London and Brighton

Ann's portrait of 'Nico with icons' won her the prestigious Baker Prize for Painting in the South West Academy Open Exhibition.

Ann lives in Colyton Devon, UK. She paints landscapes and still life, but her particular interest is portrait painting.

Ann's portrait of Sir Patrick Moore FRS

The astronomer Sir Patrick Moore FRS, still presents his Sky at Night program on BBC television (channels 1,2 and 4).

Ann painted a separate portrait of Sir Patrick Moore's beloved cat

Ann's portrait of the three Chelsea Pensioners - Bob, Michael and Fred - now has a permanent home in the Infirmary Building of the Royal Hospital Chelsea in London.

Unveiled in March 2010 by General the Lord Walker GCB CMG CBE DL, the painting can be seen by the public in the Foyer.

Figure 15-7. Boxes and borders without tables

The portrait artist Ann Roe Jones kindly gave me permission to use items from the web site I designed for her. These are used in Figure 15-7. You can view her web site at www.annroejones-artist.co.uk.

An internal style is used here for clarity only. The boxes are defined in their own <div>s and each of these has the class mainpanel. The panels are separated by the code <br class="clear">.

Listing 15-7. Creating the Structure and CSS Presentaion for a Group of Boxes (borders-boxes.html)

```
<!doctype html>
<html lang=en>
<head>
<title>Borders and boxes</title>
```

```
<meta charset=utf-8>
            meta details go here
        <style type="text/css">
        #wrapper { text-align:center;
        }
        .mainpanel {margin:auto; padding:5px; font-size:100%; text-align:center; ↵
        width:700px; border:1px solid black;
        }
        .leftcol { float:left; width:30%; text-align:center;
        }
        .rightcol {float:right; width:68%; text-align:left;
        }
        br.clear { clear:both;
        }
        p { margin-top:0; margin-bottom:6px;
        }
        .img-left { float:left; }
        .img-right {float:right; }
        #cat { float:right; margin-right:20px; margin-left: 5px;" width="69"
        }
        </style>
</head>
<body id="wrapper">
<a id="top"></a>
<div id="hdr"><h1> Borders and Boxes</h1></div>
<div class="mainpanel">
        <div class="leftcol">
        <p><img alt="Ann Roe Jones" height="194" src="images/ann150.gif" width="150"></p>
        </div>
        <div class="rightcol">
        <p> <b>Ann paints under her professional name of Ann L Roe (Jones)</b></p>
        <p><b>She is an academician</b> and trustee of the South West Academy of Fine ↵
        and Applied Arts.</p>
        <p><b>Ann studied</b> painting, art and design in France, London and Brighton.</p>
        <p><b>Ann's portrait of 'Nico with icons'</b> won her the prestigious Baker Prize ↵
        for Painting in the South West Academy Open Exhibition.</p><p><b>Ann lives in Colyton
        Devon, UK. </b>
        She paints landscapes and still life, but her particular interest is portrait ↵
        painting.</p>
        </div>
<br class="clear">
</div><br>
<div class="mainpanel">
        <div class="leftcol">
        <p><img alt="Sir Patrick Moore FRS" height="222" ↵
        src="images/patrickmoore150.jpg" width="150"> </p>
        </div>
        <div class="rightcol"><br>
        <p><b>Ann's portrait of Sir Patrick Moore FRS</b></p><p><b>The astronomer ↵
        Sir Patrick Moore FRS, </b>
        still presents his Sky at Night program on BBC television (channels 1,2 and 4).</p>
```

```
          <p id="cat"><img class="img-right" alt="Sir Patrick Moore's cat" height="91" ↩
          src="images/catthumb.jpg" >Ann painted a separate portrait of Sir Patrick Moore's ↩
          beloved cat (see inset on the right)</p>
          </div>
<br class="clear">
</div><br>
<div class="mainpanel">
          <div class="leftcol">
          <p><img alt="Chelsea Pensioners" height="153" src="images/pensioners150.jpg" ↩
          width="150"> </p>
          </div>
          <div class="rightcol"><br><p><b>Ann's portrait of the three Chelsea Pensioners</b>↩
          - Bob, Michael and Fred - The painting now has a permanent home in the Infirmary ↩
          Building of the Royal Hospital Chelsea in London.</p>Unveiled in March 2010 by ↩
          General the Lord Walker GCB CMG CBE DL, the painting can be seen by the public in ↩
          the Foyer.<br>
          </div>
<br class="clear">
</div><br>
</body>
</html>
The next section discusses the new CSS3 module for creating multiple columns.
```

The New CSS3 Module for Columns

Now that layout tables are deprecated, designers must abandon the traditional way of displaying columns of text by means of a multi-cell tables with invisible borders. Earlier in this chapter, I described how to use CSS to achieve multiple columns for containing text.

CSS3 has new module for multi-column layout, this is perhaps the most exciting time saver of all the proposed modules. When it is fully adopted, we might see an end to those ghastly web sites where the text spreads right across the screen. It will certainly be the death of table layout for columns.

The width and number of columns can be defined. The new style keywords as you would expect are, column-width and column-count. A space can be created between columns using a width called forcolumn-gap. A vertical line between columns can be created using column-rule. Content will flow from column to column like it does in publishing software.

At the time of writing, only Mozilla Firefox, Chrome, and Safari support the new multi-column module. However, Firefox, Chrome and Safari manage this by means of their own idiosyncratic hacks: -moz- for Firefox and -webkit- for Safari and Chrome. Sadly, IE 7, IE 8, and IE 9 (and Opera at the time of writing) ignore the CSS3 column styling. Therefore, CSS3 multiple columns may not be used by web designers for several years until IE 7, IE 8, and IE 9 are extinct.

■ **Note** CSS3 is not dependent on the HTML version. CSS3 enhancements will work in HTML4, XHTML, and HTML5 but only if the browser supports them. Firefox, Safari, and Chrome support multiple columns. Microsoft stated in September 2010 that IE 9 will not support CSS3 multiple columns.

Figures 15-8 and 15-9 show how the CSS3 multiple columns appear in various browsers.

Figure 15-8. *The CSS3 multi-column markup fails to display in Internet Explorer 6, 7, 8, 9, and Opera*

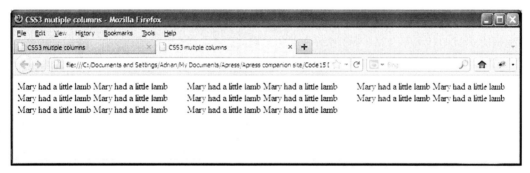

Figure 15-9. *How CSS3 multi-column displays in Mozilla Firefox, Safari, and Chrome*

In Listing 15-8, the code in bold type establishes the way that supporting browsers display the columns in these two figures.

Listing 15-8. *A Template for Content that can be Displayed in Columns Using CSS3 (css3-columns.html)*

```
<!doctype html>
<html lang=en>
<head>
<title>CSS3 mutiple columns</title>
<meta charset=utf-8>
        meta details go here
<style type="text/css">
#content { -moz-column-count: 3; -moz-column-gap: 1em;
-webkit-column-count: 3; -webkit-column-gap: 1em;
}
</style>
</head>
<body>
<div id="content">
```

```
Mary had a little lamb Mary had a little lamb Mary had a little lamb Mary had a little lamb
Mary had a little lamb Mary had a little lamb Mary had a little lamb Mary had a little lamb
Mary had a little lamb Mary had a little lamb Mary had a little lamb Mary had a little lamb
Mary had a little lamb Mary had a little lamb Mary had a little lamb Mary had a little lamb
</div>
</body>
</html>
```

CSS3 can provide vertical rules, that is, lines that separate one item from another. Figure 15-10 shows that CSS3 can provide dividing rules between paragraphs.

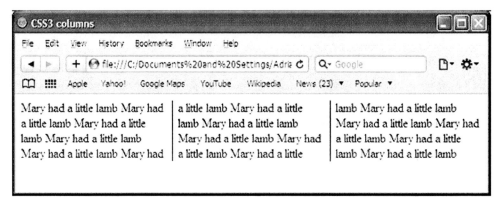

Figure 15-10. How CSS3 multi-columns displays the rules in Mozilla Firefox, Safari, and Chrome

At the time of writing, the vertical rules require the hack -moz- for Mozilla Firefox and -webkit- for Safari. In the following code snippet, the new CSS3 column module keywords for rules are shown in bold type.

```
#content { -moz-column-count: 3; -moz-column-gap: 1em; -moz-column-rule: 1px solid black;
-webkit-column-count: 3; -webkit-column-gap: 1em; -webkit-column-rule: 1px solid black;
}
```

Listing 15-10. Introducing Vertical Rules Between the CSS3 Columns (css3-3col-rules.html)

```
<!doctype html>
<html lang=en>
<head>
<title>CSS3 mutiple columns</title>
<meta charset=utf-8>
<meta details go here>
<style type="text/css">
#content { -moz-column-count: 3; -moz-column-gap: 1em; -moz-column-rule: 1px solid black;
-webkit-column-count: 3; -webkit-column-gap: 1em; -webkit-column-rule: 1px solid black;
}
</style>
</head>
<body>
<div id="content">
Mary had a little lamb Mary had a little lamb Mary had a little lamb Mary had a little lamb
Mary had a little lamb Mary had a little lamb Mary had a little lamb Mary had a little lamb
```

```
Mary had a little lamb Mary had a little lamb Mary had a little lamb Mary had a little lamb
Mary had a little lamb Mary had a little lamb Mary had a little lamb Mary had a little lamb
</div>
</body>
</html>
```

When the browser window is shrunk horizontally, the three columns reduce in width to match. They also extend downwards to accommodate all the content. If the content container has a fixed width then the columns stay the same width when the browser window is shrunk.

One wonderful day we will be able to omit the hacks and just use the following CSS3:

```
#content { column-count: 3; column-gap: 1em; column-rule: 1px solid black;
}
```

The multiple-column module will be remarkably flexible when the browsers eventually implement the next batch of features; for instance, the next snippet of CSS markup will fix the width of the columns and will adjust the number of columns to fit the content space. The column-width markup sets the column widths to at least 15 em wide. The exact number of columns will depend on the available content width.

```
#content { column-width: 15em;
}
```

In the next piece of CSS3 markup, the number of columns will be fixed, but the width of each column will change to suit the width of the content area.

```
#content { column-count: 3;
}
```

The columns can be made equal length, as follows:

```
#content { column-fill: balance;
}
```

A heading can be made to span the columns, as follows:

```
h2 { column-span: all;
}
```

The column rule (a vertical line between the columns) can be omitted or it can have various widths and colors, as follows:

```
#content {column-rule: thin solid blue;
}
```

Many other multi-column features are in the module's pipeline but are not yet finalized; nor are they available in browsers at the time of writing. They include the following:

```
column-space-distribution,    break-before:column;    break-inside:avoid-column;
and break-after:avoid-column;
```

░ **Tip** See the A List Apart web site `www.alistapart.com/articles/css3multicolumn/` for a comprehensive treatment of the new CSS3 multi-column module. See also

`http://developer.mozilla.org/en/docs/CSS3_Columns` and `www.w3.org/TR/css3-multicol/`.

Summary

This chapter provided a list of deprecated tags and attributes— items you should avoid as you design or redesign web sites. The up-arrow device was used to demonstrate the advantages of dumping deprecated items. Because tables are deprecated, several solutions were described for replacing them with CSS styling. The chapter gave solutions for problems that might arise from using CSS layouts. A way of constructing a series of boxes with borders without tables was described. Traditionally, tables with invisible borders were used to display columns of text; the chapter gave instructions for using CSS2 to replace tables and then demonstrated the new CSS3 multi-column solution.

In the next chapter you will learn how search engines work, and you will be introduced to methods for optimizing your web sites so that they will appear higher up in the search engines' results.

Search Engine Optimization

Is your web site featured in the early pages of results when you type a keyword into the search field of Bing, Yahoo!, or Google? You can improve the chances of appearing in the first few pages, but an early appearance cannot always be guaranteed without paying for a favorable position.

This chapter shows you how you might improve your rating and what to avoid. You will be given information to help you understand how search engines choose web pages that correspond with the user's search words (keywords).

Having your web site appear on a search engine's pages is a form of free advertising. However, other ways of advertising your site should not be neglected. The chapter includes advice on how to complement the work of the search engines by proclaiming the existence of your web site by other means.

Overview

Search engine optimization (SEO) can be frustrating. One of your web sites may not appear in the search listing even though it is well optimized. View the source markup of some of the web sites on the search engine's first page; you may find that some are not well-optimized. Why isn't your well-optimized site listed when the non-optimized sites are? Only the search engines (SEs) know why.

The search results seem to be inconsistent. One of my sites was at the bottom of the second page in Google and first on the second page of Bing. Two weeks later, my site had disappeared from Google but was still in the same place on Bing. A month later it had reappeared on Google at the bottom of page three. Why? I can think of no logical explanation.

SEO is more of an arcane art than a scientific process. This should not deter web designers from doing their best to optimize a web site. I have web sites listed high on page one on Yahoo!, but only on page seven of Google. This is because Yahoo! concentrates on keywords and site optimization, whereas Google depends more on the number of external links to a web site (the popularity of a web site seems to matter more to Google than whether it is useful to the searcher).

Equally frustrating is the fact that SEs take between three and five months to index a well-optimized new web site. Surprising? No, because the robots used by SEs have to crawl through 240 million existing web sites to update them. In addition to this, they crawl through almost 50 million new ones each year. About 40 million become inactive annually and may be removed from a SE's index.

Time is an important aspect. Although SEs may index a new domain in three to five months, this does not mean it will then have a good ranking in the search results. Sometimes a further five or six months must pass before your web site moves up nearer to the first page of results. Some affluent companies will purchase a well established, high-ranking domain name rather than start from scratch with a new domain. The less affluent should upload some basic content immediately rather than wait until the web site is complete. This lets the SEs index it and starts the "probationary" period while the rest of the web site is being developed,

A well-optimized web site is the equivalent of having a name plate on your street and a number on your house. On rare occasions, the postman fails to deliver your mail, but without the house number and street name, his ability to deliver your mail is greatly reduced. Without optimization, the SEs have a greatly reduced chance of indexing your web site and listing it for searchers.

A *web crawler* is the robot used by SEs to trawl though every web site, looking for keywords and key phrases. The web sites can then be indexed so that users can search for web sites possessing those keywords. Most web site hosts have a traffic monitoring system (sometime called web stats). You can use this to see when and how often a web site is crawled by the SEs.

░ **Tip** For a first-class resource, try Peter Kent's *Search Engine Optimization for Dummies* (Wiley, 2010). The techniques that Peter describes are very readable and the step-by-step instructions are crystal-clear and easy to put into practice. It contains extras on such items as pay-per-click, and a vast number of very useful resources. For a useful internet resource, see Phil Craven's web site, `http://www.webworkshop.net` Also try Term Extractor from SEOmoz at `http://www.seomoz.org/term-extractor`. This tool extracts keywords from any specific web page and mimics a search engine spider.

Beware of False Promises

Warn your clients that they will be pestered by emails from unscrupulous people for a short time after launching the web site. Even though the client's email address is encrypted or a secure contact form is used, the scammers can make a reasonable guess by trying addresses such as `info@yourwebaddress.co.uk`. They then try to persuade your client to pay for the web site to be optimized. Give your clients a copy of the following warning:

> **SCAM WARNING:** After launching a web site, owners will be contacted by spammers offering to improve their search engine optimization. If an owner is duped by this, she will pay a lot of money and the spammer will do absolutely nothing. *In fact, there is nothing the spammers can do.* Some of these dreadful individuals even claim to be working for Google, Yahoo!, or Bing, or they claim to have contacts within those organizations. One particularly nasty specimen used the telephone to contact victims. He said he worked for Google and that if the victim refused to use his "service," he would remove the web site from Google's index.

Genuine SE optimizers do exist, but they will not use spam and they will not use generic email addresses such as `@hotmail` or `@gmail`. They have a well established service that can be checked for authenticity. But why pay for a job you can do yourself with the help of this chapter?

Page Rank and Popularity

Search engines are very secretive about their search criteria and about their page ranking method. SEs may occasionally modify their rules a little, but the general principles will remain the same.

Page Rank

I have found that page rank is not a strong influence on a web site's position in a list of search results. I have web sites with poor page rank listed high in the search results and vice versa. I, therefore, ignore page rank and concentrate on a web page's position in the list of results. However, although page rank has reduced in importance recently, you might derive some benefit from monitoring the page ranking. If you would like to know more about page rank, see a detailed explanation by Phil Craven at `http://www.webworkshop.net/pagerank.html`

The word *popularity* can be considered in two ways when related to search engines. It can refer to the popularity of the web site itself, or to the popularity of the subject of the web site (that is, its keywords).

Popularity and External Links

Google and Bing place a great emphasis on a web site's popularity, which they equate to the web site's usefulness. They assume that people would not link to a useless web site. *Popularity has nothing to do with the number of hits received by a web site*. Bing and especially Google determine popularity mainly by detecting the number of external links pointing to your web site. Yahoo!, on the other hand, detects the number of keywords and the number of internally linked pages within your web site, giving results that are much more relevant to the keyword typed into the search field.

I have web pages that regularly appear on the first page of Yahoo! because the web pages are well optimized. However, using the same search words, Google and Bing do not rate them so highly simply because fewer external links point to them. Links on popular web sites that point to your site indicate that your web site must also be popular and so your site moves up the ratings. These external links have a strong effect, but unfortunately they are not directly under your control. Yahoo! relies on well-organized internal links. These will be discussed first because they are directly under your control. Fortunately, keyword content and well-organized internal links are also recognized by Bing and Google.

Popularity of Subject (and its Keywords)

If a subject is popular, you will be competing against millions of other web pages for a place in the list of search results. If you are the only company producing anti-thrombosis socks for elephants, you will be first in the results on page one. Therefore, if the web site owner could concentrate on some unique aspect of his promotion, this would help with the search engine ranking. For instance, millions of antique dealers compete for a place in the SE results. If the dealer concentrated on a special type of antique, this would narrow the search field considerably and improve the web site's ranking.

Web site designers need to know what search engines look for in order to ensure that the web site's keywords and links are optimized. The section that follows will list what the search engines look for. It then discusses the best way to implement each topic.

What Search Engines Look For

Search engines look for the following:

- Keywords and phrases (especially in the `<title>` and the `<body>` section of a page
- Well-designed internal links to all the pages on the web site
- External links in other web sites that point to your site

Keywords and Phrases

Users searching for relevant web sites use keywords and key phrases. For instance, if a user has a problem with a computer, he will probably enter the key phrase "computer problem". SEs rate the importance of keywords in the following order:

1. The keywords/phrases in the `<title>`

2. The keywords/phrases in the `<body></body>` section

3. The keywords/phrases in the `<head></head>` section (not as important to Google)

4. The keywords/phrases that appear earlier in the markup

5. Keywords/phrases in headings (`h1`, `h2`, `h3`, etc.)

6. Keywords/phrase in bold text

The Content of the First Tag

The `<title></title>` is a vitally important tag and must appear immediately after the `<head>` tag for maximum effect.

Putting your company or web site name in the title or in meta tags is not very productive unless the company is reasonably well known. If you are Tesco or Walmart, then you must put the company name in the `<title>` and `"description"` meta tags because users search well-known names. Don't waste valuable keyword space by inserting the words "Welcome to" in the title or meta tags; nobody searches for *welcome* or *welcome to*.

The Meta Tag Keywords Controversy

Some SEO gurus state that SEs index the title and the meta description, but they ignore the keywords meta tag. This view is probably still true for Google because Google omits any reference to the keywords meta tag in its search engine tips. However, Bing and Yahoo! both say the keywords meta tag is important to them. What are we to make of such conflicting information?

Google started to ignore the keywords meta tag because designers were abusing it by stuffing it with dozens of keywords. Other SEO gurus say that SEs only read a limited number of the meta tag words. We don't know the answer because SEs are extremely secretive about their methods.

I put keywords in the keywords meta tag because Bing and Yahoo! say they take note of them, and there is at least a remote possibility that Google might start looking at them again some time in the future.

Meanwhile, make sure your `<title>` tag is used to maximum effect because it is vital. Give a good and relevant `"description"` meta tag containing key phrases or keywords because this is always displayed on the results listing. Despite the controversy surrounding the `"keywords"` meta tag, you should still use it for your keywords.

■ **Tip** Body text headers such as `<h1>` `</h1>`, `<h2>` `</h2>`, and so on, are ideal locations for keywords and key phrases. Search engines give a high rating to the content of headers.

The next section will help you to choose suitable keywords and key phrases.

■ **Tip** Put your *main* keyword or key phrase first in any list of keywords. The following useful web sites will help you select keywords: Google Keyword Tool Box `http://googlekeywordtool.com`; click the first item, Google Keyword Tool) and Google Adwords Keyword Tool (`https://adwords.google.com/select/↵ KeywordToolExternal`).The Google Webmaster Tools are a must see for learning more about of search engine optimization.

Choosing Keywords and Phrases

Imagine you are the person searching for the information offered on your web site. What would you type into the search field? Ask other people what they would type in. Choosing keywords and phrases is not as easy as that, but it starts you thinking.

Suppose that during a visit to Tibet, Mr. Smith rather foolishly drove around with his car window open and he developed a painful, frozen shoulder. Fortunately, a Tibetan monk cured Mr. Smith's frozen shoulder with a quick rub down with rancid yak fat. Mr. Smith launched a web site to sell this cure. His business was registered as Smith's Health Products Ltd.

He might have chosen "rancid yak fat" as the key phrase. It would not work, because at that time he was the only person outside Tibet who knew that rancid yak fat was a cure for a frozen shoulder. No one else would dream of entering that key phrase (though a few Tibetans with laptops might).

One day in the future Mr. Smith will be able to use the key phrase "rancid yak fat" along with his current phrases. But before that can happen, the rancid yak fat cure must become well known and featured in countless magazines and TV programs. Meanwhile, he should use phrases that concern the problem and not the product.

So what should he choose? What about Smith's Health Products? This would have been totally useless; hardly anyone outside his family knows about his new enterprise. Sensible people who did know the name and web address of his firm would enter the URL into the proper place; that is, the browser's address field. If Joe Bloggs has a frozen shoulder, how would he know that a company called Smith's had a cure?

Joe Bloggs, being sensible, might search on *painful shoulders, painful shoulder, frozen shoulder, aching shoulder*, or *stiff shoulder*.

Mr. Smith would enter those four key phrases into search engines and he would find the following:

- Painful shoulder: 1,100,000 search results

- Frozen shoulder: 288,000 search results

- Stiff shoulder: 137,000 search results

- Aching shoulder: 51,000 search results

This indicated that *painful shoulder* is used by web sites four times more than the phrase *frozen shoulder*. The figures do not indicate the number of web sites containing those phrases; it tells you how many web pages contain the keyword. A huge number of those search results would highlight the fact that the key phrase appears on many pages on each web site. Many results will be duplicates or triplicates. Some results may not be very relevant; this is particularly so with Google at the moment because Google places too much emphasis on external links that may or may not be relevant.

Using the Google keyword tool and Microsoft Excel, Mr. Smith produced Table 16-1.

Table 16-1. *The Main Statistics Extracted from the Google Keyword Tool*

Keywords	Global Monthly Searches
shoulder pain	673,000
pain shoulder	673,000
frozen shoulder	201,000
shoulder injury	90,500
shoulder joint	74,000
shoulder treatment	49,500
shoulder injuries	49,500
shoulder joint pain	12,100
frozen shoulder treatment	9,900
shoulder problems	9,900
shoulder ache	9,900
painful shoulder	8,100
shoulder pain treatment	8,100

With this table, Mr. Smith would use some of the most popular key phrases between the `<head>…</head>` tags, and especially in the title and throughout his pages. He would also follow the rules in the next two sections.

Restriction on Excessive Repetition

Don't repeat a phrase (or a plural of it) in the title tags or the meta tags; for instance, don't do the following:

```
<title>shoulder pain, shoulder pain, shoulder pain, shoulder pain</title>
<meta name="description" content="shoulder pain, shoulder pain, shoulder pain, ↵
shoulder pain, shoulder pain">
        <meta name="keywords" content="shoulder pain, shoulder pain, shoulder pain, ↵
        shoulder pain, shoulder pain">
```

You can put the same word twice in different phrases in the title tag.

```
<title> shoulder pain treatment, pain shoulder, frozen joint, cure joint injuries</title>
```

You can put the same word up to four times in different phrases in the description meta tag.

```
<meta name="description" content="shoulder pain cure, pain shoulder, frozen shoulder ↵
treatment, shoulder injuries">
```

You can put the same word four times in different phrases in the keywords meta tag.

```
<meta name="keywords" content="shoulder pain treatment, pain shoulder treatment, ↵
frozen shoulder cure, cure shoulder injuries">
```

The number of key phrases is limited by the restriction on repetition. Unfortunately, if Mr. Smith consulted a thesaurus, he would find there was no other popular synonym for shoulder; therefore, Mr. Smith could only repeat the word shoulder twice in the title and four times in each meta tag. If he was selling or hiring bicycles, a number of synonyms could be used in the keywords meta tag without undue repetition, such as bicycle, bike, pushbike, and cycle.

Restrictions on the Number of Characters or Words

Limits on the number of characters or words were set because web designers were abusing the meta tags and the <body> section by stuffing them with a large number of keywords. Restrictions are as follows:

- Between the <title> </title> tags: A 60-character maximum (including spaces).
  In the <meta name="description" tag: Up to 250 characters (including spaces).

- In the <meta name="keywords" tag: A 12-words maximum.

You can put many keywords in the <body> section of a page and you can repeat them often. But don't overdo it. Most experts say the body keywords should not constitute more than 10 percent to 15 percent of the total words on a page.

Some designers think that the keywords in the head section are sufficient. This is not true. The keywords/phrases in the title are the most important, but the *keywords in the body section are more highly rated* than those in the meta tags. For maximum effect, keywords should be present in the title tag, the meta tags, and the body.

Keywords/phrases must appear between the <body>...</body> **tags.** The keywords/phrases in the body section are very important. They work in conjunction with the keywords/phrases between the <head></head> tags. The keywords/phrases must also appear between the <body> tags on every page of the web site.

The following items are keyword variations that should be considered and added to your list.

- *Singulars and plurals*: Lists and pages should include both forms of an important keyword.

- *Hyphens*: If hyphens are likely to be inserted by searchers, add the hyphenated keyword.

- *Misspellings*: If a particular keyword is commonly misspelled, add the misspelled keyword.

- *Images and links*: Add keywords in the "titles" for links. Add keywords in "alts" and "titles" for images. For instance, a diagram of a shoulder on Mr. Smith's web site might have the following HTML code:

```
<img alt="Painful shoulder" title="Painful shoulder" src="images/shoulder-pain.gif">
```

Well-Designed Internal Links

Mr. Smith would be wise to insert the most important keyword or phrase into the file names of his web pages. Mr. Smith begins with a four-page web site and he saves them with the following names:

1. index.html (this is his home page and so the page name cannot be a keyword)

2. shoulder-pain.html (this is his explanation of shoulder pain)

3. shoulder-pain-cure.html (this describes his rancid yak fat treatment)

4. shoulder-pain-form.html (this is his order form)

He could have used full stops instead of hyphens (use a maximum of three hyphens or full stops).

It follows that Mr. Smith's navigation menu would include the key phrase *shoulder pain* to link to the pages that have the key phrase in their page names:

```
<ul class="menu">
    <li><a href="shoulder-pain.html" title="Shoulder pain description"></li>
    <li><a href="shoulder-pain-cure.html" title="Shoulder pain treatment"></li>
    <li><a href="shoulder-pain-order.html" title="Shoulder pain order form"></li>
    <li><a href="index.html" title="Return to home page"></li>
</ul>
```

The menu would look something like the following:

- Shoulder pain description

- Shoulder pain cure

- Shoulder pain order form

- Shoulder pain home page

Create a sitemap because this is a powerful source of internal links. A sitemap is just a page with links to your most important pages or to all your pages. You will find instructions for creating a sitemap in the section "Sitemaps Help SEs Index a Web Site" later in this chapter.

▨ **Tip** Make sure that all pages have a link back to the home page.

External Links to Your Site

An external link on a web site that is relevant to your product has much greater value than a link from a web site with no related content. The most tactful method is to first add an advertisement to your web site and a link to the other web site. Contact the other web site owner and comment favorably on her web site. Then ask the owner if she would reciprocate by adding your link to her site.

Ask the cooperating web owner if she would add a small advertisement next to the link, like this:

```
<p><a href="http://www.best-buzzers.com">In my opinion the best quiz buzzers are found ↵
at http://www.best-buzzers.com</a></p>
```

External links must include a keyword; therefore, you must dictate what the link contains. In the previous example, the keyword was quiz buzzers. Send your preferred link and text in an email so that the cooperating owner can cut and paste it.

Ask the cooperating web site owner if she would add the link to more than one page. Try pushing your luck by asking her to put your links on relevant pages containing few other links; this increases the value of your links.

If the site content relates really well, consider purchasing a small ad on her web site, ideally with a related text link. The trading of links can become a very tiresome process, and it's often easier to manage if you purchase links on sites that relate well to your keywords.

Register with search directories. SEs pick up links from the DMOZ Open Directory Project. Submit your web site address to `http://www.dmoz.org/help/submit.html`

It is very important to select the correct category when listing in DMOZ; ensure that you are submitting at the appropriate level. DMOZ is serviced by volunteers and it can take a long time to get approved.

Contact your suppliers. Ask them to place an advertisement on their web sites; perhaps something like the following:

```
<p><a href="http://www.best-buzzers.com">Quiz buzzers made by BestBuzzers use our ↵
ElectraCo super solenoids></a></p>
```

Many companies have client lists. If you are one of the company's customers, ask to have your web address put on their client list. Another idea is to look for industry-specific web sites and directories, and industry or region-specific search engines.

Things You Should Never Do

The following list of "things you should never do" was taken from the advice pages of the three major search engines.

- Do not put links to other web sites on your home page; this would be detrimental to your own ranking.

- Do not use frames; they confuse and block web crawlers.

- Do not use JavaScript menus and JavaScript links; they prevent web crawlers from accessing your linked internal pages.

- Do not use tricks such as invisible writing; for example, white keywords on a white background. Web crawlers detect them and even detect and penalize closely related colors such as a very pale gray text on a white background.

- Do not use images for keywords/key phrases; these are invisible to SEs.

- Do not use *cookie cutters*; that is, pages that are identical or practically identical that have been added to boost the number of linked pages. SEs will not accept these and may penalize the web site.

Google says: "Don't create multiple copies of a page under different URLs. Many web sites offer text-only or printer-friendly versions of pages that contain the same content as the corresponding graphic-rich pages. To ensure that your preferred page is included in our search results, you will need to block duplicates from our spiders using a robots.txt file. For information about using a robots.txt file, please visit our information on blocking Googlebot."

http://support.google.com/webmasters/bin/answer.py?hl=en&answer=35291

▪ **Note** The page printer described in Chapter 15 of this book does not upset the search engines. Using a CSS page printer avoids this problem because there is no duplicate page.

- Do not use link farms, that is, automated systems that create hundreds of links on their web sites pointing to your pages. SEs refuse to acknowledge these links.

  Yahoo! states: *"The use of 'link farms' violates the Yahoo! Site Guidelines and will not improve your page ranking."*

  Google states: *"Don't participate in link schemes designed to increase your site's ranking or page rank. In particular, avoid links to web spammers or 'bad neighborhoods' on the web, as your own ranking may be affected adversely by those links."*

However, some SEO gurus say that certain types of link farming can work well if mixed with a solid campaign, but you need to know what you are doing to avoid upsetting the search engines.

In the next section we will examine a web page that has no search engine optimization. We can learn a lot from an example of bad practice because it highlights the common mistakes that web site designers should avoid.

A Web Site Containing No Search Engine Optimization

Figure 16-1 shows a web page that has absolutely no search engine optimization. My thanks go to Tina Farrington for allowing me to use the teddy bear photo from the web site I designed for her http://www.haynesofcolyton.co.uk

Figure 16-1. A web page that appears to contain the key phrase "teddy bears"

The obvious key phrase for this web site is *teddy bears* or *teddy bear*. At first glance, you might think that the key phrase appears five times on this page. However, the key phrases are all images, so the phrases cannot be detected by web crawlers. The designer should have used background images for the colored panels and then overlaid real text on the panels so that the SE could read the text.

Listing 16-1 illustrates the markup of a web page with no search engine optimization. The SEO faults are shown in bold type.

Listing 16-1. Demonstrating a Web Page with no Search Engine Optimization (welcome.html)

```
<!doctype html>
<html lang=en>
<head>
<title>Welcome to our web site</title>
<meta charset=utf-8>
<meta name="description" content="">
<meta name="keywords" content=" ">
        <script type="text/javascript" src="coolmenu.js"></script>
        <script type="text/javascript" src="menu_items2.js"></script>
        <link rel="stylesheet" type="text/css" href="menu_styles.css"/>
        <style type="text/css">
        #container { margin:0 auto 0 auto; width:790px;
        }
        </style>
</head>
<body>
        <div id="container">
        <div>
        <img src="images/banner.jpg" width="786px" height="224px">
```

```
        </div>
        <div>
                <script type="text/javascript">
                var m1 = new COOLjsMenu("menu1", MENU_ITEMS)
                </script>
                </div>
        <p> </p>
        <div>
        <img alt="black" height="198" src="images/black-panel.jpg" width="227">
                <img alt="yellow" height="198" src="images/yellow-panel.jpg" width="310">
                <img alt="red" height="198" src="images/red-panel.jpg" width="237">
                </div>
        </div>
</body>
</html>
```

Hide the next section and see if you can understand the SEO mistakes in the listing. If you understood all five examples of bad practice—congratulations, you have clearly absorbed the lessons of the previous section.

The SEO Faults in Listing 16-1

The next section explains the search engine optimization mistakes made in Listing 16-1.

- The title "Welcome to our web site" is not only silly, it is utterly useless. It does not contain the key phrase. The title must appropriately describe the content of the page for the benefit of the user, as well as for search engine optimization.

- The key phrase *teddy bears* does not appear anywhere in the markup, nor do the words *teddy* or *bears*.

- The meta contents did not contain the key phrase. The meta "description" tag should have described the page and the product being promoted.

- There was a chunk of JavaScript for a drop-down menu. Search engines do not read JavaScript. Nine additional pages are revealed by each button on the drop-down menu. This means that in addition to the home page, there are 20 more pages that a search engine is unable to read and index. Those pages could be full of keywords and key phrases that the SEs will never see. The JavaScript drop-down navigation menu is shown in Figure 16-2. It shows the JavaScript drop-down menu that will prevent the search engines from probing past the home page.

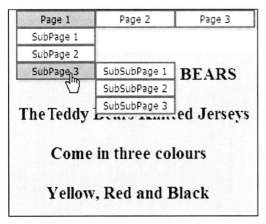

Figure 16-2. The JavaScript drop-down menu

- The header image is called banner.jpg and no alts or titles were used. Three opportunities for inserting keywords were missed. It could have read:

```
<img src="images/teddybears.jpg" alt="Colyton teddybears" title="Colyton teddybears" ↵
width="786px" height="224px">
```

The same fault can be seen in each of the three panels; for example, *black-panel.jpg* could have been:

```
<img alt="Price of teddy bears" title="price of teddy bears" ↵
src="images/teddy-bear-prices.jpg" width="227"height="198">
```

The conclusion: typing *teddy bears, teddy,* or *bears* into the search field would never find this web site.

■ **Note** If the web designer had submitted the page to W3C validation, many of the faults would have been highlighted and they could have been corrected. Always validate pages if you want the search engines to find them and index them.

It is usual to submit new web sites to the search engines. The URLs for doing this are listed in the next tip. Only submit once, otherwise the SEs will assume you are spamming. Some SEO experts prefer not to submit, but they wait for the SEs to find the web site. It is difficult to determine which is the best approach.

■ **Tip** Submit web site URLs to the three main search engines at the following addresses:

Bing: https://ssl.bing.com/webmaster/SubmitSitePage.aspx

Yahoo: http://www.search.yahoo.com/info/submit.html

Google: http://www.google.co.uk/addurl/ and http://www.google.com/submit_content.html

I do not recommend using mass submission organizations. In my experience, some of these sell the site's email address to spammers; don't risk it, do the job yourself.

Sitemaps Help SEs Index a Web Site

A sitemap can be simply a web page with a list of links to each page on the web site. The links on a simple sitemap for a small web site might look like Figure 16-3.

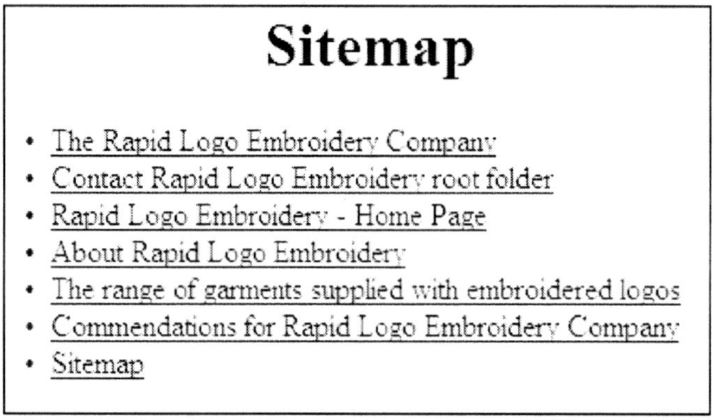

Sitemap

- The Rapid Logo Embroidery Company
- Contact Rapid Logo Embroidery root folder
- Rapid Logo Embroidery - Home Page
- About Rapid Logo Embroidery
- The range of garments supplied with embroidered logos
- Commendations for Rapid Logo Embroidery Company
- Sitemap

Figure 16-3. *A simple, but effective sitemap*

As you can see in Figure 16-3, a sitemap can be a page of text. The text consists of live links to the pages on the site. The URL of the folder containing the web site must be first in the list. Figure 16-3 was produced by Listing 16-3. The listing is not available for downloading.

Listing 16-3. *Creating a Simple Sitemap*

```
<!doctype html>
<html lang=en>
<head>
<title>Sitemap for Rapid Embroidery logos</title>
<meta charset=utf-8>
        meta details go here
        <style type="text/css">
        #container {margin:auto; width:420px; text-align:left;}
        h1 { text-align:center;
        }
        </style>
</head>
<body>
<div id="container">
   <h1>Sitemap</h1>
   <ul>
<li><a href="http://www.rapidembroidery.co.uk/">The Rapid Logo Embroidery Company ↵
root folder</a></li>
<li><a href="http://www.rapidembroidery.co.uk/logo-embroidery-contact.html">Contact ↵
Rapid Logo Embroidery</a></li>
<li><a href="http://www.rapidembroidery.co.uk/index.html">Rapid Logo Embroidery - ↵
Home Page</a></li>
<li><a href="http://www.rapidembroidery.co.uk/logo-embroidery-about.html">About Rapid ↵
Logo Embroidery</a></li>
```

```
<li><a href="http://www.rapidembroidery.co.uk/logo-embroidery-garments.html">The ↵
range of garments supplied with embroidered logos</a></li>
<li><a href="http://www.rapidembroidery.co.uk/logo-embroidery-commend.html">↵
Commendations for Rapid Logo Embroidery Company</a></li>
<li><a href="http://www.rapidembroidery.co.uk/sitemap.html">Sitemap</a></li>
</ul>
</div>
</body>
</html>
```

It is important to put a link to the sitemap on all the pages. Make the link inconspicuous because most users won't be interested in clicking that particular link. The sitemap link is best located in the web page's footer. When visitors see the sitemap link, they may interpret it incorrectly. If your web site concerns a town, a building site, or a camping site, visitors will probably assume it is a geographic map. To avoid this mistake, call the visible link something like *Web Site Directory*, but for the sake of the SEs, ensure that the actual page is called `sitemap.html`. The link listing on the home page would look something like the following:

```
<footer>
<a href="http://www.rapidembroidery.co.uk/sitemap.html">Web site Directory</a>
</footer>
```

Generated Sitemaps

If a web site has many pages, creating a page of text links would be very tedious, indeed. However, the three main search engines accept the results of free, online generators that will, in the twinkling of an eye, create a sitemap for a large web site. The preferred generator is `http://www.sitemaps.org`, but later in this section I suggest a slightly more-friendly generator called `auditmypc.com`.

Search engines will accept a plain-text sitemap like the one in Listing 16-3; however, search engines prefer to read sitemaps in XML format. The online generators produce an XML sitemap that is universal, so that it is acceptable to all search engines. Listing 16-4 is an example of a generated sitemap (this listing is not available for downloading).

Listing 16-4. Example of a Sitemap Created in XML Format Using a Generator

```
<?xml version="1.0" encoding="UTF-8" ?>
- <urlset xmlns="http://www.sitemaps.org/schemas/sitemap/0.9"
xmlns:xsi="http://www.w3.org/2001/XMLSchema-instance"
xsi:schemaLocation="http://www.sitemaps.org/schemas/sitemap/0.9
http://www.sitemaps.org/schemas/sitemap/0.9/sitemap.xsd">
- <!-- created with Free Online Sitemap Generator www.xml-sitemaps.com -->
- <url>
  <loc>http://www.rapidembroidery.co.uk/</loc>
  </url>
- <url>
  <loc>http://www.rapidembroidery.co.uk/logo-embroidery-about.html</loc>
  </url>
- <url>
  <loc>http://www.rapidembroidery.co.uk/logo-embroidery-garments.html</loc>
  </url>
- <url>
  <loc>http://www.rapidembroidery.co.uk/logo-embroidery-contact.html</loc>
  </url>
```

```
- <url>
  <loc>http://www.rapidembroidery.co.uk/logo-embroidery-commend.html</loc>
  </url>
- <url>
  <loc>http://www.rapidembroidery.co.uk/index.html</loc>
  </url>
  </urlset>
```

The generator allows you to add optional information (`lastmod`, `changefreq`, `priority`) like the next snippet, but I tend to stay with the default settings:

```
<url>
        <loc>http://www.rapidembroidery.co.uk/index.html/</loc>
        <lastmod>2011-01-01</lastmod>
        <changefreq>monthly</changefreq>
        <priority>0.8</priority>
</url>
```

The next example of a sitemap generator is an alternative to `www.sitemaps.org`.

Using Audit My PC

Make sure you are not running the web site that needs the sitemap. Go to `http://www.auditmypc.com`

This third-party generator is free (and user-friendly compared with trying to locate and use the search engines' tools). The generated sitemap is suitable for Bing, Yahoo!, and Google.

1. On the home page, click the Sitemap Generator on the top menu bar. You will see a video; don't run it but click Skip Video just above the video.

2. Click Run on the security pop-up. A window called XML sitemap tool will appear. Expand the window and type the URL for your web site.

3. Click the start-up button (a green, right arrow at the bottom left).

4. Click Export ➤ Sitemap XML.

5. Save the generated sitemap in the root folder of your web site on your hard drive. Rename it `sitemap.xml`. Then using your FTP client, upload it to the web site server's root directory.

Submitting the Sitemap to the Search Engines

Once you have generated the sitemap and uploaded it to your web site's server, you need to tell the search engines where to find it. The instructions for submitting it to Google and Bing follow:

Google

1. Log into the Google Sitemaps account at `http://google.com/webmasters/tools/` (create an account if necessary).

2. Click Add a Sitemap.

3. Enter the URL for your sitemap file; for example, `http://www.mywebsite.co.uk/sitemap.xml`.

Bing

1. Go to `http://www.bing.com/toolbox/webmaster`.

2. Sign in to Bing Webmaster Tools (use Windows Live ID login details).

3. On the Home tab, click the Add Site button and submit its URL. Verify ownership by choosing Option 1. Download an XML file named `BingSiteAuth.xml`.

4. Save it to the root folder of your web site on your hard drive.

5. Then with your FTP client, upload it to the root folder of the web site on the host/server.

6. In your browser address field, enter the URL for the XML file. Click the Verify button.

7. When it is verified, you can submit the sitemap.

8. Go to `http://www.bing.com/toolbox/webmaster/`and sign up.

9. On the Home tab page, click the web site you just verified. Click the Crawl tab ➤ Sitemaps ➤ Add Feed.

10. Enter the full URL for the sitemap like this: `http://www.yourwebsite/sitemap.xml`

11. Click Submit.

Yahoo!

This SE is now linked with Bing; therefore, a separate submission is no longer necessary. Go to Yahoo! Site Explorer for more information.

▒ **Note** In the case of *generated* sitemaps, the home page does not have a link to the sitemap. The XML file is placed in the root directory of the web site and the search engine knows where it is because you have to include this information during the process of generating the XML file.

Obtaining and submitting sitemaps can be tricky because the goalposts keep shifting. You think you have understood the process, but next time something has changed or become hidden in a maze of links and sub-links. Some interfaces have washed out colors and low-contrast colors so that tabs are not clearly visible. The general scheme seems to be: first, add a web site URL to the SE, and then verify that you are the owner of the web site. When this is verified, you can then submit the sitemap. The term *owner of the site* is not literal; it means you are the person authorized by the owner to maintain the site.

Tip See http://www.sitemaps.org/protocol.html for more information about sitemaps. This web site emphasizes the value of sitemaps and explains the sitemap protocol supported and recommend by Google, Yahoo!, and Bing.

Let People Know That Your Web Site Exists

When your web site appears on a search engine's pages, it is a form of free advertising. Your aim is to sell goods and services, to provide information, or to gain support for a cause. To maximize the number of visitors to your site, supplement the search engine results by other forms of advertising.

Note Remember that your web site's purpose is to persuade people to hire or buy your product, or to use your services; therefore, use *every* available method to send people to your web site in order to achieve this goal.

A commercial site may be ranked low, yet it gets many more visits than highly-ranked competitors. This is probably because the low-ranked site is advertised widely in trade journals, trade directories, and brochures. Don't neglect advertising your site. Regular, small advertisements in the right journals and brochures get good results.

Satisfied customers who are not necessarily computer-literate can tell others about your product. These people may then look for your product on a search engine.

On every brochure, flyer, wrapper, and all other pieces of printed matter, make sure your web site address is prominently displayed. Use a QR code on all your literature as well. This advertising medium is described in the next section.

Use a Quick Response (QR) Code

You will by now be familiar with the new type of barcode called QR code or matrix code. Modern smartphones can scan QR codes. This causes the smartphone to access a web site without the chore of tapping in the URL. A free app called a QR reader must be downloaded to the mobile device to enable it to read QR codes.

You can generate a free QR code by going to http://createqrcode.appspot.com. This Google-hosted App was devised by Jason Delport.

The form shown in Figure 16-4 will appear. You will see that I have filled in my web site URL, http://www.colycomputerhelp.co.uk You can select different image sizes, but I have chosen the default 300×300 pixels. Click Create QR Code.

Caution Do not enter any other text, or mobiles devices will think it is a text message and your web site will not load. However, if you don't want the URL to load, a QR code can also contain anything from an email address to a long piece of text.

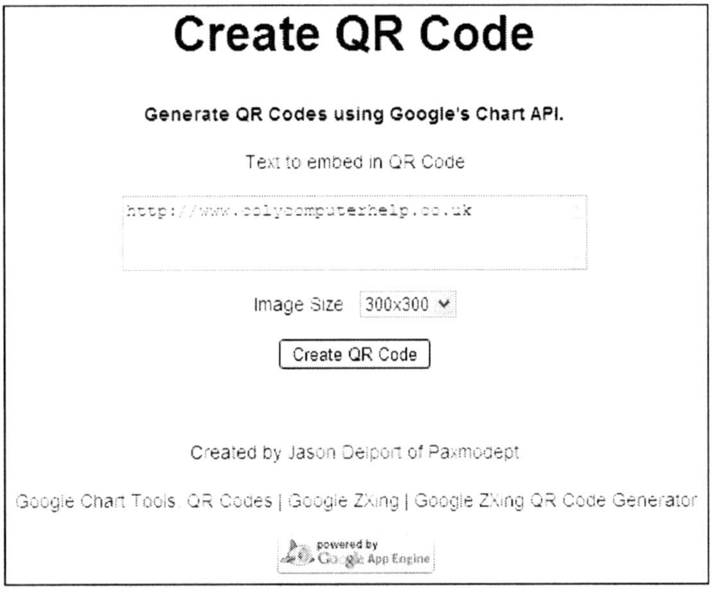

Create QR Code

Generate QR Codes using Google's Chart API.

Text to embed in QR Code

http://www.colycomputerhelp.co.uk

Image Size 300x300 ▾

Create QR Code

Created by Jason Delport of Paxmodept

Google Chart Tools QR Codes | Google ZXing | Google ZXing QR Code Generator

powered by
Google App Engine

Figure 16-4. The dialog box for entering your web site URL

The code image will appear as shown in Figure 16-5. Right-click it and save it, or copy and paste it into a document.

Figure 16-5. The QR code generated for http://www.colycomputerhelp.co.uk

You can also embed its code into a web page, although I am not sure if this is useful. To grab the code for embedding, select all of the text below the QR image starting with `http://chart…`, and paste it into the web page.

▨ **Note** See the Wikipedia QR article for an excellent explanation of the components of a QR code.

Summary

To ensure that people can find your web site, it must be advertised. This chapter dealt with the two main methods of advertising: search engines and printed matter. A third method is word of mouth.

The chapter began with an overview of search engines and a warning about the scams that afflict web site owners. You learned about page rank and how to choose keywords and phrases. There was also section describing what you must *never* do.

Advice was given on well-designed internal and external links. The example of a page that was badly designed for search engine optimization gave practical advice on what not to do. A section on sitemaps demonstrated how to produce and upload sitemaps to the search engines so that they can more easily index your web site.

This chapter suggested ways of advertising your web site, including QR codes so that smartphone users can instantly access your web site from printed documents.

In the next chapter, you will learn about three useful additions to a web site. The first section describes how to display a spam-proof email address on a page. The second section shows you how to add a visitor counter to the key pages. The final section explains methods of redirecting users to other pages or web sites.

CHAPTER 17

Printing, Counting, and Redirecting

As the title suggests, this chapter provides practical methods for implementing the following four utilities:

- Page printing

- A do-it-yourself (DIY) visitor counter

- A Google Analytics visitor counter

- Redirecting

I'll start by examining how the pitfalls of printing from the browser toolbar can be avoided and how a user can save ink and paper. Then you'll see how to create a visitor counter. Finally, I'll describe ways of redirecting to another page, or to another location on the same page, or to another web site.

Page Printing

A page can be printed from a web site page without a special style sheet by using either the printer button on the browser toolbar, or a page printer button inserted near the top of the page.

Unfortunately, both methods will print unwanted items such as background color, banner headings, menu buttons, footers, and advertisements. These items consume paper and ink unnecessarily. Also, the printer has to be set to landscape format to prevent cutting off the right side of the page. Features such as menu buttons and Go to Top arrows are quite useless on a printed document. In addition, a lengthy document may page-break at inconvenient points. The next section will demonstrate how these problems can be avoided by looking into the following topics:

- Creating a Print This Page button

- Preventing unwanted items from printing

- Simplifying the printout to save ink and paper

- Page breaks

- Printing URLs (web addresses)

- Printing check boxes

- Search engines and printable pages

- Testing CSS printable pages

Create a "Print This Page" Button

A page can be printed using the browser toolbar button, but most users appreciate a prominent Print This Page button, especially beginners. A page printer button can be inserted near the top of the page, as shown in Figure 17-1.

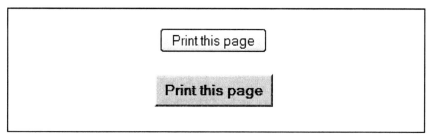

Figure 17-1. *Two types of page printer button*

For a standard Windows button (like the upper button in Figure 17-1), place this markup on the page where you want the button to appear. Only part of Listing 17-1 is given next, but the full listing is available to download from the book's page at http://www.apress.com

Listing 17-1. Partial Listing for Two Types of Page Print Button (button-types.html)

```
<div id="button">
        <input type="button" value="Print this page" onclick="window.print()"
        title="Print this page">
        </div>
```

The value (shown bold in the markup) provides the text on the button.
The CSS for the Windows style button is:

```
#button { text-align:center; }
```

For the customized lower button in Figure 17-1, use the following markup:

```
<div id=button>
<input id="printbtn" type="button" value="Print this page"
onclick="window.print()" title="Print this page">
</div>
```

The CSS for the customized button is

```
#button { text-align:center;
}
#printbtn { margin-bottom:10px; padding:5px; font-weight:bold;
background:aqua; color:black;
}
```

Prevent Unwanted Items from Printing

To strip out unwanted items when printing a page, an additional "print" style sheet must be created. This will print a page in a more convenient portrait format, in black and white, and with all the unwanted items removed.

- The main style sheet; for example, `mainstyle.css`, will dictate how the page will appear on the screen.

- The print style sheet; for example, `print.css`, will dictate how the page will print.

The print style sheet comes into play only when the Print This Page button (or the browser's Print button) is clicked.

In the `<head>…</head>` section of the HTML page, place the print style sheet link *after* the screen style sheet link, as follows:

```
<link rel="stylesheet" href="mainstyle.css" type="text/css" media="screen">
<link rel="stylesheet" href="print.css" type="text/css" media="print">
```

Simplifying the Printout to Save Ink and Paper

Figures 17-2, 17-3, and 17-4 show that a printout can have all the unnecessary items removed.

Figure 17-2. *The screen display (top half of page only)*

Figure 17-3. *First printed page*

Figure 17-4. *Second printed page*

In Figures 17-2, 17-3, and 17-4, I chose to omit the following items from the printout:

- The background color (to save colored ink).

- The header (it contains no useful information). This saves paper and ink.

- The Print This Page button, because it will not work on a printout.

- The menu buttons because they will not work on a printout.

- Headings (h1 to h6) on the screen display have large line spacing.
  I chose to reduce the text size and line height in the printout to economize on the user's paper.

- The Go to Top of Page "Up" arrow because it will not work on a printout.

- The footer because it is a set of links that will not work on a printout.

I also decided to split the columns. The screen page in this project has two columns; each column contains a different topic. Therefore, I set the printout so that it produces a different page for each column/topic. This prevents the page breaking in an inappropriate place. I achieved this by placing a page break at the top of column two.

I retained the instructional images in the printout because they would be useful to the user.

Listings 17-2a, 17-2b, and 17-2c provide the content for a two-column page and the two style sheets. The menu in this case is a horizontal menu bar with rollover buttons. It is included within the header `<div>`. No semantic tags are used so that the point of the exercise can be clearly understood without the clutter of a JavaScript hack for IE. In Listing 17-2a, most of the textual content has been omitted in order to save space and to clearly show the items targeted by the print CSS. The full page with its two style sheets can be downloaded from the Apress companion web site. The screen and print styles are shown in bold type. The `<div>`s to be ignored by the printer are also shown in bold type.

■ **Note** The printed page has a minor drawback: a multicolumn page prints each column so that it spans the whole width of the page, as seen in Figures 17-3 and 17-4.

Listing 17-2a. A Two-Column Page to Demonstrate Page Printing (twocol-printer.html)

```
<!doctype html>
<html lang=en>
<head>
<title>Two column page for printer</title>
<meta charset=utf-8>
        meta details go here
<link rel="stylesheet" type="text/css" href="twocol.css" media="screen">
<link rel="stylesheet" type="text/css" href="twocol-print.css" media="print">
</head>
<body>
<a id="top"></a>
<div id="container">
<div id="hdr"><!--the CSS removes the header from the print-out-->
<h1>Coly Computer Help</h1></div>
<ul id="hmenu"><!--the CSS removes the menu from the print-out-->
<li class="hbtnew">
<a title="Computer Jargon explained" href="glossary.php">Jargon</a></li>
        The rest of the code for the horizontal menu bar goes here
</ul>
<br>
<div id="button"><!--the CSS removes the print button from the print-out-->
<input type="button" value="Print this page" onclick="window.print()" title="Print this page">
</div><br><!--End of page printer button-->
<h3>INSTALLING &amp; CONFIGURING A FREE ANTI-VIRUS PROGRAM</h3>
<div id="leftcol">
<h3>How good is a free Anti Virus program?</h3>
<img title="XXX free" src="images/xxx-crop.jpg" alt="XXX free" width="158" height="81">
        The content of the first column goes
</div></div>
<!--LEFT COLUMN BEGINS ON A SEPARATE PAGE-->
```

```
<div id="rightcol" style="page-break-before:always;">
 <h3>Configuring a free anti-virus program</h3>
        The content of the second column goes here
</div>
</div>
<div id="ftr"><!--the CSS removes the footer from the print-out-->
<b>THIS IS THE FOOTER THAT YOU DO NOT WANT TO PRINT</b>
</div></div>
</body>
</html>
```

Some versions of Mozilla Firefox will sometimes insert a blank page due to an in-built quirk. To avoid any browser quirks, start the style sheet with a re-set, as shown in Listing 17-2b.

Listing 17-2b. The CSS Style Sheet for the Printer (twocol-print.css)

```
/*PRINT.CSS: re-set style for printing only*/
/*re-set basic styles to avoid browser compatibility quirks*/
html, h1, h2, h3, h4, h5, p { padding:0; margin:0; font-size:100%; font-weight:normal;
}
/*TO SAVE INK, set the text to black with white background*/
body { width:100%; padding:0; margin:0; float:none; color:black; background-color:white;
}
/*TO SAVE PAPER, remove the large line space beneath a heading. Set headings to 14 point*/
h1, h2, h3, h4, h5, h6 { margin-top:0; margin-bottom:0; font-weight:bold; ↵
font-size:14pt; !important
}
/*SELECT UNWANTED PRINT-OUT ITEMS, i.e., header, menu, print-button, footer and uparrow*/
#hdr, #hmenu, #button, #ftr, .uparrow { display:none;
}
/*REVEAL OUTGOING URL links on printed page. See item on Printing URLs*/
a[href^="http://"]:after {content: "(" attr(href)")";
}
/*SET PAGE BREAK class so that the printed pages do not break in undesirable places*/
.break-before { page-break-before: always;
}
```

▓ **Note** The print.css style sheet does not include any commands already covered by the main (screen) style sheet. When the page is printed, the print style sheet overrides some of the main style sheet commands.

More on Page Breaks

The previous style sheet, twocol-print.css/Listing 17-2b, contained a command to cause the page to break at the top of column two. The page can also break at the end of column one with the following CSS class:

```
.break-after { page-break-after:always;
}
```

To complete the project, the main-style listing, twocol.css, is shown in Listing 17-2c.

Listing 17-2c. Creating the Main Style for the Screen Version of the Page (twocol.css)

```css
body { background-color:#D7FFEB; font-family: "Times New Roman"; font-size: medium; ↵
color: #000000;
}
#container {text-align:center; margin: auto; width:960px;
}
img { border:0;
}
#leftcol { float: left; width: 48%; padding:2px; text-align:left;
}
#leftcol img { float:left; margin-right:5px;
}
#rightcol { float: right; width: 48%; padding:2px; text-align:left;
}
#ftr { clear: both;}/* ensure footer stays at the bottom */
#hdr { background-position:35% 20%; background-image:url('images/compbkgcrop.jpg'); ↵
background-repeat:no-repeat; width:960px; height:170px;
}
#button {margin:auto;
}
h1 { position:absolute; top:90px; left:300px; width:450px; font-family:"Times New Roman"; ↵
font-size: 300%; color: #0080a0; font-weight:bold; margin-bottom:5px;
}
.uparrow { text-align:center;
}
#hmenu { width:790px; text-align:center; margin:5px 0 10px 100px;
}
li.hbtnew {display:block; margin:auto; float:left; text-align:center; padding:3px; ↵
list-style-type:none; list-style-position:inherit;
}
li.hbtnew a {display:block; text-decoration:none; color:white; background-color:#0080a0; ↵
font-weight:bold; padding:4px;
}
li.hbtnew a { background: #0080a0;  border: 4px outset #AABAFF;
}
li.hbtnew a:hover { background: #0060a0; color:yellow;  border: 4px outset #8ABAFF;
}
li.hbtnew a:active { background:#ABCBFF; border: 4px inset #ABCBFF;
}
h3, h4, h5, h6 { margin-top:0; margin-bottom:0;
}
span.tiny {font-size: x-small;
}
.cntr { text-align:center; margin:auto;
}
.lft {text-align:left;
}
.right {text-align:right;
}
```

Printing URLs (Web Addresses)

If the web page has internal links to other pages or anchors on the same page, there is no point in printing them because they do nothing on a printed page. The next bit of CSS markup will print the URL of a web site that will be useful to the user. The printed URL will omit the underline because this can sometimes obscure an underscore in the URL. The code works in all browsers.

```
/*reveal links on printed page*/
a[href^="http://"]:after {content: "("attr(href)")"; }
```

Note that the four brackets in the middle (between the curly brackets) are ordinary curved brackets. Assuming that the following lines appear in the HTML...

```
<p>
        Click for <a title="Click for free computer help"
        href="http://www.colycomputerhelp.co.uk">Free computer help </a>
</p>
```

...the screen appearance of the URL would be as follows:

Click for <u>Free computer help</u>

The corresponding printout would be:

Click for Free computer help (http://www.colycomputerhelp.co.uk).

Printing Check Boxes

On printable pages such as an order form, square check boxes (also known as tick boxes) using Wingdings or Webdings do not work in Mozilla Firefox. However, practically every computer has the Lucida Sans Unicode symbols. The Lucida Sans Unicode check box □ displays correctly in all popular browsers. You will need to use a larger font for the box than for the text.

■ *Figure 17-5. This is how the box displays and prints in all popular browsers.*

Listing 17-5 provides a tick box that prints correctly and also displays correctly in all browsers.

Listing 17-5. A Tick Box Suitable for Printing in all Browsers (tickbox-printer.html)

```
<!doctype html>
<html lang=en>
<head>
<title>This is box styled with Unicode Lucida font</title>
<meta charset=utf-8>
<style type="text/css">
.stylebox { font:xx-large bold; font-family:"Lucida Sans Unicode"; margin-left:50px;}
</style>
</head>
<body>
<p>The tick box shown below is styled with Unicode Lucida and it is
formatted as xx-large and bold </p>
<p class="stylebox">&#9633;</p>
```

```
</body>
</html>
```

Search Engines and Printable Pages

Some web designers create a printer-friendly page that is a duplicate of the main textual content. Search engines frown on the use of duplicate pages. The following is what Google says about using duplicate pages instead of CSS printable versions of a page: "Don't create multiple copies of a page under different URLs. Many sites offer text-only or printer-friendly versions of pages that contain the same content as the corresponding graphic-rich pages. To ensure that your preferred page is included in our search results, you'll need to block duplicates from our spiders using a robots.txt file. For information about using a robots.txt file, please visit our information on blocking Googlebot."

For information on robots_text, visit:

http://code.google.com/web/controlcrawlindex/docs/robots_txt.html.

▓ **Note** The page printer described in this chapter does not upset search engines. Using a CSS page printer as shown in this chapter avoids this problem.

Test CSS Printable Pages

There is no need to waste paper and ink, even though the testing requires a reasonable amount of trial and error. Load the page into a browser and click File ➤ Print Preview to see what the printable page will look like. If the printable page includes a page break, click the right-arrow at the bottom of the print preview screen to see subsequent pages.

Press the Esc key to switch out of the Print Preview mode.

A DIY Visitor Counter

Many clients ask for a visitor counter. Having paid for the web site and its hosting, they will be anxious to know if people are visiting it. You have to choose between a third-party counter, relying on the host's counter, or putting your own DIY counter on the site.

A third-party counter means adding some code to a page. That code then links to a URL that manages the counting for you. I have found that third-party counters are sometimes subject to denial of service attacks (DOS) that put the counter out of action for a while. A site owner once told me that the site's count no longer made sense. As a result, I use the DIY counter because it is under the total control of the webmaster and not reliant on vulnerable hosts.

Most hosts provide visitor statistics, but owners are reluctant to delve into their web site's control panel. This means that the DIY counter is probably the best option. In the following sections, I will show you how to create one. It does involve the simple application of a small piece of PHP script, but this is fully explained. The main topics will be presented as follows:

- Why bother with a counter?

- Interpreting the visitor counts

- How a counter works

    - Step 1: Create a free PHP visitor counter

- Step 2: Create the "count" files

- Step 3: Use a text editor to create three, tiny, identical text files

- Step 4: Make the menus match the three, main PHP pages

- Step 5: Upload the counter to the host

- Step 6: Ensure that browsers access the new *.php pages instead of the old *.html pages

- Step 7: Test the counter

Why Bother With A Counter?

Some web designers discourage their clients from having a visitor counter. They say that counters are old-fashioned, amateurish, and pointless. These excuses usually disguise a designer's inability to optimize for search engines. They don't want their inability exposed by a low visitor count.

A visitor counter that is limited to the home page may not provide enough information for the site owner. The home page may have many hits, but if the home page is garish, messy, or obscure, users will not explore the rest of the site. The counter is only telling the site owner how many people have visited the home page, which is not very useful. The owner needs to know whether visitors were tempted to explore the other pages. Visitor counters should, therefore, be placed on other key pages, that is, the pages the owner hopes will be visited. This will tell the owner whether the home page has persuaded users to delve deeper.

Interpreting the Visitor Counts

What can we learn by looking at the visitor counts and how many pages should have counters?

Let's say the visitor counter on the home page reads 10,000. All 10,000 visitors could have taken one look at your home page and then skipped to another web site. Or they may have looked at several pages. The owner will never know whether visitors were tempted to delve deeper into the web site.

Clearly having a counter only on the home page will not be very informative. We could learn much more if counters were also placed on three other key pages. Let's call the key pages a Walker's page, a Camper's page, and an About Us page. How might we interpret the following visitor counts?

- Home page: 10,000 visitors

- Walker's page: 5,800 visitors

- Camper's page: 8,700 visitors

- About Us page: 2,300 visitors

This information shows that

- The home page is not turning away visitors because the other pages had visitors.

- The visitors are more interested in camping gear than walking equipment.

- The sum of the hits on the other pages is greater than the number of home page hits; therefore, the home page is tempting visitors to look at more than one other page.

How a Counter Works

This counter is not only free, but it is thoroughly reliable. The counter requires some PHP code, but you need no knowledge of PHP to implement it. Just insert your own file names and count numbers into the simple listing that are included in this section. The count can start at any number of the owner's choosing; in this example I chose 1000. The method is very simple and consists of a snippet of PHP code inserted into a page. When a user accesses the web page, this code triggers a small PHP file that adds 1 to the number stored in a text file. The new number (now 1001) is passed back to the web page and displayed. The process is illustrated in Figure 17-6.

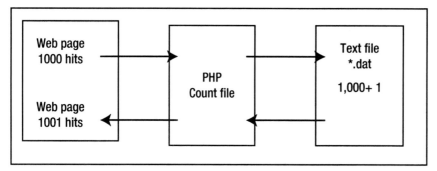

Figure 17-6. *How the visitor number is increased by one when a page is visited*

A dummy home page? Some designers create a duplicate home page named something like index-dummy.html so that all pages link to the dummy home page rather than to the real home page. This method means that, if after exploring the other pages on a web site, the visitors click back to the home page, they are sent to the dummy home page. The counter on the genuine home page does not record another unique visitor. Although this gives a more accurate visitor count, it does mean that the web site contravenes one of the search engine rules: "do not create duplicate pages." So, this technique is not recommended.

Step 1: Create a Free PHP Visitor Counter

The visitor counter featured in this chapter was devised by James Crooke of CJ Website Designs. His web site is http://www.cj-design.com.

The counter is free to use on condition that you credit him next to the visitor count. The code for doing this is listed in Step 2 of the three count*.php files.

This worked example assumes that the key pages are index.html, walk.html, and camp.html. (In this example, we will assume the owner does not want a counter on the About Us page).

■ **Note** Only the three pages listed will have a DOCTYPE. The supporting files (*.dat and count*.php) must *not* have a DOCTYPE.

---

1. Using a text editor (e.g., Notepad or Notepad++), insert the include code (shown in bold) type immediately above the closing body tag of the home page (index.html), or you could put it in the footer.

2. Save the modified index page with the name index.php, as shown in Listing 17-6.

Listing 17-6. A Home Page That Includes a Visitor Counter (index.php)

```
<!doctype html>
<html lang=en>
<head>
<title>index page with counter</title>
<meta charset= windows-1252>
        meta details go here
<link to style sheet goes here...
</head>
<body>
        the home page content goes here
    <p>
    <?php
    include("counthome.php");
    ?>
    </p>
</body>
</html>
```

■ **Caution** Because the page contains some PHP, the charset in this case must be windows-1252; otherwise, the page will not validate.

---

3. Repeat the process in the camp.html page, as follows :

```
<p>
<?php include("countcamp.php");
?>
</p>
```

4. Save the file as camp.php.

5. Repeat the process in the walk.html page.

```
<p>
<?php include("countwalk.php"); ?>
</p>
```

6. Save the file as walk.php. You now have three new .php files: index.php, camp.php, and walk.php.

Step 2: Create the Count Files

Use a text editor to create three "count" files from scratch and save them as .php files. These files are identical except for the item shown in bold type.

1. Create the first "count" file for the home page, as follows:

```php
<?php
$COUNT_FILE = "counthome.dat";
if (file_exists($COUNT_FILE)) {
        $fp = fopen("$COUNT_FILE", "r+");
        flock($fp, 1);
        $count = fgets($fp, 4096);
        $count += 1;
        fseek($fp,0);
        fputs($fp, $count);
        flock($fp, 3);
        fclose($fp);
} else {
        echo "Can't find file, check '\$file'<br>";
}
?>
<font color="#000000" size="x-small" face="Arial">
<?php echo $count;
?>
<a href="http://www.cj-design.com>&copy;CJ Counter</a>
</font>
```

2. Save the file as counthome.php.

3. Create the second "count" file for the camping page, as follows:

```php
<?php
$COUNT_FILE = "countcamp.dat";
if (file_exists($COUNT_FILE)) {
        $fp = fopen("$COUNT_FILE", "r+");
        flock($fp, 1);
        $count = fgets($fp, 4096);
        $count += 1;
        fseek($fp,0);
        fputs($fp, $count);
        flock($fp, 3);
        fclose($fp);
} else {
        echo "Can't find file, check '\$file'<br>";
}
?>
<font color="#000000" size="x-small" face="Arial">
        <?php echo $count;
        ?>
<a href="http://www.cj-design.com>&copy;CJ Counter</a>
</font>
```

4. Save the file as countcamp.php.

5. Create the third "count" file for the walking page, as follows:

```php
<?php
$COUNT_FILE = "countwalk.dat";
if (file_exists($COUNT_FILE)) {
        $fp = fopen("$COUNT_FILE", "r+");
        flock($fp, 1);
        $count = fgets($fp, 4096);
        $count += 1;
        fseek($fp,0);
        fputs($fp, $count);
        flock($fp, 3);
        fclose($fp);
} else {
        echo "Can't find file, check '\$file'<br>";
}
?>
<font color="#000000" size="x-small" face="Arial">
        <?php echo $count; ?>
        <a href="http://www.cj-design.com>&copy;CJ Counter</a>
</font>
```

6. Save the file as countwalk.php.

Step 3: Use a Text Editor to Create Three, Tiny, Identical Text Files

1. Put only the counter's start number in each file (say 0 or 1000). Do not put anything else in these files and do not insert a comma to indicate thousands.

2. Save these three files with the names home.dat, camp.dat, and walk.dat.

You now have three new PHP web pages, three .dat files, and three *count.php files.

Step 4: Make Menus Match the Three PHP Pages

On *every* page in the web site, change the menu hyperlinks so that they link to index.php, camp.php and walk.php instead of the old *.html pages.

Step 5: Upload the Counter to the Host

1. Using your FTP program, access the web site on the host server.

2. Now upload to the host server the three .dat files, the three count.php files, and the three main PHP pages.

3. Using an FTP program, in the host server's panel, right-click the new file counthome.php. On the drop-down menu, look for Properties/CHMOD and click it. Change the 644 figure to 777.

4. Repeat this for countcamp.php, countwalk.php, counthome.dat, countcamp.dat, and countwalk.dat

▓ **Note** CHMOD stands for change mode; that is, it enables you to change the access permissions on the files so that the content cannot be activated by an unauthorized person on Linux servers. The main page is left as CHMOD 664, so it is safe from interference. The other pages are set to 777 to allow the files to interact with each other, and thus change the visitor count every time someone looks at the pages. On Windows servers that support PHP, this is a little more complicated. The easiest way to do this is to place the .dat files in a sub-directory and set the sub-directory to 777.

Step 6: Ensure that Browsers Access the New *.php Pages Instead of the Old *.html Pages

This may very well be the most import step of all, as it prevents browsers accessing the old HTML files; because if two files have the same prefix, such as index.html and index.php, browsers will always choose the HTML version.

1. In the right-hand server/host pane of the FTP program, right-click the file index.html and either rename it as indexold.html or delete it. Users will now automatically access the index.php file.

2. Repeat this for the camp.html file and the walk.html file.

The counter should now function as follows: when a visitor accesses a page, this triggers one of the related files: countcamp.php or countwalk.php or counthome.php. These cause the number on the related *.dat file to be increased by one. The new number is then passed to the relevant page, where it is displayed. You now need to test the counter.

Step 7: Testing the Counter

Access the web site with a browser to ensure that the counter number is showing at the bottom of the page. If the counter number is present on the page, click the refresh icon on the browser. The number should increment by one. Access the other main pages to check that their counters work.

▓ **Note** If a PHP parsing error occurs, most likely a space has been inserted between <? and php. Delete that space so that it looks like <?php.

Track Visitors with Google Analytics

Google Analytics is an alternative to the previously described DIY counter. It provides a detailed analysis of visitors for each page, and it even records the average time visitors spend looking at each page. You will be able to discover where the visitor traffic came from; for example, a search engine, a referral, or a direct URL entry. It will even tell you which countries use your web pages the most.

Google Analytics requires you to add a piece of JavaScript to the `<head>` section of each page on your web site. The following steps will provide you with the code and help you install it:

1. To install Google Analytics, visit `http://www.google.com/analytics` and sign on. If you have a Google account, use that to sign on; otherwise, register for an account.

2. Fill in the form that appears, and tick the box to say you agree with the terms.

3. Click the Create Account button and you are given a snippet of code to inset into the `<head>` section of every page. This code is essential; Google cannot track your pages without it. Insert the snippet just before the closing `</head>` tag.

When you download the code, it will look similar to the following:

```
<script src="http://www.google-analytics.com/urchin.js" type="text/javascript">
</script>
        <script type="text/javascript">
        _uacct = "UA-67xxx9-1";
        urchinTracker();
        </script>
```

After 24 hours, you will be able to see the first visitor reports. As time goes by, the reports will become more meaningful. To access the analysis (called My Dashboard), open `www.google.com/analytics` and log in. Click on the name of your web site and the statistics are displayed.

In Google Analytics, on the left-hand menu, select Traffic Sources ➤ Keywords. This will show you a list of all the keywords people have searched in order to arrive at your site.

For help, go to `http://support.google.com/googleanalytics/?hl=en`.

Redirection

Redirection is a subset of links (or *hyperlinks* to use the full term). Links take three forms: navigation links that take the user from page to page; links within the `<head>` section of a page that connect the page to scripts or to CSS style sheets; and redirection links that don't fit into either of the other two categories.

Most users are familiar with web pages that have a set of links near the top (see Figure 17-7). These links, when clicked, cause the cursor to jump to various sections on the page. The user is redirected to a specific location on a page. Users can also be redirected to a specific place on another page. They can be redirected from one web site to another web site, and an old web site can redirect users to a later version that has a different URL.

Anchors and Links

The place that the redirection points to is called an *anchor*. Originally the anchors on a page were defined as `<a name="…"></a>`. Although `<a name="…"></a>` is not deprecated, W3C recommended in 2002 that id should be used instead of name. The code then becomes `<a id="…"></a>`. The same recommendation applies to anchors on the same page or on other pages; that is, use id not name.

The component that redirects the cursor to the anchor is a link. You will be completely familiar with links that redirect you to another page. This usually takes the following form:

```
<b>For a desciption of the tennis courts</b> Please click
<a href="tennis.html " title="Tennis court information"><b>Tennis</b></a>.
```

The next six mini-projects show that a slightly different link format is required to send the cursor to an anchor that is more specific than a whole page.

Redirecting to a Specific Place on the Same Page

A list of links at the top of a page can redirect the user to various sections on that page. This is common practice for long pages of information. Figure 17-7 shows a typical menu for moving around the same page. Clicking a link takes you to the relevant section on the page. Always place an Up arrow (or a return-to-menu link) at the end of each section to allow the user to redirect back to the menu (see Figure 17-8).

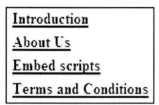

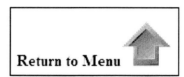

Figure 17-7. Redirection with default links   *Figure 17-8. Redirection using an Up-arrow*

The bold type in Listing 17-7 shows the location of the redirection links in these two figures. Clicking an item on the menu takes you to the relevant section. Clicking the Up arrow anywhere on the page redirects you to the menu. The full file can be downloaded from the Apress companion site.

Listing 17-7. Creating Two Types of Redirection on a Long Page (long-page-with-links.html)

```html
<!doctype html>
<html lang=en>
<head>
<title>Long page with links to items on page</title>
<charset=utf-8>
        <style type="text/css">
        #menu p { margin-top:5px; margin-bottom:0;
        }
        img { border:0;
        }
        h1 { font-size:large;
        }
        </style>
</head>
<body>
<a id="top"></a>
<div id="menu">
<p><b><a href="#intro">Introduction</a></b><a href="#intro" title="Introduction"></a></p>
<p><b><a href="#about">About Us</a></b><a href="#about" title="About Us"></a></p>
<p><b><a href="#embed" title="Embed scripts">Embed scripts</a></b></p>
<p><a href="#terms" title="Terms and conditions"><b>Terms and Conditions</b> </a></p>
</div>
<h1>EMBEDDING SCRIPTS</h1>
<a id="intro"></a>
<p>Introduction</p>
        Long block of text goes here
<p><b>Return to Menu</b><a href="#top"><img title="Return to Menu" ↵
src="images/bluearrow.gif" alt="Return to Menu"></a></p>
<a id="about"></a>
```

```
<p>About Us</p>
        Long block of text goes here
<p><b>Return to Menu</b><a href="#top"><img title="Return to Menu" ↵
src="images/bluearrow.gif" alt="Return to Menu"></p>
<a id="embed"></a>
<p>Embed scripts</p>
        Long block of text goes here
<p><b>Return to Menu</b><a href="#top"><img title="Return to Menu" ↵
src="images/bluearrow.gif" alt="Return to Menu"></p>
<a id="terms"></a>
<p>Terms and Conditions</p>
        Long block of text goes here
<p><b>Return to Menu</b><a href="#top"><img title="Return to Menu" ↵
src="images/bluearrow.gif" alt="Return to Menu"></p>
</body>
</html>
```

You need to create the arrow image in a color and size to suit your page.

For a very long block of text, you may need more than one Up arrow. Create a class for the additional Up arrow and set the top margin for that class at, let's say, 400 pixels. The Up arrows will then be spaced apart vertically, without using dozens of breaks between the Up arrows, like `<br><br><br><br><br>` or `<p> </p><p> </p><p> </p><p> </p>`, and so on.

Redirecting to a Specific Position on a Different Page in the Same Web Site

In the next example, a web page named page1.html has a link to page2.html, but the anchor is a particular place on page 2. That particular place on page2.html has a list of costs for using the tennis courts. The principle is shown in Figure 17-9.

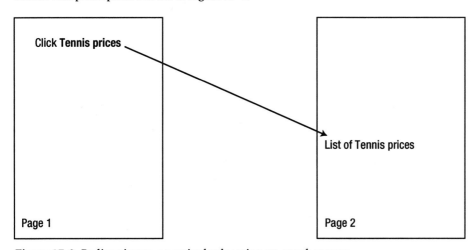

Figure 17-9. Redirecting to a particular location on another page

The redirection link in page1.html would be page2.html#tennis-prices. The complete link would be:

```
<b>For details of the cost of using the tennis courts</b> Please click ⏎
<a href="page2.html#tennis-prices" title="Tennis court hire prices"><b>⏎
Tennis prices</b </a>
```

The `href` specifies the target page (`page2.html`) and the hash symbol specifies the precise spot on the target page (`#tennis-prices`). In `page2.html`, immediately before the list of tennis court prices, you would insert the following code:

```
<a id="tennis-prices"></a>
```

When the user clicks the link on `page1.html`, the browser immediately jumps to the tennis court price list section on `page2.html`.

Redirecting from an Old Web Site to a Newer One

An owner may wish to redirect traffic from an old web site to a new site. Figure 17-10 shows a typical page for a web site that has been replaced by a new web site. As well as displaying the page, the user will be automatically redirected to the new web site within a certain number of seconds.

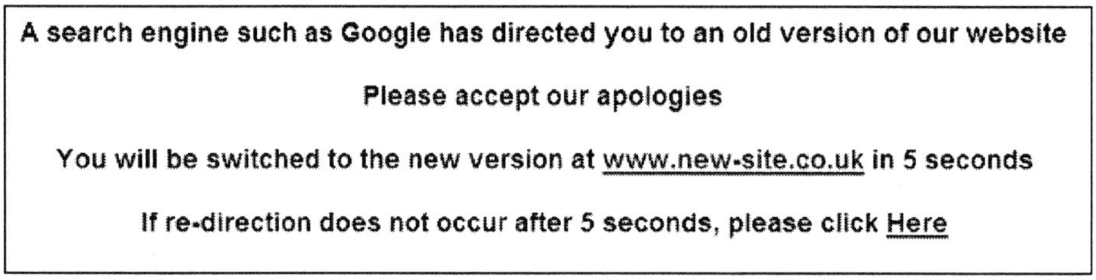

A search engine such as Google has directed you to an old version of our website

Please accept our apologies

You will be switched to the new version at www.new-site.co.uk in 5 seconds

If re-direction does not occur after 5 seconds, please click Here

---

Figure 17-10. A typical redirection page

We will now examine a typical example. Let's say that the owner is a town council in the United Kingdom. The web site is `http://www.brightville-council.com`. The council decides that the `.com` domain name is not really suitable for a UK town hall. Therefore, the council commissions you to design and produce a shiny new web site called `http://www.brightville-council.org.uk`. What is the council to do about the 100,000 people who know the old URL? And then there is the problem posed by all that literature and those directories that quote the old URL?

Also, the search engines will have indexed some of the pages of the old web site so that entering "Brightville" or "Brightville council" will access the old site.

The neatest solution is to keep the old site running for a couple of years in parallel with the new site, but you need to ensure that you have no close duplication between the old and new sites. The search engines will not tolerate duplicate web sites.

The next step requires some detective work. Use a search engine to discover which pages the search engine chooses when the keywords are entered. The pages that appear on the first three pages of results would be sufficient. Make a note of the page names because a redirection must be added to those pages.

Download copies of those pages using the FTP details for the old site. Create new versions of those pages using the markup shown in Listing 17-10 and keep the same page name. The redirection instruction is shown in bold type.

Listing 17-10 offers a simple solution to this problem by automatically notifying users and then redirecting them to the new web site. A downloadable template is not available for this listing.

Listing 17-10. Adding a Redirection to Another Web Site

```
<!doctype html>
<html lang=en>
<head>
<title>Redirection page</title>
<charset=utf-8>
<meta http-equiv="refresh" content="5; URL=http://www.brightville-council.org.uk">
        no need for any other meta content
        <style type="text/css">
        body {font-weight:bold; font-size: large; color:black; font-family:arial; ↵
        text-align:center; }
        </style>
</head>
<body>
<p>A search engine such as Google has directed you to an old version of our web site</p>
<p>Please accept our apologies</p>>
<p>You will be switched to the new version at ↵
<a href="http://www.brightville-council.org.uk"> ↵
www.brightville-council.org.uk </a> in 5 seconds</p>
<p>If re-direction does not occur after 5 seconds, please click ↵
<a href="http://www. brightville-council.org.uk /">Here</a></p>
</body>
</html>
```

Insert your own, new web site details in place of the URLs shown in bold italics. In the host where the old URL is stored, upload the revised pages to replace the old pages.

The text on the redirection message could be something like the text shown in Figure 17-10. Vary the text a little on each page so that the search engines will not be upset by duplicate pages.

Creating a "Go Back" Button

A page such as a printable form may not have a navigation menu. A redirection by means of a Go Back button would be a helpful feature. The Go Back button might look like that shown in Figure 17-9.

Figure 17-11. A typical Go Back button

Normally the Go Back button is only required on a single page of the web site, so an internal style sheet is a sensible choice. However, if you have several pages in a web site needing a Go Back button, use an external style sheet. Listing 17-11 creates the Go Back button shown in Figure 17-11. A downloadable template is not available for this listing.

Listing 17-11. Inserting a Go Back Button into a Web Page

```
<!doctype html>
<html lang=en>
<head>
<title>A Go-back-button</title>
<charset=utf-8>
```

```
        meta details go here
        <style type="text/css">
        #button {height:22px; width:125px; margin:auto; background-color:#6aaaff; ↵
        text-align:center;
        }
        /*set alternative hyperlink colours white medium bold*/
        a.button:link {color: white; text-decoration:none; font-size:100%; font-weight:bold;
        }
        a.button:hover {color: red;text-decoration: none; font-size:100%; font-weight:bold;
        }
        </style>
</head>
<body>
<div id="button">
        <a class="button" href="previous-page.html" title="Return to previous screen ↵
and full menu">GO BACK</a>
</div>
</body>
</html>
```

Replace **previous-page.html** with the file name of the page you wish to return to.

Go Back to Any Page

If the user has accessed a page from any other page at random, you will need a bit of JavaScript to achieve a redirection to the unknown page. This does duplicate the function of the browser's back button, but it might be useful, for instance, on an error-reporting page for a feedback form. The *value* of the button text would then be "Return to form".

If the user has arrived at a page called page2.html from any other page, she can return to *any* previous page with this button (see Figure 17-12).

Go to previous page

Figure 17-12. A button redirecting the user to the previous page

A user is returned to the previous page when the button is clicked.
The button is created with Listing 17-12. (This listing is not available for downloading).

Listing 17-12. Placing a Button on a Page to Redirect the User to the Previous Page

```
<!doctype html>
<html lang=en>
<head>
<title>A Go-back-to previous page button</title>
<charset=utf-8>
        meta details go here
</head>
<body>
<form method="post" action=" ">
<input type="button" value="Go to previous page" onclick="history.go(-1)">
</form>
</body>
</html>
```

Summary

This chapter dealt with three topics: page printing, a visitor counter, and redirection. The page printer code is designed to save the user's paper and ink and gives a clean printout devoid of unnecessary items such as background color, banner headings, menu buttons, advertisements, and footers.

The DIY visitor counter provides the user with a simple visual assessment of whether the web site is attracting visitors. The chapter explained why it was important to have a counter on more than one page. Instructions were provided for installing Google Analytics as an alternative to the DIY counter.

The redirection section listed and explained five types of redirection.

In the next chapter, you will learn why validation is important and how to interpret the reports provided by validators such as the W3C validator and `html5.validator.nu`.

Validation

Why You Should Validate

Validation is a frequently requested enhancement. Clients ask me to add a W3C validation logo to their pages to indicate that they have employed a competent web designer. Validation enables web designers to take pride in their accurate coding. There are also practical reasons for validating, as follows:

- Validating is another way to troubleshoot obscure problems. The designer can save time and avoid frustration by validating before testing a page in the various browsers.

- It ensures that your pages are correctly coded so that browsers do not produce odd results.

- It ensures that search engines will not be blocked by your minor coding errors.

- Disabled users will be able to access your pages. Small coding errors can baffle an automated screen reader.

- Mobile devices have reduced versions of the browsers; they cannot cope with the errors in non-validated sites.

The DOCTYPES for HTML5 and XHTML5

To validate an HTML5 page, the DOCTYPE must be set to one of the following:
For HTML5

```
<!doctype html>
<html lang=en>
<head>
<title>HTML5 test page</title>
<meta charset=utf-8>
        meta details go here
</head>
```

For XHTML5

```
<!DOCTYPE html>
<html xmlns="http://www.w3.org/1999/XHTML1.0" lang="en">
<head>
```

```
            <title>XHTML5 test page</title>
                 <meta charset="utf-8" />
                         meta details go here
            </head>
```

lang=en specifies the English language.

■ **Tip** For non-English languages, see http://www.w3schools.com/tags/ref_language_codes.asp and http://www.iana.org/assignments/language-subtag-registry

---

Logos

If a page has an accessible data table, the page must be in HTML4 or XHTML 1.0 because screen readers (at the time of writing) cannot read HTML5 tables properly (see the associated validations logos for HTML4 and XHTML1.0 in Figure 18-1).

HTML4 and XHTML 1.0 Logos

When an HTML4 or XHTML 1.0 page is validated, you are entitled to put a certificate of validation on the page to prove to your clients that you are capable of correctly coding web sites to the latest standard. You can also download a logo for a validated CSS2 style sheet. For HTML4 and XHTML 1.0, you were able to choose a logo in blue or yellow. The HTML4 and XHTML 1.0 logos are shown in Figure 18-1.

Figure 18-1. These downloadable logos are available from the W3C validator

The HTML5 logo is a bit different. We'll look at that next.

The HTML5 Logo

Figure 18-2 shows the HTML5 logo that was released in January 2011.

HTML

Figure 18-2. The HTML5 validation logo

Currently the HTML5 logo does not indicate that W3C is the authority providing the validation. You will need to state this on your page.

The HTML5 logo is available in several sizes and several configurations. The W3C logo web site is pretty but confusing. It is found at http://www.w3.org/html/logo/

▓ **Note** There is no letter "c" in the W3C URL; it is w3.org not w3c.org. It is licensed under Creative Commons Attribution 3.0 Unported. You may change the logo's color and size to match your web pages.

The Solution for a Verifiable HTML5 Logo

The HTML4 and XHTML 1.0 logos came complete with the HTML code so that users could click on the logo and receive verification that the page was genuinely validated. At the time of writing, the HTML5 logo did not have this safeguard; a webmaster could cheat and embed the HTML5 logo to pretend that the page was valid.

Meanwhile, I have devised some code to overcome this deficiency. The code can either eliminate the need to dynamically embed the HTML5 logo, or you can call it from your images folder. Enter the code shown in bold in Listing 18-2 at an appropriate place on the web page; you do not need my permission to use it.

▓ **Note** A page must be uploaded to the host to enable my logo code to produce a verification report when clicked. If you do not, an error message will tell you that the validator was unable to locate the referer.

Listing 18-2. Placing a Verifiable Logo on a Web Page (verifiable-code-1.html)

```
<!doctype html>
<html lang=en>
<head>
<title>Validation logo for html5</title>
<meta charset=utf-8>
<style type="text/css">img { border:0; } </style>
</head>
<body>
<p>
<a href="http://validator.w3.org/check?uri=referer">
<img src="http://www.w3.org/html/logo/img/mark-word-icon.png" width="64" height="64" ↩
alt="Validated HTML5" title="Validated HTML5"></a>
</p>
</body>
</html>
```

If you would prefer to load the image from an images folder in your root folder instead of from the W3C web site, download the 64-pixel logo into your images folder, and then use the following alternative code snippet (verifiable-code-2.html):

```
<p>
<a href="http://validator.w3.org/check?uri=referer">
<img src="images/html5_logo_64.png" width="64" height="64" alt="Validated HTML5" ↩
```

```
title="Validated HTML5"></a>
</p>
```

If you prefer a smaller logo, change every instance of 64 to 32 in the code snippets. You will need to download the 32-pixel version of the logo to enable the second code snippet to show the small logo.

■ **Caution** When validating HTML4, XHTML 1.0, XHTML5, or HTML5, the validation reports sometimes quote the wrong line number. The reports will refer to a line number, but you will not find the error on that line. This is normal; look for the error in a line near the one indicated, especially in earlier lines.

Using the W3C Validator

TheW3C validator and the HTML5 logos are currently in different folders and on different pages in the W3C web site. Also, a W3C logo without the necessary code does not signify that a page is valid. Hopefully these omissions will be remedied by the time this book is published.

I strongly recommend the W3C validator. Figure 18-3 shows the interface of the W3C validator, which is accessed at http://validator.w3.org.

■ **Note** No matter which DOCTYPE you use, HTML4, XHTML 1.0, HTML5, or XHTML5, the validator will recognize it and produce a report to match it. The same applies to the encoding; it will automatically detect it and validate according to whether your page is utf-8 or any of the Windows or ISO encodings.

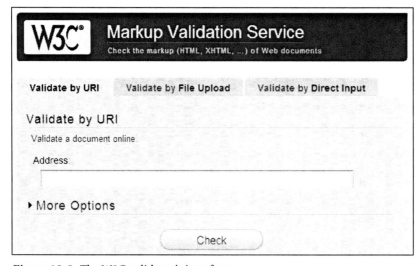

Figure 18-3. The W3C validator's interface

When you open the W3C validator in a browser, you see three tabs: Validate by URI, Validate by File Upload, and Validate by Direct Input. The following tips will help you to decide which tab you should choose:

- **If your page has already been uploaded to a web host**, choose the first tab, and either copy and paste the page's URL into the Address field or type it in; for example, http://www.mywebsite.co.uk/myhomepage.html.

  Click the Check button and wait for a few seconds. Eventually, a report will appear.

- **If the page is not yet uploaded to your web host**, click the File Upload tab, browse to the file for the page on your computer, and load it. Then click the Check button.

  Or click the Validate by Direct Input tab and paste the page's entire markup in the text area provided. Then click the Check button.

Figure 18-4 shows a successful markup.

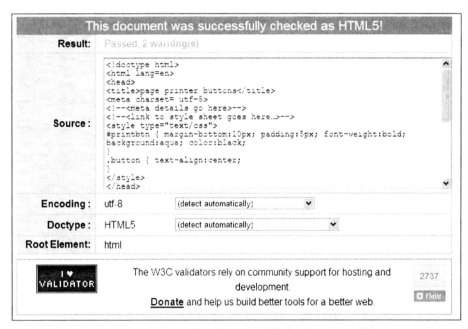

Figure 18-4. A page of markup validated successfully by the W3C validator

Figure 18-4 shows the successful validation of a page of markup that was pasted into the text area. If the validation gives one or two warnings, they can be ignored because they refer to the fact that the validator is experimental and that utf-8 is assumed automatically. The warning is not about your page.

If the validation report has a green header, then your page is valid. If it has a red header, then you have one or more errors. I think this is a poor choice of colors for accessibility because the most common form of color blindness is red/green. Regardless, the following section reviews some of the errors and suggested workarounds.

> ■ **Tip** For maximum convenience, use a text editor that indicates the line numbers and print the page markup. Put the printout beside the computer so that you can refer to the line numbers provided by the validation report.

The earlier validators for HTML4 and XHTML 1.0 checked for correct code style and for markup errors. The HTML5 validators are only concerned with markup errors. Because HTML5 is backwardly compatible, it will accept any of the earlier styles and the validator behaves accordingly. For instance, the HTML5 validator will accept `<meta charset=utf-8>`, `<META charset="utf-8">`, `<meta CHARSET=UTF-8 />`, or any combination of those styles. However, it will not validate `<meta charset=utf8>` because the missing hyphen is bad markup.

Some Typical HTML5 Validation Errors and How to Fix Them

Compared with validating HTML4 and XHTML 1.0, HTML5 documents result in fewer reported errors because the HTML5 validator only looks for bad markup; it does not check code style.

If the header of the validator's report is red, the list of problems and suggested solutions will appear below the red header.

You may be alarmed to see a large number of errors listed in a red-topped report. Don't worry, the validator always reports many errors when only a few exist in reality (many of the errors reported are duplicates).

The following sections describe some typical validation reports and the appropriate fixes.

A W3C Validation Report Found the Following Three Errors

The following is a snippet of the HTML5 markup that was submitted to the validator. I have added line numbers in parenthesis for instructional purposes only.

```
(10) <!--[if lte IE 8]><!-- conditional Javascript added -->
(11) <script src="html5.js" type="text/javascript">
(12) </script>
(13) <![endif]-->
```

The first part of the validation report was as follows:

```
Line 10, Column 23: Consecutive hyphens did not terminate a comment. -- is not permitted
inside a comment, but e.g. - - is.
<!--[if lte IE 8]><!--conditional Javascript added-->
 Line 10, Column 23: The document is not mappable to XML 1.0 due to two consecutive hyphens in
a comment.
<!--[if lte IE 8]><!--conditional Javascript added-->
 Line 13, Column 3: Bogus comment.
<![endif]-->
 Line 13, Column 11: The document is not mappable to XML 1.0 due to two consecutive hyphens in
a comment.
<![endif]-->
 Line 13, Column 12: The document is not mappable to XML 1.0 due to a trailing hyphen in a
comment.
<![endif]-->
```

Don't let the report baffle you, but start to clear away the warnings and some of the duplication as described in the following four steps.

░ **Tip** Copy the report to Notepad++ or some other text editor that displays line numbers. Then clear out the warnings. Delete the lines referring to XML because these are variations of already reported lines. This leaves a clearer field to work with (as shown next).

---

1. All warnings were removed from the report because they apply to the validator, not to the document.

2. I removed all references to XML because they duplicated the previous error messages. The following is what remained of the first section of the report:

    ```
    Line 10, Column 23: Consecutive hyphens did not terminate a comment. -- is not
    permitted inside a comment, but e.g. - - is.
    <!--[if lte IE 8]><!--conditional Javascript added-->
    <!--[if lte IE 8]><!--conditional Javascript added-->
     Line 13, Column 3: Bogus comment.
    <![endif]-->
    ```

    The report stated that consecutive hyphens are not permitted within a comment. We know that consecutive hyphens in a comment are correct, so what was the problem? The validator sees the conditional block of code as a comment. This is correct because it begins with <!-- and ends with -->. The report should have said you cannot have comments *within* comments.

3. So, I moved the comment outside and above the conditional comment and tried validating again. The amended markup is shown next.

```
<!-- conditional Javascript added -->
<!--[if lte IE 8]>
<script src="html5.js" type="text/javascript">
</script>
<![endif]-->
```

This validated successfully; only error number three remained, as follows:

```
Line 38, Column 42: Bad value 88px for attribute width on element img: Expected a digit but
saw p instead.
    title="Valid CSS!" alt="Valid CSS!" /></a>Syntax of non-negative integer:
One or more digits (0-9). For example: 42 and 0 are valid, but -273 is not.
```

Looking at the markup, it is clear that a silly mistake had been made, as shown in bold type:

```
<p><a href="http://jigsaw.w3.org/css-validator/"><img src="images/vcss-blue.gif" ↵
width="88px" height="31" title="Valid CSS!" alt="Valid CSS!"></a>↵
<span class="small"><br><br>Markup Validated by the World Wide Web Consortium</span></p>
```

4. The last section of the report said it saw a letter "p" instead of a number. Image widths in the HTML markup must be numbers only. The 88px would be fine in a CSS style sheet, but it was bad markup when included in an HTML page. After removing the px, the whole page validated successfully.

Video Files Can Produce Validation Errors and Warnings

An HTML5 file that played a video was submitted to the validator, which reported fourteen errors and two warnings. The two warnings were ignored because they related to the validator and not to the page. Twelve of the errors were the same—twelve ampersands were written as '&'. The validator recommended that the ampersands be changed to the entity &. Using Find and Replace, the twelve ampersands were changed to entities. The page was then tested in several browsers to check that it still functioned correctly; fortunately it did. The page was again submitted to the validator. The report then gave only two errors, as follows:

Line 20, Column 49: Element object is missing one or more of the following attributes: data, type.
        <object width='320' height='265' id='flvPlayer'>Attributes for element object:
Line 24, Column 9: Stray end tag embed.   </embed>

I commented out the </embed> tag and then the page was tested in browsers, and then re-submitted to the validator. This time, the only error was in line 20, where an attribute was missing in the <object> tag.

The validator recommended either a data or a type attribute. First, a Mime type was matched to the video, which was a Shockwave file.

A quick search on the internet revealed the MIME type for a Shockwave file; it was entered into the code, as shown in bold.

<object width='320' height='265' id='flvPlayer' **type="application/x-shockwave-flash">**

The amended page functioned properly in the browsers and it validated successfully.

Byte Order Mark Found

Microsoft Expression Web is one of the programs that creates markup that can produce the mysterious warning, "byte order mark found".

A byte order mark (BOM) is a sequence of bytes embedded in utf-16 pages. It makes sure that your utf-16 documents are read correctly by web browsers. Unfortunately, MS Expression Web, by default, adds a BOM to utf-8 pages or on PHP pages where a BOM is unwanted.

In MS Expression Web, to prevent a BOM being included in new pages, follow these steps:

1. Click Tools and select the Page Editor Options dialog box.

2. On the Authoring tab, look under New Documents.

3. Then under Add a byte order mark (BOM) to new utf-8 documents with these file extensions you will see a list of file extensions.

4. Clear the box next to each file extension that you would prefer not to have a BOM.

To remove a BOM from an existing page, do the following:

1. Open the document in Expression Web.

2. In Code view, right-click anywhere, and then click Encoding.

3. In the Text File Encoding dialog box, clear the box labeled "Include a byte order mark (BOM)".

4. Save the page and upload it; then re-validate it.

■ **Note** The free Notepad ++ program has a BOM removal tool. Load the page, click Format on the menu, and select Convert to UTF Without BOM. Notepad ++ also provides line numbering, color-coding, and many other great features for editing any type of web document.

Rare or Unregistered Character Encoding Detected

If you see that error message, the meta tag containing the text encoding has an error in it. The markup should read:

<charset=utf-8>

Most likely you omitted the hyphen in utf-8.

Regarding PHP pages, the inclusion of some PHP code is a common reason for the "rare or unregistered character" error message. To validate a page that contains PHP, the charset must be windows-1252, as follows:

<charset=windows-1252>

Validating Accessible Data Tables: HTML4 and XHTML 1.0 Validation Errors and Solutions

For the blind and partially sighted, any data tables must appear on an XHTML 1.0 or HTML4 page. This will be necessary until screen readers can correctly read HTML5 data tables with three or more columns.

The following section deals primarily with errors on HTML4 and XHTML 1.0 pages, but some will also apply to HTML5 pages. Only a small number of validation errors are mentioned in this section because there are 447 known errors and space is limited (visit the w3.org web sites in the following tip to see all the known error messages).

■ **Tip** For lists of validation errors and their solutions, try the web sites at http://line25.com/articles/10-common-validation-errors-and-how-to-fix-them and http://validator.w3.org/docs/errors.html. Although these URLs deal primarily with HTML4 and XHTML 1.0 validation errors, some also apply to HTML5.

You may be alarmed to see a large number of errors listed in a red-topped report. The validator finds an error at the top of the page then it cascades down the report repeating the same error report many times, sometimes using different words. For instance, when validating a page that has errors, these errors may be repeated lower down in the report as XML parsing errors. Just ignore them and they will go away when you correct the errors nearer the top of the report.

Some of the Most Common Validation Error Messages

The following are some of the most common validation error messages:

OMITTAG NO: This precedes a common error. Look for elements that are not closed properly.

```
Line 78, Column 9: end tag for "html" omitted, but OMITTAG NO was not specified.
```

The end tag for the opening <html> should appear on the last line of the page. I had omitted the tag.

The <p> tag: The most common XHTML 1.0 error is a <p> with a missing closing tag </p>.

Closing tags: Some closing tags in XHTML 1.0 are different from plain HTML4;
 must be used instead of <br>. The tag <br /> is called a self-closing tag. All XHTML 1.0 <meta> tags and <img> tags must be closed with a forward slash like this …" />. The report states closure errors like this:

```
Line 38, Column 10: end tag for "ul" omitted but OMITTAG NO was not specified.
```

That means that the closing tag angle bracket > was omitted in an HTML4/XHTML 1.0 page, or the closing tag in an XHTML 1.0 or an XHTML5 page should have been /> and not >.

When closure errors are reported, several errors will cascade through the report even though there is only one closure error. Fix the error and the cascade will vanish.

An element that is not open: The opposite of a closure error.

```
Line 87, Column 12:  end tag for element "SPAN", which is not open.
```

This may mean that you removed an inline tag such as <span> earlier in the document but forgot to delete its closing element lower down in the page.

Lowercase: Remember XHTML 1.0 markup must be all lowercase. The validator will expect to see lowercase.

Incorrect nesting: Some tag errors may be described as being in a place that is not allowed. You may have intermingled <ul> <li> elements with table elements <tr> <td>. The error message will say something like:

```
Line 33, Column 32: document type does not allow element "li" here.
```

Nesting with inline elements: In the next example, the validator is saying that block element tags like <ul> cannot be enclosed within a <span> tag.

```
Line 52, Column 4: document type does not allow element "ul" here.
        <span class="list">
        <ul>
        <li>he Haven provides sheltered housing companionship in retirement</li>
        <li>Thirteen purpose built units for single or double occupancy</li>
        </ul>
        </span>
```

The <span> tags should be eliminated and the class should be inserted into the <ul> tag.

Other *not allowed here* errors are the result of surrounding a block element with an inline tag. For instance, surrounding an unordered list with <span> tags, <b> tags, or <strong> tags.

Deprecated tags and attributes: The error report will find deprecated elements that are no longer acceptable in HTML4 or XHTML 1.0; for example:

```
Line 32, Column 7: there is no attribute "CENTER".
```

This means that *center* is no longer acceptable in HTML markup; a style sheet must be used to center elements.

Examples of the W3C validator's more helpful explanations:

```
Line 137, Column 19: value of attribute "ALIGN" cannot be "ABSBOTTOM"; must be one
of "TOP", "MIDDLE", "BOTTOM", "LEFT", "RIGHT". align="absbottom" width="199"
height="231">
```

Some attributes such as align are no longer valid for lining up text with images, only top, middle, bottom, left, and right are acceptable.

ALTs: The validator will report "alts" missing from images.

Some reports are not clear; for example:

```
Line 25, Column 39: document type does not allow element "li" here; missing one of
"ul", "ol", "menu", "dir" start-tag . <li>Home page<li>.
```

I had forgotten to put a forward slash in the closing tag like this </li> .

Some misreporting occurs like the following example:

```
Elements not allowed here
Line 23, Column 9: document type does not allow element "h2" here; missing one of
"object", "applet", "map", "iframe", "button", "ins", "del" start-tag . <h2>some
heading text was here</h2>
```

I looked at line 23 and could not find the error; the h2 element was properly closed. I then looked at nearby lines and found that on line 22, there was no closing </p> tag for a <p> element. Errors that are wrongly reported can usually be fixed by looking above and below the reported line for an unclosed <p>.

▨ **Tip** You will have concluded that reported errors are not always what they seem. You will need to work out what the report should have said by looking at lines before or after the error line. Rather like cryptic clues in a crossword puzzle, with practice you will recognize the patterns and know how to correct coding errors.

The .nu HTML5 Validator

The alternative validation web site is http://html5.validator.nu
    I found this reasonably easy to use, but its reports are not as informative as the W3C validator's. The W3C validator actually uses the .nu validator as part of its code-scanning process. I tend to use only the W3C validator, but that is probably because I am so familiar with it. You should not let my personal

preference prevent you from exploring the .nu validator. It is constantly being improved, and its interface is self explanatory. The uncluttered interface is shown in Figure 18-5.

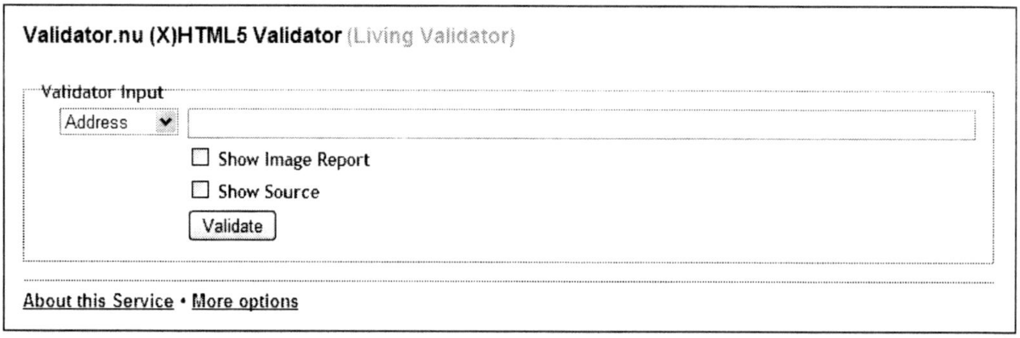

Validator.nu (X)HTML5 Validator (Living Validator)

Validator Input

Address ▼ [   ]

☐ Show Image Report
☐ Show Source
[Validate]

About this Service • More options

Figure 18-5. The .nu validator's interface

At the time of writing, the .nu validator did not provide an HTML5 logo. You will need to go to the W3C logo site for this. Then you will need to add my code snippet to enable users to check the validation.

■ **Note** At the time of writing, the W3C HTML5 and XHTML5 validator and the .nu validator were "highly experimental." Also, as time goes by, the appearance of the .nu validator changes with each update. The .nu congratulation message for an XHTML5 page states that the file checked was HTML5 and vice versa. At the time of writing, the .nu validator would only produce an HTTP ERROR 415 and it refused to validate any HTML5 files. This will hopefully be corrected by the time this book is published.

Validating CSS2

Go to http://jigsaw.w3.org/css-validator/, where you will find an interface similar to the HTML validator, but with the heading CSS Validation Service.

- **If your CSS page has been uploaded to your web host**, type in the URL of the CSS style sheet you want to validate using this format: http://www.mywebsite.co.uk/mystylesheet.css.

  Click the Check button and wait for a few seconds. Eventually, a report will appear.

- **If the CSS page is not yet uploaded to your web host**, click the File Upload tab, browse to the file for the page on your computer, and load it. Then click the Check button.

  Or click the Validate by Direct Input tab and paste the CSS page markup in the field provided. Then click the Check button.

If the markup fails to validate, you will be given hints about the errors. If it validates, you will be offered a logo to put on your page.

The following example report can be baffling:

```
29      li.btn a                Same color for background-color and border-right-color
29      li.btn a                Same color for background-color and border-top-color
29      li.btn a                Same color for background-color and border-left-color
30      li.btn a:hover          Same color for background-color and border-top-color
30      li.btn a:hover          Same color for background-color and border-left-color
30      li.btn a:hover          Same color for background-color and border-right-color
32      li.btn a:active         Same color for background-color and border-top-color
32      li.btn a:active         Same color for background-color and border-left-color
32      li.btn a:active         Same color for background-color and border-right-color
35      Same colors for color and background-color in two contexts li.btn a:active and
#footer
```

The outset border color on the menu's 3D buttons has been set the same as the background color. These warnings can be safely ignored, but if you wish, the error can be eliminated by a slight change to the outset border color to make it different from the background color.

CSS style sheets will also fail to validate if the same color is used for text and for the background of a gradient. For instance, if the background is white with a green background gradient and the text is also white. The validator ignores the gradient and compares the true background (white) with the text (white). It will report this as an error.

CSS3 Validation and Vendor Specific Errors

To validate a CSS3 style sheet, go to `http://jigsaw.w3.org/css-validator/`.

▨ **Caution** For CSS3, you must click the More Options button. Choose one of the tabs for your markup entry. Then click the drop-down arrow in the Profile field and select CSS Level 3.

- **If your CSS page has been uploaded to the web host**, type in the URL of the CSS style sheet you want to validate using this format

- `http://www.mywebsite.co.uk/mystylesheet.css`.

  Click the Check button and wait for a few seconds. Eventually, a report will appear.

- **If the CSS page is not yet uploaded to your web host**, click the File Upload tab, browse to the file for the page on your computer, and load it. Then click the Check button.

  Or click the Validate by Direct Input tab and paste the CSS page markup in the field provided. Then click the Check button.

The CSS3 validator will report errors for any vendor specific items in the style sheet; that is, items such as -mozkit- and -webkit-. This is what you would expect because the vendor-specific items are not W3C recommended; the validator's role is to check for conformance with W3C recommendations. Such errors will continue to be reported until browser vendors support CSS3 and dispense with their vendor-

411

specific hacks. By all means play with CSS3, but perhaps you should forget about CSS3 and its validation logo on clients' web sites until these hacks are no longer required and when IE 7 and IE 8 have finally expired. Meanwhile, use CSS2 on clients' web sites.

For example, a CSS style sheet was tested and the validator gave a report with a red banner. The content of a typical failure report is shown in Figure 18-6.

W3C CSS Validator results for TextArea (CSS level 3)

Sorry! We found the following errors (1)

URI : TextArea

2 td Parse Error ;0 5px }

Warnings (1)

URI : TextArea

5 You have no color set (or color is set to transparent) but you have set a background-color. Make sure that cascading of colors keeps the text reasonably legible.

Figure 18-6. The CSS validation report for a CSS3 table

I examined the code that was submitted, and found the error and the warning, as shown in bold text in the following:

```
(1) table { width: 500px; border:1px black solid; border-collapse:collapse; }
(2) td { border:1px black solid; padding:0 5px;0 5px }
(3) th { border:1px black solid; }
(4) caption { font-weight:bold; }
(5) table tr:nth-child(even) { background-color: #C8F0F0; }
(6) .right { text-align:right; }
```

In line 2 the semicolon after the 5px should have been at the end of the line as follows:

```
td { border:1px black solid; padding:0 5px 0 5px; }
```

The warning about the fifth line recommends that a text color should always be specified, as well as a background color. The line should have been:

```
table tr:nth-child(even) { background-color: #C8F0F0; color:black; }
```

When the corrected CSS code was re-validated, it gave the congratulations message, as shown in Figure 18-7. The banner in this case was green.

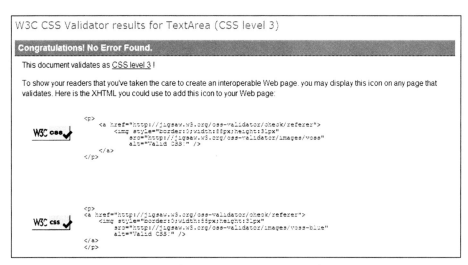

Figure 18-7. The W3C validator for CSS3 showing a successful validation

A validation logo for CSS3 was not available at the time of writing, but as you can see in Figure 18-7, you are offered the traditional CSS logos and the code that enables users to verify the validation.

Summary

In this chapter, you discovered how useful validation is for troubleshooting and for ensuring your code will function properly on all sorts of devices. A code snippet was provided to embed an HTML5 logo that enables users to check that the page has been genuinely validated. You also learned that the reports received from the validator can be rather cryptic and that some practice is necessary in order to become familiar with their meanings and the solutions.

In the next chapter, you will learn how to deal with some of the problems that arise when designing web sites. Troubleshooting is an important aspect of web development; the tips and short cuts in the next chapter will save you time and frustration.

Troubleshooting

This chapter is designed to help you track down some of those elusive problems that take up so much of a web designer's time. It covers the most common problems and testing methods. Problems not covered by this chapter can usually be solved by running the problem page through the W3C validator or by posting the problem into a search engine.

Testing Your Pages

Install the five main browsers—Internet Explorer, Mozilla Firefox, Safari, Chrome, and Opera—on your computer. Put their icons on the desktop and test your pages in each browser as you work. If you are using IE 9 you will need the IETester tool to test web sites in IE 6, IE 7, and IE 8. Or you could test with XP and IE 8 on another computer.

Some brave designers install the Apache local host on their computers to test PHP forms and counters. I have spent many frustrating hours trying to install Apache without success; sometimes it would work for two or three weeks, but eventually it failed. For a much easier and quicker solution, use Mozilla Firefox to view the PHP pages stored on your computer. To test the interactivity of a PHP feedback-form or a PHP page counter, create a test folder on one of your existing web site hosts. Then upload the interactive files to the test folder and run them; that will take about two minutes compared with hours struggling to install Apache.

Tip The nifty IETester tool is invaluable and a real time saver for testing your web pages on older versions of Internet Explorer. Download and install it from http://www.my-debugbar.com/wiki/IETester/HomePage. This tool is free, but well worth a donation. For some other good testing resources, visit Adobe BrowserLab at https://browserlab.adobe.com/en-us/features.html and the quick "version checker" at: http://netrenderer.com.

Using IETester can be puzzling. There seems to be no way of opening a web page stored in a folder on the computer. First you need to load the page in a browser. Then select and copy its address (Ctrl+C) from the browser's address field. It should start something like the following:

```
file:///C:/Documents%20and%20Settings/User/…
```

Or like `C:\Documents and Settings\User\My Documents\BOOK\Ch10 \filename`.

Open the IETester and click one of the tabs, (let's say IE 6). You will see a web address in blue in the address bar. Don't click it; just press Ctrl+V to replace the address with your file location and then press Enter. Click another tab (let's say IE 7) and repeat the Ctrl+V and press Enter. Once a page is loaded into IETester, you can click its navigation buttons and test the other pages on the site with IETester.

When using IETester, an occasional error message pops up saying the program needs to close, but this is a bug and it does not actually close the program.

Most WYSIWYG web editors have **error checking** functions. For example, MS Expression Web has an excellent error checker; pressing the F9 key in code view reveals and explains the errors step by step.

If you have a problem with **float drop or a positioning** problem, this tip might help you find the cause. Add a temporary line in the head section of the problem page like the following:

```
<style type="text/css">
* { border:1px solid red !important; }
</style>
```

When viewed in a browser, the block elements will be surrounded with a red border; this could reveal the cause of your problem.

Other testing methods and tools are included in the appropriate chapters. For example, Chapter 18 shows how to test your code for W3C compliance. Chapter 14 gives information on testing sites that are accessible to the disabled.

If a Browser Treats the Page As If It Has No DOCTYPE

This indicates that the DOCTYPE is not the first line on the page. Nothing must precede the DOCTYPE, not even an empty line. If this fault is present the browser will use Quirks mode to display the page and you probably won't like the result. However, a block of PHP code can be placed before the DOCTYPE with no adverse effect.

If You Have Positioning Problems

Elements may not appear where you want them to appear on the page. The following are some examples:

- *A left-side navigation menu appears on the right of the screen*: Try putting one or more <br> tags just before the <div> or <nav> containing the menu.

- *Images will not stay in position*: Sometimes appearing centered instead of left aligned or vice versa. Examine the style sheet and remove any image positioning style which is causing the misalignment. The style sheet may contain two image alignment instructions; the web page will obey the last one of the two.

- *A page will not display properly in a WYSIWYG web design program*: In this case view the page in various browsers, it may display properly in all of them. Some WYSIWIG programs are not entirely accurate when showing how a page will look in browsers.

If You Have a Horizontal Menu Problem

The following are the two most common horizontal menu problems:

1. One of the buttons drops out of line, especially when viewed in Internet Explorer 6.

2. One button increases in depth, or a button becomes two buttons.

These faults are shown in Figure 19-1.

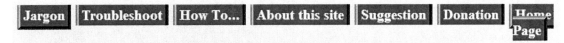

Figure 19-1. A horizontal menu with a fault on the home page button

These faults can also be caused by IE 6 because it uses a larger default font than any other browser. The larger font expands the button widths, so that the menu is too wide for its container. To cure this, you need to specify a smaller font for IE 6 only. Create a special additional style sheet called ie6style.css. It need only consist of the #container or #menu code from the mainstyle.css, but change its font size from medium to small, as shown in bold in the following:

```
#container{text-align:center; background-color:#D7FFEB; font-family: "times new roman";
    font-size: small; color: #000000; margin: auto; width:95%;}
```

In the head section of the HTML, insert a conditional link (shown in bold). Position it below the other links, as shown in the following code snippet.

```
<head>
<title>Home page …</title>
meta details go here
<link rel="stylesheet" type="text/css" href="mainstyle.css" media="screen">
<!--[if lte IE 6]>
<link rel="stylesheet" type="text/css" href="ie6style.css" media="screen">
<![endif]-->
<link rel="stylesheet" type="text/css" href="print.css" media="print">
</head>
```

There are two other issues to consider. Partially-sighted users could increase the font size with their own style sheet. Be aware of this and try to make plenty of room on the buttons for a larger text size.

If a horizontal menu refuses to center on the page, ensure that the container for the <ul> block is set to text-align:center; in the style sheet.

If You Have a Server Problem

Anti-virus alert: "Threat was blocked." This is a genuine alert because you did not deliberately build any malware into your web site. But some low-life scumbag has hacked your site and inserted a bit of JavaScript into one or more pages. Use your FTP program to download the page and look for the snippet of JavaScript. The rogue script will usually be located just after the <body> tag.

A typical rogue script looks like this:

```
<!-- ad --><script language='JavaScript' src='http://powergym.be/xxxxfs31dj.js'>↵
</script><!-- /ad -->
```

This should never happen with a decent host, but it does occur occasionally with less security conscious hosts. As a precaution always use a longer more complex password with special characters and numbers. However if the problem has occurred, the remedy is to log into your Control Panel at the host and change the FTP password to something more complex. Then use your FTP client to upload clean copies of all the infected pages. Then contact the host and complain loudly until it makes its server more secure.

If the host server suddenly won't accept your FTP password, it may be due to the same problem described in the previous paragraph; the solution is the same.

If You Have a Browser Variation Problem

If your page does not display correctly in one or more browsers, don't assume that the problem is your fault. I spent two hours chasing a problem which turned out to be a bug in Mozilla Firefox. The far right column was displayed within the middle container. By chance I viewed the page in another computer using Firefox and it was fine. The answer? Each computer had a different version of Firefox. The older Firefox version was the problem; by updating to the latest version, the page was displayed correctly. Always test on the most recent version of a browser and also on the version before it.

Another issue may be that square check boxes on printable pages or on the screen appear round in Mozilla Firefox. On the screen displaying a printable page such as an order form, square check boxes using Wingdings or Webdings do not work in Firefox. Practically every computer has the Lucida Sans Unicode symbols. By using this font for the boxes, the check boxes display correctly in all popular browsers (see Figure 19-2).

Figure 19-2. This how the box looks in all popular browsers

The code for the box is &#9633, as shown in Listing 19-2. This code enables the box to print correctly when printing a feedback form or order form containing tick boxes.

Listing 19-2. Creating a Tick Box that Displays Properly in Mozilla Firefox (tickbox-printer.html)

```
<!doctype html>
<html lang=en>
<head>
<title>This is a box styled with Unicode Lucida font</title>
<meta charset=utf-8>
<style type="text/css">
.stylebox { font:xx-large bold; font-family:"Lucida Sans Unicode"; margin-left:50px;
}
</style>
</head>
<body>
<p>The tick box shown below is styled with Unicode Lucida and it is formatted as ⏎
xx-large and bold </p>
<p class="stylebox">&#9633;</p>
</body>
</html>
```

Should We Troubleshoot Problems with IE 6 and Other Older Browsers?

It depends on the intended audience and whether it would be likely to use older browsers. Less than two percent of computer users in the United Kingdom and the United States still surf with IE 6. However, you may take on a client that does use IE 6 (for instance, some government departments and a few local government services).

Most designers are now ignoring IE 6 on the grounds that Microsoft has mounted a vigorous campaign to wean people off it. Users of Mozilla, Chrome, Safari, and Opera will usually have downloaded the latest versions of their browsers.

▧ **Tip** Visit Stat Counter Global Stat (`http://gs.statcounter.com`) to check the latest statistics and assess the trend in browser popularity. Select the bar graph version for a clearer picture of the current situation. Select the line graph version for trends.

See also `http://marketshare.hitslink.com/browser-market-share.aspx?qprid=3`. For a table of the percentage of browsers in use around the world in the year 2012, see the Appendix. The statistics from the various organizations vary. We will never know which are the most reliable, but you will be able to detect definite trends that are very useful.

Browsers Can Have Minor Display Differences

IE 6 does not recognize `max-width` and `min-width`. If the client uses IE 6 (for example, some local government departments can be stuck in a time warp) you will need to give its web site pages fixed widths.

Iron out small differences. Although the latest browsers conform to the W3C standard, some small differences are still present, especially with regard to margins and padding, these differences can be avoided by including a reset at the start of the style sheet, like the following one presented by David Sawyer McFarland in *CSS: The Missing Manual* (O'Reilly, 2009).

```
/*reset all browsers to a common standard*/
html, body, h1, h2, h3, h4, h5, h6, p, ol, ul, li, pre, code, address, variable, ↵
form, fieldset, blockquote {
 padding: 0;
 margin: 0;
 font-size: 100%;
 font-weight: normal;
}
table { border-collapse: collapse; border-spacing: 0;
}
td, th, caption { font-weight: normal; text-align: left;
}
img, fieldset { border: 0;
}
ol { padding-left: 1.4em; list-style: decimal;
}
```

Test the pages as you create them in IETester, and in IE 9, Mozilla Firefox, Chrome, Opera, and Safari.

If Strange Symbols Appear on the Screen

These could take the form of a square. Examine the markup at the place where the symbol occurs on the screen. Substitute a character entity for the symbol that is causing the problem. For instance a British £ symbol would display as a square. Replace the £ symbol with the character entity £.

If You Changed the CSS, but It Looks the Same

This can be frustrating. There are two common reasons.

The first reason is the browser cache has stored the previous style sheet and, therefore, you are seeing the results of the old style sheet. To see the page styled by the amended style sheet, use your browser's refresh button, or try Ctrl+F5 in IE and Chrome. In Firefox try Ctrl+Shift+R.

The second reason is incorrect ordering of the styles, <link>s, and JavaScript within the <head> section. The order of appearance in the markup should follow a plan.

The following snippet of code shows the correct ordering of the items enclosed in the <head> section:

```
<!doctype html>
<html lang=en>
<head>
<title>Correct order for head items</title>
<meta charset=utf-8>
meta details go here
<link rel="stylesheet" type="text/css;" href="media-sheet.css" media="handheld">
<link rel="stylesheet" type="text/css;" href="main-stylesheet.css" media="screen">
<link rel="stylesheet" type="text/css;" href="print-sheet.css" media="print">
        <style type="text/css">
                #wrapper {background: #FFF; color:#000; }
        </style>
<!--[if lte IE 8]>
<script src="html5.js">
</script>
<![endif]-->
</head>
```

The snippet of code shows that if the page links to more than one device-based style sheet, the links should be in the order handheld, screen and print. If a page has an internal style for that particular page (for instance, in the previous listing to display the page with a white background and black text) that style should be next after the main style links. Conditional styles and JavaScript should come last.

The general rule is that the last style wins. In the previous snippet, the display on a computer screen would be largely styled by the screen link, the internal style would override only the main page's color and text color. The conditional and the JavaScript would only kick in if the visitor was using IE 8 or an earlier version of IE.

If You Experience Float Drop

Floated elements can suffer from float drop; that is, an element drops below the place it was intended to occupy. This can occur in the following two related situations:

- *Static*: When a container is not wide enough to accommodate the horizontal content.

- *Dynamic*: When the browser window is shrunk horizontally by the user so that it is not wide enough to accommodate the horizontal content.

Any page with a horizontal row of fixed width elements could suffer from float drop. The page chosen for this example contains a menu block and three images in a horizontal row. Figure 19-3 shows the intended display.

I am most grateful to the artist Ann Roe Jones who kindly gave me permission to use the photographs of her very impressive portraits. The portrait images were used in a web site I designed for her. Be sure to view her web site at `http://www.annroejones-artist.co.uk`

Figure 19-3. *A display with no float drop*

Figure 19-3 has no float drop, but Figure 19-4 demonstrates float drop: the girl's portrait has slipped below the other two portraits.

Figure 19-4. One portrait has dropped below the others.

The dropped portrait leaves a big white space on the right-hand side of the other portraits. You could be forgiven for thinking that you could set the minimum width of the page's container by adding together the width of the images and the width of the menu block. However, there are hidden extras. Items like the images and the menu block probably have horizontal padding, borders, and margins. These items all add to the width. You could determine the size of these extras and set the minimum width of the container to suit.

I find it quicker and more convenient to set the maximum and minimum container width to match the most popular screen size and resolution. Then I make the horizontal elements fit within the minimum container width. This can be achieved by cropping or resizing the images in a graphics program, and/or adjusting the horizontal margins and padding of the menu block and the images.

Download the troubleshooting chapter's files and folders from the book's page at http://www.apress.com. View the file portraits-drop.html (Listing 19-4a) in a browser. Then shrink the browser's window horizontally to see the image of the girl drop below the others.

Listing 19-4a. An Example for Demonstrating Float Drop (portraits-drop.html)

```
<!doctype html>
<html lang=en>
<head>
<title>Float drop test</title>
<meta charset=utf-8>
    meta details go here
<link rel="stylesheet" type="text/css" href="portraits-drop.css">
<!--Add conditional JavaScript-->
    <!--[if lte IE 8]><script src="html5.js">
    </script>
    <![endif]-->
```

```
</head>
<body>
<div id="container">
<header>
<h1>Ann L Roe <span class="swac"> SWAc</span></h1>
</header>
<!--start of left column-->
<nav>
<ul>
    <li><a title="Portrait Paintings" href="portraits.html">Portraits</a></li>
    <li><a title="Commissions" href="commissions.html" >Commissions</a></li>
    <li><a title="Prints" href="prints.html">Prints</a></li>
    <li><a title="Latest" href="latest.html">Latest News</a></li>
    <li><a title="About Ann" href="about.html">About Ann</a></li>
    <li><a title="Return to Home Page" href="index.html">Home Page</a></li>
</ul>
</nav>
<div id="midcol-portraits">
<h3><b>SOME PORTRAITS BY ANN ROE (JONES) SWAc</b></h3>
<div id="gallery">
<figure>
    <img alt="Professor Clemments OBE" height="307" src="images/prof-h307.jpg"
    width="224">
    <figcaption><br><p>Professor Robert Clements OBE</p></figcaption>
</figure>
<figure>
    <img title="Reuben" src="images/reuben225.jpg" alt="Reuben" width="225" ↵
    height="308">
    <figcaption><br><p>Reuben</p></figcaption>
</figure>
<figure>
    <img alt="Megan" height="300" src="images/megan.jpg" width="213">
<figcaption><br><p>Megan</p></figcaption>
</figure>
<aside>
    <p > </p>
    <p ><b>All of Ann&#39;s portraits are painted <br>in oils on canvas.</b></p>
    <p >For information on commissioning a portrait, click the &#39; ↵
    Commissions&#39; button </p>
    <p >Click the &#39;Contact Ann&#39; button to request more detailed ↵
    information.</p>
</aside></div>
</div><br><br>
<footer><br>
    Footer goes here
</footer>
</div>
</body>
</html>
```

In Listing 19-4b, the container's min-width (shown in bold type) caused float drop because it was too small to contain all the horizontal elements.

In the CSS sheet (portraits-drop.css) that you downloaded from the book's page at http://www.apress.com, change the container's width from 850 pixels to 960 pixels and see how this prevents float drop.

Listing 19-4b. The CSS style sheet for Listing 19-4a (portraits-drop.css)

```
/*set attributes for consistent appearance in all browsers*/
p, ul, li, h1, h2 {margin:0; padding:0;
}
img { border:0;
}
/*add display attributes for the semantic tags*/
header, footer, section, article, nav { display:block;
}
/*A container width that prevents float drop*/
/*#container {min-width:960px; font-family:"times new roman"; font-size:medium; color:black;
margin:auto; max-width:1050px;
}*/
/* A container width that causes float drop*/
#container {min-width:850px; font-family:"times new roman"; font-size:medium; color:black;
margin:auto; max-width:1000px;
}
header {width:100%; margin:auto; height:60px; text-align:center;
}
#midcol-portraits {margin-left:165px; margin-right:15px;
}
figure { float:left; margin-right:5px; display:inline;
}
figure p { font-size:80%; height: 15px; margin:0 auto 0 auto; text-align:center; ↩
width:200px;
}
#gallery img { margin-right:20px; margin-top:5px;
}
aside { float:left; width:260px;
}
footer {clear:both; text-align:center;
}
/* set side menu position */
nav {float:left; margin-left:0; width :135px; padding:0; zoom:1;
}
/* set general side button styles */
nav ul li{ margin-bottom: 4px; text-align: center; list-style:none;
}
/* set general anchor styles */
nav ul li a { color: white; background:#D20B0D; font-weight: bold; text-decoration: none
}
/* specify state styles */
/* mouseout (default) */
nav li a { background: #D20B0D;  border: 4px outset #FFAAAA; display:block;
}
/* mouseover */
nav li a:hover { background: maroon;   border: 4px outset maroon;
}
```

```
/* onmousedown */
nav li a:active { background:#AECBFF;  border: 4px inset #AECBFF;
}
h1 {font-size:300%; font-weight:bold; color:#D20B0D; margin-top:0; margin-bottom:0; font-
family:"Calligraph421 BT"; font-style:italic; text-align:center;
}
span.swac {font-size:x-large; font-weight:bold; color:#D20B0D; ↵
font-family:"Calligraph421 BT"; font-style:italic; text-align:center;
}
h3,h4 { margin-top:0; margin-bottom:0;
}
h2 {font-size:x-large; font-weight:bold; margin-top:0; margin-bottom:0;
}
```

By changing the container's `min-width` to 890px, the float drop was prevented.

If an HTML5 Page Has No Styling in IE 7 and IE 8

You changed the style and nothing happened in the display in IE 7 and IE 8. Possible causes might be any of the following:

- The Remy Sharp JavaScript file `html5.js` has not been uploaded to the folder at the server.

- The JavaScript has not been called in the `<head>` section of the HTML page. It should be as follows:

      ```
      <!--[if lte IE 8]>
              <script src="html5.js">
              </script>
      <![endif]-->
      ```

- The following line has been omitted in the linked CSS page:

      ```
      header, nav, article, footer { display:block;
      }
      ```

- Perhaps you enclosed the conditional within the style sheet or within the style tags on an internal style. Conditionals must be part of the HTML markup.

If Data Tables Have Double Borders

Although you will no longer be using tables for page layout, tables are the recommended and essential tools for displaying data. The default table displays double lines around cell borders. This is rather unattractive and a little too fussy. Figure 19-5 shows how these borders are separated by a default 2-pixel gap.

425

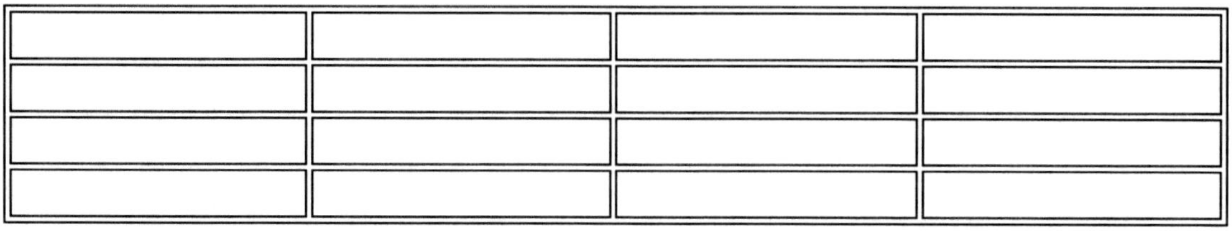

Figure 19-5. A data table with double borders

Listing 19-5 produces the double borders. The main WYSIWYG web site editors have a dialog box for tables where it is possible to eliminate the gap. Students and beginners often fail to tick the box on the dialog box that will remove the gap; usually this is because they do not yet understand the meaning of the CSS attribute `border-collapse`.

Listing 19-5. Creating a Default Data Table with Double Borders (default-table.html)

```
<!doctype html>
<html lang=en>
<head>
<title>Default table</title>
<meta charset=utf-8>
<style type="text/css">
table, tr, td { width: 600px; border: 1px solid #000000;
}
</style>
</head>
<body>
<table>
        <tr>
                <td> </td>
                <td> </td>
                <td> </td>
                <td> </td>
        </tr>
        <tr>
                <td> </td>
                <td> </td>
                <td> </td>
                <td> </td>
        </tr>
        <tr>
                <td> </td>
                <td> </td>
                <td> </td>
                <td> </td>
        </tr>
        <tr>
                <td> </td>
                <td> </td>
                <td> </td>
                <td> </td>
        </tr>
```

```
</table>
</body>
</html>
```

To remove the 2-pixel gap between the borders, change the CSS style to include the attribute border-collapse:collapse;. This merges the two borders, giving a single, unspaced line around each cell, as shown in Figure 19-6.

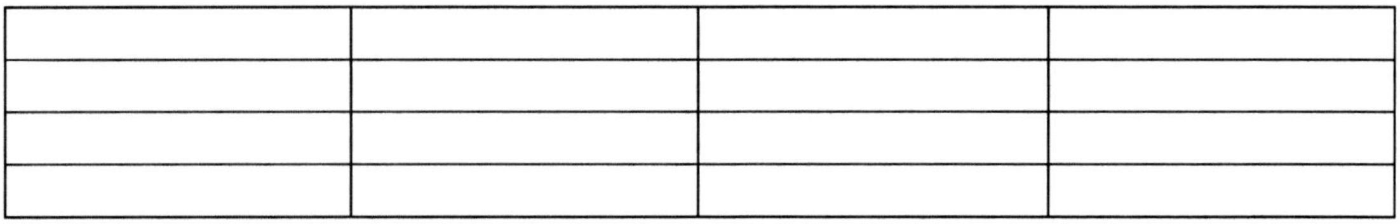

Figure 19-6. *Collapsing the double borders to single borders*

The following CSS snippet replaces the CSS style in Listing 19-5 to collapse the borders. The border-collapse item is shown in bold type (collapsed-table.html).

```
<style type="text/css">
table, tr, td { width: 600px; border: 1px solid #000000; border-collapse:collapse;
}
</style>
```

If the Site Owner Is Not Receiving Replies from the Secure Feedback Form

The owner of the web site complains that she is not receiving any feedback from the secure form (as described in Chapter 11). The cause is clearly the result of forgetting to switch the e-mail addresses in the form handler. Believe me this does happen. The web designer is so anxious to inform the owner that the form works (when tested with his own e-mail address), that he forgets to swap the addresses, or he changes the addresses but forgets to upload the revised version.

Examine the handler, if you see the following code:

```
<?php
// -------- SET THE EMAIL HEADINGS ------------------------
/* set the recipient's email address (i.e., the person you want to send the feedback to)
//$mailto = "your-client@her-isp.co.uk" ;
$mailto = "me@my-isp.co.uk" ;
```

Swap the comment-out slashes as follows:

```
<?php
// -------- SET THE EMAIL HEADINGS ------------------------
/* set the recipient's email address (i.e., the person you want to send the feedback to)
$mailto = "your-client@her-isp.co.uk" ;
//$mailto = "me@my-isp.co.uk" ;
```

And don't forget to upload the amended handler.

Summary

In this chapter, you learned how to test your pages and then how to troubleshoot a small selection of the most common problems that occur when developing a web site. If you encounter obscure problems, these can often be diagnosed and solved by validating the page as described in Chapter 18. Internet forums offer another possibility. Try entering the problem into a search engine or sign up as a member of a web designer's forum.

An appendix follows this chapter. It contains a quick reference section for CSS2 and CSS3, hints on positioning elements on a page, tips for inserting IE conditionals, instructions for ordering the HTML elements, and a table of statistics on browser popularity. It also contains advice on setting MIME types and a table of common entities.

Quick Reference, Techniques, and Useful Data

This appendix has the following three main themes:

1. *A quick reference section.* Why would readers of this book want such basic information? Because even the most experienced web designer can have momentary lapses of memory. Reminders of the basic principles in one place within one book are handy; it saves searching through several books, several chapters, or the internet.

2. *Summaries of techniques.* Some useful techniques are summarized here, such as positioning, floating, ordering markup, and ensuring the MIME types are set on your server.

3. *Tabular information.* Helpful data tables are included so that you can look up information on character entities and browser statistics.

Quick Reference Section

HTML5 and XHTML5 Quick Reference

The DOCTYPES for HTML5 and XHTML5 are much simpler than earlier forms.

For HTML5:
```
<!doctype html>

<html lang=en>
<head>
<title>HTML5 test document</title>
<meta charset=utf-8>
meta details go here
</head>
```
For XHTML5:
```
<!DOCTYPE html>
<html xmlns="http://www.w3.org/1999/xhtml" lang="en">
<head>
<title>XHTML5 test document</title>
```

```
<meta charset="utf-8" />
meta details go here
</head>
```

▩ **Note** You can use the simpler HTML5 DOCTYPE for pages marked up as XHTML5.

For languages other than English, visit `www.w3.org/International/questions/qa-choosing-language-tags.en` or `www.w3.org/blog/International/tag/qa-choosing-language-tags/`

Validating

Both DOCTYPES will validate in the W3C validator (`http://validator.w3.org`)or the .nu validator (`http://html5.validator.nu`).

At the time of writing, both validators are experimental. The .nu congratulation message for the XHTML5 check states that the file checked was HTML5, and vice versa. This should be corrected by the time this book is published. See Chapter 18, which covers validation, for full details.

If you choose to use XHTML5 markup, you should adhere to the XHTLM rules for self-closing tags and double quotes. If you prefer, as I do, to use HTML5 markup, life gets easier; you can forget self-closing tags and double quotes and lots of other former markup requirements. For instance, to specify the language, use `<html lang=en>`; to specify the character set, use `<meta charset=utf-8>`. There is no need to specify a MIME type for JavaScript because new browsers, thanks to HTML5, no longer need to be told that a JavaScript file is `type="text/javascript"`.

CSS2 Quick Reference

Try the following manuals for more information on CSS:

- *Beginning HTML and CSS with XHTML* by Craig Cook and David Schultz (Apress, 2006).

- *Pro CSS and HTML Design Patterns* by Michael Bowers (Apress, 2007).

- The second edition of *CSS: The Missing Manual* by David Sawyer McFarland (O'Reilly Media, 2009).

Many other titles are available at `http://www.apress.com`. Access the site and type "css" or "html" into the search box.

USA Spelling Must Be Used for Three Attributes

Use gray, center, and color; not grey, centre, and colour as in the United Kingdom, Australia, and New Zealand.

The Four Main Categories of CSS Selector

The following are the four main categories of CSS selector:

- id (identity)

- class
- span
- group

Identity (id)

In the CSS style sheet, an id selector is written with a hash sign; for example:

$$\text{\#credits \{font-size:small;\}}$$

Use only one of each id per page.
The target on the web page would in this case be `<div id="credits">`

Class (.)

In the style sheet, a class selector begins with a full stop; for example

```
.bigblue  {font-size:xx-large; color:blue;}
```

This class would produce a big, blue font. You can use as many of the same class as you wish per page. The target in a web page would, in this case, be

```
<p class="bigblue">The Sausage Shop</p>
```

Span \<span>

Span selectors are used inline in a page to target small elements within a larger element, such as a few words within a paragraph. A CSS example is

```
span.redfont {color:red;}
```

This would change a piece of text to the color red. A `<span>` does not add line space above and below a line of text like the tags `<div>` and `<p>`, and the headings h1, h2, h3, and so on; use as many of the same spans as you wish per page.
The HTML target in this example would be

```
<p>We hope you will visit <span class="redfont">The Sausage Shop</span> very soon</p>
```

Group Targets

Style sheet selectors can be grouped using a comma after each tag. This example sets the margins and padding on all headings to zero.

```
h1,h2,h3,h4,h4,h5,h6 {margin:0; padding:0 }
```

Specific Group Targets

Selectors can be made even more specific by choosing a selector within a selector, but with *no commas*; for example:

```
header strong {color:blue;}
```

In this case, the selector's target would be some text enclosed within a `<strong>` tag, but only if the `<strong>` tag was itself enclosed within a header tag as follows:

```
<header><strong>some text</strong></header>
```

The words `some text` would be colored blue. The jargon for this selector is *descendent selector*. The `<strong>` tag is a descendant of the `<header>` tag.

Other Targets

HTML tags such as `<img>`, `<html>`, `<body>`, and `<ul>` can be targets; they act like special `<div>`s. For instance, the following piece of styling removes borders from all images:

```
img { border:none; }
```

The next style sets the general appearance of every page on the web site.

```
body { font-family:arial; font-size:medium; background:#FFF; color:#000;}
```

Targeting Hyperlinks

The appearance and behavior of links should be determined by a style sheet. The CSS could be

```
/*set the hyperlink colour to blue and the font size to mediuml*/
a.small-normal:link { color: blue; text-decoration:none; font-weight:normal; font-size:medium;
}
a.small-normal:visited { color: blue; text-decoration: none; font-weight:normal; font-
size:medium; }
a.small-normal:hover { color: red; text-decoration: none; font-weight:normal; font-
size:medium; }
a.small-normal:active { color: blue; text-decoration: none; font-weight:normal; font-
size:medium; }
```

In this example, the targeted link would be blue to make it stand out from the default black text, and it would not be underlined because the text decoration was set to "none". The link will change from blue to red when the mouse pointer hovers over it.

The corresponding HTML for the previous style might be

```
<a title="Computer Jargon explained" href="jargon.html">Go to Jargon page</a>
```

If you would like the link to become underlined when hovered over, change the text decoration for the hover condition as follows:

```
a.small-normal:hover { color: red; text-decoration: underline; font-weight:normal; font-
size:medium; }
```

Target a Rollover Navigation Menu with 3D Buttons

The following snippet uses an unordered list to produce 3D menu buttons (Chapter 4 gives worked examples):

```
nav {position:absolute; top:100px; left:3.6%; width: 866px; padding: 5px; ↵
list-style: none; overflow: hidden; height: 35px;
}
```

```
nav li { display:inline; padding: 5px; padding-top:15px; margin:5px 0 0 2px; ↵
height:25px; width:100px;
}
nav a {height:25px; width:100px; color: #fff; font-size:80%; font-size: 100%; ↵
font-weight:bold; text-decoration: none; background-color: #72b720; ↵
border: 4px outset #5edd51; padding:5px 5px 0 5px; display: inline-block;
}
nav a:hover { font-weight: bold; background-color:green; color:white;
}
.clear { clear:both;
}
```

The :before Pseudo-Element

CSS can generate a special, highlighted piece of text and place it at the start of selected paragraphs, as shown in Figure App-1. The word *Note* was generated with white text in a colored box.

surrounding paragraph

Note: The text with the coloured background
is generated with CSS2 but is not supported by IE6 nd IE7.
The class "note" is targeted by the
pseudo-element :**before**.

surrounding paragraph

Figure App-1. *Generated content*

The pseudo-element :before is not supported by IE 7. Listing App-1 has an internal CSS style and the pseudo style for :before is shown in bold type.

Listing App-1. *Creating a Special Effect for the First Word in a Paragraph (css2-before.html)*

```
<!doctype html>
<html lang=en>
<head>
<title>Generate some content before a selected paragraph</title>
<meta charset=utf-8>
        meta details go here
        <style type="text/css">
        p { font-size: 100%; }
        .note:before { content:"Note: "; background-color:red; color:white;}
        </style>
</head>
<body>
<p>surrounding paragraph</p>
        <p class="note">The text with the coloured background<br>is generated with CSS2 ↵
        but is not supported by IE 6 and IE 7.<br>The class "note" is targeted by the ↵
        <br>pseudo-element <strong>:before</strong></p>
```

```
<p>surrounding paragraph</p>
</body>
</html>
```

A Wider Range of Named Colors

Originally, only 17 named colors were available. This number has greatly increased, and names like chocolate, darksalmon, and honeydew can be used instead of RGB or hexadecimal colors.

For a comprehensive list, visit http://somacon.com/p142.php.

Ordering Markup: What Comes First/Last in the <head> Section?

Certain items must appear in a particular order on the <head> section of the markup, otherwise you may experience unintended results. The preferred orders follow.

Linking to Different Media

```
<link rel="stylesheet" type="text/css;" href="md-sheet.css" media="handheld">
<link rel="stylesheet" type="text/css;" href="stylesheet.css" media="screen">
<link rel="stylesheet" type="text/css;" href="print-sheet.css" media="print">
```

░ **Note** The print media link should appear after the screen link. The screen link refers to the default desktop/laptop display. To remember the order, try this mnemonic: **H**ot **S**oup **P**lease (**H**andheld, **S**creen, and **P**rint).

The alternative to using a link to a special style sheet for printing is to include an @media print directive in the global style sheet that will apply to all pages. For instance, you may wish to reduce the heading sizes and line spacing on any page printed from the web site. Also, let us assume the web site uses a sans serif, 10 point font; we will change the font to 12 point Times New Roman because it is easier to read on printed matter. To do this, you would add the following code to the main external style sheet:

```
@media print {
                p { font-family: "times new roman"; font-size:12pt;
                }
                h1 { font-size:20pt; margin-bottom:0;
                }
                h2 (font-size: 14pt; margin-bottom:0;
                }
           }
```

Place Linked Styles Before Internal Styles

Place the default link statement *before* any internal style, as follows:

```
<link rel="stylesheet" type="text/css;" href="stylesheet.css">
     <style type="text/css">
             body {background: #FFF; color:#000; }
     </style>
```

Where IE Conditionals Are Located

Locate any conditional(s) styles within the <head> section. They must come *after* any linked style sheets, as follows:

```
<link rel="stylesheet" type="text/css" href="default.css" />
        <!--[if IE 6]>
        <link rel="stylesheet" type="text/css" href="style-ie6.css" />
        <![endif]-->
</head>
```

Including JavaScript

Place the JavaScript link after the linked styles and after an internal style, as follows:

```
<!doctype html>
<html lang=en>
<head>
<title>Home page</title>
<meta charset=utf-8>
        meta details go here
</head>
<link rel="stylesheet" href="default.css" type="text/css" />
                <style type="text/css">
                        body {background: #FFF; color:#000; }
                </style>
        <script type="text/javascript" src="niftycube.js"></script>
        <script type="text/javascript">
        window.onload=function(){
        Nifty("#container","big");
        Nifty("#mainpanel","same-height normal");
        Nifty("#leftcol,#rightcol", "same-height big");
        Nifty("#hdr,#ftr","normal");
        Nifty("#about li","top bottom big fixed-height");
        }
        </script>
</head>
```

Listing Video Sources in the <body> Section

Video sources in the <body> section must be listed in the following order, otherwise problems can occur with some handheld devices:

- .mp4

- .webm

- .ogv

A fallback file for IE 7 and IE 8 should be located at the end of the list.

435

Ordering the Pseudo Classes

When styling links, the order is important. It should be as follows:

- link
- visited
- hover
- active

A useful mnemonic would be Live Very Happily Always.

CSS3 Quick Reference

CSS3 has several, long-awaited enhancements. These are being perfected and released piecemeal; most browsers (other than IE 7 and IE 8) are beginning to pick them up. IE 7 and IE 8 ignore these enhancements, so that, for instance, pages with CSS3 rounded corners will display square corners. IE 9 will probably be able to utilize some of the new CSS3 enhancements.

The current list of CSS3 elements includes the following:

- Rounded corners (see Chapter 7)
- Multiple columns (see Chapter 15)
- Drop shadows (see Chapter 8)
- Drop shadows on text (see Chapter 8)
- Multiple backgrounds (see Chapter 3)
- Font selectors (see Chapter 5)
- Enhanced child selectors (see Chapter 5)
- An opacity property (see Chapter 5)
- RGBA color notation (see Chapter 5)
- A template layout module
- Border images
- Grid layout

░ **Note** This book gives worked examples for any of the modules marked with a chapter number.

Summaries of Techniques

Relative Positioning of Elements

CSS relative positioning displaces the item relative to where it would normally appear. With relative positioning, the circle on the left in Figure App-2 has been made to appear 320 pixels to the right, but the CSS code for this is not as you expect. The CSS code actually tells you where the original circle was located; that is, 320 pixels to the left and 70 pixels upwards. The CSS code is

```
#circle { position:relative; left:320px; top:70px; }
```

The best way to remember this is to assume that the dimensions for *left* and *top* are margins.

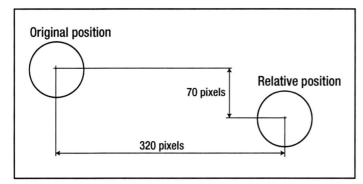

Figure App-2. *Relative positioning moves an element away from its original location*

To illustrate this, we will use a familiar image from Chapter 3. Figure App-3 shows a header with a rosette.

Figure App-3. *The location of the rosette before it was positioned*

The rosette is located against the inner left-hand edge of the header border. Listing App-3 set the *original* default position for the rosette.

Listing App-3. Superimposing a Rosette in Its Default Location (original-position.html)

```
<!doctype html>
<html lang=en>
<head>
<title>Rosette in original position</title>
<meta charset=utf-8>
        meta details go here
<style type="text/css">
body { background:#FFF url(images/green-grad.jpg) repeat-x; }
#container { margin:auto; width:920px;
}
/*add display attributes for semantic tags*/
header, footer, section, article, nav { display:block;
}
header {width:920px; height:180px; padding:0; border:10px white solid; ↵
background:url(images/header3.jpg); margin: 20px auto;
}
h1 { font-size:300%; color :white; position: relative; left:90px; width:480px; top: 55px;
}
</style>
<!--conditional JavaScript added-->
<!--[if lte IE 8]>
<script src="html5.js" type="text/javascript">
</script>
<![endif]-->
</head>
<body>
<header>
<h1>Devon's Rural Retreats</h1>
<img id="rosette" alt="Rosette" title="Rosette" height="127" width="128" ↵
src="images/rosette-128.png">
</header>
</body>
</html>
```

Relatively Position the Rosette

Logically, you would think that the rosette had to be positioned to the *right*, but as stated earlier, you need to imagine that the relative positioning dimensions are *margins*. So, using trial and error, I gave the rosette imaginary margins of 750 pixels *left* and 5 pixels *top* using the following CSS style:

```
#rosette { position:relative; left:750px; top:5px; }
```

The rosette's new position is shown in Figure App-4.

Figure App-4. *The location of the rosette after it was relatively positioned*

The relative position is applied by means of the code shown in bold type in Listing App-4.

Listing App-4. *Relatively Positioning the Rosette (re-positioned.html)*

```
<!doctype html>
<html lang=en>
<head>
<title>Rosette relatively re-positioned</title>
<meta charset=utf-8>
        meta details go here
<style type="text/css">
body { background:#FFF url(images/green-grad.jpg) repeat-x; }
#container { margin:auto; width:920px;
}
header {width:920px; height:180px; padding:0; border:10px white solid; ↵
background:url(images/header3.jpg); margin: 20px auto;
}
h1 { width:480px; font-size:300%; color :white; position: relative; left:90px; top: 55px;
}
#rosette { position:relative; left:740px; top:5px;
}
</style>
</head>
<body>
<header>
<h1>Devon's Rural Retreats</h1>
<img id="rosette" alt="Rosette" title="Rosette" height="127" ↵
src="images/rosette-128.png" width="128" />
</header>
</body>
</html>
```

Absolute Positioning of Elements

Absolute positioning locates elements relative to the following:

439

1. *The edge of the browser window.* For example

    ```
    #element { position:absolute; left:0; top:0; }
    ```

    This CSS styling would position an element so that it butts up against the far left edge and the top edge of the browser window.

2. *The edge of its nearest container.* In this case, the container must be a direct ancestor and it must also have positioning applied to it. The ancestor's positioning does not need to have any dimensions such as left, top, right or bottom.

    For example, the next CSS statements absolutely position a horizontal navigation bar within a container; the container has some positioning applied to it, in this case relative. The container's positioning can be zero, as shown bold in the first line, and it still works; in fact, the items shown bold in the first line can be omitted altogether.

```
#container {position:relative; top:0; left:0; width:950px; margin:auto; ↵
text-align:center;
}
nav { position:absolute; top:100px; left:8%; width: 785px; padding:5px; ↵
list-style: none; height: 35px;
}
```

▨ **Tip** To avoid cross-browser problems, always give a width to absolutely positioned and fixed position elements.

Display inline, block, or inline-block

Some elements are inline elements by default. To change this behavior, an element can be styled using the CSS display style attribute.

-   display:inline;: The line height, width, top, and bottom padding; and the top and bottom margins cannot be altered. Adding height or width does nothing. Padding and margins can only be added to the right and left of the content. However, the width of an element will be determined by any text and/or images enclosed by the inline element. These elements are inline by default; <span>, <a>, <label>, <input>, <img>, <strong>, <b>, <em>. List elements such as <ul>, <li> can be changed to inline, in which case they become subject to the same limitations: width, height, top, and bottom padding and top and bottom margins cannot be adjusted.

-   display:block;: Ensures that an element has top and bottom line spacing, and allows optional width, height, top, and bottom padding and top and bottom margins. In the absence of a width, the element will default to the width of its containing element, such as a sidebar column. Examples of block elements are <div>, <h1>, <h2>, <h3>, <h4>, <h5>, <p>, <form>, <dl>, <dd>, <dt>, <ul>, <li>, <ol>, <br>. Block elements sit on top of one another and are, therefore, ideal for vertical lists such as menus.

-   display:inline-block;: Removes top and bottom line spacing, but allows top and bottom padding. This is a very useful style for inline menu buttons. It was underused in the past because some older browsers did not support it.

- All three styles allow left and right padding.
- Inline elements can only contain text and other inline elements. Block elements can contain text and inline elements.

Floated Elements

Floating is another method for positioning elements. Items can be floated to the left or to the right. The default is float:none; . Floated elements should always have a width (floated *images* already have predefined width). When an element is floated, it *cannot* be given a position:absolute; or a position:relative;. The CSS is float:left; or float:right; or float:none;

▓ **Tip** Floated elements can have positive or negative margins to assist positioning.

Figure App-5 shows the top rosette floated left and the lower rosette floated right.

The rosette is floated left. The paragraph flows around the rosette. The rosette is floated left. The paragraph flows around the rosette. The rosette is floated left. The paragraph flows around the rosette. The rosette is floated left. The paragraph flows around the rosette.

The rosette is floated right. The paragraph flows around the rosette. The rosette is floated right. The paragraph flows around the rosette. The rosette is floated right. The paragraph flows around the rosette. The rosette is floated right. The paragraph flows around the rosette.

Figure App-5. *Left and right floated rosettes*

Listing App-5 creates the demonstration of the float property shown in Figure 20-5.

Listing App-5. *Demonstrating Left and Right Float (float-1.html)*

```
<!doctype html>
<html lang=en>
<head>
<title>float-1</title>
<meta charset=utf-8>
```

```
        meta details go here
<style type="text/css">
body { font-size:150%;
}
#container { width:500px; margin:auto;
}
#rosette-left { float:left;
}
#rosette-right { float:right;
}
</style>
</head>
<body>
<div id="container">
<img id="rosette-left" alt="Rosette" title="Rosette" height="127" src="images/rosette-128.png"
width="128">
<p>The rosette is floated left. The paragraph flows around the rosette. The rosette is floated
left. The paragraph flows around the rosette. The rosette is floated left. The paragraph flows
around the rosette. The rosette is floated left. The paragraph flows around the rosette.</p>
<img id="rosette-right" alt="Rosette" title="Rosette" height="127" src="images/rosette-
128.png" width="128">
<p>The rosette is floated right. The paragraph flows around the rosette. The rosette is
floated left. The paragraph flows around the rosette. The rosette is floated left. The
paragraph flows around the rosette. The rosette is floated left. The paragraph flows around
the rosette.</p>
</div>
</body>
</html>
```

The <clear> Property Applied to Floated Elements

Text flows around a floated item. Sometimes you do not want text to flow around; you would rather force the text below the floated element. This can be achieved by using the clear property; however, I am never able to remember what clears what and how right and left should be applied.

The general rule is that if an item, an image say, is floated left, give the text the CSS property clear:left;—in other words, clear the item that is floated to the left. Conversely, if an element is floated right and you do not want text to flow around it, then give the text the CSS property clear:right;.

The CSS command clear can also have the attribute both as in clear:both;. This is extremely useful for pushing an element like a footer below the columns on a page.

The example illustrated in Figure App-6 demonstrates the clear:left; and clear:right; properties.

The rosette is floated left. The paragraph has been given a class *clear-left*. The rosette is floated left. The paragraph has been given a class *clear-left*.

The rosette is floated right. The paragraph has been given a class *clear-right*. The rosette is floated right. The paragraph has been given a class *clear-right*.

Figure App-6. *The paragraphs are styled to clear the floated images.*

The code in bold type in Listing App-6 forces the text clear of the images.

Listing App-6. *Using the Clear Property (float-2.html)*

```
<!doctype html>
<html lang=en>
<head>
<title>float-2</title>
<meta charset=utf-8>
        meta details go here
<style type="text/css">
body { font-size:150%;
}
#container { width:500px; margin:auto;
}
#rosette-left { float:left;
}
#rosette-right { float:right;
}
.clear-left { clear:left;
}
.clear-right { clear:right;
}
</style>
</head>
<body>
<div id="container">
```

```
<img id="rosette-left" alt="Rosette" title="Rosette" height="127" src="images/rosette-128.png"
width="128">
<p class="clear-left">The rosette is floated left. The paragraph has been given a class <i>
        clear-left</i>. The rosette is floated left. The paragraph has been given a class
<i>clear-left</i>.</p>
<img id="rosette-right" alt="Rosette" title="Rosette" height="127" src="images/rosette-
128.png" width="128">
<p class="clear-right">The rosette is floated right. The paragraph has been given a class <i>
clear-right</i>. The
rosette is floated right. The paragraph has been given a class <i>clear-right</i>. </p>
</div>
</body>
</html>
```

Understanding MIME Types

MIME types (Multipurpose Internet Mail Extensions) tell a browser what type of file is being processed. Although originally devised for e-mailing, the standard has been extended to web sites. You see several MIME types on web pages; they appear like this: type="something". The following are typical MIME types:

HTML page: type="text/html"
JavaScript: type="text/javascript"
MP3 file: type="audio/mpeg"
SVG: type="application/svg+xml"
CSS: type="text/css"

Fortunately, web designers don't have to worry overmuch about MIME types because browsers are smart enough to know that .jpg, .gif, and .png are images and they automatically know which MIME type to apply. This will become more common in HTML5; for instance later browsers will recognize JavaScript, thus eliminating the need to state the MIME type for a script in the markup.

Server-Based MIME Types

MIME types are not always entered into a web page; some are located in the server/host. This particularly applies to audio and video for the new HTML5 recommendations.

The following notes were extracted and summarized from the web sites at http://tomraftery.com2005/01/15//creating-an.htaccess-file/ and http://www.javascriptkit.com/howto/htaccess.shtml.

▓ **Caution** Some hosts allow the web designer to add MIME type permissions to a server. You can create your own .htaccess file, but you need to find out if your host will allow you to upload it. Be warned that you must be extremely careful when changing an .htaccess file. If possible, ask your host to change it. Some hosts have a facility in their web sites' control panel for altering the file yourself. Otherwise, if you can see an .htaccess file in the host's folder, download a copy. The file is often stored as a hidden file, so you may not be able to see it. In that case, you will not be able to download it (although the dot in front of the file name signifies a hidden file, it may not be hidden at your particular host). *Always keep a backup* of the .htaccess file; if you do make a mistake, you can upload the original. Making a mistake in an .htaccess file can stop your entire site from working. If this happens, just upload the original from your backup. Neither Apress nor the author will be responsible for any mistakes you make that cause problems at your host server.

Video MIME Types

Before attempting to provide HTML5 video for a web site, be sure to contact the host server and request that the MIME types are set for .ogv, .mp4, .flv, .swf, and .webm videos files. Your videos won't play in some browsers if you neglect to do this.

The following is the snippet of code that most hosts use to set the MIME types on their servers. It lives in the .htaccess file along with other permissions called AddTypes.

```
AddType video/ogg .ogv
AddType video/mp4 .mp4
AddType video/webm .webm
AddType video/x-flv .flv
AddType application/x-shockwave-flash swf
```

▓ **Note** It is absolutely essential to use a plain text editor to create the file. The file can be created using Notebook and saved first as .htaccess.txt. Then you must remove the .txt file type by right-clicking the file and renaming it as .htaccess. It won't work if anything is written after the .htaccess file name.

- Each AddType must be on its own line with no line breaks. If your text editor wraps the text, make sure it does not insert line breaks to create the wrap.

- Use a # (hash) at the start of a line to comment-out a line.

- Multiple or single spaces are ignored, but do not use tabs.

- When uploading the file using FTP, *do not* send it in binary. You must upload it in ASCII mode.

- You should upload the .htaccess file to the folder where your home page is located (the root folder). The file then affects every single folder in the entire site.

- Using your FTP client, look for the .htaccess file that you uploaded and right-click it. Set the CHMOD to 644 or (RW-R–R–). This prevents unauthorized persons interfering with it. It also makes it usable by the server, but prevents it being seen in a browser.

■ **Tip** Your host/server may choose not to display the .htaccess file, however it is still present, so try this: in your FTP program, click the download button with no file name selected. Usually a text box will appear asking you to enter a file name. Type .htaccess and then click OK to download the file.

If your text editor refuses to allow you to rename a file like .htaccess that has a preceding dot, try viewing the file in MyComputer (or in Windows 7 view it in Computer). Then right-click the file, select Rename, type the new name, and press Enter to confirm it. Alternatively, you could upload .htaccess to your host server and rename it on the server. This will not work if the host makes the file invisible, however. Your FTP program might overcome this if it can be configured to view all files. You may not be able to see the file after you rename it in your FTP program.

After uploading your new .htaccess, you may see error messages when trying to view your web site. This means your .htaccess file was faulty. Upload the saved, good version; or in desperation you could try uploading a completely empty .htaccess file to overwrite the faulty file.

Always keep your htaccess.txt file in case you should need to make changes in the future.

A Host May Allow You to Change the .htaccess File

I use www.bargainhost.co.uk because it has a remarkable number of useful features for web designers/owners, and the support staff are the most helpful I have ever encountered. I can access the .htaccess file from the Bargain Host cPanel (Control Panel) using the following steps:

1. Login to cPanel.

2. Click on File Manager option under Files.

3. Select the home directory.

4. Select the public_html folder.

5. Select the file htaccess. Then edit the file and save it.

Internet Explorer Conditionals

Sometimes IE needs a brief but additional style sheet to overcome the browser's inability to conform to standard recommendations.

A conditional link must be placed in the head section of the HTML markup after the main link that styles the whole web site. The conditional bit is enclosed by if and endif.

If IE 6, IE 7, and IE 8 are the browsers not conforming to a particular W3C standard, then the HTML would be as follows:

```
<link rel="stylesheet" type="text/css" href="global.css">
        <!--[if lt IE 9]>
        <link rel="stylesheet" type="text/css" href="style-IE.css">
```

```
                    <![endif]-->
        </head>
```

The lt in the expression `<!--[if lt IE 9]>` means "If the browser is less than IE 9."

If IE 6 is the only browser not conforming to a particular W3C standard, then the HTML would be as follows:

```
<link rel="stylesheet" type="text/css" href="global.css" />
        <!--[if IE 6]>
        <link rel="stylesheet" type="text/css" href="style-ie6.css" />
        <![endif]-->
</head>
```

If IE 6 and IE 7 are the browsers not conforming to a particular W3C standard, then the HTML would be as follows:

```
<link rel="stylesheet" type="text/css" href="global.css" />
        <!--[if lte IE 7]>
        <link rel="stylesheet" type="text/css" href="style.ie67.css" />
        <![endif]-->
</head>
```

The lte in the expression `<!--[if lte IE 7]>` means "If the browser is less than or equal to IE 7."

▨ **Caution** You are probably used to typing "IE6", "IE7", and "IE8". Be sure to put a space between IE and the number when typing conditionals, otherwise they will be ignored by the browser.

Full details of IE conditionals can be found at `http://msdn.microsoft.com/en-us/library/ms537512(VS.85).aspx`. Also see `http://www.conditional-css.com/usage` for the conditionals for all browsers.

Data Tables

Common Character Entities

In HTML5, some characters must be represented by character entities. Table App-1 shows the most common entities.

For full details, type "ISO-8859-/entities" into a search engine.

Table App-1.

Symbol	Alphabetic Entity	Decimal Equivalent
Ampersand &	&amp;	&#38;
Space		
Tick box ◻		&#9633;
British Pound £	&pound;	
Copyright ©	&copy;	
Registered trade mark ®	&reg;	
Superscript [1]	&sup1;	
Superscript [2]	&sup2;	
Superscript [3]	&sup3;	
Quarter ¼	&frac14;	
Quote "	&quot;	
Half ½	&frac12;	
Three quarters ¾	&frac34;	
Times x	&times;	
Divide ÷	&divide;	
Degree º	&deg;	
c cedilla ç	&ccedil;	
e grave è	&egrave;	
e acute é	&eacute;	
e circumflex ê	&ecirc;	
n tilde ñ	&ntilde;	
o umlaut ö	&ouml;	
Dagger †		&#0134;
Double dagger ‡		&#0135;

Statistics for Browser Popularity

Web designers need to know which browsers the majority of their target audience is using. When deciding on our target audience, we could take magazine polls as a guideline for designing technical web sites such as tutorials and W3C information. For web sites offering news, goods, services, travel information, and for general web sites, the statistics in Table App-2 would be more applicable. Always ask your prospective client which browser she is using.

Table App-2. Statistics from http://gs.statcounter.com, February 2012

Area	IE	Mozilla	Chrome	Opera	Safari	Other
UK	44%	22%	23%	1%	9%	1%
North America	47%	22%	18%	1%	11%	1%
Europe	34%	34%	22%	4%	5%	1%

Be wary of statistics gathered by computer magazine surveys. The results do not represent the views of the general public. Instead, they give the views of a select group of computer enthusiasts. Most people and commercial concerns use Windows and the content that comes free with the operating system. Compare the UK figures for February 2012 for the two types of users in Table App-3 (*Computeractive* magazine and http://gs.statcounter.com).

Table App-3. Statistics for UK, February 2012

Area	IE	Mozilla	Chrome	Opera	Safari	Other
UK magazine	31%	39%	23%	3%	2%	2%
http://gs.statcounter	44%	22%	23%	1%	9%	1%

Table App-2 and Table App-3 do not tell the whole story. The figures for IE include good and not-so-good versions. We can ignore IE 6. If we assume that by the year 2015 users of Windows 7 and Windows 8 have become predominant, these users will probably follow their earlier preference and use whatever comes with their operating system—IE 9 and IE 10. Meanwhile (February 2012), IE 7 is only 12 percent of the United Kingdom total IE usage and is dwindling fast. IE 8 is 62 percent of the IE total and is being gradually replaced by IE 9, which in February 2012 stood at 26 percent.

Surveys are further complicated by the fact that many people now have more than one computer with a different Windows OS and different browsers on each. Government organizations sometimes lag behind the more knowledgeable general public.

For the short term, make sure that your web sites work in all browsers, including IE 7 and IE 8. Hopefully by 2015 we can forget about IE conditionals because all browsers will be more standards compliant.

▓ **Tip** When visiting http://gs.statcounter.com, select the bar graph version for a clear picture of the current situation. Select the line graph version to see the trends. See also http://marketshare.hitslink.com/browser-market-share.aspx?qprid=3.

Statistics for browser usage are also monitored by the following web sites:

- http://www.w3schools.com/browsers/browsers_stats.asp
- http://gs.statcounter.com
- http://www.netmarketshare.com/browser-market-share.aspx?qprid=0&qpcustomd=0
- http://en.wikipedia.org/wiki/Usage_share_of_web_browsers

The statistics from various organizations vary considerably. We will never know which stats are the most reliable, but you should be able to detect definite trends.

Index

CPSIA information can be obtained at www.ICGtesting.com
Printed in the USA
LVOW120118060612

284848LV00004B/30/P